Palgrave Studies in Financial Services Technology

Series Editor
Bernardo Nicoletti, Rome, Italy

The Palgrave Studies in Financial Services Technology series features original research from leading and emerging scholars on contemporary issues and developments in financial services technology. Falling into 4 broad categories: channels, payments, credit, and governance; topics covered include payments, mobile payments, trading and foreign transactions, big data, risk, compliance, and business intelligence to support consumer and commercial financial services. Covering all topics within the life cycle of financial services, from channels to risk management, from security to advanced applications, from information systems to automation, the series also covers the full range of sectors: retail banking, private banking, corporate banking, custody and brokerage, wholesale banking, and insurance companies. Titles within the series will be of value to both academics and those working in the management of financial services.

Joerg Osterrieder · Ioana Florina Coita ·
Anastas Dzurovski
Editors

Transparency in FinTech

Exploring Technological Advances, Regulation, and Societal Impact with Case Studies

palgrave
macmillan

Editors
Joerg Osterrieder
University of Twente
NB Enschede, Switzerland

Ioana Florina Coita
University of Oradea
Oradea, Romania

Anastas Dzurovski
State University St. Kliment Ohridski
Bitola, North Macedonia

ISSN 2662-5083 ISSN 2662-5091 (electronic)
Palgrave Studies in Financial Services Technology
ISBN 978-3-032-03522-6 ISBN 978-3-032-03523-3 (eBook)
https://doi.org/10.1007/978-3-032-03523-3

This Palgrave Macmillan imprint is published by the registered company Springer Nature Switzerland AG
The registered company address is: Gewerbestrasse 11, 6330 Cham, Switzerland

Preface

Artificial Intelligence supported processes are the main vehicle for Fintech market efficiency improvement. Current developments offered by Machine Learning are revolutionizing Fintech and increasing the potential for transparency. They are also imposing challenges to regulators, delivering new issues such as taxation of platforms and regulation changes in general. From the societal discourse, transparency in Fintech is not only complementary but also triggering changes within the approach to sustainable development.

Promotion of financial inclusion and directing the future innovations in the sector toward a just society and equal opportunities for all are important aspects for the complete potential to be unlocked.

Joerg OsterriederIoana Florina CoitaAnastas Dzurovski

Acknowledgement Editorial team would like to acknowledge COST Action "Fintech and Artificial Intelligence in Finance - Towards a transparent financial industry" (FinAI) CA19130 establishing a large and interconnected community across academia, public institutions and industry focusing on Financial Technology and Artificial Intelligence, improving transparency in financial services, especially in and through FinTech and also to thank MSCA Industrial Doctoral Network established within the Marie Sklodowska-Curie Actions which aims at training highly skilled doctoral candidates in Digital Finance. This book was also supported from the National Scientific Program "Petar Beron i NIE" in Bulgaria, BG-175467353-2023-14-0004 - 2023 and Fellowships for Excellent Researchers R2–R4 RRP, Slovakia, 09103-03-V04-00502- 2023.

Introduction

Five key aspects of the Fintech sector developments in Europe are analyzed: Recent technological advances in selected Fintech market segments, the regulatory perspective of technological advances' impact on transparency in Fintech (TF), the societal perspective of transparency in Fintech, the role of transparency in promoting financial inclusion, and the future of Fintech organizations and their transparency in TF, offering a perspective on current developments. Hence, the book consists of three parts: first, we research new tools offered and how they can be utilized for a more transparent Fintech market segment through Artificial Intelligence (AI) and Machine Learning (ML). Then, we research TF regulation, especially stressing taxation issues, and finally, we provide research about the impact of Fintech advances on developed countries by examining the knowledge and utilization of Fintech products by the young population and then exploring the general landscape in developing countries through case studies. We finalize the societal discourse part by researching gender dynamics.

In the first part of the book, we are bringing three interesting areas based on recent changes introduced within the areas selected through AI and ML: Integrating Health System Performance and Economic Stability, Wealth and Asset Management, and Accounting. First, we are introducing research on AI-Driven Geospatial Analysis providing evidence to enhance transparency in the Health Management System. Then, we are modeling a conceptual framework for assessing the use of AI in Wealth and Asset Management. Finally, we are researching advances in Triple-Entry

Accounting with ML and its impact on transparency by unveiling advanced analytics on the topic.

In the second part of the book, we research the regulatory perspective of technological advances' impact on TF, selecting the topics of taxation and prudential regulation. The research is directed toward the changes and challenges from the regulatory perspective caused by the impact of AI and ML on TF, selecting the topics of taxation of crowdfunding platforms as well as insurance startups and startechs. At the end of this part, we deliver an analysis of the current regulation in the field of Fintech regulations in Europe and the USA.

In the third part of the book, we have chosen the Societal Perspective: Knowledge of young people regarding Fintech products, the landscape of Fintech in developing countries, and, finally, gender dynamics in relation to TF's recent developments. We are delivering the case study "Knowledge of young people regarding Fintech products in a developed country" and another case study on Fintech from three developing countries, along with gender dynamics research through bibliometric analysis of transparency AI in Fintech.

In the fourth part of the book The Role of Transparency in Promoting Financial Inclusion, we explore how transparency can empower consumers, reduce information asymmetry, and increase trust in financial institutions, thereby promoting financial inclusion.

In the fifth part of the book, "Regulatory Perspective of Technological Advances' Impact on Transparency in Fintech," we are providing the future perspective on Fintech organizations (Fintech 5.0) and their transparency in a new era of trust-driven financial services, or resisting openness, risking market instability and regulatory intervention.

We are delighted to gather research about the topic that is changing swiftly, not only the financial sector but also the economy and society.

Contents

About the Editors

Joerg Osterrieder is a Professor of Sustainable Finance at Bern University of Applied Sciences, Switzerland, and an Associate Professor of Finance and Artificial Intelligence at the University of Twente, Netherlands. He has been working for more than 15 years in the fields of financial statistics, quantitative finance, algorithmic trading, and digitalization of the financial industry.

Ioana Florina Coita is a Lecturer in Machine Learning in Finance at the University of Oradea, Romania, and the University of Wroclaw, Poland. She also holds a position in Finance at the University of Economics in Bratislava, Slovakia.

Anastas Dzurovski is a Professor of Finance, Economics, and Law at the State University St. Kliment Ohridski, North Macedonia. He also holds a position at the Faculty of Business Economics in Skopje.

List of Contributors

Stefana (Ştefana) Belbe Babes-Bolyai University, Faculty of Economics and Business Administration, Department of Statistics-Forecasts-Mathematics, Romania

Cătălina Chinie Faculty of Business Administration in Foreign Languages, Bucharest University of Economic Studies, Romania

Miguel E. Coimbra INESC-ID/IST, Universidade de Lisboa, Portugal

Ioana Florina Coita Faculty of Economics, University of Oradea, Romania

Virgil Damian Faculty of Finance, Insurance, and Stock Exchanges, Bucharest University of Economic Studies, Romania

Flavius Cosmin Darie Faculty of Business Administration in Foreign Languages, Bucharest University of Economic Studies, Romania

Delia Deliu West University of Timişoara, Faculty of Economics and Business Administration, Timişoara, Romania

Joana Dias Faculty of Economics and INESC Coimbra, University of Coimbra, Portugal

Susanne Durst Department of Business Administration, Reykjavik University, Iceland

Alessio Faccia University of Birmingham, Dubai, UAE

Florin Grosu Faculty of Business Administration in Foreign Languages, Bucharest University of Economic Studies, Romania

Maria Iannario Department of Political Sciences, University of Naples Federico II, Italy

Szabolcs Korba Faculty of Law, Eötvös Loránd University, Budapest, Hungary

Gonçalo Leitão CISUC/LASI, Department of Informatics Engineering, Faculty of Sciences and Technology, University of Coimbra, Portugal

Codruţa Mare Babes-Bolyai University, Faculty of Economics and Business Administration, Department of Statistics-Forecasts-Mathematics, Romania

Stefania Mierlita Babes-Bolyai University, Faculty of Economics and Business Administration, Cluj-Napoca, Romania

Andreea Moldovan West University of Timişoara, Faculty of Economics and Business Administration, Timişoara, Romania

Balint Molnar Information Systems Department, Faculty of Informatics, Eötvös Loránd University, Budapest, Hungary

Pinar Nur Ankara, Medipol University, Faculty of Law, Financial Law Department, Ankara, Türkiye

Belma Ozturkkal Faculty of Economics, Social and Administrative Sciences, Kadir Has University, Türkiye

Stavros Pantos Foxhill House, Whiteknights Road, School of Law, University of Reading, United Kingdom

Daniel Traian Pele Department of Statistics and Econometrics, Bucharest University of Economic Studies, Romania

Rezarta Perri University of Tirana, Economic Faculty, Albania

Galena Pisoni York Business School, York St John University, United Kingdom

Deyan Radev Faculty of Economics and Business Administration, Sofia University "St. Kliment Ohridski,", Bulgaria

Bernardete Ribeiro CISUC/LASI, Department of Informatics Engineering, Faculty of Sciences and Technology, University of Coimbra, Portugal

Adina Viorica Rus Babes-Bolyai University, Faculty of Economics and Business Administration, Department of Political Economy, Romania

Ceylan Onay Şahin Senior Lecturer in Finance, School of Business and Law, University of Brighton, United Kingdom

Albulena Shala University of Prishtina "Hasan Prishtina", Faculty of Economics, Department of Banking and Finance, Kosovo

Catarina Silva CISUC/LASI, Department of Informatics Engineering, Faculty of Sciences and Technology, University of Coimbra, Portugal

Hanna Kristín Skaftadóttir Bifröst University, Reykjavík, Iceland

Liana Stanca Babes-Bolyai University, Faculty of Economics and Business Administration, Cluj-Napoca, Romania

Vasile Alecsandru Strat Bucharest University of Economic Studies, Romania

Alessandra Tanda Department of Economics and Management, University of Pavia, Italy

Claudia Tarantola Department of Economics, Management, and Quantitative Methods, University of Milan, Italy

Adriana Tiron-Tudor Babes-Bolyai University, Faculty of Economics and Business Administration, Cluj-Napoca, Romania

Abraham Itzhak Weinberg AI Expert, Israel

Canan Yıldırım Rennes School of Business, France

Fabian Zimmerman Department of Business Administration, Reykjavik University, Iceland

Abbreviations

AI	Artificial Intelligence
AIS	Accounting Information System
ALL	Albanian Lek
AME	Average Marginal Effects
AML	Anti-Money Laundering
ANOVA	Analysis Of Variance
API	Application Programming Interface
ASF	Financial Supervisory Authority (Romania)
ATM	Automated teller machine
AUC	Area Under the Curve
BAU	Business as usual
BCBS	Basel Committee on Banking Supervision
BD	Big Data
BDA	Big data analytics
BEAM	Bulgarian Enterprise Accelerator Market
BFA	Bulgarian Fintech Association
BGN	Bulgarian Lev
BIS	Bank for International Settlements
BNPL	Buy Now, Pay Later
BSE	Bulgarian Stock Exchange
BT	Blockchain Technology
BTC	Bitcoin
CBDC	Central Bank Digital Currencies
CBES	Climate Biennial Exploratory Scenarios
CBRT	Central Bank of Türkiye
CCAF	Cambridge Centre for Alternative Finance
CCPA	California Consumer Privacy Act

CEC	Commission of the European Communities
CEE	Central and Eastern Europe
CEEC	Central and Eastern European countries
CFPB	Consumer Financial Protection Bureau
CFTC	Commodity Futures Trading Commission (CFTC) Overview
CGAP	Consultative Group to Assist the Poor
CRO	Chief Risk Officer
DBSCAN	Density- Based Spatial Clustering of Applications with Noise
DEFI	Decentralized Finance
DLT	Distributed ledger technologies
DMA	Digital Markets Act
DORA	Digital Operational Resilience Act
DSDM	Dynamic systems development method
EBA	European Banking Authority
EBRD	European Bank for Reconstruction and Development
EC	European Commission
ECB	European Central Bank
ECLAT	Equivalence Class Transformation
EFT	Electronic Funds Transfers
EIOPA	European Insurance and Occupational Pensions Authority
ERP	Enterprise resource planning
ESFS	European System of Financial Supervision
ESG	Environmental, Social and Governance
ESMA	European Securities and Markets Authority
ESRB	European Systemic Risk Board
ETF	Exchange-traded fund
ETH	Ethereum
EU	European Union
FATF	Financial Action Task Force
FCA	Financial Conduct Authority
FI	Financial Inclusion
FIDA	Financial Data Access
FINTECH	Financial Technology
FRMA	Fintech Risk Monitoring Authority
FSB	Financial Stability board
FSC	Financial Supervision Commission
FSI	Financial Stability Institute
GDP	Gross Domestic Product
GDPR	General data protection regulation
GE	Gender Equality
GFIN	Global Financial Innovation Network
GFTC	Global Fintech Transparency Council

GIST	General Insurance Stress
GMM	Generalized Method of Moments
GTM	Grounded theory methodology
HCE	Household Consumption Expenditure
HFT	High-Frequency Trading
HLEG	High-Level Expert Group
IAIS	International Association of Insurance Supervisors
ICAAP	Internal Capital Adequacy Assessment Process
ICP	Insurance Core Principles
ICT	Information and Communication Technology
IDF	Inverse Document Frequency
IES	Insurtech Exploratory Scenario
IFW	Istanbul Fintech Week
IMF	International Monetary Fund
IPO	Initial Public Offering
IRR	Insurer Resolution Regime
IST	Insurance Stress Test
KIID	Key Investor Information Document
KNN	K-Nearest Neighbors
KVKK	Kişisel Verilerin Korunması Kanunu/Personal Data Protection Law
KYC	Know Your Customer
LM	Lagrange multiplier test
LOF	Local Outlier Factor
LSDV	Least Squares Dummy Variable
MAS	Monetary Authority of Singapore
ME	Marginal Effect
MEM	Marginal Effects at the Mean
MENA	Middle East and North Africa
MFC	Modern Finance Conference
ML	Machine Learning
MPC	Multi Party Computation
MRM	Model Risk Management
NBR	National Bank of Romania
NCA	National Competent Authority
NFSD	National Fintech Strategy Document
NISU	New Insurer Start-up Unit
NLG	Natural language Generation
NLP	Natural language Processing
NUTS	Nomenclature of Territorial Units for Statistics
NXAI	Non-explainable Artificial Intelligence
OCC	Office of the Comptroller of the Currency
OCSVM	One Class Support Vector Machine

OECD	Organisation for Economic Co-operation and Development
OLS	Ordinary Least Squares
ORSA	Own Risk and Solvency Assessment
PCI	Payment Card Industry
POS	Point-of-sale
PRA	Prudential Regulation Authority
PRISMA	Preferred Reporting Items for Systematic reviews and Meta-Analyses
PRM	Prudential Risk Management
PSD	Payment Services Directive
PSM	Periodic Summary Meeting
PSR	Payment Services Regulation
QC	Quantum Computing
QR	Quick Response
RBP	Results and Basis of Preparation
RDS	Realistic Disaster Scenarios
REA	Resource-Event-Agent
RMSE	Root-mean-square error
ROC	Receiver Operating Characteristic
RPA	Robotic Process Automation
RRP	Recovery and Resolution Planning
SDFA	Supervisory Digital Finance Academy
SDM	Spatial Durbin Model
SEA	Solvent Exit Analysis
SEC	Securities and Exchange Commission
SEEP	Solvent Exit Analysis Execution Planning
SFCR	Solvency and Financial Condition Report
SII	Solvency II Directive
SOX	Sarbanes-Oxley
SREP	Supervisory Review and Evaluation Process
SRP	Supervisory Review Process
SST	Solvency Stress Test
STEM	Science, Technology, Engineering, Mathematics
TF	Transparency in Fintech
VC	Venture Capital
WAM	Web Access Management
WEF	World Economic Forum
XAI	Explainable Artificial Intelligence
2SLS	Two-Stage Least Squares

List of Figures

Playing by the Rules": Advances in Prudential Regulation and Supervision of UK Insurance Startups and Insurtech

Fintech Regulations in Europe and USA

Regional Fintech Report for Türkiye, Romania, and Bulgaria

A Bibliometric Analysis of Transparency AI in FinTech with Emphasis on Gender Dynamics

Fintech 5.0: From Shadows to Clarity—The Future of Transparency in Financial Organizations

List of Tables

Fintech 5.0: From Shadows to Clarity—The Future of Transparency in Financial Organizations

PART I

Recent Technological Advances in the Selected Fintech Market Segments

Integrating Health System Performance and Economic Stability: A Geospatial and AI-Driven Approach to Transparency in Fintech

Stefana Belbe, Liana Stanca, Albulena Shala, Adina Viorica Rus, and Codruța Mare

S. Belbe
Department of Statistics-Forecasts-Mathematics, Faculty of Economics and Business Administration, Babes-Bolyai University, Cluj-Napoca, Romania
e-mail: stefana.cioban@ubbcluj.ro

L. Stanca
Department of Business Information Systems, Faculty of Economics and Business Administration, Babes-Bolyai University, Cluj-Napoca, Romania
e-mail: liana.stanca@ubbcluj.ro

A. Shala (✉)
Department of Banking and Finance, Faculty of Economics, University of Prishtina, Prishtina, The Republic of Kosovo
e-mail: albulena.shala@uni-pr.edu

A. V. Rus
Department of Political Economy, Faculty of Economics and Business Administration, Babes-Bolyai University, Cluj-Napoca, Romania
e-mail: adina.rus@ubbcluj.ro

C. Mare
Department of Statistics-Forecasts-Mathematics, Faculty of Economics and Business Administration, Babes-Bolyai University, Cluj-Napoca, Romania, The Interdisciplinary Centre for Data Science, Cluj-Napoca, Romania
e-mail: codruta.mare@econ.ubbcluj.ro

J. Osterrieder et al. (eds.), *Transparency in FinTech*,
Palgrave Studies in Financial Services Technology,
https://doi.org/10.1007/978-3-032-03523-3_1

1 Introduction

In the current context of the European Union, the relationship between health system performance and economic performance is becoming more and more relevant. Studies show that improving the performance of health systems can have a positive impact on economic stability and financial transparency.[1] For example, the European Union has played a significant role in recommending health system reforms and investing in these systems to improve efficiency and financial sustainability.[2]

Economic crises, such as that of 2008, have highlighted the vulnerabilities of both the economic and medical systems. Recent analyses highlight that economic downturns can increase the need for, and hinder access to, health care, thus exacerbating public health problems.[3] In this context, it is essential to understand how major economic events affect healthcare providers and how financial transparency can support more efficient healthcare systems (Prędkiewicz et al., 2022).

This study aims to analyze the relationship between health system performance and economic performance in EU countries, using advanced geospatial analysis techniques through spatial econometrics and artificial intelligence (AI). By using complex econometric models, we detect trends and anomalies in economic and medical data from 2007 to 2019.[4] We demonstrate how financial transparency can support more efficient and resilient health systems and economies through econometric analysis and AI-based models, thereby contributing to a more robust and resilient economy.[5]

The paper is structured as follows. It begins with a review of the specialized literature relevant to the subject addressed. Then, in the "Data and Methodology" section, the data sources used are presented, as well as a detailed description of the methodologies applied. This section is divided into three main parts: "Resources"—where the data collection and processing method is explained; "Econometrics processes for

[1] https://health.ec.europa.eu/system/files/2023-12/state_2023_synthesis-report_en.pdf

[2] https://health.ec.europa.eu/system/files/2023-12/state_2023_synthesis-report_en.pdf

[3] https://health.ec.europa.eu/system/files/2023-12/state_2023_synthesis-report_en.pdf

[4] https://eurohealthobservatory.who.int/publications/m/economic-crisis-health-systems-and-health-in-europe-impact-and-implications-for-policy

[5] https://eurohealthobservatory.who.int/publications/i/economic-crisis-health-systems-and-health-in-europe-country-experience-study

Enhancing Transparency"—which details the complex econometric models used, such as the Generalized Method of Moments (GMM) and the Spatial Durbin Model (SDM); and "AI processes for Enhancing Transparency"—where the machine learning (ML) algorithms and explainable AI (XAI) techniques used are explained. The next section, "Results and Discussions," presents the key findings of the analysis and interprets their significance in the context of the study objectives. Finally, the paper ends with "Conclusions, Limitations and Future Research," where major contributions are summarized, existing limitations are acknowledged and directions for further research in this field are proposed.

2 Literature Review

Effective financial regulation and good governance are predicated on transparency. Transparency serves as a foundation for financial regulation by providing legal clarity. It serves as the cornerstone for building trust, which is essential to any financial system. It reveals the principles and objectives of financial regulation and policy (Kaufmann & Weber, 2010).

Transparency in AI is frequently related to interpretability and trust in the system (Ribeiro et al., 2016). Miller (2019) suggests that assessing consumer trust in applied AI must take into account how people understand explanations and evaluate their relationship with the service or product. The limited use of many AI applications due to a lack of user trust (Linegang et al., 2006) motivates the development of XAI. Von Eschenbach (2021) considers transparency a condition for trust and the exercise of procedural rights, not an end in itself. Liu (2021) demonstrates that transparency increases trust and reduces uncertainty in AI decision systems.

Understanding AI systems requires more than just transparency because doing so runs the risk of emphasizing "seeing" above "understanding." Ananny and Crawford (2018) stated that requests for transparency "can be read as false choices between complete secrecy and total openness" in the absence of "nuanced understandings of the kind of accountability that visibility is designed to create."

Over the past few years, organizational policies, ethical principles, and regulatory developments have all placed a greater emphasis on transparency in AI. For instance, in April 2018, the EU approved a policy on AI and designated the previously stated High-Level Expert Group (AI

HLEG) to provide guidance on investment approaches as well as moral concerns pertaining to AI in Europe. The European Commission presented a coordinated "made in Europe" approach in December 2018 to promote AI research and use throughout the continent. It was not entirely the case that all member states had their own strategy in place by the middle of 2019 (Van Roy, 2020).

Studies show that transparency is the most common ethical principle for AI, essential for public trust in these systems. Transparency in AI refers to the information available about system features, components, and processes, including data, development methods, and usage. Three categories of AI transparency are distinguished: (1) technological (understanding the structure and operation of the system), (2) data (knowing the sources and purpose of collection), and (3) development and use (understanding the reasons and methods of implementation in organizations) (Tamminen, 2022).

Healthcare's significance in economic growth is underscored by its role in ensuring a healthy and productive workforce. Individuals in good health are less likely to experience work absences due to illness and are more productive contributors to the economy (Gupta et al., 2002). Multiple factors contribute to healthcare costs in developed countries, including income growth, population aging, technological advancements, and widespread access to health insurance (Nghiem & Connelly, 2017). However, data related to healthcare is sensitive and needs to be carefully addressed and assessed, increasing the need for transparency.

The literature on healthcare expenditure determinants has evolved in two phases, as Hartwig (2008) identified.

The first phase, from the mid-1970s to the mid-1990s, established the correlation between GDP and healthcare expenditures, along with the income elasticity of healthcare expenditure, demonstrating a positive correlation between GDP and HCE (Culyer, 1990; Hitiris & Posnett, 1992).

The second phase, starting in the mid-1990s, examined the relationship between healthcare expenditures and GDP over time, yielding varied results. Policymakers in emerging and transitioning economies increasingly recognize the importance of allocating resources to education and healthcare to enhance economic growth and alleviate poverty, as these allocations are pivotal in promoting equity (Bhargava et al., 2001).

Numerous studies have investigated the link between health indicators and economic growth. Bloom et al. (2001) and Wang (2011) found positive associations between health and economic growth in various country panels. Elmi and Sadeghi (2012) supported the hypothesis that health influences growth in developing countries.

Income (per capita GDP) is a crucial factor influencing healthcare spending. Cross-sectional regressions consistently show a significant income elasticity of health spending (Getzen, 2000). Various studies have explored the relationship between healthcare and income across regions, such as Latin America (Mayer, 2001) and OECD countries (Clemente et al., 2004).

Emerging economies also display positive correlations between healthcare expenditures and factors like population and income (Bedir, 2016). Darvas et al. (2018) emphasized demographic factors' influence on healthcare expenditures. A bidirectional relationship between economic growth and healthcare expenditures is observed, driven by healthcare's impact on quality of life and economic productivity (Darvas et al., 2018). The research underscores the crucial role of healthcare expenditures in economic growth, with a reciprocal relationship between the two.

Policymakers must consider these dynamics while allocating resources to promote economic development and public welfare. Understanding the intricate interplay between healthcare expenditures, economic growth, and related factors remains essential for effective policy formulation and equitable progress.

3 Data and Methodology

3.1 Resources

We address financial transparency in our proposed methodology by starting with an econometrics-based approach, in which we understand how different economic indicators influence health spending in a limited number of aggregated spatial units (39 European countries) and temporal units (13 years). We make use of resources from advanced econometrics to uncover trends, identify anomalies, and validate multivariate space-time predictive models. We then propose a system designed to scale the econometric solutions and enable analysis of financial indicators across the globe, for disaggregated spatial units and over a wide temporal interval. The system combines the advantages of the interpretability of advanced econometric methods with the predictive power and scalability of machine learning (ML) to enable transparent, comprehensive, and accurate financial analysis.

While econometrics helps us to demonstrate if a relationship is valid on a set of observed data points, we use AI to make educated guesses about the observed data points. The perspective shifts from understanding the relationship between input and output variables to applying the predictive model on real-world data and then optimizing the performance of the model via means of ML. Still, model interpretability is key in both approaches. While spatial econometrics allows for fully interpretable models, AI requires advanced explainability techniques to enable model transparency and trust.

Therefore, a key aspect of our proposed system, besides scalability, is its ability to provide clear and easy-to-understand explanations of why certain predictive models were validated and used for the inference of financial indicators at different spatial and temporal unit levels. This is achieved by combining econometrics and XAI, which identify the specific characteristics of the features that contributed to the model's predictions. In addition, the system is designed to be transparent and easily auditable, allowing for continuous monitoring of its performance and periodic updates as new data or changes in the financial environment emerge. By implementing it and keeping human expertise in the loop at every ML-assisted step, financial institutions and regulators can significantly improve their ability to make decisions based on forecasted economic downturns for different spatial and temporal units.

3.2 *Econometrics Process for Enhancing Transparency*

In the econometrics phase, we assess the relationship between health expenditure and some key economic indicators such as GDP, GDP per capita growth, public and gross debt, and life expectancy. This data was collected on a yearly basis from 2007 to 2019 for 39 European countries[6] (see Fig. 1) from Eurostat and is pre-processed to handle possible inconsistencies caused by differences in reporting standards. The dataset covers an extensive period of time, including significant economic events such as the 2008 financial crisis, thus providing a robust basis for analysis.

[6] Belgium, Bulgaria, Czech Republic, Denmark, Germany, Estonia, Ireland, Greece, Spain, France, Croatia, Italy, Cyprus, Latvia, Lithuania, Luxembourg, Hungary, Malta, Netherlands, Austria, Portugal, Romania, Slovakia, Slovenia, Finland, Sweden, United Kingdom, Iceland, Liechtenstein, Norway, Switzerland, Montenegro, Albania, Serbia, Turkey, North Macedonia, Bosnia and Herzegovina, Kosovo

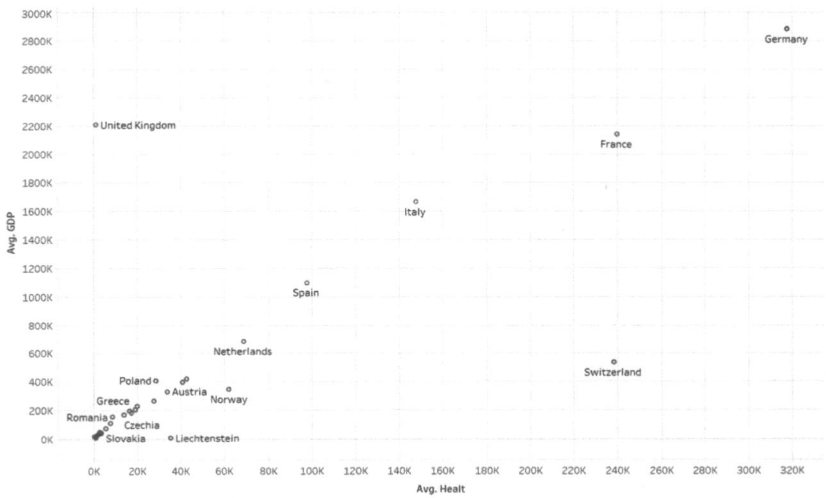

Fig. 1 Health expenses per GDP—Change in GDP and government spending on health for the period studied in EU countries

Our methodology aims to estimate the impact of economic fluctuations on health spending, using econometric techniques for panel data with fixed effects and endogenous variables. We started with a growth equation similar to those used in the literature (Caselli et al., 1996):

$$yit - yi(t - é) = \beta yi(t - é) + xit\gamma + \xi t + \eta i + vit \tag{1}$$

However, the fixed-effects model, which only considers variation over time and ignores variation across countries, can produce skewed and inconsistent estimates when analyzing data from multiple countries (Arellano & Bond, 1991). To solve this problem, we applied the Generalized Method of Moments (GMM) estimator proposed by Arellano and Bond (1991). It removes country-specific fixed effects by transforming the original equation into first-order differences. However, the OLS estimator of this transformed equation remains inconsistent due to the correlation between the lagged dependent variable and the error terms. To improve the efficiency of the GMM estimator, we used the system GMM estimator proposed by Arellano and Bover (1995) and

Blundell and Bond (1998), with the suggested alternative estimate (Roman and Bilan, 2015):

$$yit = \alpha yi(t-1) + x\prime it\gamma + \xi t + \eta i + vit \quad (2)$$

Differentiating this equation, we get:

$$\Delta yit = \alpha\Delta yi(t-1) + \Delta x\prime it\gamma + \Delta\xi t + \Delta vit \quad (3)$$

To address the problem of the correlation between Δ*yi*(*t*-1) and Δvit in Eq. 3, which makes the least squares (OLS) estimation inconsistent, we used the lagged values of the variables as instruments for the first difference equation order. This approach assumes that the error terms are not serially autocorrelated. We used moment conditions for the difference equation and for the level model, employing additional tools derived from the level equations. The validity of the instruments was assessed using the Hansen test, and autocorrelation was tested with the Arellano-Bond test. We used robust standard errors to address heteroscedasticity and treated countries as independent groups. In the final phase, we applied spatial modeling and econometric techniques to effectively capture spatial interaction effects between countries, extending panel data models to address the specific characteristics of the spatial relationships between the countries under study.

To enable space-time modeling, we preprocessed the dataset and addressed potential spatial and temporal discontinuities caused by missing measurements for certain variables. We thus created a spatial panel with 363 observations, comprising 33 spatial units represented by EU countries and 11 temporal units (2008–2018). We imputed missing values for specific countries and years by averaging the spatial neighbors of the respective variables. We reduced the set of explanatory variables to GDP, life expectancy, and net income.

To address non-linearities and heteroscedasticity, we logarithmized the variables in the final spatial econometric modeling phase. We modeled logarithmic health expenditures as functions of the logarithm of GDP, life expectancy, and net income. We generated sparse distance-based spatial weighting matrices using k-Nearest Neighbors (KNN) for an optimal number of neighbors, allowing estimation of spatial adjacency for noncontiguous units such as islands (Bivand et al., 2013; LeSage & Pace, 2009). We tested the sensitivity of the models with different k values (3, 4, 5, 6) to assess robustness to different choices of neighbors. The 3-neighbor KNN matrix proved to be the most suitable. We chose a symmetric and row-standardized weighting matrix to ensure bi-directional cross-country influences (the influence from country A to country B is the same as the influence from country B to country A) and a consistent and simplified interpretation of the results of the final spatial models.

Health spending in one country could be influenced by spending in neighboring countries. This is largely the case in the EU, as countries often learn from the health and economic practices of their geographic neighbors: if one area increases spending, neighbors may follow suit. A good example was the case of health spending caused by the increase in the Covid-19 pandemic. Therefore, we expect a spatial regression effect in the dependent variable, together with individual spatial effects given by GDP, life expectancy, and net income in neighboring countries. To model these relationships and allow the computation of fully flexible spatial spillover effects, we estimated the Spatial Durbin Model (SDM) with cross-sectional and time-specific effects, according to Eq. 4, and the Dynamic Spatial Durbin Model (DSDM) with cross-sectional and time-specific effects, according to Eq. 5 (Elhorst, 2014; LeSage & Pace, 2009; Shi & Lee, 2017). In these models, by using a row-standardized W matrix to estimate the spatial relationship between countries, the spatial autocorrelation coefficient (rho) can be interpreted as the average dependence effect of neighboring regions.

$$Y\_t = \rho WY\_t + X\_t\beta + WX\_t\theta + \mu + \alpha\_t\iota\_N + \varepsilon \tag{4}$$

$$Y\_t = \tau Y\_(t-1) + \rho WY\_t + \eta WY\_(t-1) + X\_t\beta + WX\_t\theta + \mu + \alpha\_t\iota\_N + \varepsilon \tag{5}$$

W is the n-dimensional row-standardized KNN-based spatial weights matrix and allows for the computation of the WX and WY spatial interaction effects. WX_t is the spatial lag of the explanatory variables, ρ is the coefficient of the spatially lagged dependent variable, indicating how neighboring values of the dependent variable influence its own value, and ε is the remaining independent and identically distributed vector of disturbances.

3.3 *AI Process for Enhancing Transparency*

In this methodological phase, we scale the applied econometric models between health expenditure and the economic indicators to a large number of disaggregated spatial and temporal units. We enable transparency by integrating ML algorithms, geospatial analysis, and econometrics to examine the causal relationships between health system performance, economic indicators, and financial transparency in the EU (Fig. 2). Depending on data availability, this system can be extended beyond the European landscape and the currently analyzed variables to enable complete predictive financial and economic analytics.

The first step of the process is integrating and processing detailed historical economic and health system performance data into a database with different spatial and temporal aggregation levels to enable analytics of the financial indicators described above. Once the data is integrated, the system uses ML techniques, assisted by accounting experts, to identify and address inconsistent and missing data caused by differences in reporting standards from one spatial unit (country, county, etc.) to another.

An initial spatio-temporal exploratory analysis is performed on the preprocessed database to investigate temporal and spatial autocorrelation, as well as correlations and patterns between health system and economic performance among spatial units over time, particularly during major economic events such as financial crises.

Advanced econometric models, such as the GMM and SDM, are used to analyze the preprocessed data and validate the space-time relationship between health expenses and the economic landscape. Spatial econometric techniques take into account spatial dependencies and heterogeneity in data, allowing the detection of trends and anoma-

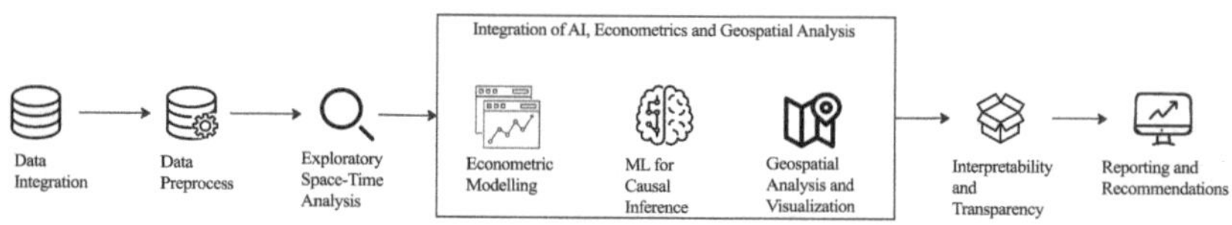

Fig. 2 AI-based Geospatial Analysis process to enable Financial Transparency

lies related to health system performance and economic indicators. In parallel, the system integrates AI via training, validating, and testing non-linear supervised ML models, including neural networks (convolutional or recurrent), support vector machines (SVMs), and decision tree-based algorithms (e.g., Random Forest or XGBoost), to discover causal relationships between health and economic indicators. The ML models are then optimized and retrained in an iterative process, adjusting parameters and incorporating new data to improve the accuracy and robustness of causal inferences. Geospatial visualization techniques are used to identify spatial patterns and regional variations in the causal relationships. The results of ML-based causal inference models and geospatial analysis are combined with the results of econometric modeling. This integrated AI, econometrics, and geospatial methodology enables the analysis of the complex causal relationships between health and economic performance, leveraging the strengths of each approach.

Another layer is added to the proposed econometrics and AI-based process to enable interoperability and transparency of all estimated models. While econometric models are interpretable by nature, XAI techniques are used to explain how data characteristics influence predictions and causal inferences in the complex ML models. We use XAI as a final step in our process to enable AI model transparency, even if this may affect accuracy to some extent.

By combining results from the econometric and ML models, the system can benefit from the econometric model's interpretability and from the ML model's predictive and scalability capabilities. While the two fields offer a different perspective and application on predictive modeling as a concept, they share the same values when it comes to model interpretability: econometrics is formulated around interpretability, while AI, and its new focus, XAI, aims to find the right methods (which could include econometrics) to help interpret the model's predictions based on the data. This is the cornerstone of financial transparency.

Findings from the integrated analysis process are finally reported, highlighting the causal effects of major economic events, such as the 2008 crisis, on the health system. Recommendations are provided on how improving different economic directions and understanding causal mechanisms can support more efficient health systems and contribute to a more robust and resilient economy.

4 Results and Discussions

Our econometrics-based analysis aims to enable financial transparency. Therefore, we start by exploring a spatial panel of key indicators reported annually for a sample of EU countries via the highly interpretable means of spatial and space-time econometrics. The data[7] used in this analytical phase show significant variation both over time and across states. Taking life expectancy as an example, while some countries report values of up to 84 years, annual per capita health expenditures range from almost $0 to nearly $400,000 per capita, reflecting significant but not extreme differences in health outcomes and investments among European nations. Differences between countries appear to be smaller, but variation within states from one period to another may indicate improvement or deterioration in some cases. Health expenditure varies widely, suggesting disparities in the financing of health systems. GDP shows annual economic fluctuations and major development gaps between EU countries. Life expectancy has little variation across countries but changes over time, indicating the impact of policies. Net income and public debt show wide variations, reflecting economic instability and inequality. The growth rate suggests convergence, but with significant cyclical fluctuations.

Correlation analysis revealed strong links between population health and economic indicators. The random-effects model showed significant relationships between health expenditures and various economic indicators, highlighting the complex interaction between economic factors and health expenditures. These findings underscore the need for comprehensive, data-driven approaches to financial transparency and health policies in the EU. To investigate the relationships between these indicators, we applied a random-effects model within the Least Squares Dummy Variable (LSDV) approach. The results of this model are shown in Table 1. The sigma_u value indicates the presence of random effects, explaining the observed variability between entities. Rho suggests that 97.4% of the total variance is due to differences between countries.

Our econometric analysis aims to improve financial transparency in the EU health sector by exploring the complex relationships between health expenditure and various economic indicators. Financial transparency, in this context, refers to the clarity and accessibility of information on the allocation and use of resources in health systems. Here, the null hypothesis

[7] https://ec.europa.eu/eurostat/databrowser/explore/all/all_themes

Table 1 Effects model encapsulates the results obtained from the applied LSDV framework

LnHealth	*Coef*	*Std.Err*	*Z*	*P>|Z|*	*[95% Conf. Interval]*	
GDP	7.3407	4.2601	1.72	0.085	−1.001	−1.5707
LifeExpectancy	0.0006	0.0067	0.09	0.929	−0.0126	0.01381
LnNetIncome	0.9317	0.0343	27.16	0.000	0.8644	0.9989
LnPublicDebt	0.1487	0.0247	6.02	0.000	0.1003	0.1972
GrossDebt	0.0004	0.0002	2.45	0.014	0.0001	0.0006
GrowthRate	−0.0065	0.0012	−5.81	0.000	−0.0086	−0.0043
_cons	−3.2557	0.4825	−6.75	0.000	−4.2014	−2.3099
sigma_u	0.2831					
sigma_e	0.04624					
rho	0.97402 (fraction of variance due to u_i)					

Source Author's.

that all the coefficients of the independent variables are equal to 0 is rejected, showing significant impacts. Health expenditures can be associated with most of the independent variables, except for life expectancy. In addition, we observe that the relationship between the variables will be maintained over time. Random effects testing requires applying the Breusch-Pagan Lagrange multiplier test (LM). The null hypothesis of the LM test is that there is no difference in the attitude toward the healthcare variable between countries ($chi^2 = 458.29$; p-value = 0.0000). This means that there are no significant differences in countries' attitudes toward the growth rate of health. Healthcare characteristics [country, t] = Xb + u [country] + e [country, t] are determined by country-specific factors (where there are t time observations for each country). So, we accept the study's null hypothesis, which states that the country's attitude toward healthcare indicators is the same. This result underlines the importance of analyzing country-specific factors to ensure adequate financial transparency at national and European levels. Cross-testing requires verification of the following hypothesis: The dimensions of the cross-section of the study are independent. The result of the Pesaran CD cross-section independence test is 6.543, with a p-value of 0.000. The absolute average value of elements outside the diagonal is 0.625. So, the null hypothesis of the study is rejected. More precisely, there is a significant correlation between the dimensions being studied. These interdependencies emphasize the

Table 2 Results of Models 1, 2 and 3

	Model1	*Model2*	*Model3*	*AR1*	*AR2*
Lag Health					
LogGDP	1.130*** (19.541)	0.712*** (9.871)	1.095*** (19.731)	1.06*** (10.431)	1.0103*** (322.361)
Log GrowthRate	0.003* (0.891)	−0.021* (−2.351)	−0.188** (−2.741)	−0.01421* (−3.081)	−0.047*** (−12.161)
PublicDebt	0.001*** (12.691)	0.001*** (13.671)	0.001*** (5.261)	0.001*** (13.811)	0.001*** (86.721)
GrossDebt	0.004** (3.961)	−0.002* (−2.261)	0.003* (2.281)	−0.005** (−3.461)	−0.0012*** (−23.301)
NetIncome	−0.002*** (−11.981)	0.001*** (3.831)	−0.001*** (−11.811)		1.151*** (95.471)
Life expectancy	−0.006* (−0.281)	0.061*** (3.991)	−0.049*** (−6.021)	0.016* (0.981)	0.069*** (51.571)
CONSt	3.711* (2.271)	3.859*** (4.441)			7.935*** (80.111)
rmse	0.7496	0.747	0.739		
N	245	245	245	245	245
No of instrument				156	186
Ar(1)*p*-value				0.632	0.944
Ar(2)-*p*-value				0.923	0.589
Hansen J test *p*-value	0.351	0.351	0.442	0.532	0.685

Notes: 1. Heteroskedasticity- and autocorrelation-robust standard errors. 2. Two-step difference GMM estimators with Windmeijer-corrected cluster—robust errors. AR(1)—Arellano-Bond test for AR(1); AR(2)—Arellano-Bond test for AR(2). t-statistics in parentheses. $p < 0.1$, $p < 0.05$, $p < 0.01$. Source: Authors' calculations using Stata

need for a holistic approach in the analysis of financial transparency, taking into account the complex interactions between different economic and health factors. The average correlation is 0.408. The data studied meets the conditions of heteroscedasticity ($chi^2 = 81{,}512.72$, $p > chi^2 = 0.0000$). Results presented in Table 1 provide a first perspective on the factors that influence health spending, thus contributing to a better understanding of financial flows in the health sector. To strengthen this analysis and improve transparency, we performed additional tests and applied advanced estimation techniques.

The results of our panel data regression analysis, using three estimation techniques, are presented in Table 2. We refer to the baseline OLS regression examining the direct relationship between health expenditure and GDP growth as Model 1 (Eq. 1), to the fixed-effects panel data model accounting for country-specific, time-invariant factors as Model 2 (Eq. 2), and to the extended fixed-effects model incorporating additional control variables as Model 3 (Eq. 3). In the estimation stage of our model parameters, we employed three different estimation techniques that are appropriate for fixed-effects panel data models with endogenous explanatory variables. Ignoring the dynamic nature of our econometric model, we initially employed more traditional instrumental variable (IV) estimation techniques, specifically two-stage least squares (2SLS) and two-stage generalized methods of moments (GMM). The regression analysis was performed using the xtivreg2 command for Stata, developed by Schaffer (2012). We can substitute life expectancy with net income and public debt, depending on the outcome. The growth rate of health expenditure was instrumented by using the first and second-lagged values to control for endogeneity. So, in our models, we instrumented the growth rate of health expenditures using first- and second-order lagged values. This approach allows us to better control factors that could obscure the real relationships between variables, thus contributing to greater transparency in understanding the financial dynamics of health systems.

In Model 1, we observed that the log GDP exhibited a significant, positive influence on L. health, showing that greater economic output is correlated with improved health outcomes. The logged growth rate showed a modest effect, suggesting a potential but comparatively weaker relationship. Public debt also manifested a noteworthy, positive relationship, implying that a country's debt situation may affect its health. Likewise, gross debt showed a positive association, indicating that higher gross debt might lead to better health outcomes. Net income displays a negative coefficient, suggesting that income levels may influence health patterns. Life expectancy, however, exhibits a marginally negative relationship, indicating that other factors may have a more substantial impact on health in this context. The constant term (CONST) demonstrates its significance, representing the baseline health level, even when other variables are absent.

In Model 2, interpreting variables is consistent with that of Model 1. Notably, log GDP continues to positively influence L. health, showing that economic output is still correlated with improved health. The impact of the logarithmic growth rate remains moderate, and public debt remains significant. Interestingly, gross debt now exhibits a negative effect, suggesting a more intricate relationship with health. Net income maintains a negative correlation, while life expectancy shows a positive correlation.

Model 3 introduces additional variables, offering a comprehensive perspective on the factors influencing health outcomes. The positive impact of log GDP remains clear, while the log growth rate now shows a substantial adverse effect, indicating a potentially significant influence on health. Public debt's impact remains consistent, while gross debt now shows a positive effect. Net income continues to exhibit a negative relationship, while the strong positive association of life expectancy reinforces its role in influencing health outcomes. The constant term (CONSt) maintains significance, showing the baseline health level. Diagnostic metrics, such as the root-mean-square error (RMSE) and the number of observations (N), contribute to the model's reliability.

Models 1, 2, and 3 show the relationship between variables and healthcare. Model 1 emphasizes the influence of economic indicators and debt on health, with net income and life expectancy showing significant correlations. Model 2 builds upon these insights, introducing additional complexities, such as the relationship between gross debt and health. Finally, Model 3 provides a comprehensive view, highlighting the negative effect of the logarithmic growth rate on health and further reinforcing the significance of life expectancy. The absence of significant p-values for the AR1 and AR2 tests in all three models confirms the validity of the results and interpretations. This comprehensive analysis contributes to a deeper understanding of the factors influencing health dynamics, aiding policymakers and researchers in making informed decisions and interventions to promote healthier societies. We included life expectancy and other macroeconomic variables in the first three models. In the last model, we also incorporated net income and other variables. The Hansen J tests confirmed the validity of our specifications, while the Arellano-Bond test for AR(2) confirmed the null hypothesis of no serial correlation. The models exhibited a solid fit for our dataset, providing valuable insights. They effectively explained a significant portion of the variations in healthcare spending across most EU Member States, with a few exceptions, such as Luxembourg, France, and Spain, requiring further investigation.

These findings highlight the complex interplay between economic factors and health spending, underscoring the need for comprehensive, data-driven approaches to financial transparency and health policies in the EU. Our model provides valuable insights for decision-makers, allowing a better understanding of the factors that influence health spending and, by implication, the health status of the population in EU countries.

The interaction between the variables is evident from our analyses. The growth rate variable, for instance, exhibited mixed effects across different models, indicating its varying impact within specific economic contexts. For example, a growth rate of 1% could result in a 10% increase in gross debt, public debt, and the log of GDP, while also causing a 10% decrease in life expectancy and net income. Intriguingly, our investigation into the relationship between healthcare expenditures and economic growth highlighted the significant influence of net income and life expectancy. Both variables showed a significant and positive impact on health, as a 1% increase in either factor corresponded to a 10% increase in healthcare. Collectively, our findings align with theoretical expectations and provide nuanced insights into the complex relationship between economic factors and health outcomes. While we observed the expected rise in health spending accompanying GDP growth, our results highlighted the complex nature of these relationships. The alignment of our findings with the proposed models and theoretical assumptions further strengthens the robustness of our study.

To assess the spatial characteristics of the variables, we plotted quartile maps for each variable in the spatial panel: Absolute GDP, Life Expectancy, Net Income, and Health Expenses. In Fig. 3, the maps generated for four years—2008, 2011, 2014, and 2018—revealed more prominent differences in the values and spatial groupings of the four quartiles between 2008 and 2011 for the health expenses, life expectancy, and net income indicators. These changes can be explained as effects of the economic crisis of 2008. Moreover, for all four years, there is a particular

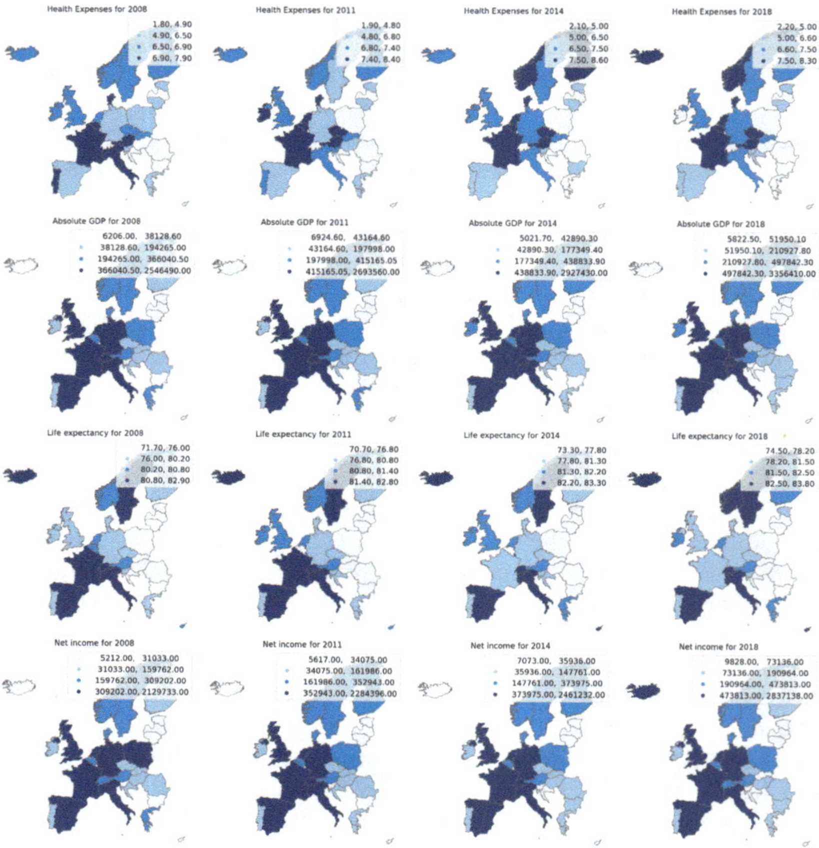

Fig. 3 Quantile maps of four interval values represented for Health expenses, GDP, Life expectancy and Net income on four years during the study period 2008, 2011, 2014 and 2018

spatial grouping of the variables, specific to spatial clustering: similar quantiles tend to be grouped together in space. We statistically tested this pattern using the pooled global Moran's I spatial autocorrelation coefficient (Beenstock & Felsenstein, 2019): for health expenses, we obtained 0.26; for GDP, 0.55; for life expectancy, 0.44; and for net income, 0.53—all values being significant at the 1% level. These results

Table 3 Results of Model 4—the Spatial Durbin Model with cross-sectional and time-specific effects

LnHealth	*Coef*	*Std.Err*	z	p >|z|
LnGDP	−0.018	0.009	−1.985	0.047
Spatial Lag LnGDP	−0.064	0.021	−3.135	0.002
LnLifeExpectancy	−0.559	0.349	−1.599	0.110
Spatial Lag LnLifeExpectancy	−0.309	0.586	−0.527	0.598
LnNetIncome	0.018	0.008	2.163	0.031
Spatial Lag LnNetIncome	−0.046	0.020	−2.298	0.022
Rho (Spatial LagLnHealth)	−0.256	0.078	−3.273	0.001
Moran I residuals	−0.024	−0.592		0.723

Source Author's

indicate a strong and positive spatial autocorrelation; hence, the indicators are influenced by neighboring countries. Such spatial effects need to be accounted for by estimating a spatial econometric model.

Results for the static and dynamic Spatial Econometric models are presented in Tables 3 and 4. We estimate SDM models with country and time-specific effects to:

1. Control for factors that are constant over time but vary across countries, ensuring that the spatial lag estimation reflects the true spatial interactions.
2. Account for differences between countries that were not explained by our set of X variables.
3. Control for factors that are constant across countries but vary over time (as was the case with the 2008 financial crisis), ensuring that the potential spatial spillover effects are due to spatial interactions and not time-specific events.

In both models, the estimate of the spatial lag of the health expenses variable is statistically significant and negative, indicating a negative spatial spillover of the dependent variable. Hence, an increase in the health expenses variable in one country is associated with a decrease in the expenses in the neighboring countries, as defined by the symmetrical and row-standardized KNN spatial weights matrix. Including the time-specific effects ensures that this negative estimate is not confounded by

Table 4 Results of Model 5 -the Dynamic Spatial Durbin Model with cross-sectional and time-specific effects

LnHealth	*Coef*	*Std.Err*	z	p > |z|
LnGDP	−0.023	0.016	−1.457	0.145
LagLnGDP	0.004	0.015	0.27	0.787
Spatial Lag LnGDP	−0.065	0.021	−3.075	0.002
LnLifeExpectancy	−0.328	0.504	−0.651	0.515
Lag LnLifeExpectancy	−0.332	0.437	−0.76	0.447
Spatial Lag LnLifeExpectancy	0.358	0.672	0.532	0.595
LnNetIncome	0.002	0.014	0.156	0.876
Lag LnNetIncome	0.021	0.015	1.411	0.158
Spatial Lag LnNetIncome	−0.05	0.020	−2.455	0.014
Rho (Spatial Lag LnHealth)	−0.241	0.082	−2.945	0.003

Source Author's

global time trends but rather reflects the genuine spatial relationship between countries over time.

The spatially lagged GDP and Net Income values are negative and significant in both models, indicative of a spatial spillover effect: an increase in these variables in one country determines a decrease in the health expenses in the neighboring countries. The negative spatial dependencies might suggest competitive or substitution effects. It could be that these 33 studied countries react to their neighbors' actions by adjusting in the opposite direction, which has critical policy implications for different economic sectors, where intercountry cooperation might be needed. Additionally, this might also point to the need to introduce into the analysis specific variables accounting for particular situations, like the ones exemplified beforehand (the 2008 financial crisis or the Covid-19 pandemic). We have already demonstrated through the spatial descriptive analysis based on maps that, for this specific dataset, there are differences in the spatial features between different years.

Our models provide evidence of significant direct and indirect effects, as indicated by the significant estimates of the coefficients of GDP and Net Income (in the case of Model 4) and their spatial lags (in both SDMs' cases). This means that the studied economic indicators impact health expenditures within the same country and, more importantly, influence the health expenditures abroad, in the nearest neighboring countries.

When setting their health policies, European countries do not act in isolation. Therefore, coordination among nations remains vital and should account for the spatial interactions in different regions in order to determine efficient policy designs. Considering these results, transparency becomes even more important.

Our mixed econometrics analysis (GMM and SDM for panel data) sheds light on the intricate connection between macroeconomic variables and health outcomes. By exploring different models and analyzing their findings, we can better understand the complex relationship between economic growth, debt, net income, life expectancy, and healthcare expenditures. These results have significant implications for policymakers and researchers who aim to promote healthier societies and make informed decisions for the well-being of nations.

4.1 Discussions

Our proposal combines traditional econometric methods with advanced AI approaches and XAI techniques to gain a more comprehensive understanding of the political economy of austerity and potential discrepancies between nominal and real spending, as suggested by Mladovsky et al. (2012). Our study examined the complex relationship between health system performance and economic performance in EU countries, with a particular focus on financial transparency. Using an innovative combination of geospatial analysis, spatial econometrics, and AI techniques, we are able to provide new and in-depth insights into these interconnections. One of the key results of our analysis is highlighting how recessions affect both the medical and economic sectors. We observed a strong link between improved health services and economic stability, suggesting that investments in health systems can have long-term positive effects on the economy. This finding underscores the importance of maintaining and even increasing investment in health, even in times of economic hardship. Our space-time analysis, which covered the period 2007–2019, including the 2008 financial crisis, revealed significant effects of major economic events on healthcare providers. These results highlight the vulnerability of health systems to economic shocks and the need for more resilient and adaptable health policies. The use of complex econometric models, such as the GMM and the SDM, allowed us to detect trends and anomalies that might have gone unnoticed through traditional methods. This approach provided a more nuanced understanding of the dynamics between health

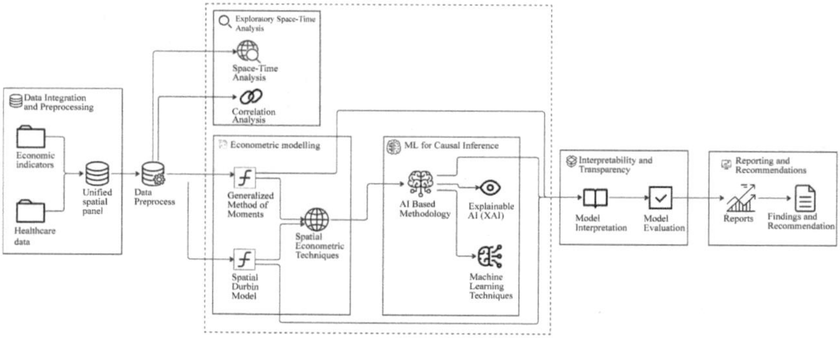

Fig. 4 Integration prototype of AI, Econometrics and Spatial Analysis for Health and Economic Systems enabling Transparency

systems and economic performance, helping to improve financial transparency in the sector. Figure 4 illustrates our integrated approach, combining AI, econometrics, and spatial analysis to enable transparency in analyzing health and economic systems.

The integrated AI-based process we proposed offers a promising perspective for scaling and analyzing the complex multidimensional connections between health systems and economic performance to address and enable financial transparency. Not only does this approach improve the accuracy of the analysis, but it also opens up new possibilities for identifying the factors that influence the performance of health systems. An important aspect of our study was the focus on interpretability, both in econometric and AI-based models. Using XAI techniques significantly improves the transparency of complex models, allowing us to better explain how data features influence predictions. This is crucial for increasing confidence in the results of the analysis and for facilitating their adoption in the policy-making process. Moreover, improving transparency in AI-based solutions can play a crucial role in mitigating the impact and managing the risks associated with an economic slowdown, especially in the healthcare sector. Increased transparency, facilitated by AI solutions, would provide better visibility into the economic landscape. Regulators and supervisors could benefit from a clearer and real-time picture of the system, enabling rapid interventions to address imminent risks and mitigate the impact of disruptions.

Our spatial econometric analysis, using SDM, provides robust evidence of the complex interactions between health system performance and economic performance in EU countries. The results reveal significant spatial spillover effects, with negative coefficients for the spatial lags of health expenditure, GDP, and net income, indicating dynamic regional interdependence. These findings support our initial hypotheses, demonstrating the impact of major economic events on the healthcare sector and highlighting the importance of financial transparency in promoting efficient health systems and a resilient economy. We enabled model interpretability via the spatial econometrics' power in capturing detailed analysis of coefficients and spatial effects. We, hence, provided a nuanced perspective on the space-time interactions in the context of the health-economy relationship in the EU and highlighted the potential of financial transparency in supporting more efficient health systems and a more resilient economy.

Financial transparency can support more efficient health systems. By providing a clear picture of how resources are allocated and used, financial transparency enables decision-makers to make more informed and effective decisions. This, in turn, helps create a more robust and resilient economy. Our observations highlight that disruptive economic events, such as the global financial crisis, have a significant impact on the volume and nature of international financial activities. Strong correlations between macroeconomic factors, such as income, GDP, and public debt, and indicators of health expenditure suggest the propagation of economic shocks across sectors and jurisdictions. This complexity underscores the need to explore data from multiple analytical perspectives to detect credible patterns and systemic anomalies.

Despite our significant results, it is important to acknowledge the limitations of our study and identify directions for future research. For example, the time horizon of the study (2007–2019, and in the case of the SDM model, 2008–2018) does not include the impact of the COVID-19 pandemic, which had profound effects on health systems and economies. Future research or an AI-based process scaled to a larger time span could capture longer-term trends and include the effects of the pandemic. We also worked with national-level data, which may mask regional or local disparities. Once again, a scaled AI-based system extended to more disaggregated spatial data could benefit from using subnational-level data for more detailed analysis. In addition, although we included a wide range of variables, we may have missed important factors that influence the relationship between health and the economy. Exploring additional variables, such as environmental or socio-cultural factors, could provide a more complete picture.

The findings of our study highlight the crucial importance of financial transparency in supporting more efficient health systems and, consequently, a more robust and resilient economy. Increased transparency, as enabled by our proposal, would provide better visibility into the complex interactions between health spending and economic performance. This study, therefore, paves the way for a new era of opportunities for researchers and policymakers in public health and economics to fundamentally reinvent how we ensure the efficiency and resilience of health systems in the global economic context.

5 Conclusions, Limitations and Future Research

This study analyzes the complex relationship between health system performance and economic performance in European Union countries, highlighting the impact on financial transparency. Using advanced spatial econometrics and artificial intelligence (AI) techniques, the research examines the effects of economic downturns on the health and economic sectors, with a particular focus on the period 2007–2019, which includes the 2008 financial crisis.

The innovative methodology combines complex econometric models (GMM and SDM) with machine learning techniques and geospatial analysis to provide a holistic perspective on the causal relationships between health, the economy, and financial transparency. The integrated approach enables spatial visualization of identified correlations and patterns, facilitating geographic interpretation.

The study reveals that health spending depends on national income but also varies between countries with similar income levels. It emphasizes the need for low-income countries to increase their health resources, while high-spending developing countries need to maximize the value of their investments. Empirical results show that reductions in health spending are not an inevitable consequence of recessions, with some less-developed European countries even experiencing steady increases in health spending. The study highlights the crucial role of financial transparency in supporting efficient health systems and a resilient economy. Limitations of the study include the heterogeneity of the health and economic systems of the analyzed EU countries, the relatively short observation period, the complexity of the relationships studied, the possible omission of relevant factors, the variability of data quality, and the trade-off between interpretability and accuracy in AI/econometric modeling, which may affect the generalizability of the conclusions.

Future research should focus on the impact of population aging, chronic disease, and lifestyle factors on health expenditures, as well as on estimating the effectiveness of these expenditures. The study provides valuable information for decision-makers regarding population needs, investments in preventive public health, and cost-effectiveness evaluation of new technologies. By prioritizing interpretability, the integrated AI/econometrics approach explains how data characteristics influence predictions of health performance indicators, economic drivers, and levels of financial transparency. Explainable AI (XAI) techniques improve model transparency, providing valuable insights for developing more informed and adaptive health and economic policies.

References

Ananny, M., & Crawford, K. (2018). Seeing Without Knowing: Limitations of the Transparency Ideal and Its Application to Algorithmic Accountability. *New Media & Society*, *20*(3), 973–989. https://doi.org/10.1177/1461444816676645

Arellano, M., & Bond, S. (1991). Some tests of specification for panel data: Monte Carlo evidence and an application to employment equations. *Review of Economic Studies*, *58*(2), 277–297. https://doi.org/10.2307/2297968

Arellano, M., & Bover, O. (1995). Another look at the instrumental variable estimation of error-components models. *Journal of Econometrics*, *68*(1), 29–51. https://doi.org/10.1016/0304-4076(94)01642-D

Bedir, S. (2016). Healthcare expenditure and economic growth. *Advances in Economic and Business*, *4*(2), 76–86. https://doi.org/10.13189/aeb.2016.040202

Beenstock, M., & Felsenstein, D. (2019). *The Econometric Analysis of Non-stationary Spatial Panel Data* (pp. 58). Springer International Publishing. https://doi.org/10.1007/978-3-030-03614-0

Bhargava, A., Jamison, D. T., Lau, L. J., & Murray, C. J. (2001). Modelling the effects of health on economic growth. *Journal of Health Economics*, *20*(3), 423–440. https://doi.org/10.1016/s0167-6296(01)00073-x

Bivand, R., Pebesma, E., & Gomez-Rubio, V. (2013). *Applied Spatial Data Analysis With R*, Second. Springer, NY. https://asdar-book.org/. ISBN: 978-1-4614-7617-7

Bloom, D. E., Canning, D., & Sevilla, J. P. (2001). The effect of health on economic growth: Theory and evidence. *National Bureau of Economic Research. World Development World Development*, *32*(1), 1–13. https://doi.org/10.3386/w8587. https://www.nber.org/papers/w8587

Blundell, R., & Bond, S. (1998). Initial conditions and moment restrictions in dynamic panel data models. *Journal of Econometrics*, *87*(1), 115–143. https://doi.org/10.1016/S0304-4076(98)00009-8

Caselli, F., Esquivel, G., & Lefort, F. (1996). Reopening the convergence debate: A new look at cross-country growth empirics. *Journal of Economic Growth*, *1*, 363–389. https://doi.org/10.1007/BF00141044

Clemente, J., Marcuello, C., Montañés, A., & Pueyo, F. (2004). On the international stability of health care expenditure functions: Are government and private functions similar? *Journal of Health Economics*, *23*(3), 589–613. https://doi.org/10.1016/j.jhealeco.2003.08.007

Culyer, A. J. (1990). Cost containment in Europe, în Health Care Systems in Transition. https://www.ncbi.nlm.nih.gov/pmc/articles/PMC4195143/pdf/hcfr-89-supp-021.pdf

Darvas, Z., Moës, N., Myachenkova, Y., & Pichler, D. (2018). *The macroeconomic implications of healthcare* (No. 2018/11). Bruegel Policy Contribution. Retrieved from https://www.econstor.eu/bitstream/10419/208018/1/1030935807.pdf

Elhorst, J. P. (2014). *Spatial Econometrics: From Cross-Sectional Data to Spatial Panels*. Springer. https://doi.org/10.1007/978-3-642-40340-8

Elmi, Z. M., & Sadeghi, S. (2012). Health care expenditures and economic growth in developed countries: Panel co-integration and causality. *Middle-East Journal of Scientific Research*, *12*(1), 88–91. https://doi.org/10.5829/idosi.mejsr.2012.12.1.6419

Getzen, T. E. (2000). Health care is an individual necessity and a national luxury: Applying multilevel decision models to analyse health care expenditures. *Journal of Health Economics*, *19*(2), 259–270. https://doi.org/10.1016/S0167-6296(99)00032-6

Gupta, S., Verhoeven, M., & Tiongson, E. R. (2002). The effectiveness of government spending on education and health care in developing and transition economies. *European Journal of Political Economy*, *18*(4), 717–737. https://doi.org/10.1016/S0176-2680(02)00116-7

Hartwig, J. (2008). What drives health care expenditure?—Baumol's unbalanced growth model revisited. *Journal of Health Economics*, *27*(3), 603–623. https://doi.org/10.1016/j.jhealeco.2007.05.006

Hitiris, T., & Posnett, J. (1992). The determinants and effects of health expenditure in developed countries. *Journal of Health Economics, 11*(2), 173–181. https://doi.org/10.1016/0167-6296(92)90033-W

Kaufmann, C., & Weber, R. H. (2010). The role of transparency in financial regulation. *Journal of International Economic Law, 13*(3), 779–797. https://doi.org/10.1093/jiel/jgq037

Kohler, U., & Kreuter, F. (2005). *Data Analysis Using Stata* (pp. 497). Stata press. ISBN-13:978-1-59718-110-5.

LeSage, J. P., & Pace, R. K. (2009). *Introduction to Spatial Econometrics.* Taylor and Francis. Chs.1 and 2.

Linegang, M. P., Stoner, H. A., Patterson, M. J., Seppelt, B. D., Hoffman, J. D., Crittendon, Z. B., & Lee, J. D. (2006). Human-automation collaboration in dynamic mission planning: A challenge requiring an ecological approach. *Proceedings of the Human Factors and Ergonomics Society Annual Meeting, 50*(23), 2482–2486. https://doi.org/10.1177/154193120605002304

Liu, B. (2021). In AI we trust? Effects of agency locus and transparency on uncertainty reduction in human–AI interaction. *Journal of Computer-Mediated Communication, 26*(6), 384–402. https://doi.org/10.1093/jcmc/zmab013

Mayer, D. (2001). The long-term impact of health on economic growth in Latin America. *World Development, 29*(6), 1025–1033. https://doi.org/10.1016/S0305-750X(01)00026-2

Miller, T. (2019). Explanation in artificial intelligence: Insights from the social sciences. *Artificial Intelligence, 267*, 1–38. https://doi.org/10.1016/j.artint.2018.07.007

Mladovsky, P., Srivastava, D., Cylus, J., Karanikolos, M., Evetovits, T., Thomson, S., & McKee, M. (2012). Health policy in the financial crisis. *Eurohealth, 18*(1), 3–6. (Retrieved August 18, 2023). https://apps.who.int/iris/bitstream/handle/10665/333155/Eurohealth-18-1-3-7-eng.pdf

Nghiem, S. H., & Connelly, L. B. (2017). Convergence and determinants of health expenditures in OECD countries. *Health Economics Review, 7*(1), 29. https://doi.org/10.1186/s13561-017-0164-4

Prędkiewicz, P., Bem, A., Siedlecki, R., et al. (2022). An impact of economic slowdown on health. New evidence from 21 European countries. *BMC Public Health, 22*, 1405. https://doi.org/10.1186/s12889-022-13740-6

Ribeiro, M. T., Singh, S., & Guestrin, C. (2016). "Why should I trust you?": Explaining the predictions of any classifier. In Proceedings of the 22nd ACM SIGKDD international conference on knowledge discovery and data mining, 1135–1144. https://doi.org/10.1145/2939672.2939778

Roman, A., and Bilan, I. (2015). An empirical analysis of the macroeconomic determinants of non-performing loans in EU28 banking sector. *Revista Economică, 67*(2), 108–127.

Schaffer, M. (2012). xtivreg28: Stata module to perform extended IV/2SLS, GMM AC/HAC, LIML, and k-class regression for panel data models (version 8). Boston College Department of Economics. Available at http://ideas.repec.org/c/boc/bocode/s456501.html

Shi, W., & Lee, L.-F. (2017). Spatial dynamic panel data model with interactive fixed effects. *Journal of Econometrics*, *197*, 323–347. https://doi.org/10.1016/j.jeconom.2016.12.001

Tamminen, P. (2022). Operationalizing transparency and explainability in artificial intelligence through.

Van Roy, V. (2020) AI watch—National strategies on Artificial Intelligence: A European perspective in 2019 (JRC Technical Report No. EUR 30102 EN/JRC119974). Publications Office of the European Union. https://doi.org/10.2760/602843

von Eschenbach, W. J. (2021). Transparency and the black box problem: Why we do not trust AI. *Philosophy and Technology*, *34*(4), 1607–1622. https://doi.org/10.1007/s13347-021-00477-0

Wang, K. M. (2011). Health care expenditure and economic growth: Quantile panel type analysis. *Economic Modeling*, *28*(4), 1536–1549. https://doi.org/10.1016/j.econmod.2011.02.008

Conceptual Framework for Assessing the Use of Artificial Intelligence in Wealth and Asset Management Offered by Fintech

Fabian Zimmermann, Miguel E. Coimbra, and Susanne Durst

1 Introduction

The financial industry has seen many developments and technological advancements, from pocket calculators to computers, leading to faster processing, with consequences such as the elimination of trading floors and the automation of many processes (Litzenberger et al., 2012). Artificial intelligence (AI), in conjunction with big data, blockchain, and quantum computing, is reshaping the financial industry (Rabah, 2018).

AI spans various research fields (Bibel, 2018) and is therefore a cross-disciplinary topic, including social sciences, ethics, engineering, and computer science. In each of these disciplines, AI is playing a significant and growing role in society. Workforce capability enhancement (Nurlia et al., 2023), faster information processing (Seng et al., 2022) and analysis

F. Zimmermann (✉) · S. Durst
Department of Business and Economics, Reykjavik University, Reykjavík, Iceland
e-mail: fabian23@ru.is
e-mail: susanned@ru.is

M. E. Coimbra
INESC-ID/IST, Universidade de Lisboa, Lisbon, Portugal
e-mail: miguel.e.coimbra@tecnico.ulisboa.pt

J. Osterrieder et al. (eds.), *Transparency in FinTech*, Palgrave Studies in Financial Services Technology,
https://doi.org/10.1007/978-3-032-03523-3_2

(Ranjan et al., 2020) are key factors of AI, contributing to a disruption of society that is ongoing at the time of writing. However, still at an early stage of its development, its fast-paced evolution fosters some misconceptions that need to be addressed. The lack of a clear roadmap for AI adaptation leads to confusion and unrealistic expectations. While there are numerous studies, such as Cowls et al. (2021), Wamba et al. (2021), *or* Kaushal and Mishra (2024), that shed light on the potential applicability and benefits of AI, most of them lack the actual feasibility and reasoning for its adaptation in an actual business setting.

The existing research regarding the use of AI stresses its innovative technological capabilities and perceived competitive advantages. While several studies, such as Kundi et al. (2023), Wang et al. (2023), or Cao (2022) mentioning that AI should be used carefully and only with human supervision when applying it in a business context, its perceived usefulness for asset management companies is still widely understated. In fact, hardly any of the existing research debates the usefulness of AI models in wealth & asset management companies. Moreover, smaller companies which do not adapt or adjust not quickly enough to incorporate AI applications could face competitiveness challenges (Borges et al., 2021; Oldemeyer et al., 2024). While this rationale might hold eventually, AI adoption in companies is still at an early stage and being among the first movers might bring its disadvantages, such as implementing systems with limited use cases in the exiting organizational setup or unrealistic expectations (Gupta et al., 2021).

Therefore, this article aims to provide a conceptual framework for AI implementations in wealth management, inducing a discussion of basic factors. It thereby takes into consideration the decision-making process of whether to adopt AI applications in a current business setting or to delay their implementation to a more statutory stage of development, where the company has developed a sharp vision of its intended use. This article stresses the importance of a profound capability and requirement analysis within wealth and asset management companies to assess the need for investments in AI applications. Thus, this article argues that technological novelties such as AI applications are not always suitable for every company. In this article, five factors were considered to conceptualize the appropriateness of AI technology for asset management companies. These factors are defined by a clear intent for the use of AI; data management, including quality and transparency; regulatory certainty; efficiency enhancement and cost reduction; and client experience and engagement. This article is structured as follows. It starts with the definition of AI and its various forms and includes a literature discussion to provide a holistic picture of the current stage of research. It is then put into context with finance and asset management, whereby the identified factors will be addressed. In the concluding section of this article, adoption criteria will be presented, offering insightful guidance by highlighting key considerations for the adoption of AI in asset management companies.

**ChatGPT is not generally seen as AI, as it is only a decision tree structure.*

2 Method

This paper makes use of the grounded theory methodology (GTM) as described by Astalin (2013) and Jabareen (2009) to develop a novel framework based on previously conducted framework attempts. This approach offers the advantage of considering already conducted research findings and building upon existing frameworks while incorporating novel aspects and addressing factors that have not yet been considered. Furthermore, it allows for the combination and adjustment of models based on the specific research area being addressed, thereby enabling the extraction of factors that might be seen as universal and retain their validity across other research fields. Thus, a novel framework based on GTM incorporates the knowledge of already conducted research and enables it to be developed further for application in other research areas. This approach is intentionally used in this paper, as frameworks for assessing the use of AI already exist in other research areas, e.g., business administration, general management, and financial services, but not specifically in the wealth and asset management area.

Thus, in the first step, a literature review, as in Paul et al. (2021), was conducted using different search engines, including web-of Science and Scopus, by employing the following key words: framework, AI, wealth and asset management, and financial services. As the focus on wealth and asset management companies revealed only a small number of relevant findings, the broadened search term "financial services" was used. Thereby, universal base factors in existing frameworks were identified and discussed within the realm of the financial sector, with consideration of their usefulness in wealth and asset management.

In the second step, a conceptual framework analysis was conducted using the proclaimed approach from Astalin (2013) by deriving existing and universal factors from the prevailing literature. This allows for the proposal of a new framework adjusted to the needs of wealth and asset management companies. For the visualization, the proposed framework is oriented on Holmström (2022) and Wirtz et al. (2020), as it provides a clear visualization of the identified factors and mathematical spheres.

3 Literature Background

The following defines the used terminology and names the basic components of AI. In addition, it briefly describes big data in conjunction with AI and its key necessity for a functional AI operation.

3.1 Artificial Intelligence

The term "artificial intelligence" embodies several research fields and draws upon various applications. As argued by Edelmann et al. (2020), from a scientific perspective, AI research stretches from mathematics (stochastic), computer science (application), cognitive and social sciences (human-like appearance) to enable the technology with human-like features (Tian et al., 2017). AI applications draw upon several other data models and assemble technology bundles in order to make the front-end of the AI application appear intelligent (Schmidt et al., 2021). As argued by Reddy and Fields (2022), as well as Sarker (2022), AI has significantly developed from simple rule-based models to highly specialized AI systems with sophisticated capabilities. These systems often comprise a bundle of technological advancements such as big data, machine and deep learning, as well as natural language processing (NLP) (Sarker, 2022).

The appearance of AI applications can vary significantly as the applied models are subject to the use case they are intended to address (Behnood & Golafshani, 2022). While AI used in human interaction may prioritize natural language processing over other methods, assessing historical market data has a strong dependency on big data capabilities (Javed Awan et al., 2021). Based on the research by Aldoseri et al. (2023) and Brem et al. (2021), AI consists of several enabling components which, depending on the applied use case, are more or less important for AI systems. These components of AI include big data, machine learning, deep learning, cognitive computing, neural networks, natural language processing, and pattern recognition. These components are not exhaustive and may be subject to changes as technology evolves. As AI applications develop, so do their underlying models. The latest versions of AI today can harness machine learning algorithms with self-generated code (Becker et al., 2023; Cao et al., 2023) to update the underlying models. Thus, AI models have the potential to incorporate self-learning capabilities to enable continuous improvements.

In conclusion, there are several relevant technologies which, when brought together, form what is described as artificial intelligence (AI). Thus, AI can vary hugely depending on the use-case it is addressing. An understanding of its capabilities is crucial to making the appropriate decisions when incorporating it into a firm's infrastructure.

3.2 *Big Data as an Enabler of Artificial Intelligence*

Artificial Intelligence, as we know it today, has been made possible by increases in computational capability and the manipulation of large volumes of information. It was formalized as an academic field of study circa 1965 and went through periods of stagnation and growth, with one of the world's first chatbots, *Eliza*, debuting in 1966 (Sharma et al., 2017). The bridging of theory into observable practice has progressed in recent decades as more powerful hardware became available, such as, for example, single-instruction multiple-data (*SIMD*) hardware (e.g., GPUs) from companies like NVIDIA.

Being able to process large volumes of information does not, by itself, constitute a value proposition for those who would employ Artificial Intelligence, as there are many details that must be tuned. Artificial Intelligence applications and logic may be used, for example, as a black box—accessing services provided via a *Software-as–a-Service* (*SaaS*) offered by an external entity. In this case, the information is fed into a system to obtain a desired output. The quality of such output may be measured in tune with the AI-supported task that is being fulfilled. For example, the performance of chat bots used for customer support may be measured with metrics such as response time to solve an issue or post-interaction user surveys. Different applications of AI, such as financial reporting and monitoring, will be subjected to other metrics of evaluation. Companies may also opt for developing their own internal AI solution for greater control of sensitive data that is critical to business processes. While this achieves finer granularity on the entire process, from data collection to value extraction, it increases operational complexity. Opting for this route requires consideration of tasks in the AI workflow, such as data collection, sanitization, and integration from multiple sources.

This requires considering the type of task that needs to be satisfied by the actual AI implementation, the type of AI model-building approach that is required, as well as the tuning of the training algorithms (e.g., the configuration of hyperparameters). In the context of in-house training, the matter of computational capability also comes into play. Should the company wishing to develop its in-house AI solution also acquire the computational capabilities to store, define, and train the models? Or should this functionality be delegated to external providers of computational power, such as those offered by Amazon, Google, and Microsoft, to name a few? This again raises the issue of potentially sensitive data being handled.

3.3 AI in Asset management

The companies referred to as wealth and asset management companies can be defined, for example, as follows by the Swiss financial market authority (2023)*: "Anyone who manages or is responsible for the safekeeping of assets held in collective investment schemes, or who represents foreign collective investment schemes [...], or manages the assets of occupational pension schemes on a commercial basis*". Thus, wealth and asset managers are firms that pool assets from numerous investors in order to invest collectively. These companies thereby serve individual investors by bundling their assets to invest in undertakings, which often require a minimum investment amount that is too high for a single investor alone (Welch, 2007). Alshaer (2023) and ChicagoSantoni de Sio and Mecacci (2021) argue that as the regulatory burden increases and the lack of a skilled workforce intensifies, smaller firms must use technological advancements to assist them with daily tasks and procedures. To stay afloat or even gain a competitive edge in the market, authors such as Nejad (2022) and Zavolokina et al. (2016) assert that it is especially crucial for asset management firms to innovate and adapt to new market movements. In the financial services sector, AI applications are perceived to be usable for front-to-back-office tasks (Coombs & Chopra, 2019; Fares et al., 2023).

The use cases of AI applications can range from market screening (Mer et al., 2024) and generation of model portfolios (Gunjan & Bhattacharyya, 2023) to actual trade execution (Addy et al., 2024) According to Mitra and

Mitra (2011) and Cohen (2022), high-frequency trading programs (HFTs) paired with web crawlers have already been used in several financial institutions. Zhou and Kalev (2019), in addition, postulate that with AI, this form of algorithmic trading is capable of analyze data and executing trades in milliseconds. In the front office, natural language processing is claimed by Olujimi and Ade-Ibijola (2023) to find direct use in client communication. Cardon et al. (2023) further claim it would allow companies to collect and track client conversations and provide extracts of each client meeting, thus giving companies with sophisticated AI models—which can incorporate pattern identification capabilities and predictive analytics—an advantage (Attaran & Deb, 2018). A similar development is claimed to occur in the back office. Cao (2022) states that AI applications can assist in compiling texts and extracting market or database information. Therefore, according to Vesna (2021), *it would* allow companies to assess risk data and highlight potential risk exposures through scenario analysis.

While the possible use-cases are vast and provide significant advantages such as cost reduction, faster data processing, and analytics (Ashta & Herrmann, 2021), it is also crucial to recognize the actual capabilities and difficulties it comes with. To assess if the implementation of an AI application is suitable, asset management companies should clarify certain questions from the beginning to avoid cost-intensive investments. Thus, we present the following framework, which aims to address these key clarification points.

4 Framework Factors

4.1 Clear Intent (Vision and Intent)

In light of technological advancements, it is often forgotten that these innovative technologies should be evaluated in conjunction with their intended use. Every new implementation follows similar procedures: it either starts with problems in the existing infrastructure or perceived significant enhancements through new applications (Kumar & Malik, 2012; Waziri et al., 2020). A clear vision of what should be achieved is crucial to avoid wasting resources. The replacement of more expensive and complex software often occurs when the pre-defined end-of-life for the software is approaching (Sakthivel, 2023). Modern technology thereby aims to replace or even enhance the existing systems. For every new implementation, it is necessary to clearly state its intent and the extent of its scope. While the intent can be of a strategic or financial nature, the scope itself defines which areas, processes, and tasks are subject to the new development.

While new advancements can be intriguingly interesting, their actual use case needs to be proven and tested. As argued by Van Assen et al. (2020) and Slota et al. (2020), there could be hype around AI and its perceived usefulness at the current stage. Therefore, the intended use of the new application must be clear from the beginning before attributing significant development budgets to the perceived useful solution.

4.2 Data Management

Data Security

Data security is a crucial factor for every new application and existing software (Bertino, 2016). Especially for wealth and asset management companies, data security plays a pivotal role in safeguarding client data (Fang et al., 2017). While AI is perceived to increase the security of existing networks, it can also become a security risk if misused.

According to (Becue et al., 2021) AI can protect against cyber threats by monitoring incoming attacks and learning from data patterns that can indicate such threats. This is based on the ability to analyze and draw conclusions from historical data. Li (2018) and Zaman et al. (2021) claim that AI can also execute countermeasures against incoming threats and set up security protocols. Thus, the use of AI for data encryption ensures that only authorized personnel can access sensitive data. Taherdoost (2022) further postulates that, for the purpose of data transfers, AI and encryption applications can contribute to the security of the IT infrastructure. However, as some of the software within a company may connect to entities in the outside world (e.g., other financial institutions or data providers), this poses a potential data security threat.

Based on Hoppner and Streatfeild (2023), the scope of its use and development can range from operating only in a confined network system with no access points to the outside, up to a system with full access to external databases and even the internet. Thus, there is concern regarding the safekeeping of data (Carmody et al., 2021). However, even when AI models might operate autonomously in a confined system, they are still an additional application adding to the complexity of a firm's IT infrastructure. Only data that can be accessed outside of a firm should be fed into AI applications (Hu et al., 2021; Zaman et al., 2021) or data that is non-sensitive. As such, criteria are not defined for a variety of data, such as client information or private financial information, making it necessary to either anonymize the information or not use it at all. Data security is, therefore, the crucial point when it comes to AI implementations, especially in wealth and asset management companies. Thus, it is likely that AI application use is extremely limited for some firms, or it cannot be used at all.

Data Quality

As the security of data is a crucial factor, so is the quality of the output produced. According to Zhang and Lu (2021), AI data analytical tools can handle large datasets and extract information through pattern recognition models. As further confirmed by Khanra et al. (2020), deep learning and big data analytics can generate more accurate and transparent output. Since the analysis of large datasets is complicated and would require significant manual validation time, it is crucial that the data generated by AI is accurate and reliable (Cheong, 2024).

As argued by Cao (2022) and Cao et al. (2024), advanced accuracy is also crucial for the compiling of texts and reports. The generation of market reports relies on the accuracy of their content. The AI application thereby makes use of natural language processing (NLP) to understand natural texts and human language. Furthermore, natural language generation (NLG) is used to structure the output and generate a readable result (Xing et al., 2018).

However, despite its fast processing, some time still needs to be dedicated to proof-reading and plausibility checking of the generated output (Hall et al., 2022). One crucial factor when it comes to data quality is bias-free output generation (Ntoutsi et al., 2020). An additional risk mentioned by Ying (2019) is that too much data input is observed to be detrimental, as it can lead to overfitting and confusion of the applied model. The availability of greater volumes of information in this big data world is important, and so is the computational ability to process it. But discernment must accompany data curation, training of models, and their testing. To ensure the generated output is transparent and flawless, machine learning models are required to be trained with accurate input data. As the saying goes, "garbage in, garbage out," it is important to know what the appropriate input data is. For financial institutions, such as wealth and asset management companies, manual plausibility checks might still be required, especially for generated outputs that can have significant reputational or economic impact (Maple et al., 2023).

Data Transparency
As indicated by Futia and Vetrò (2020), Hofmann et al. (2018), Vilone and Longo (2021), and Dwivedi et al. (2023), with a continuing collection of information and, therefore, new data points, it might become increasingly difficult to comprehend the root cause of AI-generated outputs.

As AI technology is complex, its key functionality must be understood. This is crucial to assess how information was generated and what the potential shortcomings are (Meena & Mishra, 2023; Weber et al., 2023). Authors like Schiff et al. (2020) and Allam and Dhunny (2019) raise concerns that the complexity of AI might lead to the blind adoption of applications, resulting in a loss of control and understandability. Consequently, the individual employee risks losing the "big picture" as well as an understanding of traditional processes (Enholm et al., 2022).

Whereby AI, on the one hand, adds to the complexity through its various capabilities and applicational use cases, on the other hand, it also contributes to a better understanding of problems through a more accurate assessment of big data and its structuring in an understandable way (Zhai et al., 2021). For the understanding and interpretation of data, AI applications rely on interpretable machine learning models, explaining how conclusions are drawn using linear models or decision-trees (Nielsen, 2022; Sahu et al., 2023). Furthermore, Salah et al. (2019) assert that blockchain is another contributor to the transparency of AI-generated output. Thus, blockchain can ensure the origin and traceability of data (Ilbiz & Durst, 2019). Thereby, the combination of various technologies can help to make sense of difficult-to-comprehend data or fuzzy processes.

4.3 *Regulatory Certainty*

As the regulations regarding the use of artificial intelligence vary from country to country, the regulatory landscape for each country a company operates in needs to be assessed. As described by Georgiadis and Poels (2021), every implementation that involves the use of client data or bears financial and data security risks requires legal backing. With AI still being at an early stage, the regulatory landscape is rather limited and not fully developed. Therefore, AI applications might be subject to already existing regulations. As for data and privacy protection, the regulatory landscape has developed significantly with regulations such as GDPR or CCPA. However, industry-specific regulations can also additionally apply, such as, for example, data security standards in the payment card industry (PCI) or accurate financial reporting requirements under Sarbanes-Oxley (SOX) (Hamdani et al., 2021).

As mentioned by authors such as Meurisch and Mühlhäuser (2021), and Addis and Kutar (2018), the new developments in AI leave companies either at risk of breaching existing regulations, such as data protection legislation, or entirely lacking accountability for AI-performed actions when blindly making use of AI applications. However, if regulations exist, it is crucial to adhere to them or obtain the required licensing. Therefore, the AI application needs to fulfill the mandatory standards and have the appropriate recognition in an auditing process (Falco et al., 2021).

Country-specific regulations should be considered, especially when handing over sophisticated processes, such as the investment process or client data handling, to automated engines (Buczynski et al., 2021).

4.4 *Effectiveness*

Efficiency

According to (Bisht et al., 2022) the time for each work step and process has already been reduced by faster technology; however, it would still be possible to push the boundaries of reducing processing time even further. Tasks that still require human interaction are prone to being subjected to technological advancements or automation. According to Makridakis (2017), this is especially the case for tasks in which humans are the limiting factor. In wealth and asset management companies, these are heavily manual tasks such as market screening, compiling market reports and documentation, and analyzing large datasets (often via Excel, Matlab, or R), which bear a risk of human errors (Chorafas, 2011; Phoon & Koh, 2017; Singh & Kaur, 2017). Furthermore, studies such as Baviskar et al. (2021), (Dwivedi et al., 2021) and Shin et al. (2022) reveal that a significant amount of time is spent on rudimentary tasks such as formatting, filling out work plans, scheduling, and planning.

Through the introduction of big-data analytics, simple, phrased requests can be handled efficiently by AI, which would otherwise take humans significantly longer to analyze. The screening capabilities allow the identification of keywords efficiently and can reduce analysis and research time (Yugal, 2021). Big-data analytics enhances not only the analysis capabilities but also the ability to recognize patterns and allows the interlinking of potential causes of their occurrence. For generated output, AI applications can be used to validate the results by using multi-factor models, providing a holistic insight into potential shortcomings (Černevičienė & Kabašinskas, 2022). Despite its advantages, Meyer and Oosthuizen (2023) and Abedin (2022) argue that through the continuous addition of new analysis possibilities, a statutory stage could be reached in which over-perfectionism could slow down entire processes.

Cost Reduction
According to Kokina and Blanchette (2019), AI offers the possibility to automate these labor-intensive processes. However, training is required to make appropriate use of the technology and to validate its generated outcomes (Schöning & Pfisterer, 2023). Therefore, it is crucial to conduct a proper cost-benefit analysis. Despite implementation costs and required training, AI can foster, over time, a lower cost structure (Ashta & Herrmann, 2021). In addition, once certain tasks are set up correctly and performed by AI without interruption, they become less error-prone and thereby also reduce the costs of failure and correction (Mandala et al., 2022). Thus, the overall perceived benefit of AI comes from the cost-saving aspect, as time-consuming or labor-intensive processes can be automated.

Enhanced Accuracy
While timesaving and cost reductions are some of the dominantly addressed reasons for the use of AI, its enhanced accuracy for rudimentary tasks is often neglected. For instance, human creation of market reports might occasionally lack in-depth analysis, or investment reports might fail to provide a holistic picture. AI is capable of delivering continuous, consistent outputs (Vandewinckele et al., 2020). While this deviation might be insignificant for certain tasks, for other tasks, such as predictive models, it can have significant impacts overall. According to Zakaria et al. (2023), AI can overcome "human-error" and contribute to more accurate and consistent outputs. Plausibility checks combined with big data analytics allow companies to generate better and more reliable output (Subudhi, 2019). Especially for big-data analysis, technologically advanced

applications can be more accurate and faster than human data analysts (Bose et al., 2023; Vassakis et al., 2018), thereby contributing to greater efficiency by reducing manual feedback loops and cost-intensive troubleshooting.

4.5 Client

An assumption about AI, addressed by several authors, is its client-interacting capabilities, which can replace human call centers and support staff (Graßmann & Schermuly, 2021; Nasir et al., 2021). This assumption about AI applications intensified through the widespread emergence of ChatGPT and real-time chatbots, avatars, or simply voice assistants (Dwivedi et al., 2021; Rane, 2023).

For wealth and asset management companies, the use of automated client interaction can be beneficial, especially when dealing with rudimentary requests (Suta et al., 2020). According to Luo et al. (2022) and Adamopoulou and Moussiades (2020), through AI, client interaction can largely be enhanced, and the user experience intensified.

While most wealth and asset management companies are low-staffed, forms of engagement that can reduce the manual workload add significant benefits (Darbyshire, 2024; Martens & Tolan, 2018). These benefits can range from client meeting recordings as word-to-text protocols enabled through natural language processing to direct client interactions when handling client orders. Furthermore, the automated suggestion of investment strategies and tailored investment advice is another possible positive way of incorporating AI. Additionally, benefits could also originate from automated portfolio monitoring and automated allocation.

While the use of AI applications can make a difference and lead to a competitive edge in client interaction, it also carries inherent disadvantages. Smaller asset managers benefit from close and direct client contact, but the use of generic AI interactions can weaken the client relationship if not carefully implemented. As mentioned in Luo et al. (2022), more complex client requests that require human assistance will increase the time consumption on the client's end when dealing with chatbots, which might not provide the required answers quickly enough. Furthermore, Vlasceanu et al. (2023) and Arman and Lamiya (2023) noted that a general challenge could be creating a user experience that is distinguishable from competitors despite the generic AI interactions.

5 Conceptual Framework for AI in Asset management

The proposed framework is based on previous readiness framework attempts for AI implementations and combines them with wealth and asset management. Thereby, it draws on AI introduction frameworks by utilizing their dominant components.

In particular, the proposed framework draws upon the previously conducted research from Wirtz et al. (2020), Holmström (2022), Wirtz et al. (2022), as well as Brem et al. (2021), Zhu et al. (2024), Reim et al. (2020), and Zhou et al. (2022), Nortje and Grobbelaar (2020). The derived factors above are indicators for the implementation of AI applications and are discussed in the realm of wealth and asset management. They provide guidance on whether the implementation of AI applications can be considered potentially beneficial for a wealth and asset management company. The following table summarizes these crucial indicators and addresses key considerations, as well as their applicability and widespread use cases.

The proposed framework comprises the identified factors from the literature review and formulates acceptance criteria as described in Table 1. In contrast to the proposed model from Wirtz et al. (2020), the revised model replaces challenges with the effectiveness of AI, as the challenges are part of the intersection between the five identified factors (Fig. 1).

The proposed model places the clear intended use of AI at the center of the framework, as it serves as the starting point for assessing and making decisions regarding the use of AI from both a strategic and operational point of view. Thus, it follows the general decision-making approach for technology implementations. More emphasis is placed on client interaction and experience, as this factor is crucial in wealth and asset management. The framework, furthermore, accentuates data management from a data quality and transparency perspective to ensure the reliability of the generated output data. As mentioned, the challenges arise at the intersections between the factors (Fig. 2).

Regulatory challenges could arise between the technological feasibility and the regulatory limitations for data use and storage within the client's sphere. Therefore, the above-mentioned country-specific regulatory landscape might pose a challenge for companies trying to make effective use of collected data. Thus, difficulties could emerge between the optimal utilization of available data and the regulatory limitations on storing and using them.

Table 1 Framework to test the usefulness of AI in Asset Management Companies

Key considerations	*Acceptance criteria*	*Unacceptance criteria*	*Cases*
Clear intent			
Clear intent (vision & intent)	Clear use case the AI application is used for	General curiosity with no immediate business reason	For example, AI is used to generate annual market reports and investor statements
Data management			
Data security	Enhances or does not jeopardize existing data security	Sensitive data leakage unauthorized third-party access	For example, client data is not accessible by unauthorized third parties
Data quality (output reliability)	Increasing data quality or maintaining high quality	Wrong, incomplete, or biased data	For example, better outcomes due to the elimination of wrong/misleading data
Data transparence (explainability)	Explainable processes and proceedings	Uncertainty regarding decision making processes	For example, AI decisions are explainable and comprehensive
Regulatory			
Regulatory certainty	Regulatory certainty regarding the use of AI systems is insured	No regulatory clarity of responsibilities and accountability	For example, decisions taken by AI to execute trades are either the responsibility of software provider of the asset management company
Effectiveness			
Efficiency	Reduction of work steps, leaner process	No work step reduction, complexity increments, and more feedback looks are required	For example, the use of AI chatbots reduced the client interaction work steps. 4 eye principle got eliminated as AI does the validation
Cost reduction	Foreseeable cost reductions	No amortization trough cost reduction	For example, the implementation of AI in compiling investment outlook publications leads to cost reductions

(continued)

Table 1 (continued)

Key considerations	*Acceptance criteria*	*Unacceptance criteria*	*Cases*
Enhanced accuracy	Maintaining output constancy, without variations	No change in analysis and manufacturing time	For example, consistent output allowing precise decision-making
Client			
Client experience	Client interaction can be automated/ enhance	Client interaction becomes worse and too complex	For example, client experience is enhanced through multiple touchpoints and 24/7 service possibility
Client engagement	Client self-service possible	Client engagement becomes a regulatory and administrative burden	For example, rudimentary client request such as guiding through documents, or the online banking platform are handled by AI

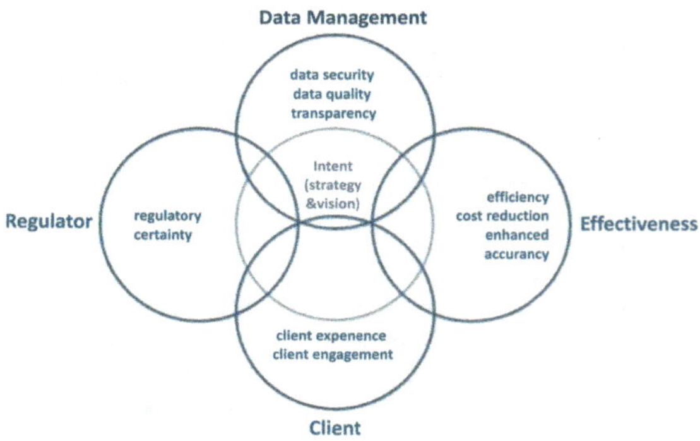

Fig. 1 Framework for the use of artificial intelligence (AI) in WAM. Adjusted from Wirtz et al. (2020)

Furthermore, challenges are also likely to arise between data management and the effectiveness factor, whereby the quality of data and transparency need to be ensured to allow efficient operation. Therefore, accuracy is also dependent on the collected client data, its consistency and transparency.

Fig. 2 Challenges and key considerations

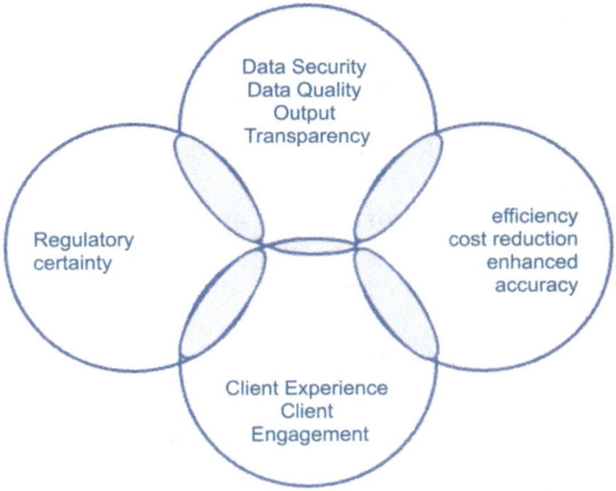

6 Conclusion

The current AI developments indicate high potential for its use in the financial sector. While some large financial institutions already make use of the technology, it is largely unused in smaller financial firms. In the years to come, it is perceived that its use will increase and become a daily tool among workforces. Thereby, it might help wealth and asset management companies in daily tasks and enhance existing processes.

Despite its promising benefits, AI applications are still at an early development stage. Companies should not get carried away by the current developments and make hasty decisions. While the potential use cases might be apparent and there might be a clear intent for what it should be used for, there is still uncertainty regarding data management and maintenance within smaller companies. To make full use of the technology, several input points, e.g., the internet, databases, and third-party servers, might be required. As regulatory clarity is not provided in every instance, there might be risks of potential legal breaches and security violations. Even in instances where regulatory clarity is provided, data security and cyber security remain of crucial importance. Above all, the generated output must be transparent and reliable to be useful. The appropriate training of the workforce involved is, therefore, crucial. It is recommended that companies clarify the scope of AI applications first and narrow down their intended use cases and capabilities. Furthermore, clarity about the regulatory landscape and the enforcement of data protection regulations in the area where the company is operating is crucial to avoid legal breaches. While taking time and making a decisive decision, it should be recognized that there is also the possibility of a first-mover advantage by making use of innovative technology. This not only provides the above-mentioned benefits but also creates awareness of being at the forefront of the technology among industry peers, which can have a positive market effect. As the AI market is growing, it is crucial for wealth and asset management companies to select the appropriate application. The decision for one AI application over another might be derived from the intended use of the AI application, as not every AI model fulfills all potential requirements. Furthermore, as costs and efficiency play a significant role when adopting AI applications, recurring costs for maintenance and training should be considered. Thus, setting up an amortization calculation is crucial to predict the cost efficiency and financial usefulness of an AI application.

To conclude this article, it needs to be mentioned that there might be firm-specific reasons why a different approach for the adoption of AI applications in wealth and asset management companies might be used. Attractive first-adopter trial implementations with low or even no costs, personal connections to an application provider, or even the firm's own expertise to develop or set up such an AI application could be reasons to deviate from a best practice approach. Thus, the ideas discussed in this paper and its proposed framework provide various controversies, opening the gates for further research and analysis regarding the appropriateness of AI applications. One suggestion is to assess the five proposed criteria in a case study set up to further investigate their usability in wealth and asset management companies. Furthermore, the criteria could also be applied to companies of varied sizes or even financial institutions with different setups, such as banks, loan brokers, or financial market data providers, thus providing more clarity about the appropriate practices in each market.

References

Abedin, B. (2022). Managing the tension between opposing effects of explainability of artificial intelligence: A contingency theory perspective. *Internet Research*, *32*(2), 425–453.

Adamopoulou, E., & Moussiades, L. (2020). An overview of chatbot technology. In *IFIP international conference on artificial intelligence applications and innovations* (pp. 373–383). Springer.

Addis, M. C., & Kutar, M. (2018). The general data protection regulation (GDPR), emerging technologies and UK organisations: Awareness, implementation, and readiness.

Addy, W. A., Ajayi-Nifise, A. O., Bello, B. G., Tula, S. T., Odeyem, O., & Falaiye, T. (2024). Algorithmic trading and AI: A review of strategies and market impact. *World Journal of Advanced Engineering Technology and Sciences, 11*(1), 258–267.

Aldoseri, A., Al-Khalifa, K. N., & Hamouda, A. S. (2023). *Re-think Data Strategy and Integration for Artificial Intelligence: Concepts, Opportunities and Challenges*. MDPI AG. https://doi.org/10.20944/preprints202305.1565.v2

Allam, Z., & Dhunny, Z. A. (2019). On big data, artificial intelligence and smart cities. *Cities, 89*, 80–91.

Alshaer, M. (2023). A systematic review of the use of artificial intelligence in managing innovation in E-Government organizations worldwide. *International Journal of Technology and Systems, 8*(2), 65–81.

Arman, M., & Lamiya, U. R. (2023). ChatGPT, a product of AI, and its influences in the business world. *Talaa: Journal of Islamic Finance, 3*(1), 18–37.

Ashta, A., & Herrmann, H. (2021). Artificial intelligence and fintech: An overview of opportunities and risks for banking, investments, and microfinance. *Strategic Change, 30*(3), 211–222.

Astalin, P. K. (2013). Qualitative research designs: A conceptual framework. *International Journal of Social Science & Interdisciplinary Research, 2*(1), 118–124.

Attaran, M., & Deb, P. (2018). Machine learning: The new'big thing'for competitive advantage. *International Journal of Knowledge Engineering and Data Mining, 5*(4), 277–305.

Baviskar, D., Ahirrao, S., Potdar, V., & Kotecha, K. (2021). Efficient automated processing of the unstructured documents using artificial intelligence: A systematic literature review and future directions. *IEEE Access, 9*, 72894–72936.

Becker, B. A., Denny, P., Finnie-Ansley, J., Luxton-Reilly, A., Prather, J., & Santos, E. A. (2023, March). Programming is hard-or at least it used to be: Educational opportunities and challenges of ai code generation. In *Proceedings of the 54th ACM Technical Symposium on Computer Science Education V. 1* (pp. 500–506).

Bécue, A., Praça, I., & Gama, J. (2021). Artificial intelligence, cyber-threats and Industry 4.0: Challenges and opportunities. *Artificial Intelligence Review, 54*(5), 3849–3886.

Behnood, A., & Golafshani, E. M. (2022). Artificial intelligence to model the performance of concrete mixtures and elements: A review. *Archives of Computational Methods in Engineering, 29*(4), 1941–1964.

Bertino, E. (2016). Data security and privacy: Concepts, approaches, and research directions. In *2016 IEEE 40th Annual Computer Software and Applications Conference (COMPSAC)* (Vol. 1, pp. 400–407). IEEE.

Bibel, W. (2018, July). On a scientific discipline (once) named AI. In *Ijcai* (pp. 5143–5149).

Bisht, D., Singh, R., Gehlot, A., Akram, S. V., Singh, A., Montero, E. C., ... Twala, B. (2022). Imperative role of integrating digitalization in the firms finance: A technological perspective. *Electronics, 11*(19), 3252.

Borges, A. F., Laurindo, F. J., Spínola, M. M., Gonçalves, R. F., & Mattos, C. A. (2021). The strategic use of artificial intelligence in the digital era: Systematic literature review and future research directions. *International Journal of Information Management, 57*, 102225.

Bose, S., Dey, S. K., & Bhattacharjee, S. (2023). Big data, data analytics and artificial intelligence in accounting: An overview. *Handbook of Big Data Research Methods, 0*, 32.

Brem, A., Giones, F., & Werle, M. (2021). The AI digital revolution in innovation: A conceptual framework of artificial intelligence technologies for the management of innovation. *IEEE Transactions on Engineering Management, 70*(2), 770–776.

Buczynski, W., Cuzzolin, F., & Sahakian, B. (2021). A review of machine learning experiments in equity investment decision-making: Why most published research findings do not live up to their promise in real life. *International Journal of Data Science and Analytics, 11*, 221–242.

Cao, L. (2022). AI in finance: Challenges, techniques, and opportunities. *ACM Computing Surveys (CSUR), 55*(3), 1–38.

Cao, S. S., Jiang, W., Lei, L., & Zhou, Q. (2024). Applied AI for finance and accounting: Alternative data and opportunities. *Pacific-Basin Finance Journal*, 102307.

Cao, Y., Li, S., Liu, Y., Yan, Z., Dai, Y., Yu, P. S., & Sun, L. (2023). A comprehensive survey of ai-generated content (aigc): A history of generative ai from gan to chatgpt. arXiv preprint. arXiv:2303.04226.

Cardon, P. W., Ma, H., & Fleischmann, C. (2023). Recorded business meetings and AI algorithmic tools: Negotiating privacy concerns, psychological safety, and control. *International Journal of Business Communication, 60*(4), 1095–1122.

Carmody, J., Shringarpure, S., & Van de Venter, G. (2021). AI and privacy concerns: A smart meter case study. *Journal of Information, Communication and Ethics in Society, 19*(4), 492–505.

Černevičienė, J., & Kabašinskas, A. (2022). Review of multi-criteria decision-making methods in finance using explainable artificial intelligence. *Frontiers in Artificial Intelligence, 5*, 827584.

Cheong, B. C. (2024). Transparency and accountability in AI systems: Safeguarding wellbeing in the age of algorithmic decision-making. *Frontiers in Human Dynamics*, *6*, 1421273.

ChicagoSantoni de Sio, F., & Mecacci, G. (2021). Four responsibility gaps with artificial intelligence: Why they matter and how to address them. *Philosophy and Technology*, *34*, 1057–1084.

Chorafas, D. N. (2011). *Wealth Management: Private Banking, Investment Decisions, and Structured Financial Products*. Elsevier.

Cohen, G. (2022). Algorithmic trading and financial forecasting using advanced artificial intelligence methodologies. *Mathematics*, *10*(18), 3302.

Coombs, C., & Chopra, R. (2019). Artificial intelligence and data analytics: Emerging opportunities and challenges in financial services.

Cowls, J., Tsamados, A., Taddeo, M., & Floridi, L. (2021). A definition, benchmark and database of AI for social good initiatives. *Nature Machine Intelligence*, *3*(2), 111–115. Chicago.

Darbyshire, M. (2024). Talent shortfall limits funds' ability to sell wealthy clients on 'alts': Asset managers struggle to hire salespeople as they move into more complex products. *The Financial Times Limited, 2024*.

Dwivedi, R., Dave, D., Naik, H., Singhal, S., Omer, R., Patel, P., & Ranjan, R. (2023). Explainable AI (XAI): Core ideas, techniques, and solutions. *ACM Computing Surveys*, *55*(9), 1–33.

Dwivedi, Y. K., Hughes, L., Ismagilova, E., Aarts, G., Coombs, C., Crick, T., ... Williams, M. D. (2021). Artificial Intelligence (AI): Multidisciplinary perspectives on emerging challenges, opportunities, and agenda for research, practice and policy. *International Journal of Information Management*, *57*, 101994.

Edelmann, A., Wolff, T., Montagne, D., & Bail, C. A. (2020). Computational social science and sociology. *Annual Review of Sociology*, *46*(1), 61–81. Chicago.

Enholm, I. M., Papagiannidis, E., Mikalef, P., & Krogstie, J. (2022). Artificial intelligence and business value: A literature review. *Information Systems Frontiers*, *24*(5), 1709–1734.

Falco, G., Shneiderman, B., Badger, J., Carrier, R., Dahbura, A., Danks, D., ... Yeong, Z. K. (2021). Governing AI safety through independent audits. *Nature Machine Intelligence*, *3*(7), 566–571.

Fang, W., Wen, X. Z., Zheng, Y., & Zhou, M. (2017). A survey of big data security and privacy-preservi. *IETE Technical Review*, *34*(5), 544–560.

Fares, O. H., Butt, I., & Lee, S. H. M. (2023). Utilization of artificial intelligence in the banking sector: A systematic literature review. *Journal of Financial Services Marketing*, *28*(4), 835–852.

Futia, G., & Vetrò, A. (2020). On the integration of knowledge graphs into deep learning models for a more comprehensible AI—Three challenges for future research. *Information*, *11*(2), 122.

Georgiadis, G., & Poels, G. (2021). Enterprise architecture management as a solution for addressing general data protection regulation requirements in a big data context: A systematic mapping study. *Information Systems and e-Business Management*, *19*, 313–362.

Graßmann, C., & Schermuly, C. C. (2021). Coaching with artificial intelligence: Concepts and capabilities. *Human Resource Development Review*, *20*(1), 106–126.

Gunjan, A., & Bhattacharyya, S. (2023). A brief review of portfolio optimization techniques. *Artificial Intelligence Review*, *56*(5), 3847–3886.

Gupta, R., Kukreja, G., Gupta, A., & Tyagi, L. (2021). Artificial Intelligence fostering fintech: Emerging trends and use cases. In *Cybersecurity in Emerging Digital Era: First International Conference, ICCEDE 2020, Greater Noida, India, October 9–10, 2020, Revised Selected Papers 1* (pp. 61–73). Springer International Publishing.

Hall, S. W., Sakzad, A., & Choo, K. K. R. (2022). Explainable artificial intelligence for digital forensics. *Wiley Interdisciplinary Reviews: Forensic Science*, *4*(2), e1434.

Hamdani, S. W. A., Abbas, H., Janjua, A. R., Shahid, W. B., Amjad, M. F., Malik, J., & Khan, A. W. (2021). Cybersecurity standards in the context of operating system: Practical aspects, analysis, and comparisons. *ACM Computing Surveys (CSUR)*, *54*(3), 1–36.

Hofmann, R. R., Mueller, S. T., Klein, G., & Litman, J. (2018). Metrics for explainable AI: Challenges and prospects. *arXiv preprint arXiv:1812.04608*.

Holmström, J. (2022). From AI to digital transformation: The AI readiness framework. *Business Horizons*, *65*(3), 329–339.

Hoppner, T., & Streatfeild, L. (2023). Chatgpt, Bard & Co.: An introduction to ai for competition and regulatory lawyers. *An Introduction to AI for Competition and Regulatory Lawyers* (February 23, 2023), 9.

Hu, Y., Kuang, W., Qin, Z., Li, K., Zhang, J., Gao, Y., … Li, K. (2021). Artificial intelligence security: Threats and countermeasures. *ACM Computing Surveys (CSUR)*, *55*(1), 1–36.

Ilbiz, E., & Durst, S. (2019). The appropriation of blockchain for small and medium-sized enterprises. *Journal of Innovation Management*, *7*(1), 26–45.

Jabareen, Y. (2009). Building a conceptual framework: Philosophy, definitions, and procedure. *International Journal of Qualitative Methods*, *8*(4), 49–62.

Javed Awan, M., Rahim, M. S. M., Nobanee, H., Munawar, A., Yasin, A., & Zain, A. M. (2021). Social media and stock market prediction: A big data approach. *Computers, Materials and Continua*, *67*(2), 2569–2583.

Kaushal, S., & Mishra, D. (2024, March). Strategic implications of AI in contemporary business and society. In *2024 2nd International Conference on Disruptive Technologies (ICDT)* (pp. 1469–1474). IEEE.

Khanra, S., Dhir, A., & Mäntymäki, M. (2020). Big data analytics and enterprises: A bibliometric synthesis of the literature. *Enterprise Information Systems, 14*(6), 737–768.

Kokina, J., & Blanchette, S. (2019). Early evidence of digital labor in accounting: Innovation with Robotic Process Automation. *International Journal of Accounting Information Systems, 35*, 100431.

Kumar, A., & Malik, S. C. (2012). Stochastic modeling of a computer system with priority to PM over S/W replacement subject to maximum operation and repair times. *International Journal of Computer Applications, 43*(3), 27–34.

Kundi, B., El Morr, C., Gorman, R., & Dua, E. (2023). *Artificial Intelligence and Bias: A Scoping Review* (pp. 199–215). AI and Society.

Li, J. H. (2018). Cyber security meets artificial intelligence: A survey. *Frontiers of Information Technology & Electronic Engineering, 19*(12), 1462–1474.

Litzenberger, R., Castura, J., & Gorelick, R. (2012). The impacts of automation and high frequency trading on market quality. *Annual Review of Financial Economics, 4*(1), 59–98.

Luo, B., Lau, R. Y., Li, C., & Si, Y. W. (2022). A critical review of state-of-the-art chatbot designs and applications. *Wiley Interdisciplinary Reviews: Data Mining and Knowledge Discovery, 12*(1), e1434.

Makridakis, S. (2017). The forthcoming Artificial Intelligence (AI) revolution: Its impact on society and firms. *Futures, 90*, 46–60.

Mandala, G. N., Buddhi, D., Arumugam, M., Harbola, S., Othman, B., & Almashaqbeh, H. A. (2022, April). A critical review of applications of Artificial Intelligence (AI) and its powered technologies in the financial industry. In *2022 2nd International Conference on Advance Computing and Innovative Technologies in Engineering (ICACITE)* (pp. 2362–2365). IEEE.

Maple, C., Szpruch, L., Epiphaniou, G., Staykova, K., Singh, S., Penwarden, W., ... Avramovic, P. (2023). The AI revolution: Opportunities and challenges for the finance sector. *arXiv preprint arXiv:2308.16538.*

Martens, B., & Tolan, S. (2018). *Will This Time Be Different? A Review of the Literature on the Impact of Artificial Intelligence on Employment.* Incomes and Growth.

Meena, R., & Mishra, A. (2023). Need for Artificial Intelligence (AI) to be explainable in banking and finance: Review of AI applications, AI Black Box, Xai Tools and Principles: *Review of AI Applications, AI Black Box, Xai Tools and Principles.*

Mer, A., Singhal, K., & Virdi, A. S. (2024). A review of the role of artificial intelligence in banking and stock market trading. *Finance Analytics in Business: Perspectives on Enhancing Efficiency and Accuracy*, 175–198.

Meurisch, C., & Mühlhäuser, M. (2021). Data protection in AI services: A survey. *ACM Computing Surveys (CSUR), 54*(2), 1–38.

Meyer, W., & Oosthuizen, R. (2023, June). Verification & validation methods for complex AI-enabled cyber-physical learning-based systems: A systematic

literature review. In *2023 IEEE International Conference on Engineering, Technology and Innovation (ICE/ITMC)* (pp. 1–7). IEEE.
Mitra, L., & Mitra, G. (2011). Applications of news analytics in finance: A review. *The Handbook of News Analytics in Finance*, 1–39.
Nasir, A., Shaukat, K., Iqbal Khan, K., Hameed, A., Alam, I., M., T., & Luo, S. (2021). Trends and directions of financial technology (Fintech) in society and environment: A bibliometric study. *Applied Sciences*, *11*(21), 10353.
Nejad, M. G. (2022). Research on financial innovations: An interdisciplinary review. *International Journal of Bank Marketing*, *40*(3), 578–612.
Nielsen, S. (2022). Management accounting and the concepts of exploratory data analysis and unsupervised machine learning: A literature study and future directions. *Journal of Accounting & Organizational Change*, *18*(5), 811–853.
Nortje, M. A., & Grobbelaar, S. S. (2020). A framework for the implementation of artificial intelligence in business enterprises: A readiness model. In *2020 IEEE International Conference on Engineering, Technology and Innovation (ICE/ITMC)* (pp. 1–10). IEEE.
Ntoutsi, E., Fafalios, P., Gadiraju, U., Iosifidis, V., Nejdl, W., Vidal, M. E., Staab, S. (2020). Bias in data-driven artificial intelligence systems—an introductory survey. *Wiley Interdisciplinary Reviews: Data Mining and Knowledge Discovery*, *10*(3), e1356.
Nurlia, N., Daud, I., & Rosadi, M. E. (2023). AI implementation impact on workforce productivity: The role of AI training and organizational adaptation. *Escalate: Economics and Business Journal*, *1*(01), 01–13.
Oldemeyer, L., Jede, A., & Teuteberg, F. (2024). Investigation of artificial intelligence in SMEs: A systematic review of the state of the art and the main implementation challenges. *Management Review Quarterly*, 1–43.
Olujimi, P. A., & Ade-Ibijola, A. (2023). NLP techniques for automating responses to customer queries: A systematic review. *Discover Artificial Intelligence*, *3*(1), 20.
Paul, J., Merchant, A., Dwivedi, Y. K., & Rose, G. (2021). Writing an impactful review article: What do we know and what do we need to know? *Journal of Business Research*, *133*, 337–340.
Phoon, K., & Koh, F. (2017). Robo-advisors and wealth management. *The Journal of Alternative Investments*, *20*(3), 79–94.
Rabah, K. (2018). Convergence of AI, IoT, big data and blockchain: A review. *The Lake Institute Journal*, *1*(1), 1–18.
Rane, N. (2023). ChatGPT and similar generative artificial intelligence (AI) for smart industry: Role, challenges and opportunities for industry 4.0, industry 5.0 and society 5.0. *Challenges and Opportunities for Industry*, *4*.
Ranjan, S., Gupta, D. R., & Gupta, D. A. (2020). Artificial intelligence in financial acumen: Challenges and opportunities. *Cosmos Journal of Engineering & Technology*, *10*(1), 1–5.

Reddy, B., & Fields, R. (2022, April). From past to present: A comprehensive technical review of rule-based expert systems from 1980–2021. In *Proceedings of the 2022 ACM Southeast Conference* (pp. 167–172).

Reim, W., Åström, J., & Eriksson, O. (2020). Implementation of artificial intelligence (AI): A roadmap for business model innovation. *Ai*, *1*(2), 11.

Sahu, S. K., Mokhade, A., & Bokde, N. D. (2023). An overview of machine learning, deep learning, and reinforcement learning-based techniques in quantitative finance: Recent progress and challenges. *Applied Sciences*, *13*(3), 1956.

Sakthivel, S. (2023). A critical review of cost-benefit analysis for business software investments. *American Journal of Business*, *38*(4), 229–247.

Salah, K., Rehman, M. H. U., Nizamuddin, N., & Al-Fuqaha, A. (2019). Blockchain for AI: Review and open research challenges. *IEEE Access*, *7*, 10127–10149.

Sarker, I. H. (2022). AI-based modeling: Techniques, applications and research issues towards automation, intelligent and smart systems. *SN Computer Science*, *3*(2), 158.

Schiff, D., Rakova, B., Ayesh, A., Fanti, A., & Lennon, M. (2020). Principles to practices for responsible AI: Closing the gap. *arXiv preprint arXiv:2006.04707*.

Schmidt, A., Mayer, S., & Buschek, D. (2021, May). Introduction to intelligent user interfaces. In *Extended Abstracts of the 2021 CHI Conference on Human Factors in Computing Systems* (pp. 1–4).

Schöning, J., & Pfisterer, H. J. (2023). Safe and trustful AI for closed-loop control systems. *Electronics*, *12*(16), 3489.

Seng, J. K. P., Ang, K. L. M., Peter, E., & Mmonyi, A. (2022). Artificial intelligence (AI) and machine learning for multimedia and edge information processing. *Electronics*, *11*(14), 2239.

Sharma, V., Goyal, M., & Malik, D. (2017). An intelligent behaviour shown by chatbot system. *International Journal of New Technology and Research*, *3*(4), 263312.

Shin, Y., Kim, S., & Lee, Y. H. (2022). AI musculoskeletal clinical applications: How can AI increase my day-to-day efficiency? *Skeletal Radiology*, *51*(2), 293–304.

Singh, I., & Kaur, N. (2017). Wealth management through robo advisory. *International Journal of Research-Granthaalayah*, *5*(6), 33–43.

Slota, S. C., Fleischmann, K. R., Greenberg, S., Verma, N., Cummings, B., Li, L., & Shenefiel, C. (2020). Good systems, bad data?: Interpretations of AI hype and failures. *Proceedings of the Association for Information Science and Technology*, *57*(1), e275. Chicago.

Subudhi, S. R. I. H. A. R. I. (2019). Banking on artificial intelligence: Opportunities & challenges for banks in India. *International Journal of Research in Commerce, Economics & Management*, *9*(7).

Suta, P., Lan, X., Wu, B., Mongkolnam, P., & Chan, J. H. (2020). An overview of machine learning in chatbots. *International Journal of Mechanical Engineering and Robotics Research*, *9*(4), 502–510.

Swiss Financial Market Authority. (2023). Asset management: Managers of collective assets. https://www.finma.ch/en/authorisation/asset-management/.

Taherdoost, H. (2022). Blockchain technology and artificial intelligence together: A critical review on applications. *Applied Sciences*, *12*(24), 12948.

Tian, Y. H., Chen, X. L., Xiong, H. K., Li, H. L., Dai, L. R., Chen, J., & Gao, W. (2017). Towards human-like and transhuman perception in AI 2.0: A review. *Frontiers of Information Technology & Electronic Engineering*, *18*, 58–67.

Van Assen, M., Banerjee, I., & De Cecco, C. N. (2020). Beyond the artificial intelligence hype: What lies behind the algorithms and what we can achieve. *Journal of Thoracic Imaging*, *35*, S3–S10.

Vandewinckele, L., Claessens, M., Dinkla, A., Brouwer, C., Crijns, W., Verellen, D., & van Elmpt, W. (2020). Overview of artificial intelligence-based applications in radiotherapy: Recommendations for implementation and quality assurance. *Radiotherapy & Oncology*, *153*, 55–66.

Vassakis, K., Petrakis, E., & Kopanakis, I. (2018). Big data analytics: Applications, prospects and challenges. *Mobile big data: A roadmap from models to technologies*, 3–20.

Vesna, B. A. (2021). Challenges of financial risk management: AI applications. *Management: Journal of Sustainable Business and Management Solutions in Emerging Economies*, *26*(3), 27–34.

Vilone, G., & Longo, L. (2021). Classification of explainable artificial intelligence methods through their output formats. *Machine Learning and Knowledge Extraction*, *3*(3), 615–661.

Vlasceanu, C. F., Valentin, T. A., & Țigu, G. (2023). The fusion of advanced technology: Artificial intelligence and virtual reality in the cruise industry and global hospitality organizations. *Revista de Management Comparat International*, *24*(4), 650–665.

Wamba, S. F., Bawack, R. E., Guthrie, C., Queiroz, M. M., & Carillo, K. D. A. (2021). Are we preparing for a good AI society? A bibliometric review and research agenda. *Technological Forecasting and Social Change*, *164*, 120482.

Wang, H., Fu, T., Du, Y., Gao, W., Huang, K., Liu, Z., ... Zitnik, M. (2023). Scientific discovery in the age of artificial intelligence. *Nature*, *620*(7972), 47–60.

Waziri, T. A., Yakasai, B. M., & Yusuf, I. (2020). On some discounted replacement models of a series system. *Life Cycle Reliability and Safety Engineering*, *9*, 291–301.

Weber, P., Carl, K. V., & Hinz, O. (2023). Applications of explainable artificial intelligence in finance—a systematic review of finance, information systems, and computer science literature. *Management Review Quarterly*, 1–41.

Welch, S. (2007). Coming to portfolios near you: Investment ideas you should be paying more attention to. *The Journal of Wealth Management, 10*(2), 63.

Wirtz, B. W., Weyerer, J. C., & Kehl, I. (2022). Governance of artificial intelligence: A risk and guideline-based integrative framework. *Government Information Quarterly, 39*(4), 101685.

Wirtz, B. W., Weyerer, J. C., & Sturm, B. J. (2020). The dark sides of artificial intelligence: An integrated AI Governance framework for public administration. *International Journal of Public Administration, 43*(9), 818–829. Informa UK Limited. https://doi.org/10.1080/01900692.2020.1749851

Xing, F. Z., Cambria, E., & Welsch, R. E. (2018). Natural language based financial forecasting: A survey. *Artificial Intelligence Review, 50*(1), 49–73.

Ying, X. (2019). An overview of overfitting and its solutions. *Journal of Physics: Conference Series, 1168*, 022022. IOP Publishing.

Yugal, L. (2021). Business analytics: Trends and challenges. *Integrated Emerging Methods of Artificial Intelligence & Cloud Computing*, 236–243.

Zakaria, S., Manaf, S. M. A., Amron, M. T., & Suffian, M. T. M. (2023). Has the World of finance changed? A review of the influence of artificial intelligence on financial management studies. *Information Management and Business Review, 15*(4 (SI) I), 420–432.

Zaman, S., Alhazmi, K., Aseeri, M. A., Ahmed, M. R., Khan, R. T., Kaiser, M. S., & Mahmud, M. (2021). Security threats and artificial intelligence based countermeasures for internet of things networks: A comprehensive survey. *IEEE Access, 9*, 94668–94690.

Zavolokina, L., Dolata, M., & Schwabe, G. (2016). The FinTech phenomenon: Antecedents of financial innovation perceived by the popular press. *Financial Innovation, 2*, 1–1.

Zhai, X., Chu, X., Chai, C. S., Jong, M. S. Y., Istenic, A., Spector, M., … Li, Y. (2021). A review of artificial intelligence (AI) in Education from 2010 to 2020. *Complexity, 2021*, 1–18.

Zhang, C., & Lu, Y. (2021). Study on artificial intelligence: The state of the art and future prospects. *Journal of Industrial Information Integration, 23*, 100224.

Zhou, H., & Kalev, P. S. (2019). Algorithmic and high frequency trading in Asia-Pacific, now and the future. *Pacific-Basin Finance Journal, 53*, 186–207.

Zhou, J., Chen, C., Li, L., Zhang, Z., & Zheng, X. (2022). FinBrain 2.0: When finance meets trustworthy AI. *Frontiers of Information Technology & Electronic Engineering, 23*(12), 1747–1764.

Zhu, H., Vigren, O., & Söderberg, I. L. (2024). Implementing artificial intelligence empowered financial advisory services: A literature review and critical research agenda. *Journal of Business Research, 174*, 114494.

Empowering Triple-Entry Accounting with Machine Learning and Blockchain: Unveiling Transparency Through Advanced Analytics

Abraham Itzhak Weinberg and Alessio Faccia

1 Introduction

Traditional double-entry bookkeeping, a longstanding cornerstone of accounting practices, has historically governed financial record-keeping methodologies (Sangster, 2016). Its enduring legacy, spanning centuries, has provided a structured framework for tracking.

Financial flows between two entities or accounts. However, as the intricacies of global business transactions and regulatory frameworks have evolved, the inherent limitations of this conventional system have become increasingly pronounced, revealing a lack of the transparency and auditability demanded in contemporary business landscapes. In response to these challenges, the concept of "Triple-Entry (TE) accounting" has

A. I. Weinberg (✉)
AI-WEINBERG, AI Experts, Tel Aviv, Israel
e-mail: aviw2010@gmail.com

A. Faccia
University of Birmingham Dubai, Dubai, UAE
e-mail: alessio.faccia@gmail.com

J. Osterrieder et al. (eds.), *Transparency in FinTech*, Palgrave Studies in Financial Services Technology,
https://doi.org/10.1007/978-3-032-03523-3_3

Table 1 Comparison of double-entry bookkeeping and triple-entry accounting

Double-Entry Bookkeeping	*Triple-Entry Accounting*
• Records each transaction with two equal and offsetting entries (debits and credits)	• Records each transaction with three entries- the traditional double entries plus an additional digital certificate or record cryptographically recorded on a distributed ledger like blockchain
• Maintains the accounting equation that Assets = Liabilities + Equity	• Provides a single, shared, immutable record on the ledger
• Entries are recorded privately in a company's own journals and ledgers	• Ledger provides transparency—all entries are visible to permissioned participants on the network
• Prone to errors or possibility of manipulation as records can be altered	• Reduces risks of fraud, hidden dealings, or manually altered past records • Transactions can be verified in real-time by independent parties on the network • Automated reconciliation simplifies auditing and improves compliance

emerged as a compelling solution to enrich and modernize accounting practices (Sarin, 2022; Sgantzos et al., 2023), as can be seen in Table 1.

In comparing the various models of accounting, it is evident that while traditional and emerging systems aim to enhance the accuracy and transparency of financial records, each model presents distinct differences and limitations. One of the early systems proposed to shift from double entry was the so-called 'Russian Triple-Entry System,' proposed by Fedor Esersky, which focuses on continuous inventory updates across three books, but its relevance has diminished with the adoption of perpetual inventory systems, making its additional bookkeeping efforts redundant (Faccia et al., 2020). Later, Yuji Ijiri's Momentum Accounting introduces a third axis, 'force,' to capture wealth in addition to income, yet it does not incorporate a third accounting book, limiting its practical application (Ijiri, 1986). More recently, Ian Grigg's Triple-Entry Accounting integrates cryptography to eliminate reconciliation by using a shared transaction repository (Grigg, 2005). However, this model is largely focused on payment systems and lacks integration with broader accounting principles such as accruals, posing challenges to its widespread adoption; not even the more recent publication from the author has overcome the issue (Grigg, 2024).

Another model, the Resource-Event-Agent (REA), proposed by McCarthy, aims to enable a computer software model for an enterprise information system by focusing on inter-enterprise shared ledger systems. However, it replaces, rather than integrates with, existing AIS/ERP systems, limiting its compatibility with current infrastructures (McCarthy, 1982). The X-Accounting model, developed by Faccia, advances these concepts by integrating blockchain technology and AI to create a 'Triple-Axis' system that enhances accountability and real-time auditing (Faccia et al., 2020).

Despite its potential, this model requires significant infrastructure upgrades and government enforcement, highlighting the complexity of fully implementing such advanced systems within existing accounting frameworks. Triple-Axis X-Accounting is an advanced accounting model that enhances traditional double-entry bookkeeping by adding a third axis: a blockchain-generated hash. This model records each transaction in three ways: (1) Debit and Credit Entries: The traditional method of recording transactions in two accounts. (2) Blockchain Hash: A cryptographic hash unique to each transaction, ensuring it is securely recorded and immutable. (3) AI-Driven Adjustments: Automation through artificial intelligence for real-time auditing, compliance checks, and adjusting entries. This third axis (the blockchain hash) provides a tamper-proof, time-stamped record, making each transaction traceable and transparent across all participating entities.

The use of AI further streamlines the accounting process by automating routine tasks and enabling continuous auditing. X-Accounting works by integrating these components into a shared ledger accessible to all relevant parties, ensuring that all records are consistent, secure, and up–to-date. This model not only improves the security and accuracy of financial records but also facilitates real-time compliance and scalability, making it an efficient and modern solution for complex accounting needs (Faccia et al., 2020; Faccia & Mosteanu, 2019; Faccia et al., 2021).

By integrating a third entry alongside the traditional debits and credits, TE accounting extends the narrative of financial transactions by encapsulating non-financial contextual data, elucidating the comprehensive who, what, where, when, and why behind each financial exchange. This innovative approach not only enhances transparency by rendering financial decisions and their underlying rationale auditable but also fortifies defenses against fraudulent activities seeking to obscure transactional specifics (Grigg, 2005). Furthermore, the inclusion of supplementary metadata fosters opportunities for advanced analytics to extract deeper insights into organizational performance, risk management, and operational efficiencies. In an era characterized by a "trust but verify" ethos, the enhanced transparency and evidence-based nature of TE accounting serve to bolster credibility with critical external stakeholders, including investors, regulators, and auditors (Groblacher & Mizdrakovic, 2019).

Nevertheless, the mere accumulation and storage of enriched transactional data are insufficient without systematic analysis through the lens of advanced analytics. Here, the integration of ML emerges as a pivotal enabler, automating the detection of patterns, relationships, and anomalies across both financial and contextual dimensions. This infusion of data science techniques into oversight processes not only elevates transparency and compliance efforts but also propels strategic decision-making to unprecedented levels, equipping organizations to navigate the multifaceted challenges of today's intricate business environment with newfound clarity and agility (Chowdhury, 2021).

While the idea of TE accounting aims to increase transparency, its full potential can only be achieved by leveraging advanced analytics on the richer transactional data (Ibanez et al., 2023; Petratos, 2024). Capturing additional metadata through a third accounting entry addresses only part of the challenge—the real value comes from what organizations can uncover by systematically analyzing these combined financial and contextual records. Traditional audit and reporting practices may not be sufficient for making full sense of the large volumes and complexity inherent in TE accounting data. This is where integrating ML techniques can help automate the process of discovery (Dixit et al., 2024). For example, classification algorithms could help identify common patterns and anomalies across attributes like customer segments, product categories, geographical regions, or time periods. Clustering approaches may group entities or transactions based on similarities in their multiple dimensions. These analytical insights can then shine a light on areas warranting deeper scrutiny, as inconsistencies or outliers come to the surface.

Another benefit of the analytics layer is connecting seemingly disparate pieces of information (Qadir & Muhamed, 2022). For instance, correlating specific contextual attributes with downstream financial metrics could reveal important drivers of profitability, revenue, or costs that may not be apparent simply through manual examination. Such enriched associative links between various transactional attributes are what truly drive strategic decision-making value. Advanced algorithms are well-equipped to unveil these subtle yet meaningful multivariate relationships buried in vast volumes of interlinked data. Transparency is crucial for trust, accountability, security, and true decentralization in Decentralized Finance (DeFi) systems such as blockchains, since it helps promote adoption and integrity of these new open financial networks. TE accounting fills in the gaps of DeFi and blockchains (Schuldt & Peskes, 2023). The transparency, immutability, and verifiability of TE accounting perfectly complement the decentralized nature of DeFi applications and blockchains. It provides essential accounting functionality for this new digital financial system.

1.1 Triple Entry Accounting and Smart Contracts

Within TE accounting, the connection with smart contracts is crucial for various aspects (Faccia & Mosteanu, 2019). A smart contract is defined as a transaction protocol designed to autonomously execute, govern, or record events and actions based on the conditions of a contract or agreement (Zou et al., 2019). TE accounting utilizes a distributed ledger, typically a blockchain, to capture the third entry, guaranteeing an unchangeable transaction history (Inder, 2023). The comparison between TE accounting and smart contracts can be seen in Table 2.

In parallel, smart contracts empower the automation of transaction conditions and executions, executing contractual clauses that self-verify and self-execute. This automation cultivates trustless verification, removing the necessity for intermediaries and heightening transparency. Moreover, by embedding terms in smart contracts, the automation of reconciling TE bookkeeping entries reduces manual errors and labor.

The secure storage of records within smart contracts on a distributed ledger ensures the trustworthiness of financial reporting. Auditors benefit from streamlined auditing processes by inspecting immutable ledger records generated through smart contract executions. Furthermore, real-time updates facilitated by smart contracts amplify visibility and enable instant record reconciliation. Conditional payments delineated in smart contracts ensure the automatic fulfillment of payment obligations upon meeting predefined conditions, thereby optimizing processes effectively.

1.2 The Role of Triple-Entry Accounting and Alternatives

TE accounting is regarded as a crucial advancement for several reasons. It enhances transparency and trust by documenting financial transactions

Table 2 Comparison of triple-entry accounting and smart contracts

	Triple-Entry Accounting	*Smart Contracts*
Distributed Ledger	Can use any distributed ledger (blockchain, Directed Acyclic Graph) (Schuldt & Peskes, 2023)	Requires a blockchain or smart contract platform
Verification	Transactions verified by participants	Transactions verified by network consensus
Immutability	Ledger entries are immutable	Code and execution are immutable
Transparency	Transactions are transparent	Code, execution, and state are transparent
Automation	Manual accounting processes	Processes are automated through code
Conditional Actions	No conditional logic	Include conditional logic through code
Governance	Requires trusted central authorities	Fully decentralized governance
Fraud Prevention	Reduces alteration risk	Reduces alteration and misconduct risk
Auditing	Simplifies auditing process	Enables programmatic auditing of execution
Limitations	Privacy, scaling, and interoperability	Bugs, centralization of platforms

from three distinct viewpoints: the involved parties and an impartial third ledger, fostering greater confidence in the accuracy of financial records. Moreover, it enables comprehensive traceability of value flow, surpassing the limitations of traditional double-entry systems by tracking how value circulates through interconnected transactions, yielding deeper insights.

Additionally, its compatibility with distributed ledger technologies like blockchain facilitates independent verification of transactions without a central authority, aligning well with principles of transparency. Furthermore, TE accounting extends to sustainability considerations, encompassing natural, social, and relationship capital alongside monetary flows, potentially aiding in environmental, social, and governance reporting for overall sustainability impact assessment. Lastly, it serves as a robust tool for mitigating fraud and errors, with the third ledger acting as a vigilant checkpoint to identify inconsistencies or inaccuracies, thereby reducing mistakes and fortifying fraud prevention mechanisms.

Table 3 Pros and Cons of triple-entry accounting

Pros	*Cons*
Increased transparency and auditability of financial records	Higher compliance costs compared to traditional double- entry bookkeeping
Improved accuracy and ability to detect errors or fraud early	Increased complexity of financial record-keeping systems and processes
Better suited for distributed ledger technologies due to independent verification	Potential issues synchronizing updates across all three ledgers in real-time
Standardizes capturing of multi-step transactions and non- financial impacts	Privacy and confidentiality may be reduced with full transparency of records
Facilitates tracking value flows through entire systems of interconnected parties	Immaturity of standards and lack of experience operating TE systems in practice
Promotes trust in accounting through consensus-based self- verification	Reporting frameworks still evolving to translate additional data captured into meaningful reporting
Might be overkill for simpler organizations or transactions that don't require full transparency	

1.3 Pros and Cons of Triple-Entry Accounting

TE accounting offers several advantages and disadvantages worth considering, as can be seen in Table 3. On the positive side, it enhances transparency and auditability by introducing an additional verification layer, improving accuracy and enabling early detection of errors or fraud through easily identifiable ledger inconsistencies.

It is well-suited for distributed ledger technologies, standardizes the recording of complex transactions, and enables the tracking of value flows across interconnected systems. Moreover, it fosters trust in accounting practices by promoting consensus-based self-verification. Conversely, adopting TE accounting can incur higher compliance costs, complicate financial record-keeping processes, and pose challenges in synchronizing updates across all three ledgers in real-time. The full transparency of records may reduce privacy and confidentiality, while the immaturity of standards and lack of operational experience with TE systems present additional hurdles. Furthermore, reporting frameworks are still evolving to effectively translate the captured data into meaningful reports, and for simpler organizations or transactions not requiring full transparency, TE accounting may be excessive. In essence, while TE accounting enhances transparency, integrity, and interoperability[1], it also introduces complexities, costs, and potential synchronization and privacy issues compared to traditional methods, with standards and practical experience still in development.

1.4 *Why Is Triple-Entry Accounting so Important for Blockchain?*

TE accounting holds immense significance for blockchain due to its intrinsic alignment with the decentralized nature of blockchain technology (Faccia & Mosteanu, 2019). By incorporating a third independent ledger to verify transactions, TE accounting enhances transparency and trust within blockchain networks, which is crucial for ensuring the accuracy and integrity of financial records. This additional layer of verification not only mitigates fraud and errors but also complements the decentralized and distributed nature of blockchain by providing a reliable mechanism for validating transactions across the network without the need for a central authority. Furthermore, the traceability of value flow inherent in TE accounting complements blockchain's ability to securely track and record the movement of assets, making it an essential tool for enhancing the efficiency, security, and reliability of blockchain transactions.

1.5 *The Importance of Transparency in Blockchain Technology*

Transparency plays a critical role in blockchain technologies for several key reasons (Cai, 2021). In decentralized blockchain systems, where a central authority is absent, transparency is essential to enable all participants to independently verify the validity and sequencing of transactions, fostering a trustless environment where reliance on third parties is unnecessary. The immutability characteristic of blockchains, which aims to maintain an unchangeable record, relies on transparency in rule-based operations and comprehensive transaction histories for users to continuously validate the integrity and accuracy of the ledger.

Moreover, the auditability aspect is crucial for regulators and auditors who seek assurance that blockchains function as transparent public ledgers,

[1] Blockchain interoperability allows for different blockchain systems to communicate and exchange data, messages, and digital assets with one another.

facilitating asset tracking, error and fraud detection, and compliance monitoring. Additionally, transparency in decentralized blockchains ensures censorship resistance by making data equally visible to all users, unlike centralized systems that are vulnerable to data manipulation or concealment. Furthermore, in blockchain protocols like Bitcoin, which operate without trusted third parties, transparency into the consensus protocol and transaction confirmation process is vital for users to ascertain the finality of transactions. This transparency also fosters accountability by making all data, algorithms, and transaction processes open for public scrutiny, incentivizing protocols to operate with integrity and minimizing the risk of unintended flaws or manipulations that could erode users' trust in the system.

1.6 Alternatives for Transparency in accounting and blockchain Systems

In exploring alternatives to transparency in accounting, several avenues diverge from the conventional norm of full disclosure (Alkan, 2021). Compliance reporting focuses on meeting regulatory requirements with minimal information, reducing transparency by providing only essential data. Private or restricted ledgers keep accounting records confidential, diminishing visibility and trust due to the absence of independent verification on public distributed ledgers. Estimates and approximations involve using rounded figures and aggregated data rather than precise numbers, offering reduced transparency while potentially sufficing for certain applications. Selective disclosure entails releasing high-level metrics instead of granular transaction data, limiting the transparency scope to streamline information dissemination. Third-party attestation involves independent auditors verifying accuracy instead of complete transparency on distributed ledgers, introducing a trusted intermediary (Dai & Vasarhelyi, 2017). Proprietary formats store records in closed formats, hindering transparency and impeding interaction for independent participants. Manual reconciliation, involving periodic rather than real-time balance checks, lowers the frequency and reliability of transparency. Anonymized metadata shares transaction details without identifiers, reducing linkability and contextual clarity compared to the full transparency of counterparties and items.

When considering alternatives to TE accounting within blockchain systems, various approaches emerge that offer different paths toward transaction verification and accuracy (Bonson & Bednarova, 2019; Fullana & Ruiz, 2021; Rizal Batubara et al., 2019). Cryptographic proofs, such as zero-knowledge proofs[2], cryptographically validate transaction accuracy without exposing full transaction details, providing verification without complete transparency. Auditing committees could replace the TE system by periodically selecting committees to review transactions, adding trusted third-party auditors into the verification process. Off-chain data availability involves storing transaction payloads off-chain while maintaining light client-verifiable commitments on-chain, enabling verification through sampling rather than for each transaction.

Selective disclosure focuses on releasing high-level summaries instead of granular transaction details, emphasizing transparency through analytics over raw data. Privacy technologies like homomorphic encryption[3] computations on private data without revealing content, offering verification without accessing raw data (Shrestha & Kim, 2019). Blockchain sampling validates random blocks periodically instead of real-time validation for every transaction, reducing overhead at the expense of real-time assurance (Elommal & Manita, 2021). Despite these alternatives, most compromise transparency to some extent or introduce additional parties and assumptions compared to the self-auditing nature of TE accounting. Thus, TE accounting remains the most direct approach to achieve transparency, integrity, and decentralization simultaneously within blockchain systems.

2 Foundations of Triple-Entry Accounting

Double-entry bookkeeping, a foundational practice within accounting, has long been relied upon for maintaining financial records with precision (Cai, 2021). This system's integrity is upheld by ensuring that debits align with credits and transactions are recorded twice, instilling consistency in financial documentation (Rahmawati et al., 2023). Although double-entry bookkeeping excels in balancing accounts, it falls short in providing a comprehensive understanding of transaction contexts, such as the parties involved, the nature of exchanges, and the timing and rationale behind transactions. In response to this limitation, the principles of TE accounting have been introduced to augment traditional practices (Cai, 2021).

[2] A zero-knowledge proof or protocol is a technique through which one party can demonstrate to another party the truth of a given statement without revealing any details beyond the validity of that statement.

[3] Homomorphic encryption is a cryptographic method enabling computations to be conducted on encrypted data without the need for decryption.

This innovative approach integrates a third "entry" dedicated to capturing non-financial metadata alongside debit and credit entries. By intertwining financial data with crucial contextual details, TE accounting offers a more holistic view of organizational activities, propelling insights beyond those achievable through traditional double-entry systems. This rich contextual foundation serves as a robust platform for leveraging advanced analytics methodologies, enabling organizations to derive deeper insights and make well-informed strategic decisions based on a wealth of interconnected data points.

2.1 *Limitations of Traditional Double-Entry Bookkeeping*

Traditional double-entry bookkeeping, while a stalwart in accounting practices, grapples with several key limitations that TE accounting seeks to rectify (Chowdhury, 2021; Hambiralovic & Karlsson, 2018). The current system lacks transparency, as it focuses solely on monetary exchanges between accounts, omitting vital contextual details crucial for verifying transactions and detecting anomalies. Furthermore, the inability to connect financial data with non-financial information creates a disjointed perspective on transactions, impeding comprehensive analysis and audit trails.

This deficiency not only obscures potential fraud and errors but also complicates compliance adherence, as the absence of transaction context can hinder regulatory assessments. Moreover, the limited viewpoint provided by the traditional double-entry system restricts strategic analysis by overlooking interconnected attributes like location, product, and customer data, which are essential for obtaining deeper operational insights. Finally, the system's inability to trace asset provenance across successive transactions undermines the clarity and integrity of historical financial records, weakening independent verification and heightening the risk of unnoticed anomalies.

2.2 *Overview of Triple-Entry Accounting: Principles and Framework*

The principles and framework of TE accounting represent a significant advancement over traditional double-entry systems (Groblacher & Mizdrakovic, 2019; Rahmawati et al., 2023). By expanding beyond the financial debits-and-credits paradigm, TE accounting introduces a third "entry" dedicated to capturing contextual metadata for each transaction, offering a comprehensive view of the "why" behind financial flows (Sarin, 2022).

In this framework, financial elements are recorded conventionally as debits and credits, while non-financial attributes such as parties involved, transaction locations, item descriptions, and tags are meticulously defined as metadata fields. Each transaction is uniquely identifiable through shared reference keys, ensuring a robust linkage between financial and contextual entries that are both immutable and transparent. This model not only bolsters auditability and transparency but also facilitates deeper insights and analytics by providing a unified and verifiable view of both financial and contextual activities. By enabling the seamless integration of financial and non-financial data in a structured and immutable manner, TE accounting not only fortifies compliance and audit processes but also serves as a resilient foundation for advanced analytics approaches within accounting practices.

3 The Role of Advanced Analytics in Triple-Entry Accounting

While TE accounting enriches transactional insights by interlinking financial and metadata records, the mere accumulation of this comprehensive data is insufficient without systematic analysis and value extraction mechanisms. Organizations necessitate automated and intelligent processes to sift through vast amounts of information effectively. This is where the integration of advanced analytics driven by ML emerges as crucial. Traditional manual auditing and reporting may overlook intricate patterns, correlations, and anomalies embedded within multifaceted datasets, whereas ML algorithms excel at uncovering hidden insights and knowledge from complex data structures.

Techniques like prediction, classification, clustering, and association rule mining can be harnessed to unearth strategic and tactical insights, enabling organizations to forecast future outcomes, identify anomalies, segment entities, discover relationships, and optimize processes. By automating compliance monitoring, enhancing fraud detection, and facilitating informed decision-making, this analytical fusion empowers auditors, managers, and regulators with scalable tools for continuous oversight, strategic planning, and assurance of organizational integrity. By leveraging the cognitive capabilities of ML within transparent TE accounting frameworks, a new era of analytical prowess emerges, promising to redefine accountability, governance, and value generation across industries navigating the complexities of today's data-driven business landscape.

3.1 Motivation for Applying Machine Learning and Data Mining

The integration of ML and data mining into TE accounting data unveils a spectrum of compelling reasons driving this technological fusion. ML's prowess lies in unearthing obscured patterns and relationships within vast and diverse transaction datasets, offering insights beyond human perception. Predictive models, a hallmark of ML, furnish a methodical approach to foresee outcomes, predict risks, identify anomalies, and estimate future financial trajectories based on historical metadata trends. By automating monitoring processes and anomaly detection, ML algorithms provide continuous oversight, swiftly flagging irregularities and conserving manual efforts. This proactive monitoring extends to auditing and governance realms, ensuring real-time alignment with policies rather than sporadic assessments, fostering a culture of perpetual compliance adherence.

Moreover, ML-generated patterns and predictive guidance equip managers with evidence-based support for strategic decision-making across various organizational domains. Addressing the challenges posed by extensive data volumes inherent in TE accounting, ML excels in extracting intelligence from interconnected datasets at a scale surpassing traditional tools. Additionally, ML classifiers and rules play a pivotal role in streamlining compliance efforts, systematically checking for violations and mitigating oversight costs associated with manual reviews. By spotlighting outliers and enhancing forensic capabilities, ML becomes instrumental in combating fraud and errors, bringing to light both intentional and unintentional financial reporting discrepancies. Furthermore, the iterative learning process facilitated by ML fosters organizational knowledge enhancement over time, with insights garnered from feedback loops contributing to the model's accuracy as it delves into recurring and novel transactions alike.

3.2 Benefits of Transparency, Insights, and Fraud Detection

Empowering TE accounting with ML yields a myriad of advantages spanning transparency, insights, and fraud detection. By integrating ML into the accounting framework, visibility into the full transaction context is enhanced through the interconnectedness of financial and metadata records, with ML algorithms further enhancing transparency by automatically identifying anomalies and outliers (Awosika et al., 2024). This fusion also fortifies compliance and governance efforts through real-time monitoring, alerts, and the application of classification and rules to pinpoint regulatory issues at a detailed level.

Strategic decision-making gains a competitive edge as data-driven predictive patterns and associations offer objective guidance, shedding light on optimization opportunities across various dimensions. The process of continuous organizational learning is facilitated through feedback loops, refining models and knowledge over iteratively analyzed data, thereby influencing well-informed planning and decision-making over the long term.

Moreover, automated fraud and error detection mechanisms enable the identification of unusual profiles and transactions beyond set thresholds, reducing oversight costs while bolstering forensic investigation support. Proactive risk prediction is enabled through predictive models that forecast potential risks, liabilities, and problematic areas, allowing for preemptive controls to be implemented, thus strengthening risk mitigation strategies compared to reactive post-event approaches. Ultimately, this amalgamation of TE accounting with ML not only enhances credibility for stakeholders by providing intelligent oversight but also minimizes disruptions stemming from compliance issues or reporting inaccuracies, solidifying the strategic benefits across governance, compliance, and decision-making functions within organizations.

4 A Machine Learning Approach

The methodology for representing TE data as features involves converting financial records into target or output variables, while metadata attributes are reshaped into predictive input features. Categorical variables are managed through dimensional modeling techniques, and data irregularities are addressed using feature encoding methods (Cho et al., 2020; Ucoglu, 2020). Various algorithms and models are then employed for different purposes: classification models such as logistic regression (Bekoe et al., 2018), decision trees (Nawaiseh & Abbod, 2021), and neural networks (Sanchez-Serrano et al., 2020) are utilized to predict transaction types or outcomes, while clustering algorithms like K-means (Sahoo & Sahoo, 2021), hierarchical clustering (Thiprungsri, 2019), and Density-Based

Spatial Clustering of Applications with Noise (DBSCAN) (Bhattacharya & Lindgreen, 2020) are used to identify natural segments within similar records.

Association rule mining techniques (Sawangarreerak & Thanathamathee, 2021), such as Apriori (Ioannou et al., 2021) and Equivalence Class Transformation (ECLAT) (Tsapani et al., 2020), are applied to uncover correlations, and anomaly detection algorithms, including Isolation Forests (Bakumenko & Elragal, 2022), Local Outlier Factor (LOF) (Kuna et al., 2014), and One-Class Support Vector Machine (OCSVM) (Wilfred, 2021), are employed to detect outliers.

Predictive modeling methods like linear or logistic regression (Nawaiseh & Abbod, 2021), Recurrent Neural Networks (RNNs) (Jan, 2021), and time-series analysis are utilized for forecasting purposes. Model evaluation is carried out using realistic train/test datasets, with performance metrics tailored to each specific problem, such as accuracy, precision, recall for classification tasks (Nawaiseh & Abbod, 2021), silhouette score for clustering (Byrnes, 2019), confidence and support for associations (Suppiah & Arumugam, 2023), and F-score (Miharsi et al., 2024), Receiver Operating Characteristic (ROC) Area Under the Curve (AUC) (Carrington et al., 2022) for anomalies, with strategies in place to combat overfitting and data imbalances. This systematic approach aims to transform TE data into actionable intelligence using a diverse array of ML algorithms, tailored to the unique analytical objectives at hand.

4.1 Methodology for Representing Triple-Entry Data as Features

In the methodology for representing TE data as features, financial records are designated as target or label variables, with debit and credit amounts potentially being predicted or classified as the output or label, while fields such as account and transaction ID serve as unique identifiers (Dixit et al., 2024; Ibanez et al., 2021). Metadata attributes[4] are converted into predictive features, with categorical variables like location encoded using techniques such as one-hot encoding[5], dates transformed into integer

[4] Attributes that describes data.

[5] A technique that converts categorical data into numerical by creating binary columns for each category, marking 1 for presence and 0 for absence.

time deltas or periods encoded using one-hot encoding, and text fields processed using methods like TF-IDF[6] or word embeddings[7].

Dimensional modeling manages categorical variables by creating separate tables for textual fields like product or customer, extracting categorical variables from these dimension tables, and employing one-hot encoding (Sarwar et al., 2023). Feature engineering[8] plays a crucial role in structuring inputs appropriately, involving the grouping of related fields into composite features when meaningful, normalization to standardize numeric ranges[9] like debit amounts, and handling missing values or sparse attributes. Feature selection techniques are utilized for dimensionality reduction[10], identifying unimportant or correlated inputs through methods like Analysis of Variance (ANOVA) (Surana & Bhanawat, 2022)[11] and employing recursive feature elimination to enhance algorithm performance. This structured approach enables ML algorithms to uncover valuable patterns and relationships within TE data, facilitating tasks such as classification, clustering, and prediction for various analytical objectives.

5 The Relationship Between Triple-Entry Accounting and Multiparty Computation

Multiparty Computation (MPC), also known as the protocol of oblivious transfer, has the objective of developing techniques that enable parties to collaboratively compute a function using their inputs while maintaining the privacy of those inputs (Evans et al., 2018). MPC fits well with blockchains by enabling privacy-preserving and decentralized computations in a transparent and incentive-compatible manner—all of which are

[6] An acronym for Term Frequency-Inverse Document Frequency, quantifies the relevance of a word in a text by comparing its frequency across a corpus.

[7] Represents a word as a real-valued vector, encoding its meaning such that words closer in the vector space are likely to share similar meanings.

[8] A supervised ML processing, where raw data is converted into a more efficient set of inputs, with each input consisting of multiple attributes, referred to as features.

[9] A scaling technique used to standardize the values of numeric columns in the dataset to a uniform scale.

[10] The process of reducing data from a high-dimensional space to a low-dimensional space while preserving key properties of the original data.

[11] A test employed to ascertain variances between research findings across three or more distinct and unrelated samples or groups.

important requirements for many blockchain use cases (Zhou et al., 2021).

TE accounting and MPC can be complementary technologies. TE alone cannot replace the cryptographic security guarantees provided by MPC-based solutions for multiparty computations on blockchains, as can be seen in Table 4. MPC is still needed for that core functionality (Cao et al., 2024; Ibanez et al., 2021; McCallig et al., 2019). The differences between the two lie in their core functionalities: MPC stands out as a groundbreaking method facilitating secure computations among multiple parties without exposing their private inputs, ensuring a high level of confidentiality. This technique, underpinned by robust cryptographic principles, offers security assurances even in scenarios where some parties may collude or act maliciously. In contrast, TE Accounting, a system tailored for the immutable and auditable recording of financial transactions, lacks the same comprehensive security guarantees intrinsic to MPC. While TE Accounting excels in maintaining transaction records on a decentralized ledger, it falls short in enabling secure distributed computations akin to the capabilities provided by MPC.

Table 4 Comparison of triple-entry accounting and multiparty computation for privacy- preserving analysis of transaction data

	Triple-Entry Accounting	*Multiparty Computation*
Approach	Links financial transactions to contextual metadata and stores permanently	Computes on private inputs without directly revealing them through secure sharing
Scope	Focuses on accounting domains and transparency	General technique for private joint analysis by multiple parties
Data Management	Collects and archives all records	Computes without long-term storage of private inputs/outputs
Privacy	Provides transparency of record contents	Preserves privacy of inputs during distributed computation
Implementation	Leverages database technologies	Relies on cryptographic secure computation protocols
Use Cases	Auditing, compliance, analytics on public records	Collaborative analysis of sensitive private data
Strengths	Allows archiving and transparency	Preserves privacy during joint analysis
Weaknesses	No long-term input privacy	No permanent archive of results

They can be combined to create a robust framework: MPC protocols offer a secure avenue for computing transactions and business logic, with the outcomes subsequently documented on-chain[12] in a triple-entry format for enhanced transparency. Integrating zero-knowledge proofs (Sun et al., 2021), generated via MPC, with TE accounting could furnish mathematical verification of transaction validity. Moreover, on-chain MPC could uphold regulatory compliance logic, channeling the results into TE accounting systems for comprehensive governance and oversight.

MPC and TE accounting possess complementary strengths: MPC excels in secure computations, while TE accounting ensures transparency. By integrating the two, MPC can manage confidential on-chain computations, while TE accounting securely records the outputs in an immutable manner, leveraging the strengths of both systems for a comprehensive and efficient solution.

5.1 *The Potential of Integrating Triple-Entry Accounting with Multi-Party Computation*

MPC can significantly enhance triple-entry accounting on blockchain networks through various applications, such as privacy-preserving audits and compliance checks, securing records linkage, regulatory calculations, fraud detection, dispute resolution, running encrypted queries, and risk modeling.

Privacy-preserving audits and compliance checks can be conducted using MPC, allowing sensitive financial data, such as transactions and Know Your Client (KYC) records[13] to undergo auditing or compliance logic checks without disclosing the underlying information. The pass/fail results can then be securely recorded in the TE system.

MPC also enables secure record linkage, facilitating the linking of related records, such as transactions across different parties or systems, in a privacy-preserving manner. This linkage supports functionalities such as netting and reconciliation within the TE logs. Furthermore, MPC can power fraud detection algorithms, enabling the private execution of complex ML/AI models on transaction data to identify issues, with the findings reported anonymously in the triple-entry format.

[12] A transaction that is exclusively registered and validated within the primary blockchain.

[13] KYC, short for Know Your Customer or Know Your Client, is the mandatory process where banks verify clients' identities to ensure authenticity.

Regulatory calculations, including determining prudential standards and capital adequacy ratios, can be privately computed using MPC on financial data before public reporting. In the event of disputes, MPC protocols can be employed to verify facts or compute ledger states privately, aiding in dispute resolution while minimizing data disclosure.

Users can utilize encrypted queries through MPC to run queries on the triple-entry ledger, extracting private analytics without revealing the queries or results. Lastly, for risk modeling purposes, MPC can be leveraged to analyze counterparty risk measures, conduct stress tests, and perform portfolio analyses privately, enhancing risk assessment across the network.

6 Discussion

Empowering TE accounting with ML presents a domain of possibilities and considerations. The benefits of analytics are profound, as TE accounting generates extensive structured financial and metadata that can be harnessed for advanced analytics using ML and AI. This utilization unlocks insights and applications that enhance transparency, decision-making processes, and governance practices. Nevertheless, addressing privacy concerns is crucial. Implementing proper techniques, such as anonymization and secure MPC, is essential to safeguard individual privacy while still enabling ML on aggregated TE data for analytical advantages. Regulatory considerations play a pivotal role in this landscape. Regulators must establish standards and guidelines concerning data privacy, model governance, and other pertinent issues to ensure the ethical and compliant use of ML with sensitive financial records. Moreover, leveraging analytics on TE data, coupled with alternative data sources, could revolutionize financial inclusion by facilitating the assessment of credit risk for individuals lacking traditional credit histories, thereby fostering broader financial inclusivity.

The integration of ML could also give rise to new business models. Startups may emerge, offering TE accounting and analytics as a service through innovative approaches like blockchain technology, which can significantly benefit compliance, auditing practices, and risk management functions within organizations. As this transformation unfolds, the workforce landscape in accounting, auditing, and related domains is likely to evolve. While certain job roles may change, the overall demand for skilled professionals is expected to rise with the integration of advanced analytics capabilities. This shift also demands new skill sets within these industries. Ensuring model security is paramount in this data-driven landscape. Defenses against adversarial attacks on ML systems are imperative to prevent the manipulation of risk and fraud analyses derived from TE data. Moreover, the importance of explainability in models becomes increasingly significant to guarantee that stakeholders can comprehend and validate the analyses derived from these sophisticated systems.

6.1 Key Implications and Organizational Impact

Empowering TE accounting with ML carries significant implications and potential organizational impacts. Through advanced analytics, there is a notable increase in transparency and trust, fostering deeper insights that enhance accountability and stakeholder trust. Compliance and governance are bolstered as ML can automatically detect anomalies and non-compliant patterns, reinforcing internal controls and risk management practices. Auditing processes are optimized with continuous monitoring and customized alerts, reducing manual efforts for auditors and enabling proactive issue identification. Predictive decision-making becomes feasible through forecasting trends, risks, and anomalies, facilitating a shift from reactive to preventative strategies.

Process automation and efficiencies are realized as tasks, such as reconciliations, are automated end-to-end using ML-powered workflow tools, freeing up resources for more strategic endeavors. Cultivating a data-driven culture becomes paramount, en-Enabling widespread data access and self-serve analytics that nurture evidence-based strategies and discussions centered around data points. Workforce reskilling becomes imperative as employees require training on new tools, analytics skills, and revised work methodologies, potentially leading to job disruptions. Transition costs pose a challenge, necessitating upfront investments in platforms, reskilling initiatives, and change management efforts that require adequate budget allocations and organizational support.

Vendor management strategies become crucial as organizations may consider outsourcing certain capabilities, introducing risks related to data security and model reliability that demand robust governance frameworks. The debate between centralized and decentralized systems emerges, where decentralized structures can enhance collaboration, but centralized control often aids in compliance efforts. Navigating these implications and organizational impacts effectively is essential for harnessing the full potential of TE accounting empowered by ML in the modern business landscape.

6.2 *Addressing Key Challenges in Data and Systems: Quality, Scalability, and Beyond*

Empowering TE accounting with ML poses key challenges that necessitate careful consideration alongside potential solutions for effective implementation. Data quality emerges as a critical issue, with TE data often being noisy, incomplete, or erroneous. Employing ML techniques such as data cleaning, imputation, and validation is essential to enhance data quality and reliability. Scalability presents another hurdle, given the massive volume of TE data. Leveraging distributed ML platforms capable of efficiently processing vast datasets on cloud infrastructure can address scalability concerns effectively.

Model bias and fairness represent significant challenges, with the potential for certain groups to be unfairly treated by ML models. Techniques like adversarial debiasing

During training sessions, it can help mitigate biases and promote fair outcomes (Singh et al., 2021). Privacy and security concerns surrounding sensitive financial data necessitate stringent access controls and the adoption of privacy-preserving techniques like federated[14].

Or differential privacy[15] when utilizing data for ML purposes, ensuring regulatory compliance is paramount, requiring well-defined governance frameworks covering data usage, model oversight, explainability, and more. Collaborating with regulators and establishing partnerships can provide essential oversight and regulatory guidance.

Interpretability of ML models[16] is crucial for validation and recourse, emphasizing the importance of unveiling how insights are derived. Implementing explainable AI methods enhances model interpretability and transparency. Integration challenges arise when amalgamating TE data, ML platforms, and analytics tools, demanding meticulous system

[14] Offers privacy protections at the individual record level, guaranteeing privacy for each of a client's data records against adversaries.

[15] Provides a mathematical framework that allows statistical details about datasets to be shared while protecting individual privacy.

[16] Refers to the degree to which cause and effect can be observed within a system.

design and change management practices. Utilizing microservices[17] can streamline integration processes and facilitate smoother transitions. The absence of standardized benchmarks poses a challenge for evaluating model performance. Industry consortia play a vital role in establishing benchmarking standards and facilitating performance evaluations[18].

Moreover, the skills shortage across multidisciplinary fields encompassing accounting, data science, and compliance underscores the importance of developing a talent pool equipped with the requisite skills. Training programs and collaborations with academic institutions are instrumental in bridging these skill gaps and nurturing a workforce adept at navigating the complexities of TE accounting empowered by ML. Addressing these challenges with strategic solutions is fundamental to realizing the full potential of this transformative integration within organizational frameworks.

7 Conclusions

This chapter delves into the application of ML in empowering TE accounting systems, enhancing transparency, analytics, and decision-making capabilities across organizations and industries. By adhering to proper guidelines and technical safeguards, ML can substantially bolster transparency while preserving privacy. Key implications encompass evidence-based strategic planning, continuous auditing, proactive risk management, and the introduction of new revenue models. Simultaneously, reshaping workforce skills and establishing standards for model integrity are pivotal for success. Overall, the integration of ML with TE accounting holds promise for transforming financial transparency, leading to improved governance, reduced financial crimes, and a more informed global economy.

Looking ahead, this work underscores the contributions of applying ML to enhance TE accounting systems, yet unresolved challenges persist. Maturing techniques are necessary to address issues surrounding data privacy, regulatory oversight, and decentralized governance. Further

[17] Comprises loosely coupled, fine-grained services that communicate via lightweight protocols.

[18] An in-processing adversarial training technique simultaneously trains a predictor and discriminator. The predictor aims to accurately predict the target variable while mitigating bias, as identified by the discriminator.

engagement with standards bodies and policymakers is crucial. Additionally, targeted use cases and datasets are needed to explore applications in diverse sectors such as supply chain, insurance, and financial markets. Future research should delve into scalable, privacy-aware ML architectures optimized for distributed financial graphs to deepen understanding at a technical level.

Continued interdisciplinary research has the potential to fortify global accountability through transparent, learning-driven applications of TE bookkeeping.

References

Alkan, B. S. (2021). Real-time blockchain accounting system as a new paradigm. *Muhasebe Ve Finansman Dergisi*, 41–58.

Awosika, T., Shukla, R. M., & Pranggono, B. (2024). Transparency and privacy: The role of explainable ai and federated learning in financial fraud detection. *IEEE Access*.

Bakumenko, A., & Elragal, A. (2022). Detecting anomalies in financial data using machine learning algorithms. *Systems*, *10*(5), 130.

Bekoe, R. A., Owusu, G. M. Y., Ofori, C. G., Essel-Anderson, A., & Welbeck, E. E. (2018). Attitudes towards accounting and intention to major in accounting: A logistic regression analysis. *Journal of Accounting in Emerging Economies*, *8*(4), 459–475.

Bhattacharya, I., & Lindgreen, E. R. (2020). A semi-supervised machine learning approach to detect anomalies in big accounting data. In *ECIS*.

Bonson, E., & Bednarova, M. (2019). Blockchain and its implications for accounting and auditing. *Meditari Accountancy Research*, *27*(5), 725–740.

Byrnes, P. E. (2019). Automated clustering for data analytics. *Journal of Emerging Technologies in Accounting*, *16*(2), 43–58.

Cai, C. W. (2021). Triple-entry accounting with blockchain: How far have we come? *Accounting & Finance*, *61*(1), 71–93.

Cao, S. S., Cong, L. W., & Yang, B. (2024). Distributed ledgers and secure multiparty computation for financial reporting and auditing. National Bureau of Economic Research, Tech. Rep.

Carrington, A. M., Manuel, D. G., Fieguth, P. W., Ramsay, T., Osmani, V., Wernly, B., Bennett, C., Hawken, S., Magwood, O., Sheikh, Y., et al. (2022). Deep roc analysis and auc as balanced average accuracy, for improved classifier selection, audit and explanation. *IEEE Transactions on Pattern Analysis and Machine Intelligence*, *45*(1), 329–341.

Cho, S., Vasarhelyi, M. A., Sun, T., & Zhang, C. (2020). Learning from machine learning in accounting and assurance. 1–10.

Chowdhury, E. K. (2021). Financial accounting in the era of blockchain-a paradigm shift from double entry to triple entry system. *Available at SSRN 3827591*.

Dai, J., & Vasarhelyi, M. A. (2017). Toward blockchain-based accounting and assurance. *Journal of Information Systems, 31*(3), 5–21.

Dixit, P., Harwani, H., Amarsela, R., Patel, K., Patel, M. J., et al. (2024). Incorporating triple entry accounting as an audit tool—enhancing modern accounting systems. *Journal of Informatics Education and Research, 4*(2).

Elommal, N., & Manita, R. (2021). How blockchain innovation could affect the audit profession: A qualitative study. *Journal of Innovation Economics & Management*, I103–27.

Evans, D., Kolesnikov, V., Rosulek, M., et al. (2018). A pragmatic introduction to secure multi-party computation. *Foundations and Trends® in Privacy and Security, 2*(2-3), 70–246.

Faccia, A., & Mosteanu, N. R. (2019). Accounting and blockchain technology: From double-entry to triple-entry. *The Business & Management Review, 10*(2), 108–116.

Faccia, A., Mogteanu, N. R., & Leonardo, L. P. (2020). Blockchain hash, the missing axis of the accounts to settle the triple entry bookkeeping system. In *Proceedings of the 2020 12th International Conference on information management and engineering* (pp. 18–23).

Faccia, A., Sawan, N., Eltweri, A., & Beebeejaun, Z. (2021). Financial big data security and privacy in x-accounting. A step further to implement the triple-entry accounting. In *Proceedings of the 6th International Conference on information systems engineering* (pp. 7–12).

Fullana, O., & Ruiz, J. (2021). Accounting information systems in the blockchain era. *International Journal of Intellectual Property Management, 11*(1), 63–80.

Grigg, I. (2005). Triple entry accounting. *Systemics Inc*, 1–10.

Grigg, I. (2024). Triple entry accounting. *Journal of Risk and Financial Management, 17*(2), 76.

Groblacher, M., & Mizdrakovic, V. (2019). Triple-entry bookkeeping: History and benefits of the concept. In *Proceedings of the 2019 International Scientific Conference, (Finiz)* (pp. 58–61).

Hambiralovic, M., & Karlsson, R. (2018). Blockchain accounting in a tripple-entry system.

Ibanez, J. I., Bayer, C. N., Tasca, P., & Xu, J. (2023). Rea, triple-entry accounting and blockchain: Converging paths to shared ledger systems. *Journal of Risk and Financial Management, 16*(9), 382.

Ibanez, J. I., Bayer, C. N., Tasca, P., & Xu, J. (2021). The efficiency of single truth: Triple-entry accounting. *Available at SSRN 3770034*.

Ijiri, Y. (1986). A framework for triple-entry bookkeeping. *Accounting Review*, 745–759.

Inder, S. (2023). Triple entry accounting with blockchain technology. In *Digital Transformation, Strategic Resilience, Cyber Security and Risk Management* (Vol. 111, pp. 123–131). Emerald Publishing Limited.

Ioannou, A., Bourlis, D., Valsamidis, S., & Mandilas, A. (2021). A framework for information mining from audit data. In *Global, regional and local perspectives on the economies of Southeastern Europe: Proceedings of the 11th International Conference on the Economies of the Balkan and Eastern European Countries (EBEEC) in Bucharest, Romania, 2019* (pp. *223–242*). Springer.

Jan, C.-L. (2021). Using deep learning algorithms for cpas' going concern prediction. *Information*, *12*(2), 73.

Kuna, H. D., Garcla-Martinez, R., & Villatoro, F. R. (2014). Outlier detection in audit logs for application systems. *Information Systems*, *44*, 22–33.

McCallig, J., Robb, A., & Rohde, F. (2019). Establishing the representational faithfulness of financial accounting information using multiparty security, network analysis and a blockchain. *International Journal of Accounting Information Systems*, *33*, 47–58.

McCarthy, W. E. (1982). The rea accounting model: A generalized framework for accounting systems in a shared data environment. *Accounting Review*, 554–578.

Miharsi, D., Gamayuni, R. R., & Dharma, F. (2024). Analysis of the utilization of altman z-score, beneish m-score, and f-score model in detecting fraudulent of financial reporting: A literature review. *Journal of Management, Accounting, General Finance and International Economic Issues*, *3*(2), 353–364.

Nawaiseh, A. K., & Abbod, M. F. (2021). Financial statement audit utilising naive bayes networks, decision trees, linear discriminant analysis and logistic regression. In *The importance of new technologies and entrepreneurship in business development: In the context of economic diversity in developing countries: The impact of new technologies and entrepreneurship on business development* (pp. *1305–1320*). *Springer*.

Petratos, P. (2024). Triple-entry accounting and system integration. *Journal of Risk and Financial Management*, *17*(2), 45.

Qadir, A. M. A., & Muhamed, R. A. A. (2022). Blockchain technology and accounting: The triple-entry affecting transparency. *Telematique*, 4950–4958.

Rahmawati, M. I., Sukoharsono, E. G., Rahman, A. F., & Prihatiningtias, Y. W. (2023). Demistifying of triple-entry accounting (tea): Integrating the block. In *Ninth Padang International Conference on Economics Education, Economics, Business and Management, Accounting and Entrepreneurship (PICEEBA 2022)*. (pp. 23–31). Atlantis Press.

Rizal Batubara, F., Ubacht, J., & Janssen, M. (2019). Unraveling transparency and accountability in blockchain. In *Proceedings of the 20th Annual International Conference on Digital Government Research* (pp. 204–213).

Sahoo, G., & Sahoo, S. S. (2021). Accounting fraud detection using k-means clustering technique. In *Machine Learning and Information Processing: Proceedings of ICMLIP 2020.* (pp. 171–180). Springer.

Sanchez-Serrano, J. R., Alaminos, D., Garcia-Lagos, F., & Callejon-Gil, A. M. (2020). Predicting audit opinion in consolidated financial statements with artificial neural networks. *Mathematics*, *8*(8), 1288.

Sangster, A. (2016). The genesis of double entry bookkeeping. *The Accounting Review*, *91*(1), 299–315.

Sarin, V. (2022). Triple entry accounting. Example and benefits. https://www.eduyush.com/blogs/digital-skills/triple-entry-accounting. (Online; Accessed 12 May 2023).

Sarwar, M. I., Nisar, K., Khan, I., & Shehzad, D. (2023). Blockchains and triple-entry accounting for b2b business models. *Ledger*, *8*.

Sawangarreerak, S., & Thanathamathee, P. (2021). Detecting and analyzing fraudulent patterns of financial statement for open innovation using discretization and association rule mining. *Journal of Open Innovation: Technology, Market, and Complexity*, *7*(2), 128.

Schuldt, L. T., & Peskes, M. (2023). Decentralized finance-how triple-entry accounting and distributed ledger technology is revolutionizing the world of financial services from a business perspective. IUCF Working Paper, Tech. Rep.

Sgantzos, K., Hemairy, M. A., Tzavaras, P., & Stelios, S. (2023). Triple-entry accounting as a means of auditing large language models. *Journal of Risk and Financial Management*, *16*(9), 383.

Shrestha, R., & Kim, S. (2019). Integration of iot with blockchain and homomorphic encryption: Challenging issues and opportunities. In *Advances in Computers* (Vol. 115, pp. 293–331). Elsevier.

Singh, A., Gupta, A., Wadhwa, H., Asthana, S., & Arora, A. (2021). Temporal debiasing using adversarial loss based gnn architecture for crypto fraud detection. In *2021 20th IEEE International Conference on Machine Learning and Applications (ICMLA).* (pp. 391–396). IEEE.

Sun, X., Yu, F. R., Zhang, P., Sun, Z., Xie, W., & Peng, X. (2021). A survey on zero-knowledge proof in blockchain. *IEEE Network*, *35*(4), 198–205.

Suppiah, K., & Arumugam, D. (2023). Impact of data analytics on reporting quality of forensic audit: A study focus in malaysian auditors. In *E3S Web of Conferences* (Vol. 389, pp. 09033). EDP Sciences.

Surana, G., & Bhanawat, S. S. (2022). Awareness of blockchain technology-based accounting system among professionals. *IUP Journal of Accounting Research & Audit Practices*, *21*(4), 34–49.

Thiprungsri, S. (2019). Cluster analysis for anomaly detection in accounting. In *Rutgers Studies in Accounting Analytics: Audit Analytics in the Financial Industry* (pp. 87–110). Emerald Publishing Limited.

Tsapani, E., Tenidou, E., Pappas, D., & Valsamidis, S. (2020). Knowledge mining from accounting data as imechanism for decision support. *Journal of Engineering Science & Technology Review*, *1*, 112–177.

Ucoglu, D. (2020). Current machine learning applications in accounting and auditing. *Pres- sAcademia Procedia*, *12*(1), 1–7.

Wilfred, K. (2021). A big data approach to accounting fraud detection using data envelopment analysis and one class support vector machine. *University of Toronto (Canada)*.

Zhou, J., Feng, Y., Wang, Z., & Guo, D. (2021). Using secure multi-party computation to protect privacy on a permissioned blockchain. *Sensors*, *21*(4), 1540.

Zou, W., Lo, D., Kochhar, P. S., Le, X.-B. D., Xia, X., Feng, Y., Chen, Z., & Xu, B. (2019). Smart contract development: Challenges and opportunities. *IEEE Transactions on Software Engineering*, *47*(10), 2084–2106.

Balancing Innovation and Regulation: Fintech, Sandboxes, and Competition Law

Cristina Poncibò and Laura Zoboli

1 Introduction: Pro-competitive Regulation in the Digital Economy

The European Commission has embraced a strategic approach to fostering competition in digital services markets, including financial technologies ('FinTech'), by implementing asymmetrical, sector-specific regulation. This approach, often referred to as pro-competitive regulation, aims to address the unique challenges posed by digital platforms and emerging technologies.[1] A cornerstone of this strategy, which we have selected as the key sample for our analysis, is the Regulation of the European

[1] O. Borgogno, G. Colangelo, *Data, Innovation and Competition in Finance: The Case of the Access to Account Rule* in European Business Law Review, 2020, 31, pp. 573–610.

C. Poncibò (✉)
University of Turin, Turin, Italy
e-mail: cristina.poncibo@unito.it

L. Zoboli
IE University, Madrid, Spain
e-mail: laura.zoboli@unibs.it

J. Osterrieder et al. (eds.), *Transparency in FinTech*, Palgrave Studies in Financial Services Technology,
https://doi.org/10.1007/978-3-032-03523-3_4

Parliament and of the Council on Fair and Contestable Markets in the Digital Sector, known as the Digital Markets Act (DMA).[2]

The DMA reflects the European Union's clear departure from a laissez-faire regulatory philosophy, particularly in the context of the digital economy.[3] The EU has identified the lack of proactive public intervention as a long-term risk to the proper functioning of the single market. By introducing ex-ante obligations for gatekeepers—large digital platforms that act as bottlenecks to market access—the DMA signals a shift toward a regulatory framework that prioritizes fairness and accessibility. However, this proactive approach is not without its challenges. The speed of technological innovation and the risk of creating a burdensome and fragmented regulatory framework pose significant concerns, particularly for small and medium-sized enterprises (SMEs) and financial institutions. The potential increase in compliance costs could inadvertently hinder innovation and burden end-users.[4]

The decision to implement such detailed regulation stems from the European institutions' skepticism about the effectiveness of traditional competition law mechanisms in addressing the dominance of digital platform operators, particularly gatekeepers. Traditional competition law, reliant on ex-post enforcement, often struggles to keep pace with the rapid developments in the digital economy. Notable cases, such as the EU's protracted investigations into Google and Amazon, highlight the limitations of addressing anti-competitive practices retrospectively. The DMA, in contrast, represents a paradigm shift: it introduces ex-ante prohibitions and obligations, allowing regulators to proactively address potential issues before they distort the market.

In the context of FinTech, the DMA has significant implications for both gatekeepers and smaller market participants. Gatekeepers are subjected to stringent obligations aimed at preventing practices such as tying, self-preferencing, and unfair data usage. Meanwhile, non-gatekeepers, including

[2] Regulation (EU) 2022/1925 of the European Parliament and of the Council of September 14, 2022 on fair and contestable markets in the digital sector and amending Directives (EU) 2019/1937 and (EU) 2020/1828 (Digital Markets Regulation), in OJ L 265, 12.10.2022, pp. 1–66, ELI: http://data.europa.eu/eli/reg/2022/1925/oj.

[3] R.E. Matland, *Synthesizing the Implementation Literature: The Ambiguity-Conflict Model of Policy Implementation*, in Journal of Public Administration Research and Theory, 1995, 5(2), pp. 145–174.

[4] W. A. Kaal, *Dynamic Regulation for Innovation*, in M. Fenwick et al. eds., *Perspectives in Law, Business & Innovation*, Springer, New York, 2016.

innovative FinTech firms and traditional financial institutions, stand to benefit from a more level playing field. For instance, the DMA's focus on data sharing, interoperability, and fair contractual terms is expected to open new avenues for competition and collaboration in the digital finance sector.

However, as the financial and digital sectors increasingly converge, questions arise about whether the DMA's prescriptive framework is sufficiently adaptable to the rapid pace of FinTech innovation. Regulatory sandboxes, which have gained traction globally in jurisdictions such as the UK, Singapore, and Australia, present an alternative model for navigating this complex landscape. These controlled environments allow firms to test innovative financial products and services under the supervision of regulators, offering a balance between fostering innovation and ensuring consumer protection. Notable examples include the UK's Financial Conduct Authority (FCA) sandbox, which has facilitated the development of groundbreaking payment technologies, and Singapore's sandbox, which has supported initiatives in blockchain and digital banking.

This chapter examines whether regulatory sandboxes could complement or even offer a more effective alternative to the DMA's rigid ex-ante framework. It explores how these experimental frameworks enable firms to address market entry barriers, test innovative solutions, and manage risks in a way that maintains fair competition and consumer trust.[5] By analyzing the interplay between sandboxes, FinTech regulation, and EU competition law, the chapter seeks to identify a more flexible yet robust regulatory approach to the evolving challenges of digital finance.

2 Regulatory Sandboxes: Pioneering-Innovation Friendly Governance

Regulatory sandboxes have emerged as an innovative mechanism within the broader regulatory landscape, particularly in the FinTech sector, where such mechanisms have been used by public authorities to regulate innovative services while safeguarding critical interests, including consumer protection and competition.[6] Unlike traditional regulatory approaches, sandboxes provide firms—ranging from start-ups to

[5] EMA, Regulatory Sandbox, 2020, https://www.ema.gov.sg/Sandbox.aspx.

[6] D. Arner, J. Barberis, R. P. Buckley "Fintech, Regtech and the Reconceptualization of Financial Regulation" 37 *Northwestern Journal of International Law and Business* (2017), 373–385.

established players—with a controlled environment to test novel financial products and services under the supervision of regulatory authorities. These frameworks often include temporary exemptions from certain legal requirements, allowing for risk-managed innovation.

The rationale behind regulatory sandboxes lies in their ability to foster innovation by enabling public and private actors to better understand the market dynamics shaped by emerging financial technologies.[7] By allowing experimentation with fewer regulatory constraints, sandboxes empower regulators to fulfill their functions more effectively, including mitigating risks to financial and market stability. Furthermore, they serve as a platform for stakeholders—including regulators, industry participants, and institutional actors—to collaborate in identifying and addressing the barriers and challenges associated with new digital services. In this context, sandboxes function as test cases that demonstrate the agility and flexibility required to close regulatory gaps, enhancing their proactive and dynamic nature.[8]

The European Parliament, in its study on regulatory sandboxes and innovation hubs, has emphasized the potential of these frameworks to improve the effectiveness of regulatory measures through learning and experimentation.[9] Innovation is, therefore, a core element of regulatory sandboxes, not only in FinTech but also in other sectors. Regulators operating sandboxes effectively assume the role of governing innovation, treating it as a key entry threshold.[10] However, the interpretation of innovation and its associated criteria varies significantly between legal

[7] D. Arner, J. Barberis, R. P. Buckley 'Fintech, Regtech and the Reconceptualization of Financial Regulation' 37 Northwestern Journal of International Law and Business (2017), 373–385.

[8] Agile Governance: Reimagining Policy-making in the Fourth Industrial Revolution," World Economic Forum, (2018) http://www3.weforum.org/docs/WEF_Agile_Governance_Reimagining_Policy-making_4IR_report.pdf.

[9] R. Parenti, "European Parliament study on regulatory sandboxes and innovation hubs for FinTech," PE 652.752, 2020.

[10] A theoretical analysis related to the application of regulatory sandboxes in artificial intelligence regulation can be found in S. Ranchordas, Experimental Regulations for AI, in *Morals & Machines* 2021. One can then find some studies related to experiments already carried out in the field, with specific regard to the "Tokku" special zone for robotics in Japan, see: Y.H. Weng et al, Intersection of "Tokku" Special Zone, Robots, and the Law: A Case Study on Legal Impacts to Humanoid Robots, in *Int. J. of Soc. Rob.*, 2015.

systems and industries, reflecting the diversity of policy priorities across jurisdictions and sectors.[11]

The United Kingdom has been a leader in implementing regulatory sandboxes, with its Financial Conduct Authority (FCA) launching one of the first frameworks in 2016. This sandbox has facilitated the development of groundbreaking solutions in areas such as payment technologies, blockchain applications, and digital identity systems, providing a collaborative environment that attracts participants ranging from start-ups to large financial institutions. The UK's sandbox has also embraced an international dimension through the Global Financial Innovation Network (GFIN), enabling cross-border testing and regulatory alignment across multiple jurisdictions. This feature underscores its role not only as a tool for fostering domestic innovation but also as a strategic asset for positioning the UK as a global FinTech hub, especially in the post-Brexit context.

Singapore has adopted a similarly forward-looking approach, but with a distinct emphasis on aligning sandbox operations with broader national objectives, such as green finance and regional financial connectivity. The Monetary Authority of Singapore (MAS) has leveraged its sandbox to promote blockchain-based solutions for cross-border payments, as well as digital banking innovations. Moreover, its "sandbox express" initiative enables less complex experiments to bypass lengthy approval processes, significantly reducing time-to-market for new products. This model highlights Singapore's commitment to balancing regulatory rigor with efficiency, ensuring that the sandbox environment remains both innovative and competitive.

However, the success of regulatory sandboxes is not without challenges. One critical concern is whether their *selective nature grants unfair advantages to participants at the expense of competitors.* Firms admitted to sandboxes often benefit from reduced compliance costs and accelerated market entry, enabling them to allocate resources toward research, development, and marketing. By contrast, firms excluded from the sandbox face higher regulatory burdens and longer timeframes to achieve the same outcomes, potentially disrupting the level playing field in the market.

At the same time, the *proliferation of sandboxes across jurisdictions* has raised concerns about regulatory arbitrage, as firms may gravitate toward

[11] D. M. Ahern, "Regulators Nurturing FinTech Innovation: Global Evolution of the Regulatory Sandbox as Opportunity Based Regulation," 60 *European Banking Institute Working Paper Series* (2020).

jurisdictions offering more lenient or favorable sandbox conditions.[12] The UK's GFIN initiative attempts to address this challenge by fostering cross-border collaboration, but its success depends on the willingness of other jurisdictions to align their regulatory policies.

Another dimension of complexity arises, in more general terms, from the *interaction between sandboxes and competition law*. While sandboxes encourage innovation, they can also affect market dynamics by altering consumer behavior, pricing structures, or the distribution of market power. Innovations tested in sandboxes may lead to regulatory revisions or even the creation of entirely new competition rules to address the implications of emerging technologies. This underscores the importance of continuous collaboration between regulators, competition authorities, and market participants to ensure that sandboxes contribute positively to innovation and fair competition.

To achieve their full potential, regulatory sandboxes must strike a careful balance between fostering innovation and maintaining market fairness. Their design must account for diverse goals, such as lowering barriers to entry, ensuring consumer protection, and promoting competitive neutrality. By addressing these considerations, sandboxes can evolve into versatile tools that shape a dynamic and inclusive regulatory environment capable of supporting the sustained growth and stability of the FinTech sector.[13]

3 Regulatory Sandboxes and Competition Law: A Collaborative Framework for Emerging Markets

The growing interest in promoting competition policy through pro-competitive regulation is increasingly evident in discussions surrounding regulatory sandboxes.[14] These tools offer a unique opportunity for public authorities to establish a regulatory framework during the inception of new markets. Such a framework can integrate not only economic

[12] D. M. Ahern, Regulators Nurturing FinTech Innovation: Global Evolution of the Regulatory Sandbox as Opportunity Based Regulation, in *European Banking Institute Working Paper Series*, 2020, 60.

[13] D. M. Ahern, cit.

[14] J. Kálmán, *Ex Ante Regulation? The Legal Nature of the Regulatory Sandboxes or How to Regulate before Regulation Even Exists* (November 21, 2022) http://dx.doi.org/10.2139/ssrn.3255850.

objectives but also broader societal goals, including sustainability. By setting the "rules of the game" at an early stage, regulatory sandboxes can help prevent the concentration of economic power in digital markets and the creation of entry barriers that stifle competition.

Despite their potential, the relationship between competition law and regulatory sandboxes remains underexplored in academic literature. Public authorities, however, have demonstrated confidence in the dual capacity of sandboxes to foster innovation and enhance competition in fast-moving digital markets. Competition is explicitly identified as a goal of many sandboxes. For instance, the Financial Conduct Authority in the UK launched its regulatory sandbox in 2015 to promote effective competition in digital financial services markets.[15] This initiative was designed to enable the FCA to work directly with innovators, thereby ensuring consumer welfare while fostering competition in financial services, particularly for small and medium-sized enterprises (SMEs).

At their core, regulatory sandboxes aim to prioritize innovation as the primary objective, with competition emerging as a secondary but complementary goal.[16] Effective regulation of the FinTech sector is critical to sustaining innovation, and sandboxes allow regulators to monitor the sector's rapid evolution without stifling its potential. These frameworks also ensure necessary protections for consumers, businesses, and other stakeholders participating in or affected by the experimental activities.

The significance of regulatory sandboxes in promoting both innovation and competition has been corroborated by global studies. A notable example is the CGAP-World Bank study (2019), which surveyed sixty-two

[15] FCA, "Regulatory sandbox lessons learned report" (2017) https://www.fca.org.uk/publications/research/regulatory-sandbox-lessons-learned-report.

[16] L. Bromberg, A. Godwin, I. Ramsay, 'Fintech Sandboxes: Achieving a Balance between Regulation and Innovation', 28 *Journal of Banking and Finance Law and Practice* (2017), 314–336. For example, one safeguard might be to limit the range of consumers who can access the product or service during the testing phase. In both Denmark and the United Kingdom, innovative products were accessible only to consumers active in the local market. The rationale for these restrictions is that the lack of coordination or prior interaction with the host authority could pose risks regarding compliance with local customer disclosure or other consumer protection requirements. In addition, the competent authority monitoring the sandbox test may not have sufficient proximity to monitor testing outside its jurisdiction. (Section 2.3 of the BSG's July 2017 report on regulatory sandboxes https://www.eba.europa.eu/documents/10180/807776/BSG+Paper+on+Regulatory+Sandboxes_20+July+2017.pdf.

financial sector regulators between February and April 2019.[17] The study highlighted how sandboxes foster collaboration between emerging FinTech companies and regulators, building mutually beneficial relationships at an early stage. Regulators gain valuable insights into the characteristics and operations of innovators, while companies better understand the regulatory requirements they must comply with after the experimental phase.[18] Importantly, competition policy was explicitly identified as one of the objectives of regulatory sandboxes in this study, further emphasizing their dual role in fostering innovation and competitive market dynamics (Fig. 1).

While public authorities have expressed optimism about the potential of regulatory sandboxes to contribute to the governance of digital services markets, empirical research in this area is still in its infancy. It will take time to produce robust, data-driven assessments of these tools' effectiveness.[19] Nevertheless, national authorities have warmly embraced sandboxes,

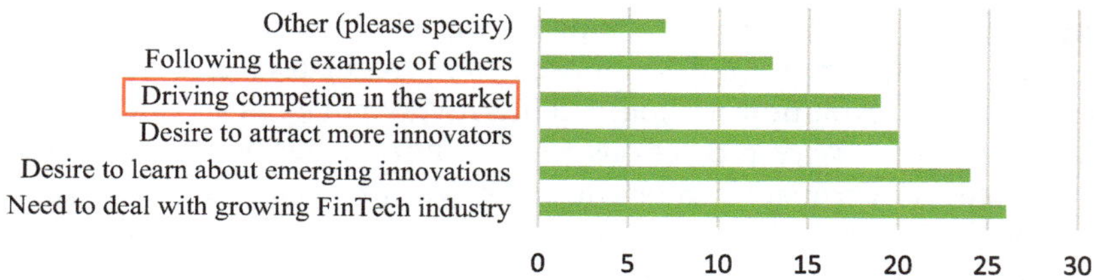

Fig. 1 Motivations driving implementation of innovations facilitators. *Source* CGAP-World Bank study (2019)

[17] CGAP-World Bank: Regulatory Sandbox Global Survey (2019), https://www.findevgateway.org/sites/default/files/publication_files/surevy_results_ppt_cgap_wbg_final_20190722_final.pdf.

[18] S. Appaya, I. Jenik, CGAP-World Bank: Regulatory Sandbox Global Survey (2019), https://www.findevgateway.org/sites/default/files/publication_files/surevy_results_ppt_cgap_wbg_final_20190722_final.pdf, 12.

[19] For example, as pointed out by D. Arner, J. Barberis, and R. P. Buckley ("Fintech, Regtech and the Reconceptualization of Financial Regulation" 37 *Northwestern Journal of International Law and Business* (2017), 373–385), the first sandbox experience in the United Kingdom involved only a tiny fraction of the total number of financial services firms, a significant number of which are now in liquidation or insolvent.

recognizing their capacity to revisit and adapt the proportionality principle of EU law. By enabling greater flexibility and regulatory activism, sandboxes offer a more innovation-friendly approach that aligns with the rapid pace of technological development.

Competition among jurisdictions has also emerged as a noteworthy phenomenon in the regulatory sandbox landscape. Inspired by the UK's pioneering example, numerous jurisdictions have developed their own sandboxes to attract innovative businesses and start-ups. This competitive dynamic reflects a broader trend among national authorities to position their legal systems as the most favorable for FinTech and digital services. However, distinguishing between truly innovative regulatory practices and mere promotional announcements is crucial to ensuring the effectiveness of these tools. In some cases, the emphasis on marketing a jurisdiction as "innovation-friendly" risks overshadowing substantive progress in effectively regulating digital markets.

Digital services markets, particularly financial services, have become central to experimentation with regulatory sandboxes. The ability to balance flexibility with oversight is critical to their success. Sandboxes offer a means to navigate the complexities of regulating rapidly evolving technologies while addressing public interest goals such as consumer protection, fair competition, and sustainability. Going forward, it is essential to integrate these experimental tools into a coherent regulatory strategy that both fosters innovation and ensures a level playing field in digital markets.

4 FinTech and Sandboxes: Transforming Financial Services Regulation

As mentioned, regulatory sandboxes have gained significant prominence in the FinTech sector, where they play a pivotal role in shaping regulation for technology-driven financial services that regulators are not yet fully equipped to address. The UK Financial Conduct Authority pioneered this approach in Europe by launching its regulatory sandbox in 2016, setting a benchmark for other jurisdictions. The FCA's sandbox emerged as a response to the rapid growth of the financial technology sector, introducing a new regulatory methodology that aims to balance competing objectives: promoting innovation, ensuring consumer welfare, mitigating market risks, and fostering competition on the merits.

A fundamental objective of financial market regulation should be to promote competition based on merit, ensuring that all firms adhere to the same rules and incur similar costs.[20]

Regulatory sandboxes support this goal by providing an environment where firms can innovate to differentiate themselves from competitors, rather than exploiting gaps in existing regulations—gaps that are often closed retroactively. This dynamic fosters sustainable innovation that aligns with broader market principles.

While the success of regulatory sandboxes is closely tied to the financial and banking sectors, their application has expanded to other industries, including transportation (e.g., drones and autonomous vehicles), energy, and health.[21] Public authorities are increasingly using sandboxes to address the inherent limitations of traditional regulatory approaches. Notably, EU institutions are considering the development of a pan-European regulatory sandbox under the European Blockchain Partnership, which would address complex issues such as data portability, inter-enterprise data exchange, digital identity, and smart contracts.[22] Similarly, the European Commission has framed a regulatory sandbox for artificial intelligence (AI) under Title V of the Artificial Intelligence Act.[23]

The AI sandbox aims to create controlled environments where innovative AI technologies can be tested within a defined timeframe and under the supervision of relevant national authorities.[24] However, unlike

[20] L. Bromberg, A. Godwin, I. Ramsay, "Fintech Sandboxes: Achieving a Balance between Regulation and Innovation," 28 *Journal of Banking and Finance Law and Practice* (2017), 314–336.

[21] Council Conclusions on Regulatory sandboxes and experimentation clauses as tools for an innovation-friendly, future-proof and resilient regulatory framework that masters disruptive challenges in the digital age, November 16, 2020 https://data.consilium.europa.eu/doc/document/ST-13026-2020-INIT/en/pdf.

[22] European Commission, "Legal and regulatory framework for blockchain" (2022) https://digital-strategy.ec.europa.eu/en/policies/regulatory-framework-blockchain.

[23] Proposal for a Regulation of the European Parliament and of the Council laying down harmonized rules on artificial intelligence (Artificial Intelligence Act) and amending certain legislative acts of the Union, {SEC(2021) 167 final}.

[24] Regulatory sandboxes in the field of artificial intelligence are also mentioned in: Council of EU, 'Conclusions on Regulatory sandboxes and experimentation clauses as tools for an innovation-friendly, future-proof and resilient regulatory framework that masters disruptive challenges in the digital age' (2020); Commission, 'EU Coordinated Plan on AI' (2018 and

traditional sandboxes, this framework would not exempt participants from compliance with existing EU regulations, including the General Data Protection Regulation (GDPR).[25] This approach has raised concerns, as it risks undermining a key incentive for companies to participate in such experimental frameworks—namely, the opportunity to operate with relaxed regulatory constraints.

Each jurisdiction follows its own path in creating regulatory sandboxes, reflecting diverse legal, economic, and cultural contexts. Consequently, the term "regulatory sandbox" encompasses a wide variety of experimental frameworks.[26] Jurisdictions often adopt a trial-and-error approach to determine the most effective model for their unique regulatory and business environments. This divergence is evident within the EU, where sandboxes differ significantly based on the regulatory frameworks applied during trials. For example, the European sandbox for AI-related services adopts stricter compliance requirements, while other jurisdictions implement more flexible frameworks.

Several recurring patterns emerge across different legal systems, which can be analyzed through the lens of competition protection. First, there are traditional sandboxes, which are accessible to enterprises that meet certain predefined criteria and are interested in testing new digital services in a controlled environment. These are distinct from case-specific sandboxes, which are tailored to individual use cases and involve a small, selected group of enterprises.

Additionally, some sandboxes maintain the existing regulatory framework without relaxing compliance rules during the trial period. This approach, as seen under the AI Act, is often used when sensitive issues, such as personal data protection, are involved.[27] Maintaining full

its 2021 review); EU Parliament 'Resolution of 12.02.2019'; G20, 'Ministerial Statement on Trade and Digital Economy' (2019).

[25] Regulation (EU) 2016/679 (General Data Protection Regulation), in OJ L 119, 04.05.2016.

[26] Jurisdictions where customized regulatory relaxation is allowed include the State of Arizona (United States), Brunei, Canada, Hong Kong, Indonesia, Malaysia, and Singapore, see D. M. Ahern, "Regulators Nurturing FinTech Innovation: Global Evolution of the Regulatory Sandbox as Opportunity Based Regulation," 60 *European Banking Institute Working Paper Series* (2020).

[27] See, for example, Datatilsynet (Norwegian Data Protection Authority), 'Sandbox for responsible artificial intelligence' (2021); CNIL (Commission nationale de l'informatique et des libertés), 'Bac à sable données personnelles' (2021).

compliance during trials mitigates concerns about preferential treatment for sandbox participants and ensures fair competition for firms excluded from the sandbox. This model reduces the risk of anticompetitive effects arising from the creation of regulatory sandboxes.

In contrast, a second recurring model involves regulatory sandboxes that allow public authorities to relax certain rules during experimentation. The FCA's sandbox provides a theoretical framework for this approach, enabling regulators to waive specific requirements temporarily.[17] However, the extent of regulatory relaxation varies significantly between jurisdictions. For example, the Netherlands employs a more permissive sandbox for testing innovative energy solutions. In this context, cooperatives and energy associations participating in the sandbox have been authorized to derogate from certain national energy regulations, offering a concrete example of a sandbox that prioritizes flexibility to foster innovation.[28]

The diversity in sandbox models highlights the importance of tailoring regulatory frameworks to the unique needs of each jurisdiction and industry. While strict compliance requirements ensure consistency and fairness, more flexible approaches can create opportunities for groundbreaking innovation, especially in sectors where existing regulations may stifle creativity. Both models have their merits, and the choice between them should depend on the regulatory goals and risks associated with the specific market or technology.

5 The UK Financial Conduct Authority's Sandbox: A Global Benchmark

The UK Financial Conduct Authority (FCA) launched its regulatory sandbox in 2016 as a pioneering initiative in Europe, creating an experimental space where companies could test FinTech services under controlled conditions. Unlike traditional market entry pathways, this sandbox allowed participants to mitigate legal risks related to non-compliance with regulations on data protection, consumer rights, and other sensitive areas.[29]

[28] E.C. van der Waal, A.M. Das, T. van der Schoor, *Participatory Experimentation with Energy Law: Digging into a Regulatory Sandbox for Local Energy Initiatives in the Netherlands*, in Energies, 2020, 13(2), 458, https://doi.org/10.3390/en13020458.

[29] Financial Conduct Authority, 'Regulatory Sandbox' (2015) https://www.fca.org.uk/publication/research/regulatory-sandbox.pdf ("This paper is a report to Her Majesty's Treasury on the feasibility and practicalities of developing a regulatory sandbox that is

A key feature of the FCA sandbox was its collaborative approach, which enabled the regulator to work directly with innovators before these services reached the broader market. This partnership ensured that experimental products aligned with existing regulatory standards while minimizing potential harm to consumers and market stability. Prospective participants were required to demonstrate the novelty of their solutions and their ability to deliver measurable, long-term benefits to consumers, reinforcing the sandbox's focus on fostering innovation with practical value.

Of particular relevance to our discussion is the FCA's explicit inclusion of consumer and competition protection among the primary objectives of the sandbox, alongside the promotion of innovation. This tripartite focus underscores the UK's strategic positioning as a hub for FinTech innovation, coupled with a regulatory framework that balances market openness with protective oversight. By creating an environment conducive to testing and refining innovative services, the FCA signals its intent to attract FinTech firms while maintaining a competitive and well-regulated financial marketplace.[30]

The sandbox operated with several key parameters that ensured its effectiveness and credibility. Each experimental phase lasted for a limited duration, typically three to six months, allowing for a focused timeframe for testing while maintaining momentum for market entry. The FCA also ensured a robust participation framework by admitting a sufficient number of participants to generate statistically significant insights while embedding safeguards to protect consumers. Furthermore, remedial measures and protection mechanisms were integrated into the sandbox framework to address potential harm that might arise during experimentation.[31]

a 'safe space' in which businesses can test innovative products, services, business models and delivery mechanisms without immediately incurring all the normal regulatory consequences of engaging in the activity in question. We believe there is opportunity to expand Project Innovate and introduce a regulatory sandbox. In this report, we set out our plans for implementing the sandbox and proposals for how we can work with industry and the Government to further support businesses.").

30 M. Fenwick, W.A. Kaal, E.P.M. Vermeulen, "Regulation Tomorrow: What Happens When Technology is Faster than the Law?", 6 *American University Business Law Review* (2017).

31 C. Poncibò, L. Zoboli, "Sandboxes and Consumer Protection: The European Perspective," *International Journal on Consumer Law and Practice* (2020).

Since its launch, the FCA's model has been widely emulated, influencing the creation of regulatory sandboxes in both the FinTech sector and other areas of the economy across numerous jurisdictions. For example, similar approaches have been adopted in Singapore and Australia, where the focus on consumer protection and competition enhancement echoes the FCA's foundational principles. Additionally, the FCA's emphasis on fostering a mutually beneficial relationship between regulators and innovators has set a benchmark for sandbox design globally.

This case demonstrates how a well-constructed regulatory sandbox can simultaneously promote innovation, protect consumers, and enhance competition. The FCA's framework highlights the potential for regulatory experimentation to address the dynamic challenges of digital markets while establishing a precedent for other regulators to follow. However, as sandboxes continue to proliferate across jurisdictions, questions remain about how best to harmonize these frameworks to ensure global interoperability without stifling localized innovation.

6 The United States: Challenges and Opportunities in Adopting Regulatory Sandboxes

From a comparative perspective, it is notable that public authorities in the United States appear less enthusiastic and proactive about the regulatory sandbox model than their counterparts in other jurisdictions. Federal initiatives in this area have been limited, despite recognition from some policymakers of the need to catch up with the global regulatory competition. For instance, the U.S. Treasury Department has called for swift action to address the growing regulatory gap, urging the adoption of tools that can foster innovation while maintaining regulatory oversight.[32]

The primary obstacle to the adoption of regulatory sandboxes in the United States lies in its fragmented statutory and regulatory framework for financial supervision. The U.S. system involves multiple layers of federal and state regulators, each with overlapping or exclusive jurisdiction in specific areas.[33] This fragmentation complicates the development and implementation of consistent regulatory sandbox models. In response to

[32] U.S. Department of the Treasury (2018), 13.

[33] U.S. Department of the Treasury (2018), 13–14.

this challenge, the Treasury Department has advocated for regulatory tools that nurture innovation across jurisdictions in a more harmonized manner.

In 2018, the Consumer Financial Protection Bureau (CFPB) became the first federal agency to design a sandbox tailored to the FinTech sector.[34] This initiative offered participants a two-year exemption from the enforcement of financial regulations by federal or state authorities and from certain consumer protection rules. However, the proposal proved controversial. Consumer advocacy groups voiced concerns that such exemptions could weaken safeguards for consumers and potentially lead to exploitative practices.[35]

In contrast, the Office of the Comptroller of the Currency (OCC) adopted a different strategy in 2019 with its "Innovation Pilot Program".[36] This program emphasized small-scale, short-term experiments conducted in collaboration with companies engaged in innovation.[37] Under the OCC framework, only supervised entities were eligible to apply, enabling them to address legal or regulatory uncertainties that might hinder the development of innovative financial services.[38] Participants were required to meet specific criteria, such as promoting

[34] The EFPB was established in the wake of the financial crisis to provide integrated oversight of consumer protection across the financial sector.

[35] J. Kelly, A 'fintech sandbox' might sound like a harmless idea. It's not', in *Financial Times* (2018), https://www.ft.com/content/3d551ae2-9691-3dd8-901f-c22c22667e3b.

[36] The OCC is an independent branch of the U.S. Department of the Treasury that establishes, regulates, and supervises all national banks and federal savings associations, as well as branches and federal agencies of foreign banks. The OCC carries out its mission by issuing banking rules and regulations and providing legal interpretations and guidance on banks' business decisions governing their practices; by visiting and examining the banks it oversees; by evaluating applications for new bank charters or branches; for other proposed changes in the banks' corporate structure or operations and by foreign banks wishing to operate in the United States under an OCC charter; imposing corrective measures, when necessary, on OCC-operated banks that fail to comply with laws and regulations or otherwise engage in unsafe or unsound practices; protecting consumers by ensuring that banks give fair access and equal treatment to customers and comply with consumer banking laws.

[37] OCC Innovation Policy Program (2019) https://www.occ.gov/topics/supervision-and-examination/responsible-innovation/occ-innovation-pilot-program.pdf.

[38] Entities supervised by the OCC are national banks, federal savings associations, their subsidiaries, and federal branches and agencies of foreign banking organizations. FinTech companies cannot independently enroll in the OCC's program.

financial inclusion or mitigating micro- or macro-prudential risks, while ensuring adequate consumer protection.

Unlike the CFPB sandbox, the OCC's program did not offer exemptions from federal laws, including liability provisions. Despite significant pressure from the financial and technology industries to include liability exemptions for activities conducted during the pilot program, the OCC maintained its initial stance, emphasizing full compliance with federal regulations.[39]

Interestingly, this approach echoes the position adopted by European authorities for their regulatory sandboxes in artificial intelligence. Similar to the OCC's framework, the European model also provides for the liability of participants during experiments, which has sparked debate about whether this undermines a key incentive for participation. A central appeal of regulatory sandboxes lies in their ability to provide exemptions or limitations on liability, allowing firms to innovate without fear of punitive consequences for unintended regulatory breaches.

The divergence between the CFPB and OCC models highlights the broader challenges of implementing sandboxes within the fragmented U.S. regulatory landscape. While the CFPB attempted to create a relatively permissive framework, its initiative faced resistance from consumer groups and was constrained by broader regulatory dynamics. The OCC, on the other hand, adopted a more cautious and restrictive approach, prioritizing consumer protection and regulatory compliance over innovation incentives.

These differences illustrate the tension between promoting innovation and maintaining stringent oversight, a recurring theme in regulatory sandbox debates. For the United States to fully harness the potential of regulatory sandboxes, addressing the fragmentation of its financial supervisory system will be crucial. A harmonized approach that balances innovation, consumer protection, and competition may help the U.S. remain competitive in the global regulatory arena.

[39] The OCC assesses the legality of any activity proposed under the Program prior to any live testing.

7 The Benefits of Regulatory Sandboxes: Catalyzing Competition and Consumer Protection

Analyzing the benefits inherent in experimental regulation, particularly regulatory sandboxes, is crucial to understanding their transformative potential, especially in the context of technological advancements. Regulatory experimentation represents a distinct departure from traditional ex-ante regulatory approaches, such as those exemplified by the Digital Markets Act. Unlike the DMA, which imposes a rigid framework of obligations on large digital platforms, regulatory sandboxes enable a dynamic process of testing, impact assessment, and iterative refinement before implementing formal regulatory measures.[40]

This approach holds particular promise when viewed through the lens of competition and consumer protection, especially in sectors like FinTech, where innovation often outpaces traditional regulatory frameworks. While the DMA focuses on compliance with predefined obligations, sandboxes provide an alternative—or at least complementary—mechanism to address the challenges posed by digital markets and nascent sectors reliant on emerging technologies. By fostering a measured and context-specific approach to regulation, sandboxes can mitigate the risks of over-regulation, which may inadvertently stifle innovation in fast-evolving environments.

The experimental nature of regulatory sandboxes is particularly well-suited to FinTech markets. These markets are characterized by rapid technological advancement, significant investment in innovative business models, and evolving consumer expectations. The sandbox model allows for a tailored investigation of specific financial products and services, enabling regulators to assess the potential impact of rules before they are broadly applied. This adaptability is crucial in FinTech, where rigid regulations might otherwise inhibit the introduction of technologies such as blockchain, digital payments, or AI-driven financial advisory tools.

Moreover, sandboxes facilitate a collaborative approach between regulators and FinTech innovators. Traditional regulatory frameworks often create a distance between rule-makers and market participants, but sandboxes bridge this gap by fostering dialog and cooperation. Through sandbox experiments, regulators gain practical insights into how financial

[40] T. Sachs, L'évaluation d'un dispositif juridique: l'exemple d'une loi experimentale, in *Rivista Italiana di diritto del lavoro* (2011).

innovations operate, while firms receive guidance on navigating complex compliance requirements. This interaction not only informs better regulatory design but also ensures that FinTech firms can bring their products to market without unnecessary delays or legal risks.

The logic underlying regulatory sandboxes reflects the recognition that static regulations may fail to achieve their intended objectives in dynamic markets. In sectors like FinTech, where consumer behaviors and technological capabilities are continuously evolving, traditional regulations may quickly become outdated or counterproductive. Sandboxes address this challenge through a trial-and-error model, wherein public authorities monitor and adapt frameworks based on real-world outcomes. This iterative approach is especially valuable in FinTech, where the risks of regulatory missteps—such as stifling payment system innovation or inadvertently favoring incumbents over challengers—are particularly acute.

From a competition perspective, sandboxes offer significant advantages. In FinTech, where new entrants often challenge established financial institutions, sandboxes provide a level playing field for innovation by reducing regulatory barriers to entry. By allowing smaller players to experiment within a controlled environment, sandboxes encourage competition based on the merits of innovation rather than the ability to navigate complex regulatory systems. This fosters a dynamic market where consumers benefit from a broader range of choices, improved pricing models, and innovative financial solutions.

From the perspective of consumer protection, sandboxes also demonstrate their value by identifying and addressing potential risks in a controlled environment. In the FinTech sector, where products such as peer-to-peer lending platforms or decentralized finance (DeFi) services may expose users to unique risks, sandboxes allow regulators to proactively address vulnerabilities without impeding market development. This ensures that regulatory interventions remain proportionate and targeted, balancing the need for innovation with the imperative to safeguard consumers.

In addition to these benefits, sandboxes provide valuable data for assessing the broader economic and social impacts of FinTech innovations. For example, sandboxes can reveal how digital payment systems affect financial inclusion or how AI-driven lending platforms impact credit accessibility for underserved communities. This data-driven approach allows regulators to craft policies that not only promote competition and innovation but also align with broader societal goals.

In summary, regulatory sandboxes embody a forward-looking approach to governance, designed to navigate the complexities of digital markets and emerging technologies. Particularly in FinTech, where innovation and disruption are the norm, sandboxes offer a flexible, data-driven framework for achieving competitive, consumer-centric outcomes. By allowing for experimentation and collaboration, they address the shortcomings of rigid regulatory models and provide a pathway to balanced and effective regulation that fosters sustainable growth in the financial sector.

7.1 *Dynamic and Proactive Regulation*

Regulatory sandboxes represent a significant departure from traditional regulatory frameworks, offering a dynamic and proactive approach to governing digital markets. These mechanisms challenge conventional regulatory paradigms by embedding principles of adaptability, responsiveness, and collaboration into the regulatory process. First and foremost, regulatory sandboxes emphasize proactive, dynamic, and reactive regulation, enabling public authorities to respond more effectively to the rapid pace of technological change.

A defining feature of regulatory sandboxes is their reliance on an empirical and flexible methodology. This approach allows regulators to tailor their interventions based on real-world data gathered during controlled experiments, distinguishing these mechanisms from more rigid regulatory frameworks, such as the mentioned DMA.[41] Unlike static regulatory approaches that impose a fixed set of obligations, sandboxes adapt to the specific characteristics of individual markets and technologies, enabling regulators to refine their frameworks iteratively. This flexibility is especially critical in sectors like FinTech, where technologies evolve rapidly and disrupt traditional market dynamics.

The regulatory sandbox is often seen as a reasonable compromise in addressing the urgency of regulating innovative services. Emerging technologies, such as distributed ledger technologies (DLTs) and blockchain, exemplify the challenges posed by nascent markets. While these technologies hold immense potential, they are often underdeveloped and poorly understood at the time of their introduction, making premature or overly

[41] D. M. Ahern, Regulators Nurturing FinTech Innovation: Global Evolution of the Regulatory Sandbox as Opportunity Based Regulation, 60 *European Banking Institute Working Paper Series* (2020).

prescriptive regulation counterproductive.[42] Regulatory sandboxes provide a structured yet flexible environment where such technologies can be tested, allowing regulators to evaluate their risks and benefits before crafting permanent rules.

By enabling experimentation and iterative learning, regulatory sandboxes offer a way to bridge the gap between innovation and oversight. This balance is particularly valuable in digital markets, where the stakes are high and the risks of misregulation—such as stifling innovation or entrenching existing power dynamics—are significant. Through their dynamic and proactive nature, sandboxes not only address the challenges of rapidly evolving technologies but also promote a regulatory culture that values collaboration, adaptability, and empirical evidence.

7.2 Public Authorities Can Learn From Experiments

Regulatory sandboxes facilitate a unique and valuable collaboration between participants—typically innovators and firms—and the regulators or monitoring authorities overseeing these experiments. This collaborative aspect is one of the key reasons for the growing adoption of sandboxes across jurisdictions. It reflects the willingness of regulators and competition authorities to learn directly from participants who possess first-hand expertise and familiarity with emerging technologies and market dynamics.

For regulators, this process provides an opportunity to continuously evaluate the adequacy of existing legal frameworks in light of evolving market realities. By engaging with innovators during sandbox experiments, public authorities can gather empirical data and insights into new services and technologies, which can inform the development of higher-quality regulations. Importantly, these regulations tend to adopt a pro-innovation approach, balancing the need for oversight with the flexibility required to accommodate rapid technological change.

The information, practices, and data exchanged during sandbox experiments are instrumental in helping authorities design and structure future regulatory or statutory interventions. This process not only enhances the technical competence of regulators but also allows them to anticipate potential challenges and opportunities associated with emerging technologies. For example, in FinTech, understanding the practical implications of

[42] W.G. Ringe, C. Ruof, A Regulatory Sandbox for Robo Advice, in *European Banking Institute Working Paper* (2018), 26, p. 52.

blockchain-based payment systems or decentralized finance models through sandbox trials enables regulators to tailor their interventions more effectively.

From the perspective of participating economic actors, regulatory sandboxes provide a secure environment to test innovative business models and technologies. Participants often benefit from temporary exemptions from certain regulatory constraints—such as those related to data protection or licensing requirements—allowing them to refine their offerings without the immediate pressure of full compliance. This safe testing environment can lead to a significant reduction in regulatory and normative barriers to market entry, enabling smaller firms and start-ups to compete more effectively with established incumbents.

The mutual learning and capacity-building processes inherent in sandbox experiments are, therefore, highly beneficial for both regulators and participants. For regulators, the experimentation phase enhances their understanding of emerging markets and builds their "capability" to address future challenges in a proactive and informed manner. For participants, the opportunity to engage with authorities during sandbox trials provides valuable insights into compliance requirements, market dynamics, and consumer expectations, ultimately strengthening their readiness for full market entry.[43]

This dynamic underscores the broader potential of sandboxes as tools for fostering not only innovation but also a deeper, more collaborative relationship between regulators and market participants. By promoting this exchange of knowledge and expertise, regulatory sandboxes contribute to the development of a regulatory ecosystem that is both adaptive and responsive to the needs of emerging markets.

8 Regulatory Sandboxes: Analysis of Competitive Risks

While regulatory sandboxes have been embraced with enthusiasm by many jurisdictions, they are not without limitations, which could impact their effectiveness in practice.[44] One significant challenge lies in the

[43] G. Frazier, N. Walter, Regulatory Sandboxes: How Federal Agencies Can Take Part in Cooperative Federalism and Catalyze Innovation and Economic Growth Through Exercise of Their Exemptive Authority (2020) https://doi.org/10.2139/ssrn.3561263.

[44] ESA, "FinTech: Regulatory sandboxes and innovation hubs' (2019) https://www.eba.europa.eu/sites/default/documents/files/documents/10180/2545547/154a7ccb-06de-4514-a1e3-0d063b5edb46/JC%202018%2074%20Joint%20Report%20on%20Regulatory%20Sandboxes%20and%20Innovation%20Hubs.pdf, 35–36.

inherent difficulty of determining whether specific services meet the innovation requirements necessary for inclusion in the sandbox. Establishing a predictable and fair system that ensures only genuinely innovative companies gain access to the testing phase is complex. This evaluation demands that public authorities possess not only the necessary technical and legal expertise but also sufficient financial and human resources dedicated to the task.

These challenges do not negate the potential benefits of sandboxes, but they highlight the need for further empirical research and deeper reflection by academics and regulators. To date, there remains a lack of comprehensive studies that evaluate the long-term impact of regulatory sandboxes on competition and innovation, leaving room for improvement in their design and implementation.

8.1 The Risk of Favoring Companies Participating in the Experiment

From another perspective, regulatory sandboxes carry the risk of inadvertently granting an advantage to companies admitted to the experimental phase at the expense of non-admitted competitors or new entrants. If participation in a sandbox creates a competitive edge—such as faster market authorization or reduced regulatory burdens—this could disadvantage other firms and ultimately reduce competition in the market. This is particularly concerning in markets characterized by rapid innovation, where barriers to entry are already high.

In a competitive market, such preferential treatment could lead to unintended consequences. For example, a company allowed to test a product in a sandbox and secure rapid approval might gain a significant advantage over competitors that must navigate the standard regulatory process. This discrepancy risks creating a two-tier system where firms admitted to the sandbox benefit disproportionately, while others face greater hurdles to compete effectively.[45]

A key concern is the discretion granted to public authorities in deciding which companies gain access to sandboxes. Without clear and transparent admission criteria, the selection process could distort competition and

[45] H. J. Allen, *Sandbox Boundaries*, in Vanderbilt Journal of Entertainment & Technology Law, 2020, p. 299.

undermine the goal of creating a level playing field. To address these risks, it is essential for authorities to ensure maximum transparency in their decision-making processes.

Another consideration is the scope of exemptions granted to sandbox participants. While limited exemptions from legal risks are necessary to encourage innovation, overextending these exemptions could compromise financial stability and consumer protection. Regulators must strike a careful balance between fostering experimentation and mitigating associated risks, ensuring that sandboxes remain tools for innovation without jeopardizing broader regulatory objectives.[46]

Transparency and clarity are also critical in the guidance provided by public authorities to companies participating in sandboxes. Without clear rules and expectations, the experimental phase may fail to achieve its intended goals, leaving public authorities disappointed in their ability to balance key objectives such as innovation, competition, and consumer protection.

In conclusion, while regulatory sandboxes hold significant promise as mechanisms for fostering innovation and collaboration, their implementation requires careful consideration of the competitive risks they pose. By ensuring transparency, maintaining proportionality in exemptions, and fostering a level playing field, public authorities can address these challenges and maximize the potential of sandboxes as tools for sustainable market development.

8.2 The Risk OF Fictitious Distortion OF Competition

Regulatory sandboxes inherently involve a participant selection process, and this creates the potential for selected firms to gain an advantage or even an exclusive position in the relevant market once the experimental phase concludes successfully.[47] By establishing an "artificial market"

[46] In a comparative perspective, see C. Tsai, C. Lin, H. Liu, The Diffusion of the Sandbox Approach to Disruptive Innovation and Its Limitations, in Cornell International Law Journal, 2020, 53, pp. 262–295. In particular, the authors point out that the implementation of regulatory sandboxes transplanted from common law jurisdictions to different national contexts may reflect regulatory inertia, regulatory capture, and path dependence. The authors argue that these problems could make a country's rule of law and regulatory strategy unstable and affected by unenforceability, uncertainty, and under-implementation.

[47] We can distinguish between regulatory sandboxes and private sandboxes. Although they are used for "testing" purposes, industry-run sandboxes can also pursue strategic competitive goals. In this case, it is not the state that invites industry to test its innovations, but it is the

managed and controlled by public authorities, sandboxes can inadvertently influence the natural competitive process. While their primary intent is to foster innovation, the structure of sandboxes may simultaneously generate both positive and negative externalities throughout their operation.

One notable concern is the possibility of a notional distortion of competition among participants. For instance, some commentators have raised the issue that sandboxes may facilitate anticompetitive behavior, such as algorithmically controlled collusion or cartel-like arrangements among rivals. In particular, pseudonymous or algorithmic participants could be harder to monitor, potentially complicating the authority's ability to identify or address such behavior.[48]

That said, while the risk of sandboxes enabling the organization or implementation of cartel agreements appears abstract and remote, it cannot be entirely dismissed. Enterprises participating in sandboxes should be fully informed about the competition law risks associated with the experimental phase. One significant issue is the exchange of information among competitors within the sandbox environment, which could inadvertently lead to anticompetitive outcomes. Public authorities, therefore, must establish clear guidelines and robust safeguards to ensure that any such risks are proactively addressed.

By maintaining strict oversight and ensuring transparency in sandbox operations, regulators can mitigate these risks while preserving the benefits of collaboration and innovation. In practice, this includes clearly delineating permissible information exchanges and ensuring that participants are educated about compliance with competition law during the sandbox phase.

a. The Risk of Creating Barriers to Entry

A further concern related to regulatory sandboxes is their potential to create barriers to entry in the broader market. Firms that benefit from participation in a sandbox may be able to allocate resources to goals

industry incumbent that brings together public and private institutions around its platform. Although they are conceptually the same as regulatory sandboxes, both the nature and risks of private actors' sandboxes are different.

[48] T. Schrepel, *Predatory innovation in antitrust law*, Larcier, Bruylant Press, 2018.

beyond research or regulatory compliance, gaining a competitive edge. In contrast, competitors who are excluded from the sandbox often must invest greater economic and technical resources to achieve similar outcomes, potentially delaying or deterring their market entry.

This disparity, often referred to in the literature as the "sandbox paradox," highlights the tension between incentivizing firms to participate in regulatory experiments and preserving fair competition.[49] While sandboxes offer participating firms valuable incentives—such as temporary immunity from certain legal risks or reduced regulatory burdens—these advantages can inadvertently weaken market competition once the experimental phase concludes.[50]

For instance, firms emerging from sandboxes with established market positions and tested innovations may be better positioned to dominate a given sector, leaving competitors who lacked access to similar advantages at a structural disadvantage. This imbalance risks undermining the positive effects of competition, such as improved pricing, innovation, and consumer choice.

To address this paradox, public authorities must carefully balance the incentives offered to sandbox participants with the broader goal of maintaining a level playing field. This includes limiting the extent of competitive advantages granted during the experimental phase and ensuring that firms outside the sandbox are not disproportionately disadvantaged. Additionally, transparency in the admission process and equitable treatment of market participants can help prevent the sandbox from becoming a tool for entrenching market incumbents or creating insurmountable barriers for new entrants.

By carefully managing these risks, regulatory sandboxes can fulfill their potential as a mechanism for fostering innovation and competition without compromising the integrity of the markets they aim to enhance.

[49] B. Knight and T. Mitchell, *The Sandbox Paradox: Balancing the Need to Facilitate Innovation with the Risk of Regulatory Privilege*, in South Carolina Law Review (2021), 72 (2), pp. 445–475.

[50] Although most jurisdictions offer a sandbox free of charge, there are costs associated with performing the tests. However, for some sandbox entities, regulator feedback on applicable regulations reduces legal fees, which may equal or even exceed the costs associated with sandbox testing.

9 Conclusions: Toward a Forward-looking Regulatory Framework

This chapter has examined the adoption of regulatory sandboxes in FinTech markets as a pro-competitive tool to enforce EU competition law. The analysis reveals that the goal of creating competitive digital markets through sandboxes aligns with the broader principles of experimentalist governance.[51] Regulatory sandboxes represent an evolving approach to balancing innovation and regulation—a challenge particularly relevant in FinTech, where rapid technological advancements require both flexible oversight and robust protections.

Balancing Innovation and Regulation: FinTech, Sandboxes, and EU Competition Law has emerged as a critical theme throughout this chapter. Regulatory sandboxes are not merely technical instruments but are emblematic of a broader reimagining of the regulatory state's role in fostering innovation while safeguarding competition and consumer interests. The structure and design of a sandbox directly influence its effectiveness. Some participants reap considerable benefits—such as reduced legal risks and market entry advantages—while others face higher costs or barriers to entry, leading to uneven outcomes.

This divergence underscores that experimentation is not a neutral activity; it involves critical policy decisions about how to balance innovation with fairness. The fragmented adoption of sandboxes across jurisdictions further illustrates the experimental nature of these mechanisms, with variations in objectives, methods, and outcomes. The diversity of these approaches reflects the empirical research and monitoring role of public authorities, who must tailor sandbox designs to meet the specific needs of competition policy and emerging technologies.

Regulatory sandboxes create a space of convergence between competition policy and regulatory frameworks. They blur the traditional distinctions between ex-ante and ex-post interventions, introducing a hybrid

[51] C. F. Sabel, J. Zeitlin, Jonathan, *Learning from Difference: The New Architecture of Experimentalist Governance in the European Union*, in Sabel and Zeitlin (eds), *Experimentalist Governance in the European Union: Towards a New Architecture*, Oxford: Oxford University Press, 2010, pp. 1–28. On this point see also Y. Svetiev, *Experimentalist Competition Law and the Regulation of Markets*, Hart, Oxford, 2020.

approach that is both anticipatory and reactive.[52] Regulation shapes the boundaries of competition law, while competition law informs the evolution of regulatory interventions.

This interplay represents a form of co-evolution between the two disciplines, transcending the conventional dichotomy between regulation and competition. Sandboxes, therefore, shift the focus from a narrow view of compliance and enforcement to a broader framework for fostering fair and innovative markets. They redefine competition policy as a forward-looking tool that enables public authorities to set the "rules of the game" for emerging digital services, benefiting both businesses and end consumers.

The analysis also highlights how innovation, particularly digitization, is driving the expansion of public regulatory intervention. In the EU, the shift toward ex-ante regulation—exemplified by the Digital Markets Act (DMA)—reflects the growing reliance on regulatory frameworks to govern nascent markets. However, this trend raises questions about the adaptability of such models in the face of ongoing technological and social transformations.

There is a risk that the DMA, with its prescriptive approach, may struggle to achieve its intended outcomes in practice. While regulatory sandboxes offer a more flexible and innovative alternative, their success depends on their design and implementation. European and national competition authorities, such as the Greek Competition Authority's initiatives on sustainability, are already extending their reach into broader objectives, demonstrating the versatility of sandboxes as tools for addressing societal challenges beyond competition.

Regulatory sandboxes have the potential to deliver significant benefits for competition policy in FinTech. They foster collaboration among stakeholders, enhance the learning capacity of public authorities, and provide a controlled environment for testing and refining innovative services and technologies. By reducing legal risks and lowering barriers to entry, sandboxes can create a level playing field for new entrants and support the development of competitive market conditions.

However, these benefits come with risks. Regulatory sandboxes can inadvertently favor participants over non-participants, distort market dynamics, or introduce new challenges for consumer protection.

[52] D. A. Zetzsche et al, *Regulating a Revolution: From Regulatory Sandboxes to Smart Regulation*, in Fordham J. Corp. & Fin. L., 2017, 31, p. 23.

Additionally, the discretionary power of public authorities in selecting participants and defining exemptions requires robust safeguards to ensure transparency, fairness, and accountability.

The findings of this chapter suggest that regulatory sandboxes can complement traditional regulatory tools like the DMA, offering an adaptable mechanism for addressing the challenges of rapidly evolving markets. The use of experimental regulation is reshaping competition law, moving toward a model of anticipatory competition policy. This approach positions competition authorities at the forefront of market governance, assigning them greater responsibilities in shaping the rules for nascent markets.

In conclusion, regulatory sandboxes are not just a response to the complexities of digital markets but a transformative tool for rethinking the relationship between innovation, regulation, and competition. They represent an opportunity to align public and private interests, enabling markets to evolve in a way that is both innovative and equitable. As digital finance and other technology-driven sectors continue to grow, regulatory sandboxes will play an increasingly pivotal role in shaping the future of competition law and market governance.

References

Ahern, D. M. (2020). Regulators nurturing FinTech innovation: Global evolution of the regulatory sandbox as opportunity based regulation. *European Banking Institute Working Paper Series*, 60.

Allen, H. J. (2020). Sandbox boundaries. *Vanderbilt Journal of Entertainment & Technology Law*, 2994.

Appaya, S., & Jenik, I. (2019). CGAP-World Bank: Regulatory sandbox global survey. https://www.findevgateway.org/sites/default/files/publication_files/surevy_results_ppt_cgap_wbg_final_20190722_final.pdf

Arner, D., Barberis, J., & Buckley, R. P. (2017). Fintech, regtech and the reconceptualization of financial regulation. *Northwestern Journal of International Law and Business, 37*, 373.

Borgogno, O., & Colangelo, G. (2020). Data, innovation and competition in finance: The case of the access to account rule. *European Business Law Review, 31*, 573.

Bromberg, L., Godwin, A., & Ramsay, I. (2017). Fintech sandboxes: Achieving a balance between regulation and innovation. *Journal of Banking and Finance Law and Practice, 28*, 314.

CNIL. (2021). Bac à sable données personnelles. https://www.cnil.fr/fr/lebac-a-sable-de-la-cnil accessed 10 May 2025.

Council of the European Union. (2020). Conclusions on regulatory sandboxes and experimentation clauses as tools for an innovation-friendly, future-proof and resilient regulatory framework that masters disruptive challenges in the digital age. ST 13026/2020 INIT. https://data.consilium.europa.eu/doc/document/ST-13026-2020-INIT/en/pdf. Accessed 10 May 2025.

Datatilsynet (Norwegian Data Protection Authority). (2021). Sandbox for responsible artificial intelligence. https://www.datatilsynet.no/en/about-us/sandbox-for-artificial-intelligence/. Accessed 10 May 2025.

European Commission. (2018). Coordinated plan on artificial intelligence. Coordinated Plan on Artificial Intelligence 2021 Review (2021). https://digital-strategy.ec.europa.eu/en/policies/european-approach-artificial-intelligence. Accessed 10 May 2025.

European Commission. (2021). Proposal for a regulation of the European Parliament and of the council laying down harmonised rules on artificial intelligence (Artificial Intelligence Act) and amending certain union legislative acts. COM(2021) 206 final, SEC. 167, final. https://eur-lex.europa.eu/legal-content/EN/TXT/?uri=CELEX%3A52021PC0206. Accessed 10 May 2025.

European Commission. (2022). Legal and regulatory framework for blockchain. https://digital-strategy.ec.europa.eu/en/policies/regulatory-framework-blockchain. Accessed 10 May 2025.

European Parliament. (2020). Study on regulatory sandboxes and innovation hubs for FinTech. *PE*, *652*, 752.

European Parliament. Resolution of 12 February 2019 on a comprehensive European Industrial Policy on Artificial Intelligence and Robotics (2018/2088(INI)). https://www.europarl.europa.eu/doceo/document/TA-8-2019-0081_EN.html. Accessed 10 May 2025.

European Supervisory Authorities (EBA, EIOPA, ESMA). (2019). Joint report on regulatory sandboxes and innovation hubs. JC 2018 74. https://www.eba.europa.eu/sites/default/documents/files/documents/10180/2545547/154a7ccb-06de-4514-a1e3-0d063b5edb46/JC%202018%2074%20Joint%20Report%20on%20Regulatory%20Sandboxes%20and%20Innovation%20Hubs.pdf. Accessed 10 May 2025.

FCA. (2015). Regulatory sandbox. https://www.fca.org.uk/publication/research/regulatory-sandbox.pdf

FCA. (2017). Regulatory sandbox lessons learned report. https://www.fca.org.uk/publications/research/regulatory-sandbox-lessons-learned-report

Fenwick, M., Kaal, W. A., & Vermeulen, E. P. M. (2017). *Regulation tomorrow: What happens when technology is faster than the law?* (pp. 6). American University Business Law Review.

Frazier, G., & Walter, N. (2020). Regulatory sandboxes: How federal agencies can take part in cooperative federalism and catalyze innovation and economic growth through exercise of their exemptive authority. https://doi.org/10.2139/ssrn.3561263 accessed 10 May 2025.

G20. (2019). Ministerial statement on trade and digital economy. Tsukuba, Japan. https://www.meti.go.jp/press/2019/06/20190610003/20190610003-1.pdf. Accessed 10 May 2025.

Kaal, W. A. (2016). Dynamic Regulation for Innovation. In M. Fenwick, W. A. Kaal, & E. P. M. Vermeulen (Eds.), *Perspectives in Law, Business and Innovation*. Springer.

Kálmán, J. (2022). Ex Ante regulation? The legal nature of the regulatory sandboxes or how to regulate before regulation even exists. https://doi.org/10.2139/ssrn.3255850

Kelly, J. (2018). A "Fintech Sandbox" might sound like a harmless idea. *It's Not*'. Financial Times. https://www.ft.com/content/3d551ae2-9691-3dd8-901f-c22c22667e3b

Knight, B., & Mitchell, T. (2021). The sandbox paradox: Balancing the need to facilitate innovation with the risk of regulatory privilege. *South Carolina Law Review*, *72*(2), 445.

Matland, R. E. (1995). Synthesizing the implementation literature: The ambiguity-conflict model of policy implementation. *Journal of Public Administration Research and Theory*, *5*(2), 145.

OECD. (2018). Agile Governance: Reimagining Policy-making in the Fourth Industrial Revolution. http://www3.weforum.org/docs/WEF_Agile_Governance_Reimagining_Policy-making_4IR_report.pdf. Accessed 10 May 2025.

Office of the Comptroller of the Currency (OCC). (2019). *Innovation Policy Program*. https://www.occ.gov/topics/supervision-and-examination/responsible-innovation/occ-innovation-pilot-program.pdf. Accessed 10 May 2025.

Poncibò, C., & Zoboli, L. (2020). Sandboxes and consumer protection: The European perspective. *International Journal on Consumer Law and Practice*.

Ranchordas, S. (2021). Experimental regulations for AI. *Morals & Machines*.

Regulation (EU) 2016/679 (General Data Protection Regulation). (2016). OJ L119/1.

Regulation (EU) 2022/1925 of the European Parliament and of the Council on Fair and Contestable Markets in the Digital Sector (Digital Markets Act). (2022). OJ L265/1.

Ringe, W. G., & Ruof, C. (2018). A regulatory sandbox for robo advice. European Banking Institute Working Paper.

Sabel, C. F., & Zeitlin, J. (2010). Learning from difference: The new architecture of experimentalist Governance in the European Union. In S. & Z. (Eds.),

*Experimentalist Governance in the European Union: Towards a New Architecture**. Oxford University Press.

Sachs, T. (2011). L'évaluation d'un dispositif juridique: L'exemple d'une loi expérimentale. Rivista Italiana di diritto del lavoro.

Schrepel, T. (2018). *Predatory Innovation in Antitrust Law*. Larcier, Bruylant Press.

Svetiev, Y. (2020). *Experimentalist Competition Law and the Regulation of Markets*. Hart, Oxford.

Tsai, C., Lin, C., & Liu, H. (2020). The diffusion of the sandbox approach to disruptive innovation and its limitations. *Cornell International Law Journal*, *53*, 262.

US Department of the Treasury. (2018). *A Financial System That Creates Economic Opportunities: Nonbank Financials, Fintech, and Innovation*. https://home.treasury.gov/system/files/136/A-Financial-System-That-Creates-Economic-Opportunities—Nonbank-Financials-Fintech-and-Innovation.pdf. Accessed 10 May 2025.

van der Waal, E. C., Das, A. M., & van der Schoor, T. (2020). Participatory experimentation with energy law: Digging into a regulatory sandbox for local energy initiatives in the Netherlands. *Energies*, *13*(2), 458.

Weng, Y. H., Sun, Y., & Jang, M. (2015). Intersection of "Tokku" special zone, robots, and the law: A case study on legal impacts to humanoid robots. *International Journal of Social Robotics*, *7*(5), 841.

Zetzsche, D. A., et al. (2017). Regulating a revolution: From regulatory sandboxes to smart regulation. *Fordham Journal of Corporate & Financial Law*, *23*, 31.

PART II

Regulatory Perspective of Technological Advances' Impact on Transparency in Fintech

"Playing by the Rules": Advances in Prudential Regulation and Supervision of UK Insurance Startups and Insurtech

Stavros Pantos

1 Introduction

In this research, the existing supervisory approach and regulatory view considering risk management practices and expectations against Pillar 2 of Solvency II for insurtech are critically discussed and analyzed.[1] The focus is especially on the Own Risk and Solvency Assessment (ORSA) and recovery planning,[2] building on prior findings about stress and scenario testing (S&ST) methodologies and practices from fast-growing firms and fintech (Pantos, 2023) and model risk management (MRM) (Pantos, 2024). By collectively analyzing these areas, recommendations

[1] Please note that following the UK's review of Solvency II, and the restatement of assimilated law from PRA's CP5/24 (PRA, 2024i) and PS15/24 (PRA, 2024j), the new UK prudential regime for insurers will be known as 'Solvency UK' (PRA, 2024i: par. 1.20; 2024j: par. 1.9). However, in this paper Solvency II is referenced for consistency, since PRA's policy material and publication continue to refer to the UK regime as Solvency II (PRA, 2024j: par. 1.9; 2024i: par. 1.18–1.20).

[2] From the Insurer Resolution Regime (IRR) and the Solvent Exit Analysis (SEA) and Execution Planning (SEEP).

S. Pantos (✉)
School of Law, University of Reading, Reading, UK
e-mail: s.pantos@pgr.reading.ac.uk

J. Osterrieder et al. (eds.), *Transparency in FinTech*, Palgrave Studies in Financial Services Technology, https://doi.org/10.1007/978-3-032-03523-3_5

about the development of regulatory-prescribed stress testing exercises are presented, building on the most recent PRA's 2022 Insurance Stress Test (IST) (PRA, 2023c) and in preparation for forthcoming exercises.[3] These are combined with the realistic disaster scenarios (RDS) developed for the London Market by Lloyd's of London (Lloyd's of London, 2023a, 2024a) as an additional regulatory-led recurring stress testing exercise. In relation to stress and scenario testing, particular attention should be placed on insurers and insurtechs not invited to participate in the IST, with proposals to address the associated gaps in supervising their risk management capabilities in the areas of stress testing, the ORSA, and MRM.

Recommendations for the design and development of the prudent supervisory approach to insurtechs' risk management practices are included. This is in line with the underlying objective of this study, which is to examine the impact of insurance startups and insurtech on traditional insurance models from a regulatory and supervisory perspective, considering that a key stakeholder of insurtech is the regulator (Xu & Zweifel, 2020). Particularly regarding risk management practices and the prudential supervisory expectations based on the PRA's Rulebook[4], and in line with the Lloyd's of London Principles[5] for the London market. The analysis presented in this chapter comments on the gaps identified in the PRA's latest approach to insurance supervision (PRA, 2023a) and the New Insurer Start-up Unit (NISU) Guide from 2023 (PRA, 2023b). The proposed developments support advances in insurance supervision, toward for their effective application to insurance start-ups and insurtech. These are broadly aligned with the regulation and digital transformation[6] recommendations of Insurtech

[3] The next Life Insurance Stress Test (LIST) will run in 2025 (PRA, 2024a) whereas the next General Insurance Stress (GIST), the dynamic general insurance stress test (DyGIST) has been postponed and will be launched in 2026 instead (PRA, 2023d, 2024b).

[4] Referring to the Insurance Rules for both insurance firms not subject to and subject to the Solvency II Directive.

[5] Primarily the Solvency principles, Capital (#7), Liquidity (#8) and Investments (#9), with the Governance, Risk Management and Reporting principle (#10). (Lloyd's of London, 2023b, 2024b, 2024c).

[6] Insurtech driving capabilities are presented in Fig. 3 of Sosa and Montes (2022), following from a graphical demonstration of the insurance sector structure in Fig. 2 (Sosa & Montes, 2022). For more detail on the relationship between process vs. product innovation from Insurtech introduction, see Fig. 4 of Sosa and Montes (2022).

UK's roadmap[7] (Insurtech UK, 2024). Using the UK (re)insurance industry as a case study, this chapter provides insights into advances in the prudential supervision of insurtech and insurance start-ups.

This chapter is structured as follows: It presents the challenges introduced by insurtech, before commenting on the supervisory approach at the UK level. Specifically, it reviews the PRA's approach to insurance supervision, comments on the gaps around insurtech, and then moves to the NISU Guide, highlighting the areas for development. Then, the core components of prudential risk management and supervision are covered in detail, before concluding with the recommended proposals and supervisory advances.

2 UK Insurtech

2.1 *The Insurance Market And Background*

Before commenting on the regulatory and supervisory approaches describing the UK insurance sector and defining insurtech, it is important to briefly discuss the insurance market. The structure of the UK insurance market consists of three categories, according to Thoyts (2010). These are the buyers (private individuals, industry and commerce, and state-funded organizations), the intermediaries (brokers, consultancies), and the insurers (proprietary insurance companies, mutual insurance companies, and Lloyd's of London syndicates) (Thoyts, 2010). Insurance companies are segmented by the type of products they offer, split into General insurers, Life insurers, and Composite insurers, offering both life and general insurance products (Thoyts, 2010). Lloyd's of London[8] is a unique, world-leading insurance marketplace, with different syndicates, brokers, and managing general agents operating within it. Managing general agents (MGAs) are agents or brokers given underwriting authority from an insurer (Neale et al., 2020). Regulation and supervision of insurance companies are linked to their type. The types of insurance market regulation, according to Thoyts (2010), are (i) systemic, (ii) conduct of business, and (iii) prudential, with

[7] In particular, Recommendation #1 about "the PRA maintaining momentum in evolving the regulatory regime to the needs and structure of insurtechs" and Recommendation #3 with "regulators deploying a progressive, enabling approach to emerging technologies" (Insurtech UK, Insurtech UK, 2024).

[8] Please see Fig. 6.1 of Thoyts (2010) for a description of the Lloyd's of London market and the different flow of capital and premium across its different participants.

prudential referring to the "regulation of the overall financial position of the market", as stated by Thoyts (2010), which is the focus of this study.

Insurtech has different definitions as a term[9]. In particular, the OECD defines insurtech as new technologies bringing innovation to the insurance sector while impacting the regulation of the insurance market (OECD, 2017). Insurtech, originating from the terms "insurance" and "technology", refers to the application of technology to the insurance business (Cosma & Rimo, 2024). Its definition[10] stems from using digital technologies and innovation to improve processes and operations within the insurance business model (Eti et al., 2024). Insurtech is the sub-industry of fintech focusing on insurance (Kalifa, 2021). The UK insurtech sector is considered a world-leading industry (Allanson et al., 2023), explaining the importance of its prudent regulation and supervision. There are different categories of insurtech operating in the UK, according to Insurtech UK[11] (2024), segmented into the following based on their focus: (a) Managing General Agents, (b) Platform, (c) Claims, (d) Data & Analytics, (e) Brokers, and (f) Managing Risks.

Considering the developments observed in the insurance industry, shaped by consolidation and collaboration with insurtech in the form of partnerships, enhancements to the underlying prudential framework are required. The supervisory approach should evolve to address the challenges introduced by the relationship between insurance startups and traditional insurers. Insurtech strives to develop technological innovations, using digital technologies, leading to improvements in the insurance business model[12]. Through partnerships with traditional re-insurers, they provide tailored solutions to support different processes and parts of the insurance value chain[13]. To comprehend the implications of insurtech, the

[9] Please see Table 2 of Gómez and Pineda (2023) for a list of different definitions based on scholarly articles from the literature.

[10] Please see Gómez and Pineda (2023) for an analysis of the term with underpinning scientific approach in defining it.

[11] More detail about the exact Insurtech in the UK is available from Insurtech UK (https://insurtechuk.org/), that is the trade association of the UK Insurtech sector.

[12] For the technology relevant to insurtech, ranging from mobile technology and applications, blockchain and AI, please see Box 2 of OECD (2017).

[13] Please see Yan et al. (2018) for more detail on the insurtech activities with their associated trends and their benefits to the insurance model, using certain specific examples.

components of the insurance value chain should first be understood[14], to capture the impact of digitalization (Elling and Lehmann, 2018; Noordhoek, 2021). Insurtech has already transformed the insurance sector and will continue to play a fundamental role in its transformation[15] via different solutions being developed and technological innovations applied (Gómez & Pineda, 2023). According to Eti et al. (2024), various advantages to the insurance industry are offered through the deployment and application of insurtech systems. These advantages relate to claims management, pricing and underwriting, product design, and development, among others[16] (Eti et al., 2024).

Insurtech is acquired mainly by traditional reinsurers and insurers[17], aiming to improve their efficiency, while at the same time desiring to innovate and disrupt the insurance market (Neale et al., 2020). Venture capital firms and fintech also participate in the insurtech space via acquisitions (Neale et al., 2020). Often insurtechs partner with multiple reinsurers competing in the same sub-sector. To account for the effective supervision of those activities and partnerships toward establishing the overarching prudential framework without hindering innovation, different approaches and advances are described. These are linked to the supervision of big techs' activities in insurance, with the applicable regulatory requirements in the areas of insurance underwriting, digital distribution, and service provision (Ocampo et al., 2023). The study by Xu and Zweifel (2020) presents an indicator system for evaluating insurtech innovations[18]. The application of (new) technologies in insurance, with innovations from startups and insurtechs, leads to the emergence of new risks

[14] Please see Fig. 1 and Table 1 from Noordhoek (2021), adapted from Elling and Lehmann (2018).

[15] For the implications of insurtech to the insurance sector in terms of its structure, please see Fig. 3 of Gómez and Pineda (2023).

[16] Marketing and distribution, and policy management are also noted as key areas where insurtech could support insurance business using advanced technology (Eti et al., 2024: Table 2).

[17] Especially from insurers with more business written in less complex insurance lines of business, with larger investments in insurance technology according to the findings of Neale et al. (2020).

[18] Please see Table 1 of Xu and Zweifel (2020) with three levels and dimensions of layers for the evaluation of insurtech (Layer I: Management and Operations; Level of Technology; User Experience).

from the innovative products introduced (Cosma & Rimo, 2024; Xue & Zweifel, 2020). Insurtech opportunities in the digital transformation of insurance usually include product development, distribution, administrative and claims management, as well as pricing and underwriting (Wilamowicz, 2019). Insurtech developments appear to significantly disrupt the competitiveness of the insurance market in favor of larger insurers, offering increased competitiveness, with smaller insurers more prone to adverse disruption (Chang, 2023).

2.2 *Challenges*

The challenges introduced by insurtech in relation to the regulatory environment have already been examined in different studies. Marano (2019) highlights the capability of the current regulatory framework in dealing with insurtech. In responding to technological advancements from insurtech, the development of regulations is required (Wilamowicz, 2019). The regulatory challenges are linked to the type of activity[19] of the insurtech, considering the applicable regulatory requirements (Ocampo et al., 2023). Regulatory concerns have been triggered by the increase and growth of insurtech, based on the new risks[20] potentially introduced (Ostrowska, 2021). To address such concerns, it requires either the application of existing regulation without changes or the introduction of a separate regime (Ostrowska, 2021). Ostrowska (2021) demonstrates the principle of proportionality for the regulation of insurtech. Ostrowska (2021) argues for adapting existing rules and policy approaches to insurtech business models, instead of introducing new regulation and causing major regulatory changes. The legal issues linked to insurtech could be segmented into three major categories: privacy, cyber security, and access/fairness (Wilamowicz, 2019). Supervisory practices should evolve to address those challenges introduced by the relationship between insurance startups and traditional insurers. Risk management of digital insurance is noted by

[19] Graph 4 provides that distinction, in relation to the activities of big tech companies within insurance (Ocampo et al., 2023). The same principles could be considered for insurance startups and insurtech.

[20] For the risks originating from insurtech's activity, from the point of view of customers/policyholders, as well as regulators and supervisors, please see the study of Ostrowska (2021).

Cosma and Rimo (2024) as a future research direction, and in particular, the response of regulators to the rise of insurtech, with this point validating the importance of this study. At the same time, the disruption from insurtech is perceived as an opportunity for regulatory reform and redesign of the supervisory approach and toolkit (Michaels and Homer, 2018). The recommendations to the regulatory framework presented in the subsequent sections aim to incorporate innovations without creating obstacles for insurance startups and insurtech, accommodating their business structure and model (Ostrowska, 2021).

3 Insurance Regulation and Supervision

Financial regulation has as its purpose the improvement of the system's function, explaining the importance of the design of financial regulation (Armour et al., 2016). Prudential regulation is one of the core strategies of financial regulation, linked to governance regulation with risk management (Armour et al., 2016). Armour et al. (2016) define prudential regulation as aiming to seek the safety and soundness of the regulated entity and the overall market (distinguishing between micro-prudential and macro-prudential). Dhumale (2001) underlines that solvency is the main task of prudential supervision by regulatory authorities. Prudent supervision and regulation of the insurance market are vital, since its soundness is linked to the legal and supervisory structure (Oyetayo, 2015). The regulator is the authority with the power to set the rules, whereas the supervisor is the authority undertaking the monitoring (Löfvendahl & Yong, 2018). In this case, the PRA is the insurance regulator and supervisor from a prudential perspective. For the London Market, Lloyd's of London partially plays that role, supporting the PRA. In the UK, the Prudential Regulation Authority (PRA) is the regulator and supervisor of prudential nature for insurance companies. The PRA's approach to prudential regulation and supervision is detailed in its guidance for insurance undertakings (PRA, 2023a), reflected in different publications, such as its annual business plan and "Dear CEO" letters, while also captured in speeches by policy makers. The PRA has continued to strengthen its supervisory approach, based on its latest report, updated in January 2023 (PRA, 2023a). Armor et al. (2016) argue that regulation should be dynamic, matching the industry it regulates. This cannot be more true for insurtech, with advances in technology and new and emerging risks, thus regulation following suit with amendments and enhancements (Armour et al., 2016), as also flagged in the recommendations of Insurtech UK (2024).

3.1 *Approach*

Principles-based regulation is the adopted financial regulation in the UK (Walsh, 2008). Principles-based regulation at the UK level, initially started with the Financial Services Authority (FSA)[21], refers to outcomes-focused supervision (Ferran, 2009). Principles-based regulation is defined as an outcomes-based regulation, having high-level principles or broadly stated rules, setting standards for the regulated business instead of prescriptive rules, according to Black et al. (2007) and Black (2008). Principles-based regulation is defined as the system where desired outcomes are listed, with regulators providing guidance on how regulated entities could meet them (Walsh, 2008). For instance, the "Dear CEO" letters issued by the PRA are examples of principles-based regulation (Black et al., 2007 and Black 2008). Risk-based regulation could complement principles-based regulation (Ferran, 2009), especially in supervision, by focusing on the areas with the highest risk (Ferran, 2009). At the UK level, the risk-based, proportionate, and targeted approach to regulation is highlighted (Ferran, 2009), with this approach potentially applicable to insurtech. The benefits of a combination of proportionate regulation and risk-based regulation have been highlighted in relation to insurance regulation, based on Solvency II (Löfvendahl & Yong, 2018). In this study, the focus is placed on risk-based regulation, which in effect should shape supervision (but not risk-based supervision[22]). A third alternative, in addition to principles-based and rules-based regulation, the "institutions-based" regulation, is offered as a new paradigm (Walsh, 2008), on the basis that the optimal regulatory regime combines both principles and rules (Walsh, 2008). This approach could be considered and adopted for insurtech. A fourth approach, added beyond rules-based regulation, is the "incentives-based" approach (Dhumale, 2001). In the case of insurtech, the "incentives-based" regulation, providing more freedom and enabling the

[21] The FSA was the predecessor of the PRA and the FSA.

[22] Löfvendahl and Yong (2018) distinguish and clarify the risk-based regulation vs. risk-based supervision.

growth and scale of insurtech, could be considered. This is linked to the recommendations from Insurtech UK (2024).

The concept of proportionality in insurance regulation, as introduced by Löfvendahl and Yong (2018), could also characterize the approach to insurtech regulation as another dimension. The principle of proportionality in the regulation of insurtech has been examined in the literature (Marano & Siri, 2021; Ostrowska, 2021). Proportionality means applying less complex requirements based on certain criteria that should be met. It refers to regulators classifying insurtech and insurance startups based on specific criteria and imposing differentiated regulatory requirements (Löfvendahl & Yong, 2018). Proportionality is embedded in the Insurance Core Principles (ICPs) of the International Standards on Insurance Supervision, as set by the International Association of Insurance Supervisors (IAIS) (IAIS, 2019; Löfvendahl & Yong, 2018). The principle of proportionality refers to the regulatory requirements applied proportionally to insurtech, based on its risk profile (Ostrowska, 2021). It is argued that the correct application of proportionality for insurtech should be made based on the insurtech's operations (Ostrowska, 2021). These approaches to the prudential regulation and supervision of insurtech shape the dimensions of developments noted in the subsequent sections.

3.2 Developments for Insurtech

Findings concerning the PRA's overarching approach to supervising insurtech are discussed. These are accompanied by proposed developments in adapting and adjusting the supervisory approach for insurtech. Starting from the most recent "Dear CEO Letters" documenting the insurance supervision priorities, there are no references to the approach in supervising insurtech and insurance startups (that are within the scope of supervision with authorization in place). This is evident from the letters issued in 2023, 2024, and 2025, respectively (PRA, 2023e, 2024c, 2025). Operational resilience was highlighted in 2023 (PRA, 2023e) and then again in 2024 (PRA, 2024c), but only recently was this linked to other operational risks potentially connected to insurtech, such as cyber and outsourcing (PRA, 2025). This is tied to the forthcoming Cyber Stress Test, with the overarching approach in managing information and communication technology (ICT) and cyber risks (PRA, 2025). These are key risks for insurtech and insurance startups, but not enough attention is given to them. The UK insurance sector takes opportunities linked to technological developments, with this being vital for firms in assessing their financial and operational capabilities to adapt and grow (PRA, 2024c). However, insurtech and insurance startups are neither mentioned, nor is the approach to supervise them addressed. A similar pattern is evidenced in the PRA's report detailing its approach to insurance supervision, without any references to insurtech and insurance startups (PRA, 2023a). In the latest approach to insurance supervision, the impact categories have been reduced to four instead of five (PRA, 2018, 2023a). Proportionate application of the supervisory approach is explained, referring to insurers posing a very low risk to the PRA's objectives, supervised on a portfolio basis, analyzing regulatory returns on a peer basis (PRA, 2023a: par. 138–143). Despite the update on the potential impact categories, it is not clarified where insurtech and insurance startups fit in (PRA, 2023a: par. 38–42). Based on the definition of "Category 4," it could be assumed that insurtech should be considered under that category (PRA, 2023a: par. 39). However, an explanation should be provided. Arguably, another "special category" could also be introduced, extending the scope of "Category 4" to capture insurance startups and insurtech. In addition to amending paragraph 39, adding a new category or explaining how insurtech fits within the existing four impact categories, further explanations should be added regarding the indication of the supervisory interaction and level anticipated, as in paragraph 42 (PRA, 2023a). In particular, the approach for insurtech should be distinguished based on the allocated category. The PRA's risk assessment framework[23] has also been refined in the latest report to capture operational resilience considerations (PRA, 2018, 2023a). The Risk Element Framework capturing the PRA's approach to risk assessment has been amended (PRA, 2023a: Fig. 1). This is a positive development toward addressing operational and non-financial risks linked to insurtech activities and operations, but without any detailed explanation. Effectively, the internal risk assessments and frameworks should be developed in line with this, inclusive of the approaches for insurtech. Perhaps it is assumed that insurtech falls out of the scope of Solvency II, with this guide and its requirements not being applicable at all (PRA, 2023a: par. 37). Even if that's the case, it should be noted, with commentary on insurtech being regarded as a "Non-Solvency II firm",

[23] Thoyts (2010) explains the initial risk-based approach in applying Solvency II the Financial Services Authority (FSA), the PRA and FCA predecessor, followed in applying Solvency II principles, the "ARROW" and "ARROW" process (please see Fig. 5.4).

Fig. 1 Insurtech Supervisory Approach

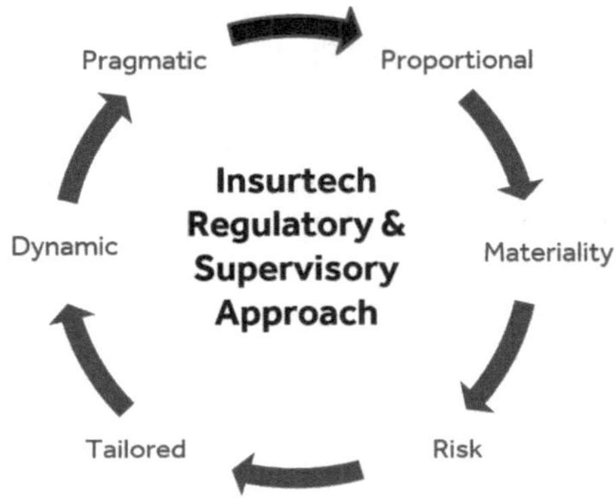

justifying that differentiation. That clarification should also be made in the PRA's Rulebook, with a separate section explaining this. Nevertheless, the argument remains about considering insurtech under Solvency II, providing more details around their supervisory approach in the PRA's guide (PRA, 2023a). An alternative could be adding a separate sub-section in the "Proportionate application of the supervisory approach" (PRA, 2023a: par. 132–155). Effectively, certain paragraphs about insurtech and insurance startups could be introduced if these cannot be factored into prior sections. Figure 1 below depicts the forces shaping the regulatory and supervisory approach toward insurtech, based on the developments required from the PRA.

3.3 *New Insurer Start-up Unit Guide*

The critique of PRA's approach to insurtech supervision should consider the guidance from the New Insurer Start-up Unit (NISU), jointly developed with the FCA (PRA and FCA, 2023), focusing on specific aspects of prudential regulation. The OECD states that regulatory barriers of a prudential nature to authorization for insurtech exist (OECD, 2017). Regulatory requirements are noted as a barrier preventing new participants from entering and competing in the insurance sector (Gómez & Pineda, 2023). Collaboration between insurtech and regulators is required to allow for innovations in the insurance sector (Wilamowicz, 2019). The regulatory sandbox approach introduced by the FCA in the UK supports cooperation between insurtech and regulators, assisting the market entry and authorization process (OECD, 2017). In parallel, NISU was set up by the PRA and the FCA to support new insurers entering the UK market, providing guidance in the following stages: (i) Early Stages, (ii) Pre-Application, (iii) Application, and (iv) After Authorization (PRA and FCA, 2023). This guidance could be utilized by new London market entrants but is not designed for Lloyd's of London managing agents and thus is not tailored to their authorizations (PRA and FCA, 2023). Instead, specific guidance[24] from Lloyd's of London should be consulted (Lloyd's of London, 2023a), based on new entrant's appetite to enter Lloyd's with alignment to the Lloyd's principles for doing business (Lloyd's of London, 2022, 2023b, 2024a, 2024b).

These guides are helpful but could be enhanced, especially in the case of the NISU, by including more information about prudential risk management expectations. Linked to the category impact firm from the PRA's approach to insurance supervision (PRA, 2023a), the NISU guide should clarify whether the insurtech or insurance startup is subject to the Solvency II Directive, commenting on the distinction between "SII firms" and "non-directive firms" (PRA and FCA, 2023: pp. 6, "Will my firm be subject to the Solvency II Directive?"). This distinction is crucial, as it determines the remaining components around the core requirements in relation to prudential risk management. Gaps are observed in the expectations around risk management in the NISU. There are no references to the ORSA, stress testing (IST), and MRM under stage (i) (PRA and FCA, 2023: pp. 7, "What will your insurer do and how will it do it?"). Moving to stage (ii) of the NISU, the business plan, viability, and financial resources with capital and risk management are listed under the "Challenge Session" (PRA, 2023a: pp. 15, "What do you need to know and do?"). However, again, any reference or signposting to the ORSA, IST, MRM, etc., is missing. This changes under stage (iii). The draft ORSA Report is mentioned under the assessment for Solvency II firms and described as the "internal process undertaken to assess adequacy

[24] Please see the guide for applicants considering establishing a management at Lloyd's published by Lloyd's of London. The 6 steps of the application process are detailed in that guide: (1) contacting the new entrants team; (2) qualitive submission; (3) detailed plan presentation; (4) Lloyd's Council in-principle approval; (5) delivery of operational and administrative aspects; and (6) final approval and launch (Lloyd's of London, 2023a).

of risk management and current and prospective solvency positions under normal and severe stress scenarios" (PRA, 2023a: pp. 18, "What we will assess?"). For the 'non-directive' firms, the ORSA is not a requirement, but an equivalent risk assessment report should be produced, covering a review of the capital, management, and governance requirements (PRA, 2023a: pp. 18, "What we will assess?"). More clarity about the components of that risk assessment should be included, along with confirmation of the conditions when the insurtech and insurance startup is under Solvency II and when it is a non-directive firm. The PRA's supervisory approach is documented for stage (v) with the standard supervisory timetable for a new insurer and the Periodic Summary Meeting (PSM), but expectations around the ORSA timeline are not included (PRA and FCA, 2023a: pp. 23–24). The same applies to the IST participation, with no detail around stress and scenario testing expectations. The timeline should be updated to reflect this for the IST, perhaps noted with a checkpoint at the PSM (PRA and FCA, 2023a: pp. 23–24). The above developments aim to support insurtech and insurance startups utilizing the NISU guide, with more detail around the underlying prudential risk management requirements. This is linked to the proportional approach on the basis of materiality for the prudential risk management requirements. Insurtech UK (2024) highlights the need for a regulatory regime enabling more new entrants, based on an agile and accelerated process with an effective regime for smaller firms. This explains the importance of providing more detailed guidance and support in that area.

4 Prudential Supervision Of Insurtech

In extending the developments discussed above, the advances and proposals for the prudential supervision of insurtech are segmented by the (prudential) risk management component. The key risks of an insurance company are underwriting, credit, market, liquidity, and operational (Thoyts, 2010). Therefore, how insurtech impacts those risks should be understood to shape the core elements of prudential regulation and supervision. The focus of this study is placed on Pillar 2 of Solvency II, consisting of risk management, the ORSA, and the Supervisory Review Process (SRP) (Siri and Van den Hurk, Siri & Van den Hurk, 2022). Recommendations for each of those four elements

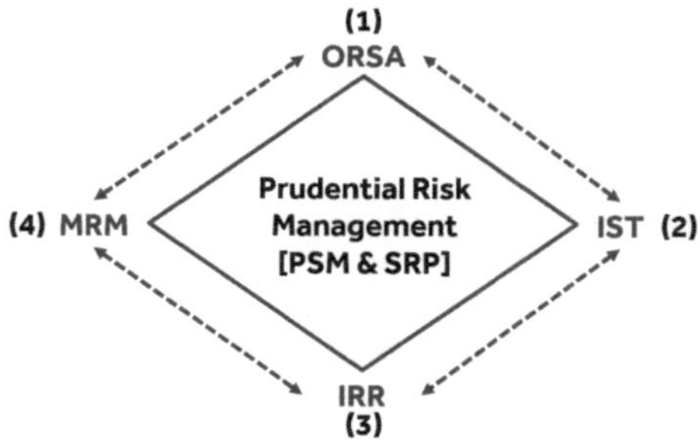

Fig. 2 Insurance Prudential Risk Management Components

of prudential risk management, as shown in Fig. 2 below, are included before summarizing all requirements and commenting on their interconnectivity.

4.1 *Solvency II Orsa*

A proportional approach to the application of the Solvency II requirements is conditional on the risk profile, risk complexity, scale, and nature of the business and operations of the insurtech (Ostrowska, 2021). These criteria—nature, scale, and risks—shape the risk profile of the insurtech and are effectively used to calibrate the application of Solvency II proportionality (Ostrowska, 2021). The proposed amendments to the ORSA requirements, as captured in the PRA's guidance (PRA, 2024d: Supervisory Statement 19/16), are interlinked with the concept of proportionality. A proportionate annual ORSA was initially introduced by the Dutch Association of Insurers and Insurance Ireland (2019) under the proportional application of Solvency II. The ORSA should be proportionate to the size, business mix, and complexity of an insurer, based on a survey of several authorities about supervisory reporting, with often reduced frequency of an ORSA Report (>1 year) (Löfvendahl & Yong, 2018). Ostrowska (2021) argues the importance of proportionality for supervisory reporting duties, referring to the Solvency and Financial Conditions Report (SFCR) and the ORSA. This is to reduce the burden on the insurtech if it is deemed that its effective supervision could be conducted without these reports or at a specific frequency (Ostrowska, 2021).

PRA's SS19/16 ORSA guidance presents the ORSA supervisory report components, produced in a forward-looking manner, capturing the current risk profile and considering stress testing as a tool for assessing risks to which they are exposed and assisting in quantifying potential impact (PRA, 2024d: par. 2.1, 2.2, 2.3). This covers the business plan and strategy timelines, reflecting the specific risk profile and governance mechanisms (PRA, 2024e: par. 7.1). This is also explained in PRA's Approach to Insurance Supervision (PRA, 2023a: par. 75–77). Supervisory Statement SS41/15 states that PRA will review ORSA reports on a risk-based and proportionate basis as part of its supervisory process (PRA, 2024e: par. 7.3). Building on lessons from the banking sector at the EU level[25], the same approach should be followed for the insurance sector, and insurtech in particular. Replicating this approach for insurers, with a pragmatic ORSA, an "ORSA light" defined for insurtech and insurance startups is recommended. This pragmatic approach aims to cover PRA's ORSA requirements (PRA, 2024d: par. 2.2–2.3, 2024e: par. 7.1). Similar to guidelines[26] on the pragmatic supervisory review and evaluation process in light of the COVID-19 crisis developed by the European Banking Authority for the EU banking sector (EBA, 2020), further developments in updating PRA's SS19/16, SS41/15, and the Approach to Supervision to clarify expectations are required. These should also be reflected in the PRA's and FCA's NISU guide, with updated references. The CRO Forum (2012) initially commented on a flexible, principle-based approach for the ORSA Report, conditional on the undertaking's needs. Certain common design features of the ORSA Report are discussed by the CRO Forum (2012), which are prevalent for the ORSA light. A key feature of these is providing assurance on the undertaking's risk strategy (CRO Forum, 2012), which should be core in the "ORSA light". An indicative outline with a table of contents[27] for the ORSA Report is presented by the CRO Forum (2012). In the "ORSA light," these sections should be simplified and effectively focus on covering the strategy and business plan

[25] Arguing that "a pragmatic SREP delivers appropriate supervision for the crisis" according to a member of the Supervisory Board of the ECB (McCaul, 2020).

[26] Please EBA's final report guidelines on the pragmatic 2020 supervisory review and evaluation process in light of the COVID-19 crisis (EBA, 2020).

[27] Consisting of the following: 1. Current Solvency Assessment and Analysis by Risk Type, 2. Business Planning and Projected Solvency Assessment; 3. ORSA Assessment; 4. Description of the Undertaking; 5. Risk and Capital Management Framework; 6. Internal Model Overview (CRO Forum, 2012).

of the insurtech, its key risks, risk profile, and the underpinning risk management processes and approach (i.e., risk framework, risk assessments, etc.), with the evaluation under different severe but plausible scenarios. The "ORSA light" should contain, at a minimum, the following common aspects of the ORSA Report, as highlighted in the CRO Forum (2023). These are: (i) the risk identification and assessment of all material risks, in a forward-looking manner; (ii) the risk measurement and risk methodology, based on the risk profile; (iii) performing stress and scenario tests; and (iv) the risk management framework with underpinning processes and procedures. The proposed "ORSA light" exhibits similarities to the proportionate ORSA from Annex 3 of the Dutch Association of Insurers and Insurance Ireland (2019). However, not all components should be expanded, with a pragmatic approach to the level of detail and analysis presented in the ORSA. This should focus on the business plan and strategy, risk profile, and capital position, with different stress and scenario tests used to evaluate the current and future (risk) position.

4.2 *Insurance Stress Testing*

Stress and scenario testing, including reverse stress testing, is part of the risk management expectations under Solvency II (Marano and Grima, Marano & Grima, 2022). Stress testing is defined as the analysis of implications to the re-insurer resulting from adverse developments of one or multiple risks and risk factors, according to the CRO Forum (2023). Stress and scenario testing is a key element of the ORSA, as highlighted in the PRA's guidance (PRA, 2023a, 2024d, 2023e). A recent guide published by the CRO Forum (2023) presents insights on ORSA Stress and Scenario Testing, particularly regarding the interaction of its different components with the Enterprise Risk Management Cycle. The different types of stress and scenario tests available for insurers are described in the CRO Forum's (2023) report. These include single risk factor stress tests, multiple risk factor stress tests, reverse stress tests, quantitative and qualitative scenarios, and exploratory stress tests (CRO Forum, 2023). The scenarios for insurtech should address the main risks they face. This is also true for established re-insurers, capturing their key risks along with their cross-section with risk interconnectivity from different risk drivers and vulnerabilities (CRO Forum, 2023). The scenarios typically capture (a) insurance shocks; (b) financial market events; (c) operational risks and incidents; (d) legal and regulatory challenges;

(e) catastrophes (natural or man-made); (f) operational resilience, business continuity, and disaster recovery; and (g) other scenarios for new and emerging risks (e.g., climate change, COVID-19) (CRO Forum, 2023). It is important that scenarios for insurtech cover some of these risks based on the insurtech's exposure and risk profile. These should capture the key risks of the insurance undertaking in a forward-looking approach for current and future risks (Marano and Grima, 2022), especially considering non-financial risks, and in particular operational risks, such as IT, cyber, and operational resilience-related risks. The insurtech's key risks linked to their activities should be reflected in the stress and scenario tests undertaken (Pantos, 2023). Beyond the scenarios for insurtech, the scenarios for their traditional reinsurer partner should also be adapted and adjusted accordingly. Considering the partnership and relationship between insurtech and the re-insurer, the scenarios should focus on (a) the risks introduced by insurtech (if new to the risk profile of the re-insurer) and (b) how the existing risk profile evolves based on that partnership.

In addition to the stress and scenario tests performed as part of the ORSA, another type of testing should be highlighted: the regulatory prescribed stress tests, designed by the PRA, noted as the "Insurance Stress Test" (IST). The IST is a (usually) biennial exercise and involves asking the largest regulated life and general insurers to provide information about the impact of a range of stress scenarios on their business (PRA, 2023c). Developing the IST is a key priority for the PRA, with the objective to (a) assess sector resilience to severe but plausible adverse scenarios, (b) guide supervisory activity, and (c) enhance the PRA's and firms' ability to respond to future shocks (PRA, 2023c). The PRA's IST objectives, as documented in the "Dear CEO Letter" of insurance supervision priorities, are (1) assessing sector resilience, (2) supporting capacity building in risk management, and (3) guiding supervisory activity (PRA, 2023c, 2023e). The IST exercise is split into scenarios for life insurers (LIST) and for general insurers (GIST) (PRA, 2023c). It consists of a combination of market and underwriting risk shocks, natural catastrophes, and operational risk stresses[28] (PRA, 2020; 2023c). Its aim is to test the resilience of the general insurance sector and to identify shortcomings in the calculation and assessment of tail events, with the same

[28] Note that the PRA IST 2019 included the first exploratory climate change scenario (PRA, 2020; 2023c), whereas the cyber underwriting stresses were introduced at the PRA IST 2022 for the first time (PRA).

approach applied to life insurance (PRA, 2020; 2022a; PRA, 2023c). The IST in 2022 was the fourth PRA exercise for general insurers and the second exercise for life insurers since the introduction of Solvency II introduction[29] (PRA, 2023c). A dynamic general insurance stress test (DyGIST), involving the simulation of a sequential set of adverse events over a short period of time to assess solvency/liquidity resilience and risk management effectiveness (plus management actions), initially planned for 2025, has been postponed to 2026 (PRA, 2024b). The life insurance equivalent stress test (LIST), planned for the same period, has already been launched (PRA, 2025).

PRA is pursuing a forward-looking, proportionate, and judgment-based approach to insurance supervision, using the tool of stress and scenario testing, referring to the IST, to assess resilience (PRA, 2023a, 2023c, 2023e). However, there are no provisions for smaller insurers and insurtechs outside the scope of the GIST and the LIST. This contradicts the PRA's approach for the banking industry, where there is an equivalent to the macroprudential stress tests for smaller banks and building societies. Effectively, for the banking institutions outside the concurrent stress testing, not participating in the Annual Cyclical Scenario (ACS) or the Solvency Stress Test (SST) from the Bank of England, scenarios are provided[30], with the PRA anticipating observing their completion as part of the Internal Capital Adequacy Assessment Process (ICAAP). It is recommended that the PRA provides insurance-focused scenarios for smaller re-insurers and insurtechs not in scope of the IST. These scenarios could be exploratory and initially of a qualitative nature, and ideally, should be linked to developments in the stress testing practices and capabilities of those institutions, supporting them in building their approach toward prudent risk management applications. An example in that direction associated with the IST is the Results and Basis of Preparation (RBP) qualitative return introduced for the first time in 2022 to accompany the IST quantitative returns (PRA, 2022a, 2023c). Therefore, the non-IST

[29] The GIST was run in 2015, 2017, 2019 and 2022, whereas the LIST in 2019 and 2022 (and currently in 2025).

[30] For more information about those scenarios, please access the "Stress Testing" section of the Bank of England and the PRA's website: https://www.bankofengland.co.uk/stress-testing.

participating institutions could start developing an RBP equivalent as part of the scenarios the PRA could prescribe for them. In the past couple of years, the Bank of England and the PRA have developed exploratory scenarios, looking at other risks outside the IST, such as climate and liquidity, among others[31]. Therefore, exploratory scenarios should be developed for insurtechs and insurance startups. This insurance and insurtech exploratory scenario or scenarios ("IES") should also play a supporting mechanism, as part of their journey, covering NISU's stages from (i) to (iv) (PRA and FCA, 2023). The IES should complement existing stress and scenarios identified and performed at the insurtech level. That's why it is important to improve existing practices and capabilities in designing an appropriate stress testing framework. Thus, the development of a framework for stress testing and solvency assessment, with projections encompassing a range of severe yet plausible scenarios, is crucial for insurance startups and insurtechs (PRA, 2023a). For the risk assessment, a range of stress-testing techniques proportionate to the nature, scale, and complexity of their business is anticipated (PRA, 2023a: par. 84). In the PRA's approach to insurance supervision, internal approaches to stress testing and undertaking bespoke stress tests, potentially reviewed for Category 1 and 2 insurers, are noted (PRA, 2023a: par. 108). This should be extended to Category 3 and 4, but with clarification on expectations, proportionality, and, overall, with a tailored approach for insurance startups and insurtechs. The same approach could be adopted for the London Market and Lloyd's of London. Initially, this could involve updating the requirements under most of Lloyd's Principles (Lloyd's, 2023b, 2024a, 2024b). This should apply to the performance, solvency, and operational principles when referring to the use of stress and scenario testing, and perhaps most importantly under #10 "Risk Management" (Lloyd's of London, 2023b, 2024a, 2024b). This should be reflected in the Realistic Disaster Scenarios (RDS) developed by Lloyd's (2023c, 2024c). In the RDS specification, more guidance about the attempt to perform the RDS scenarios could be introduced. Then, in a similar manner to the IES, a section on "insurtech-related risks" could be included for the insurance startups and

[31] The Climate Biennial Exploratory Scenarios (CBES), at which the largest life and general insurers (inclusive of ten Lloyd's of London syndicates) participated (PRA, 2021, 2022b), and the Liquidity Biennial Exploratory Scenarios (LBES) (BoE, 2021).

insurtechs operating in the London market. Finally, beyond the RBP equivalent, exploratory scenarios for smaller re-insurers and insurtechs, and effectively their IST-like scenario(s) in the IES, the PRA could provide more guidance for the entities attempting to replicate the IST. This could support them in better understanding stress and scenario testing practices, learning from the IST exercise, and using an idiosyncratic version as part of their BAU risk management practices and the ORSA.

4.3 Recovery and Resolution

Stress and scenario testing are linked to recovery and resolution planning. In particular, the ORSA scenarios could be utilized as part of the recovery plan and also to design the resolution plan. Figure 2 of the CRO Forum (2023) graphically illustrates their connection in relation to the capital ratio and position, with recovery and resolution being below the buffer set. Insurers in solvent run-off requirements are included in the supervisory approach (PRA's Approach to Insurance Supervision, PRA, 2023a: paras. 149–150). Implications from insurtech should be reflected in run-off rules within recovery and resolution planning, with regular stress and scenario tests performed (as part of the ORSA) to validate their application (PRA, 2023a). Recovery and resolution measures, which are also closely linked, are core elements of the governance of insurers (Siri and Van den Hurk, 2022). The Insurance Core Principles (ICPs) from the IAIS are linked to recovery and resolution (ICP #12: "Exit from the Market and Resolution") (Siri and Van den Hurk, 2022; IAIS, 2019). Another ICP from the IAIS that is relevant to recovery and resolution planning is ICP #16: "Enterprise Risk Management for Solvency Purposes" (Siri and Van den Hurk, 2022; IAIS, 2019). The recovery plan consists of outlining the available actions that allow insurers to withstand a severe crisis, using different scenarios to inform this (Houben & van Voorden, 2014). Resolution plans, on the contrary, focus on wind-down, with the continuation of activities (Houben & van Voorden, 2014). Recovery and resolution planning, originating from the banking sector, are linked to the Solvent Exit Analysis (SEA) and Execution Planning (SEEP) (PRA, 2024f, 2024g, 2024H) and the overarching Insurer Resolution

Regime[32] (IRR)[33] (HM Treasury, 2023a, b). The SEA and SEEP for insurance startups and insurtech should be proportionate, in a similar manner to the ORSA. Effectively, a "SEEP light", containing the relevant and material components, should be applied if applicable, as the PRA anticipates (PRA, 2024H: par. 3.14). In particular, the action plan for the solvent exit should detail financial, operational, and conduct obligations (PRA, 2024H: para. 3.14). The "SEEP light" is derived from a pragmatic SEA, capturing risks and conditions leading to a solvent exit (PRA, 2024f, 2024g, 2024H). What is key for insurance startups and insurtech is identifying and documenting the key vulnerabilities. For insurance startups and insurtech, these vulnerabilities vary by type, business model, activities, and operations. The FCA Handbook (i.e., wind-down guide) might be more relevant in some cases compared to the PRA Rulebook.

4.4 *Model Risk Management*

The final component of prudential risk management examined captures models utilized and their management. This is another example highlighting the amendments to the insurance regulatory framework, linked to model risk management regarding the sound risk management and governance of pricing and risk modeling (Marano & Siri, 2021). The guidance developed by the PRA at the UK level focuses on model risk management (MRM) for banks (PS6/23, SS1/23), and not re-insurance undertakings (PRA, 2023f, 2023g). However, the same principles in managing model risks during their lifecycle should apply to re-insurers (PRA, 2023g: par. 2.9–2.10). Arguably, this risk management approach should concern all models designed, developed, deployed, and used by the reinsurer, in theory referring to all models underpinning the core insurance processes, such as underwriting, pricing, risk management, and reinsurance[34]. This should extend beyond the internal capital model for capital management and the solvency capital requirements, especially considering

[32] In particular about recovery and resolution with order recovery or exit (par. 26), with pre-resolution planning par. 4.72) (HM Treasury, 2023b).

[33] Note that Lloyd's of London is not in scope of the IRR (HM Treasury, 2023a: par. 2.7, A.9, 2023b: par. 4.21–4.31).

[34] Please see Fig. 4 of Pantos (2024) about the model governance in insurance cases, when commenting on AI uses application and techniques.

insurance startups and insurtech, where different models are utilized, ranging from the application of artificial intelligence (AI) and machine learning (ML) to big data analytics. Considering that insurance startups and insurtech use advanced technologies and often focus their operations entirely on their application, or even on a single element of the insurance value chain (e.g., AI for underwriting decisions), it is vital to ensure that model risk management principles are adopted. The PRA's five MRM principles[35] should be considered and applied proportionally (PRA, 2023g: par. 3.1–3.3), incorporating a framework and building structure for the oversight of those models, with prudent risk management in place (e.g., model risk controls) (PRA, 2023g). In particular, the first three MRM principles, along with their sub-principles, capture model identification, risk classification, governance, and model development, implementation, and use for insurance startups and insurtech (PRA, 2023g: par. 3.1, sec. 4). Looking at those MRM principles and sub-principles, documentation on how these are considered and evidence of adherence to them should be provided by the insurtech. The ORSA is probably the formal regulatory report that could contain that information, along with the relevant framework and policy documents. Producing an attestation on the applicability of the MRM principles and their alignment with insurtech's practices is also recommended. Complementing the findings of an earlier study on AI prudential supervision and regulation (Pantos, 2024), insurance MRM guidance should be introduced by the PRA. Beyond the need to introduce explicit insurance-specific MRM guidance, provisions for insurance startups and insurtech should also be developed. Therefore, separate guidance clarifying the PRA (and the FCA) expectations for insurtech, in relation to the models that are part of their processes and operations, is a recommendation for consideration. This guidance should explain the MRM principles that are relevant and applicable to insurtech (if different compared to those for re-insurers and banks) and outline the supervisory expectations as part of regular supervision. As commented above for the ORSA, the RRP, and the IST, equally MRM requirements should remain proportional, conditional on the risks and type (plus authorization stage, if applicable) of the insurtech. The insurance MRM

[35] These are the following: Model Identification and Model Risk Classification (Principle #1); Governance (Principle #2); Model Development, Implementation, and Use (Principle #3); Independent Model Validation (Principle #4); Model Risk Mitigants ((Principle #5) (PRA, 2023g: par. 3.1).

guide should clarify expectations for insurtech and insurance start-ups in adopting and applying those principles for their models.

4.5 *Advances and Proposals*

The regulatory environment of insurtech in the UK should support innovation (Allanson et al., 2023; Insurtech UK, 2024). However, updates to the insurance regulatory framework to account for insurtech are required (Marano & Siri, 2021). These updates should be linked to technology and data, with the integrated environment and ecosystem facilitated via the introduction of insurtech (Marano & Siri, 2021). Developments in risk governance and amendments to the insurance regulatory framework for the Solvency II regime should be based on the innovations, data, and technologies emerging from insurtech (Marano & Siri, 2021). Insurtech-specific risks should be incorporated into the approach to insurance supervision with a pragmatic, tailored, and proportionate approach to supervision, as outlined in the Periodic Summary Meeting (PRA, 2023a). The ORSA and IST expectations, combined with the MRM requirements and the RRP/SEA-SEEP, should be linked to the evolving business model and associated risks of insurtech, assessing risk profiles and transmission channels. The prudential risk management requirements should be tailored to the type of insurtech, based on the categories defined by Insurtech UK (2024), to create differential requirements. In terms of components of prudential risk management applicable to the type of insurtech: the ORSA is applicable to "Managing General Agents", whereas the IST (IES) applies to "Managing General Agents" and "Brokers", with IRR[36] and MRM applicable to all five categories ("Managing General Agents"; "Platform"; "Claims"; "Data & Analytics"; "Brokers"; "Managing Risk") (Insurtech UK, 2024).

The recommendations for the prudential supervision of insurtech, as described in the previous sub-sections regarding the four components of prudential risk management, are summarized in the following table. Effectively, this provides guidance for "ORSA light", develops IST-specific exercises (the IES), and adopts a proportionate approach to MRM and IRR/SEA-SEEP for insurtech under Solvency II, all within

[36] For the IRR, referring to the RRP, SEA-SEEP, an extension to the disaster recovery, business continuity and operational resilience should be considered for Platform, Claims and Managing Risk.

Table 1 Insurance Prudential Risk Management Components—Developments

PRM Pillar	*Developments*
ORSA	– Introduce the proportional "ORSA light" for insurtech/insurance startups – Prescribe the minimum standards for the "ORSA light"
IST	– Scenarios capturing key risks, vulnerabilities and their cross-section – Develop IST exercise specifically for Insurtech/insurance startups – Results and Basis of Preparation (RBP) equivalent with qualitative analysis – Design exploratory scenario (IES); with equivalent at RDS for Lloyd's of London
IRR	– Use stress and scenario tests for recovery and resolution planning (RRP) – Conduct pragmatic Solvent Exit Analysis (SEA) – Produce "SEEP light" (Solvent Exit Execution Plan) – Link IST with proportionate contingency, reflected in the ORSA Report
MRM	– Develop MRM for insurers; with special guidance on insurance startups/insurtech – Attestation on consideration, adoption and application of MRM Principles – Reporting of MRM adherence in the ORSA Report

a pragmatic PSM framework. Additionally, it includes producing an equivalent proportionate approach for 'non-directive' firms. An overarching requirement regarding risk governance, not presented below, is the development and establishment of internal frameworks, policies, and procedures around: (i) the Solvency II Own Risk and Solvency Assessment, (ii) Stress Testing, (iii) Model Risk Management, and (iv) Resolution with Solvent Exit (Table 1).

Based on the above developments, the prudential supervisory expectations should also consider the stage of the insurance startup and insurtech. Looking at the four stages under NISU's guide from the PRA and the FCA (2023) and the potential impact category (PRA, 2023a), supervisory expectations of a prudential nature based on the four components (ORSA, IST, MRM, IRR) should be pragmatic and proportionate to the stage. Providing flexibility and expecting less at the (i) early stage, evolving through the (ii) pre-application and the (iii) application stage, before reaching (iv) the post-authorisation stage (PRA and FCA, 2023). Specifically, the ORSA light should start after the (i) early stage, with more detail when reaching the (iv) post-authorization stage, as discussed at the PSM. A similar approach should be adopted for the IST, IRR, and

MRM, all commencing at the (ii) pre-application stage, initially developing internally the underpinning framework and policies. More consideration of those requirements should be given at the (iii) application stage. Post-authorization, the IES with RBP should describe the stress testing expectations, with these reflected in the ORSA Report, capturing how MRM principles are adhered to. This should complement the MRM principles' attestation. In the ORSA Report, the SEA outcome with the SEEP light should also be included at that stage (iv).

These recommendations are in line with what Insurtech UK (2024) already flagged, highlighting the requirement for evolving regulation based on the structure and scale of insurtech. The proposals presented should be read in conjunction with other regulatory and supervisory recommendations[37]. Simplified rules for insurance startups and insurtech are recommended based on the prudential supervision components discussed (Löfvendahl & Yong, 2018).

Beyond the underlying risk management practices of prudential risk management, it should be noted that a risk management function should be established for the insurtech to provide oversight and lead the completion of the underpinning activities shaping prudential risk management, such as the ORSA, stress testing, etc. (Marano & Grima, 2022). The structure of the risk and actuarial functions of insurtech is an area closely linked to the prudential risk management components discussed, which could be examined in subsequent studies, since these functions provide oversight from a prudential perspective (Marano & Siri, 2021). This is in line with Solvency II requirements regarding setting a risk management system, model risk management, delivering the ORSA, and developing a risk register (Marano and Grima, 2022).

Reviewing the conduct supervision based on the FCA's approach could be an extension of this study, together with analyzing regulatory and supervisory advances from other jurisdictions, such as Europe, with the approach from the European Insurance and Occupational Pensions Authority (EIOPA). Finally, beyond the supervisory expectations for insurance startups and insurtech, the requirements for traditional re-insurers could be reviewed and subjected to developments. Considering the advances from insurtech and their partnerships, it would be interesting to examine in detail how their relationship shapes

[37] A key example as highlighted in report from the Geneva Association is the implementation of a technology-agnostic regulatory framework to support technological advancements in the future (Noordhoek, 2021).

the underlying regulatory and supervisory framework. When examining different scenarios or performing the ORSA to understand the implications of insurtech, under a prudential lens, for traditional re-insurers.

References

Allanson, E., Comina, A., Richelli, P., & Zaharieva, L. (2023). *The United Kingdom: The nexus of insurtech*. McKinsey & Company.

Armour, J., Awrey, D., Davies, P., Enriques, L., Gordon, J. N., Mayer, C., & Payne, J. (2016). *Principles of financial regulation*. Oxford University Press.

Black, J. (2008). Forms and paradoxes of principles-based regulation. *Capital Markets Law Journal, 3*(4), 425–457. https://doi.org/10.1093/cmlj/kmn026

Black, J., Martyn Hopper, M., & Band, C. (2007). Making a success of Principles-based regulation. *Law and Financial Markets Review, 1*(3), 191–206. https://doi.org/10.1080/17521440.2007.11427879

BoE. (2021). *Financial Policy Summary and Record of the Financial Policy Committee Meeting on 11 March 2021*. Financial Policy Committee, Bank of England. Accessed 26 March 2021.

Chang, V. Y. L. (2023). Do InsurTech startups disrupt the insurance industry? *Finance Research Letters, 57*, 104220. https://doi.org/10.1016/j.frl.2023.104220

Cosma, S., & Rimo, G. (2024). Redefining insurance through technology: Achievements and perspectives in Insurtech. *Research in International Business and Finance, 70*, 102301. https://doi.org/10.1016/j.ribaf.2024.102301

CRO Forum (2012). *CRO forum paper on the own risk and solvency assessment (ORSA): Leveraging regulatory requirements to generate value*. The CRO Forum.

CRO Forum. (2023). *ORSA stress and scenario testing: Best practice for assessing risks*.The CRO Forum.

Dhumale, R. (2001). Incentive v. rule-based financial regulation: A role for market discipline. In E. Ferran & C. Goodhart (Eds.), *Regulating financial services and markets in the twenty-first century*. Hart Publishing.

Dutch Association of Insurers and Insurance Ireland (2019). *A proportionality toolbox for solvency II discussion paper*. The Dutch Association of Insurers and Insurance Ireland.

EBA (2020). Guidelines on the pragmatic 2020 supervisory review and evaluation process in light of the COVID-19 crisis. Final report on the pragmatic 2020 SREP, EBA/GL/2020/10, European Banking Authority. Accessed 23 July 2020.

Eling, M., & Lehmann, M. (2018). The impact of digitalisation on the insurance value chain and the insurability of risks. *The Geneva Papers on Risk and Insurance-Issues and Practice, 43*, 359–396.

Eti, S., Dinçer, H., Meral, H., Yüksel, S., & Gökalp, Y. (2024). Insurtech in Europe: Identifying the top investment priorities for driving innovation. *Financial Innovation*, *10*, 38. https://doi.org/10.1186/s40854-023-00541-y

Ferran, E. (2009). Principles-based, risk-based regulation and effective enforcement. In T. Michel, H. De Wulf, C. Van der Elst, & R. Steennot (Eds.), *Perspectives in company law and financial regulation*. Cambridge University Press.

Gómez, I. S., & Pineda, Ó. M. (2023). What is an InsurTech? A scientific approach for defining the term. The American risk and insurance association. *Risk Management and Insurance Review*, *26*(2), 125–173. https://doi.org/10.1111/rmir.12243

HM Treasury (2023a). *Introducing an insurer resolution regime: Government response to consultation*. HM Treasury, UK Government. August 2023.

HM Treasury. (2023b, January). *Introducing an insurer resolution regime: Consultation*. HM Treasury, UK Government.

Houben, A., & van Voorden, H. (2014). Insuring the financial system against insurers: A macroprudential framework. In J. Monkiewicz & M. Małecki (Eds.), *Macroprudential supervision in insurance theoretical and practical aspects*. Palgrave Macmillan.

IAIS. (2019). Insurance corpore principles and common framework for the supervision of internationally active insurance groups. *IAIS ICPs and ComFrame, updated November 2019, international association of insurance Supervisors*.

Insurtech UK (2024). A roadmap for UK insurtech growth. Insurtech UK. Retrieved from: https://insurtechuk.org/ Accessed 31 December 2024.

Kalifa, R. (2021). *Kalifa review of UK Fintech. Independent report on the UK Fintech sector by Ron Kalifa OBE, policy paper*. HM Treasury.

Lloyd's of London. (2022). *New entrants December 2022*. Lloyd's new entrant appetite. Lloyd's of London.

Lloyd's of London. (2023a). *Establishing a management agent at Lloyd's: A guide for applicants*. Lloyd's of London.

Lloyd's of London. (2023b). *Principles for doing business at Lloyd's*. Lloyd's of London.

Lloyd's of London (2023c, January). *RDS 2023: Realistic disaster scenarios scenario specification*. Lloyd's of London.

Lloyd's of London. (2024a, November). *Principles for doing business at Lloyd's: Summary of revisions*. Lloyd's of London.

Lloyd's of London. (2024b, November). *Principles for doing business at Lloyd's*. Lloyd's of London.

Lloyd's of London. (2024c, January). *RDS 2024: Realistic disaster scenarios scenario specification*. Lloyd's of London.

Löfvendahl, G., & Yong, J. (2018). *Proportionality in the application of insurance solvency requirements.* No. 14, FSI Insights on Policy Implementation No. 14. Financial Stability Institute, Bank for International Settlements.

Marano, P. (2019). Navigating InsurTech: The digital intermediaries of insurance products and customer protection in the EU. *Maastricht Journal of European and Comparative Law, 26*(2), 294–315. https://doi.org/10.1177/1023263X19830345

Marano, P., & Grima, S. (2022). The risk management system, the risk culture and the duties of the insurers' directors. In P. Marano & K. Noussia (Eds.), *The governance of insurance undertakings. Corporate law and insurance regulation, AIDA Europe research series on insurance law and regulation 6.* Springer. https://doi.org/10.1007/978-3-030-85817-9_7

Marano, P., & Siri, M. (2021). Regulating insurTech in the European Union. *The capco institute journal of financial transformation, 54,* 166–177.

McCaul, E. (2020). A pragmatic SREP delivers appropriate supervision for the crisis. Blog post by Elizabeth McCaul, member of the supervisory board of the ECB, 12 May 2020, The supervision blog, European Central Bank. Retrieved from https://www.bankingsupervision.europa.eu/press/blog/2020/html/ssm.blog200512~0958bc57fc.en.html Accessed 31 December 2024.

Michaels, L., & Homer, M. (2018). Regulation and Supervision in a Digital and Inclusive World. In D. L. K. Chuen & R. H. Deng (Eds.), *Handbook of blockchain, digital finance, and inclusion, volume 1: Cryptocurrency, fintech, insurtech, and regulation.* Academic Press, Elsevier.

Neale, F. R., Drake, P. P., & Konstantopoulos, T. (2020). InsurTech and the disruption of the insurance industry: Western risk and insurance association. *Journal of Insurance Issues, 43*(2), 64–96.

Noordhoek, D. (2021). *Regulatory considerations for digital insurance business models.* The Geneva Association, Issue Brief March 2021.

Ocampo, D. G., Taneja, J., Yong, J., & Zhu, J. (2023). *From clicks to claims: Emerging trends and risks of big techs foray into insurance.* No 51, FSI insights on policy implementation. Financial Stability Institute, Bank for International Settlements.

OECD. (2017). *Technology and innovation in the insurance sector.* Organisation for Economic Cooperation and Development.

Ostrowska, M. (2021). Regulation of insurTech: Is the principle of proportionality an answer?. *Risks, 9*(10), 185. https://doi.org/10.3390/risks9100185

Oyetayo, Y. (2015). Principles-based regulations: A model for legal reform in the nigerian insurance industry. *Journal of African Law, 59*(1), 64–84. https://doi.org/10.1017/S0021855315000029

Pantos, S. (2023). Designing stress tests for UK fast-growing firms and fintech. *Risks, 11*(2), 31.

Pantos, S. (2024). Supervisory approaches to AI regulation in insurance: The case of the UK prudential framework. In E. Magnaghi & E. Veglianti Eds., *Organizations and Technology for Sustainability*. CRC Press, Taylor & Francis.

PRA. (2018). *The prudential regulation authority's approach to insurance supervision*. Prudential Regulation Authority, Bank of England.

PRA (2020). *Dear CEO Letter sent to participating firms Insurance Stress Test 2019 and Covid-19 stress testing: feedback for general and life insurers*. 17 June, 2020, Prudential Regulation Authority, Bank of England.

PRA. (2021). *Key elements of the 2021 biennial exploratory scenario: Financial risks from climate change*. Prudential Regulation Authority, Bank of England. Accessed 8 June 2021.

PRA. (2022a). *Insurance stress test 2022. Requirements for the "Results and basis of preparation" report*. Prudential Regulation Authority, Bank of England. Accessed 4 May 2022.

PRA. (2022b), 24 May 2022. *Results of the 2021 climate biennial exploratory scenario (CBES)*. Prudential Regulation Authority, Bank of England.

PRA. (2023a). *The prudential regulation authority's approach to insurance supervision*. Prudential Regulation Authority, Bank of England.

PRA. (2023b). *New insurer start-up unit guide: What you need to know from the PRA and the FCA*. Prudential Regulation Authority, Bank of England.

PRA. (2023c). *Dear CEO letter: Insurance stress test 2022 feedback*. Prudential Regulation Authority, Bank of England.

PRA. (2023d). *PRA statement on the dynamic general insurance stress test in 2025*. Prudential Regulation Authority, Bank of England.

PRA. (2023e). *Dear CEO letter: Insurance supervision: 2023 priorities*. Prudential Regulation Authority, Bank of England.

PRA. (2023f). *Model risk management principles for banks*. Policy Statement, PS6/23, Prudential Regulation Authority, Bank of England. Accessed 17 May 2023.

PRA. (2023g), Supervisory Statement, SS1/23. *Model risk management principles for banks*. Prudential Regulation Authority, Bank of England. Accessed 17 May 2023.

PRA. (2024a). *Life insurance stress test (LIST) 2025: Request for technical input*. Prudential Regulation Authority, Bank of England.

PRA. (2024b). *Update on the dynamic general insurance stress test*. Prudential regulation authority, bank of England. Retrieved from: https://www.bankofengland.co.uk/news/2024/december/update-on-the-dynamic-general-insurance-stress-test Accessed 31 December 2024.

PRA. (2024c). *Dear CEO Letter: Insurance supervision: 2024 priorities*. Prudential Regulation Authority, Bank of England.

PRA. (2024d), *November 2024, updating November 2016, Supervisory Statement SS19/16*. Solvency II: ORSA. Prudential Regulation Authority.

PRA. (2024e). *Solvency II: Applying EIOPA's Set 2, System of governance and ORSA guidelines.* November 2024, updating December 2021, Supervisory Statement SS41/15. Prudential Regulation Authority.

PRA. (2024f). *Solvent exit planning for insurers.* Consultation Paper CP2/24, Prudential Regulation Authority. Accessed 23 January 2024.

PRA. (2024g). *Solvent exit planning for insurers.* Policy Statement PS20/24, Prudential Regulation Authority. Accessed 18 December 2024.

PRA. (2024H). *Solvent exit planning for insurers.* Supervisory Statement SS11/24, Prudential Regulation Authority. Accessed 18 December 2024.

PRA. (2025). *Dear CEO letter: Insurance supervision: 2025 priorities.* Prudential Regulation Authority, Bank of England.

PRA and FCA. (2023). New insurer start-up unit guide. What you need to know from the PRA and the FCA. Prudential regulation authority and financial conduct authority, Bank of England.

Siri, M., & Van den Hurk, A. (2022). Recovery and resolution of insurance companies and director's Duties. In P. Marano & K. Noussia (Eds.), *The governance of insurance undertakings. Corporate law and insurance regulation, AIDA Europe research series on insurance law and regulation 6.* Springer. https://doi.org/10.1007/978-3-030-85817-9_7

Sosa, I., & Montes, Ó. (2022). Understanding the InsurTech dynamics in the transformation of the insurance sector. The American risk and insurance association. *Risk Management and Insurance Review, 25*(1), 35–68. https://doi.org/10.1111/rmir.12203

Thoyts, R. (2010). *Insurance Theory and Practice.* Taylor & Francis.

Walsh, J. H. (2008). Institution-based financial regulation: A Third Paradigm. *Harvard International Law Journal, 49*(2), 381–412.

Wilamowicz, A. (2019). The great fintech disruption: InsurTech. *Banking & Finance Law Review, 34*(2), 215–238.

Xu, X., & Zweifel, P. (2020). A framework for the evaluation of InsurTech. The American risk and insurance association. *Risk Management and Insurance Review, 23*(4), 305–329. https://doi.org/10.1111/rmir.12161

Yan, T. C., Schulte, P., & Chuen, D. L. K. (2018). InsurTech and FinTech: Banking and insurance enablement. In D. L. K. Chuen & R. H. Deng (Eds.), *Handbook of Blockchain, Digital Finance, and Inclusion, Volume 1: Cryptocurrency, FinTech, InsurTech, and Regulation.* Academic Press, Elsevier.

Fintech Regulations in Europe and USA

Bálint Molnár, Galena Pisoni, Hanna Kristín Skaftadóttir, and Szabolcs Korba

Conversely, the US approach encourages rapid innovation but often lacks comprehensive safeguards. The paper concludes by emphasizing the need for agile, balanced regulation that supports fintech growth while addressing systemic risks and regulatory fragmentation.

B. Molnár (✉)
Faculty of Informatics, Information Systems Department,
Eötvös Loránd University of Budapest, Budapest, Hungary
e-mail: molnarba@inf.elte.hu

G. Pisoni
York Business School, York St John University, York, UK
e-mail: g.pisoni@yorksj.ac.uk

H. K. Skaftadóttir
Bifröst University, Reykjavík, Iceland
e-mail: hannak@bifrost.is

S. Korba
Faculty of Law, Eötvös Loránd University of Budapest, Budapest, Hungary
e-mail: korba@inf.elte.hu

J. Osterrieder et al. (eds.), *Transparency in FinTech*,
Palgrave Studies in Financial Services Technology,
https://doi.org/10.1007/978-3-032-03523-3_6

1 Introduction

The fields of Information Technology (IT), Computer Science (C.Sc), and business technology in finance, particularly in the form of FinTech (Financial Technology), have evolved significantly. FinTech plays a crucial role in the digital economy, which is largely based on the Internet. While FinTech services are fundamentally rooted in traditional financial operations, the extensive use of modern technologies enhances the efficiency of various transactions and offers cost-effectiveness for underserved business entities. To understand the current state of FinTech, it is essential to review the latest development trends and the entities that fall under the supervision of regulatory authorities.

The rapid evolution of financial technology (fintech) has transformed global financial markets, prompting the need for regulatory frameworks that balance innovation, competition, and consumer protection. Fintech emerged as a post-crisis paradigm, reshaping financial services and regulatory approaches in various jurisdictions, particularly in the European Union (EU) and the United States (US) (Arner et al., 2015). One of the key regulatory developments in the EU has been the introduction of open banking under the Revised Payment Services Directive!(PSD2), which has fostered competition by enabling third-party access to banking data (Borgogno 2021). This approach contrasts with the US, where fintech regulation remains fragmented, with no centralized framework equivalent to PSD2.

Regulatory approaches to crypto assets further highlight the divergence between the EU and the US. The European Commission has pursued comprehensive regulatory measures to integrate crypto assets into the financial system (European Commission: Crypto-assets). The EU's approach is characterized by its structured legislative efforts, such as the General Data Protection Regulation (GDPR), which governs data privacy in fintech operations ("European-Parliament" "and" "of the Council", 2025). Additionally, the Fintech Action Plan outlines the EU's commitment to fostering a competitive and innovative financial sector through regulatory reforms ("European-Parliament" "and" "of the Council" FinTech action plan, 2018). In contrast, the US regulatory landscape remains decentralized, with oversight split among multiple agencies, including the Office of the Comptroller of the Currency (OCC), which enforces compliance measures for fintech firms (Office of the Comptroller of the Currency, 2016).

Another critical area of differentiation is digital resilience and cybersecurity. The EU has introduced the Digital Operational Resilience Act (DORA) to ensure financial institutions maintain robust digital infrastructure ("European-Parliament" "and" "of the Council", 2025). This proactive regulatory stance contrasts with the US approach, which relies more on sector-specific enforcement actions rather than comprehensive legislative mandates. Similarly, sustainable finance has gained prominence in EU regulation, integrating environmental, social, and governance (ESG) principles into fintech policy frameworks ("European-Parliament" "and" "of the Council", 2025).

Despite these differences, regulatory convergence is emerging in certain areas, such as data-driven finance and RegTech. The EU has adopted a prescriptive regulatory framework that fosters innovation while ensuring financial stability (Zetzsche, 2019). Meanwhile, discussions around RegTech and SupTech in both regions highlight the need for consistent regulatory principles that balance supervision with technological advancements (McCarthy, 2022). Moreover, regulatory sandboxes have been proposed as a mechanism to encourage fintech innovation in the EU, with scholars advocating for a structured and guided approach (Ringe and Ruof, 2020).

This paper explores the key differences between EU and US fintech regulations, examining their impact on competition, innovation, data privacy, crypto assets, and regulatory enforcement. By analyzing regulatory frameworks in both jurisdictions, this study aims to provide insights into the benefits and challenges associated with different approaches to fintech governance.

1.1 Methodology

To systematically analyze the articles in our study, we employed a structured data extraction approach, focusing on key regulatory dimensions in fintech. Our process ensured that we captured relevant details from each study, including jurisdictional scope, regulatory frameworks, and their implications for innovation and market entry.

First, we identified the specific fintech domain examined in each study. This included areas such as RegTech, SupTech, crypto assets, and mobile payments. We extracted the exact terminology used by the authors to describe the regulatory focus, ensuring consistency with their descriptions. If multiple fintech areas were discussed, we recorded them in order of prominence based on the study's emphasis. To determine the precise regulatory domain analyzed, we reviewed the introduction, methodology, and findings sections of each paper.

Next, we documented the jurisdictional scope by listing all jurisdictions explicitly mentioned in the regulatory analysis. We categorized each study as either comparative (analyzing multiple jurisdictions), single-jurisdiction focused, or providing a global regulatory overview. Additionally, we captured references to key regulatory bodies or institutions, such as the European Banking Authority or the European Commission, to understand which regulatory authorities were central to the study's analysis.

To characterize the regulatory approach, we examined whether the study described top-down or bottom-up regulatory models and whether the stance toward fintech innovation was supportive or restrictive. We looked for explicit descriptions in the findings, discussion, or conclusion sections, and if multiple characterizations were present, we listed them in order of prominence.

We also extracted the key regulatory challenges identified in each study, prioritizing those explicitly stated in the findings or discussion sections. These challenges included legal uncertainties, technological development barriers, and regulatory gaps. When multiple challenges were presented, we ranked them based on their significance as interpreted by the study's authors.

Finally, we analyzed how regulatory frameworks impact fintech innovation and market entry. We focused on the studies' assessments of whether regulations facilitate or hinder technological development and innovation. We carefully examined the findings, discussion, and conclusion sections for direct statements about the implications of regulatory policies. Where possible, we used direct quotes to capture the nuanced perspectives provided by the authors.

By following this systematic approach, we ensured a comprehensive extraction of data, allowing for a thorough analysis of fintech regulation across different jurisdictions and regulatory frameworks (Table 1).

The European Union (EU) emerged as the primary regulatory focus across all ten studies. However, three studies extended their analysis to additional jurisdictions. Specifically, one study conducted a global comparison, another compared the UK with the EU, and one examined regulatory differences between the US and China. One study also referenced other jurisdictions but did not specify them explicitly. Among the included studies, analytical papers were the most common, accounting for six out of ten studies. One study employed a quantitative approach, but no

Table 1 Characteristics of included studies

Study	*Research Focus*	*Regulatory Scope*	*Study Type*	*Key Findings*
McCarthy (2022)	Regulatory approaches to RegTech and SupTech	EU and UK	Comparative study	Distinct variations in EU and UK approaches; balance needed between top-down and bottom-up regulation
Ringe & Ruof (2020)	Proposal for EU fintech regulatory sandbox	EU	Analytical paper	Guided sandbox approach could benefit EU fintech regulation; current framework inadequate for new technologies
Vezzoso (2018)	Impact of PSD2 on fintech and competition	EU	Analytical paper	PSD2's access to-account (XS2A) rule facilitates fintech innovation; potential template for broader data access regimes
Zetzsche et al. (2019)	Impact of EU regulatory reforms on data-driven finance	EU	Analytical paper	EU reforms have unintentionally driven RegTech adoption; creating ecosystem balancing various objectives
Ferrarini (2017)	Regulation of crowd-funding and payment services	EU, with references to other jurisdic-tions	Analytical paper	Regulation of crowdfunding shows trade-offs between investor protection and innovation; PSD1 and PSD2 promote competition
Ferreira & Sandner (2021)	EU regulatory approach to crypto assets	EU	Analytical paper	EU moving towards comprehensive regulation of crypto assets; current regulatory gap contributes to legal uncertainty
Hutukka (2024)	Comparative analysis of	EU, US, China	Comparative study	Distinct regulatory approaches in EU, US,

(continued)

Table 1 (continued)

Study	*Research Focus*	*Regulatory Scope*	*Study Type*	*Key Findings*
	fintech regulation			and China; convergence in some areas like data protection
Kapsis (2020)	Critical review of EU fintech regulation	EU	Critical review	EU's current approach is conservative and favors incumbents; more flexible framework needed

purely qualitative studies or systematic reviews were identified. A notable finding came from the study on the impact of PSD2 on the PayTech sector, which reported that PSD2 had a positive effect on the PayTech industry in Europe, leading to a rapid surge in PayTech start-ups following its implementation.

2 Fintech Regulation in the USA and EU

The rapid growth of fintech has necessitated an evolution in regulatory approaches. According to Zetzsche et al. (Zetzsche et al. 2019), the fintech sector encompasses a wide array of services, including payments, lending, investment, and insurance, all of which operate within a complex regulatory landscape. The authors argue that traditional regulatory frameworks often struggle to keep pace with the innovative nature of fintech, leading to calls for adaptive regulatory measures that can foster innovation while ensuring consumer protection and financial stability. In the United States, the regulatory environment is characterized by a fragmented approach, with multiple federal and state agencies overseeing various aspects of fintech operations (Magnuson, 2018). This decentralized framework can create challenges for fintech companies, as they must navigate a patchwork of regulations that differ by state and service type. In contrast, the European Union has pursued a more harmonized regulatory approach, exemplified by the European Commission's (2018) Fintech Action Plan (European-Parliament" "and" "of the Council", 2018) which aims to create a unified regulatory framework across member states.

The regulatory frameworks for fintech in the USA and EU reflect divergent philosophies and priorities. In the United States, regulation tends to prioritize innovation and competition, often at the expense of comprehensive consumer protection (Arner et al., 2016). This approach is evident in the Office of the Comptroller of the Currency's (OCC) special-purpose national bank charter for fintech companies, which aims to facilitate access to banking services while maintaining regulatory oversight ("Office of the Comptroller of the Currency", 2016). However, critics argue that this model may lead to regulatory arbitrage, where fintech firms exploit gaps in oversight to operate without sufficient accountability (Magnuson, 2018). Conversely, the European Union's regulatory framework emphasizes consumer protection and risk mitigation. The EU's General Data Protection Regulation (GDPR) and the Payment Services Directive 2 (PSD2) exemplify this focus, as they impose stringent requirements on data privacy and payment security (European Commission, 2019). Zetzsche et al. (2017) highlight the EU's commitment to fostering a secure and transparent fintech ecosystem, arguing that these regulations not only protect consumers but also enhance trust in fintech services (Zetzsche, 2017).

The regulatory landscape for financial technology (fintech) in the United States (USA) and the European Union (EU) differs significantly due to their distinct legal frameworks, regulatory philosophies, and market structures. While both jurisdictions aim to foster innovation while ensuring consumer protection and financial stability, their approaches diverge in key areas such as licensing, data privacy, consumer protection, and compliance requirements.

3 Thematic Analysis of Analyzed Papers

Our thematic analysis of the included studies reveals a diverse range of research focuses and regulatory themes in the fintech sector. The most common area of study was fintech regulation, appearing in two studies, while other topics included PayTech, crowdfunding, payment services, crypto-assets, RegTech, SupTech, regulatory sandboxes, PSD2, competition, and data-driven finance.

3.1 EU Regulatory Framework and Open Banking (PSD2)

Several studies have examined the impact of PSD2 on the PayTech sector, emphasizing its pro-competitive effects. Borgogno and Manganelli (2021) highlighted that PSD2's access-to-account (XS2A) rule fosters competition by enabling new fintech entrants to access customer banking data (Borgogno and Manganelli, 2021). Vezzoso (2018) further suggested that this rule facilitates innovation within the payment sector (Vezzoso 2018). However, Ferrarini (2017) pointed out trade-offs, noting that while PSD1 and PSD2 encourage competition, they also create challenges in balancing innovation with investor protection (2017).

The European Union has taken a proactive, rules-driven approach to fintech regulation, exemplified by its open banking framework. The Revised Payment Services Directive (PSD2), adopted in 2015 and effective from 2018, mandated that banks open up customer account data to licensed third-party providers with customer consent, thereby establishing a stable regulatory foundation for open banking in Europe (Preziuso et al., 2023). This regime introduced new categories of third-party providers, such as payment initiation and account information service providers, to foster competition and innovation in payments by breaking banks' monopoly over customer financial data Preziuso et al. (2023).

In practice, PSD2's implementation significantly accelerated the open banking paradigm, although inconsistent national transposition led to some fragmentation and interpretative disputes between banks and fintech firms regarding access rules. To address these issues, the European Commission introduced an update in 2023 with a proposed third Payment Services Directive (PSD3) alongside a directly applicable Payment Services Regulation (PSR). This legislative package is characterized as an "evolution not a revolution"—aiming to harmonize implementation across Member States and refine open banking requirements without uprooting the existing framework (Cambounet 2023). For example, the PSR would unify technical standards and supervision to reduce the variability in API quality and enforcement seen under PSD2's country-by-country approach (Cambounet 2023).

At the same time, the EU is looking beyond payments: a proposed Financial Data Access (FIDA) regulation seeks to expand open banking into a broader "open finance" model, extending consumers' data portability rights to other financial products like savings, mortgages, insurance, and pensions (Nolan, 2025). These developments reflect the EU's comprehensive regulatory strategy—continuously updating rules to spur fintech innovation while safeguarding consumers—firmly entrenching open banking and, increasingly, open finance as central pillars of the European financial regulatory landscape (Cambounet 2023; Nolan, 2025).

3.2 Data Protection and Privacy Approaches

Studies emphasized the EU's strict approach to data protection, particularly its implications for fintech regulation. Zetzsche et al. (2019) highlighted how the EU's stringent data protection rules create a secure and trustworthy environment for fintech innovation, albeit with potential compliance costs (Zetzsche, 2019). Additionally, Hutukka (2024) observed an emerging convergence in data protection policies across the EU, US, and China, suggesting a possible shift toward global alignment (Hutukka, 2024).

Data protection regimes in Europe and the United States diverge significantly, shaping distinct fintech privacy approaches. The European Union's General Data Protection Regulation (GDPR), in force since 2018, establishes a comprehensive, high-standard privacy framework that applies across all sectors (Pop, 2025). GDPR enshrines robust principles (like data minimization and purpose limitation) and grants individuals rights over their data (e.g., rights to access, portability, and erasure), with strict consent requirements and hefty penalties for non-compliance (Pop, 2025). By contrast, the US lacks a single overarching data privacy law at the federal level; instead, it relies on a patchwork of sector-specific regulations (Pop, 2025). In the financial sector, for instance, the Gramm-Leach-Bliley Act imposes certain privacy notice obligations on banks, and newer state laws (such as California's Consumer Privacy Act) have begun introducing GDPR-like rights. Still, U.S. privacy protections remain more fragmented and generally less expansive in scope than Europe's (Pop, 2025).

This regulatory contrast creates different operating conditions for fintech firms: EU fintech providers must build compliance frameworks around GDPR's uniform and stringent requirements, whereas U.S. fintechs navigate a complex mosaic of federal and state privacy rules that vary by data type and jurisdiction (Pop, 2025). Notably, both jurisdictions aim to give consumers greater control over their data, even if the legal mechanisms differ (Winch, 2025). Europe's

PSD2 incorporated data protection principles by requiring explicit customer consent for third-party access to account data, complementing the GDPR's broader rights (Winch, 2025). Open banking thus operates alongside privacy laws: while opening financial data to third-party fintech apps raises security and privacy concerns, proponents argue that open banking and data protection can be compatible, as both seek to empower users regarding their data (Winch, 2025).

Europe's rigorous privacy regime has set a global benchmark, influencing other jurisdictions. U.S. policymakers are increasingly considering stronger privacy safeguards, suggesting a slow convergence toward higher data protection standards, even as differences persist in the transatlantic approach (Pop, 2025). Fintech companies must carefully balance innovation in data-driven services with compliance with these differing privacy expectations, ensuring consumer trust and data rights are maintained across both markets.

3.3 Crypto-Asset Regulation

The regulatory landscape for crypto assets remains an evolving area in EU policymaking. Ferreira and Sandner (2021) noted that the EU is progressing toward a comprehensive regulatory framework for crypto assets but identified regulatory gaps that contribute to legal uncertainty and weak investor protection (Ferreira and Sandner, 2021).

Crypto-Asset Regulation in the United States

As of April 2025, the U.S. still lacks a federal stablecoin law. However, bipartisan proposals like the Clarity for Payment Stablecoins Act (U.S. Congress, 2023) and a bill from Senator Hagerty (2020) aim to require 100% reserve backing, regular audits, and temporary restrictions on algorithmic stablecoins. They differ mainly in regulatory oversight—some assign it to federal institutions like the Fed or OCC, while others allow licensed non-bank entities to issue stablecoins under state supervision. While no law has yet been passed, momentum suggests legislation could materialize by late 2025. In the meantime, regulators such as the SEC and CFTC have acted under existing statutes, contributing to legal uncertainty (U.S. Commodity Futures Trading Commission, 2021; U.S. Securities and Exchange Commission, 2023.

Crypto-Asset Regulation in the European Union (EU)

The Markets in Crypto-Assets (MiCA) regulation took effect in June 2024. It requires EU-based stablecoin issuers to be licensed, fully reserve-backed, and compliant with disclosure, audit, and governance standards ("European-Parliament" "and" "of the Council", 2025). Interest payments to token holders are banned to prevent the tokens from being classified as securities. Tokens that reach certain thresholds in volume or market cap are subject to enhanced oversight by the European Banking Authority. MiCA is expected to support adoption, especially in fintech, while limiting issuer profitability due to yield restrictions (Legal Nodes, 2023). Historically, the EU took a more hands-off, market-driven approach, relying on industry-led data-sharing arrangements (or even practices like screen-scraping) in the absence of direct regulation (Carr et al., 2020).

Such differences mean that a fintech product or business model that easily fits Europe's single market (benefiting from EU "passporting" rights, which allow a financial license obtained in one member state to operate across the EU) may encounter hurdles in the U.S.'s fragmented system of state-by-state licensing and sectoral rules (Carr et al., 2020). Conversely, a U.S. fintech leader must adapt to stricter compliance demands when entering Europe, including obtaining EU authorizations and conforming to standards like PSD2. These regulatory mismatches can increase compliance costs and complexity, reflecting varying local priorities.

Transatlantic differences in data access rules illustrate this divergence: the European approach (through PSD2 and upcoming FIDA) creates an affirmative right for consumers to share data, enforced by financial regulators, whereas the U.S. approach (embodied in the Consumer Financial Protection Bureau's pending rules under Dodd-Frank Section 1033) emphasizes consumer access but with a lighter-touch implementation and ongoing debate over scope and security responsibilities (Nolan, 2025). According to recent analysis, the EU and US data-sharing regulations are "diverging in style, scope, and ambition," with Europe pushing a broader mandate and the U.S. opting for narrower, more market-oriented rules (Nolan, 2025). This regulatory divergence can influence where fintech firms launch new services and how they structure operations. It has been noted that the United States currently hosts more fintech firms than Europe, but Europe's fintech sector is growing quickly in the wake of its supportive regulatory framework (Nolan, 2025). In the long run, the outcomes of these divergent regulatory choices could shape global fintech leadership and innovation trends (Nolan, 2025).

From an industry perspective, the lack of common standards across jurisdictions adds complexity and compliance burdens for fintech companies operating globally. Firms must tailor their products to each regulatory environment—for instance, adjusting data handling practices, capital requirements, or licensing status—which can slow expansion and create operational inefficiencies. Regulators themselves acknowledge these challenges: fragmented rules can inadvertently encourage "jurisdiction shopping" or limit the scalability of fintech innovations. Indeed, analysts project that regulatory divergence will persist in the near term, continuing to drive high operational and compliance challenges for firms until greater international alignment is achieved (KPMG, 2024). At the same time, some convergence may occur in response to emerging technologies and risks. For example, the EU and the U.S. are grappling with regulating cryptocurrency and stablecoins, and there is growing dialog in international forums about best practices for fintech oversight. However, navigating incompatible or overlapping regulatory regimes remains a core strategic task for fintech companies seeking global market access (KPMG, 2024). The most successful firms will likely remain adaptable to diverse regulatory expectations, investing in compliance expertise to meet each jurisdiction's requirements while advocating for more harmonized standards where possible (KPMG, 2024).

4 Innovation and Market Implications

The "Impact of PSD2 on PayTech Sector" study reported an increase in PayTech start-ups following its implementation. Borgogno and Manganelli (2021) emphasized that the XS2A rule played a crucial role in fostering competition by reducing barriers to entry (Borgogno, 2021).

However, the impact of fintech regulations on market access was mixed. PSD2 lowered barriers in certain sectors, such as PayTech, while Ringe and Ruof (2020) suggested that regulatory sandboxes could further ease market entry (Ringe and Ruof, 2020). Conversely, Ferreira and Sandner (2021) noted that regulatory uncertainty in the crypto sector could discourage new entrants (Ferreira and Sandner, 2021).

Regulatory frameworks also influence fintech adoption. Zetzsche et al. (2019) reported that EU regulatory reforms have unintentionally driven RegTech adoption, as firms seek compliance solutions

Table 2 Regulatory impact analysis

	EU Approach	*Global Approach*	*Market Impact*
Open Banking	Prescriptive(PSD2, XS2Arule)	Varied (e.g., UK-led, market-driven in US)	Increased competition, surge in PayTech start-ups
Data protection	Stringent (General Data Protection Regulation)	Generally less strin gent, some conver gence	Enhanced trust, potential compliance burden
Crypto Assets	Moving	Varied (e.g., more permissive in some jurisdictions)	Current, regulatory gap causing uncertainty
RegTech/ SupTech	Emerging focus, variations across EU	Growing focus globally, varied approaches	Unintended acceleration of RegTech adoption
Regulatory Sandboxes	Proposed "guided sandbox" approach	Widely adopted (e.g., UK FCA sandbox)	Potential to reduce barriers to entry and foster innovation
Crowdfunding	Balancing investor protection and innovation	Varied approaches	Trade-offs between protection and innovation
Overall Fintech Approach	Comprehensive, potentially	Varied (e.g., more principles-based in US)	Mixed impact on innovation and market entry

(Zetzsche et al. 2019). However, Kapsis (2020) argued that the legal framework must be more flexible to accommodate fintech growth at the necessary pace (Kapsis, 2020) (Table 2).

The European Union (EU) regulatory environment has had positive and negative effects on fintech market dynamics. On the positive side, pro-competitive policies such as open banking under the revised Payment Services Directive (PSD2) have spurred greater competition and new market entry—studies document a surge in fin-tech start-ups (particularly in payments, or "PayTech" firms) following the adoption of PSD2 in 2015, even if that spike was somewhat temporary (Polasik et al., 2020). Enhanced data protection rules have also played a constructive role: compliance with the General Data Protection Regulation (GDPR) is credited with safeguarding customer data and strengthening consumer trust in digital finance, which is expected to support long-run fintech adoption (Aldboush and Ferdous, 2023). Additionally, the rise of regulatory technology (RegTech) and supervisory technology (SupTech) solutions in Europe indicates compliance-driven innovation. Financial institutions and regulators have accelerated their use of tech tools to meet new requirements, a trend observed by the Financial Stability Board. Most supervisory authorities now have a SupTech or data strategy in place, with usage "growing significantly" in recent years (Financial Stability Board (FSB), 2020).

Furthermore, many EU jurisdictions have implemented regulatory sandboxes to allow fintech innovators to test products in a controlled environment. Such sandboxes appear to reduce barriers to entry and encourage experimentation; empirical research finds, for example, that introducing regulatory sandboxes has had "very positive" effects on fintech venture investment by reducing regulatory uncertainty (Goo and Heo, 2020). These aspects of the EU framework open banking, data protection, RegTech/SupTech adoption, and sandboxes have provided impetus to fintech innovation and growth in several sectors.

However, significant challenges persist under the EU's fintech regulatory framework. Compliance burdens in areas like data protection remain non-trivial, especially for smaller firms. Early analyses of GDPR's impact on fintech indicate that while the regulation aimed for transparency, in practice, privacy disclosures became longer and more complex, calling into question whether the GDPR's consumer protection goals have been fully met (Dorfleitner et al., 2023). In emerging domains such as crypto-assets, regulatory uncertainty has been a hurdle: before recent EU initiatives (e.g., the Markets in Crypto-Assets regulation), the crypto sector lacked a unified rulebook, and this lack of clarity constrained growth and innovation in that space (EIT Digital, 2023). Policymakers have also faced difficult trade-offs between safeguarding investors and fostering innovation—a notable example is the crowdfunding sector. Crowdfunding platforms have broadened access to finance, but overly stringent investor-protection rules can unintentionally stifle these new financing models. Indeed, research suggests that maximizing investor protection (through heavy disclosure or limits) may "hurt small firms" by making it harder for them to raise funds via equity crowdfunding (Hornuf and Schwienbacher, 2017). This illustrates the tension regulators must balance: while strong consumer and investor safeguards are essential for trust and stability, they can impose compliance costs that weigh more heavily on new entrants. The EU's fintech regulatory framework has produced mixed results for innovation and market entry. Specific fintech segments have benefited from regulatory clarity and enhanced consumer confidence (for instance, payments and open banking services). In contrast, other areas have faced constraints due to fragmented rules or heavy compliance demands. Going forward, authorities recognize the need to continually calibrate this balance, coordinating policies to manage the trade-offs between financial innovation and objectives like consumer protection, privacy, and market integrity (Feyen et al., 2021).

5 Enterprise and Technology Architecture in FinTech Ecosystem

The FinTech regulation tries to implement governance over a complex architecture. We outline the most relevant components in Fig. 1.

1. Transaction Finalization Layer: This layer consists of the blockchain and its native protocol asset (e.g., Bitcoin [BTC] on the Bitcoin blockchain and Ether [ETH] on the Ethereum blockchain). It enables the network to securely store ownership data and ensures that any state changes conform to the blockchain's defined ruleset.

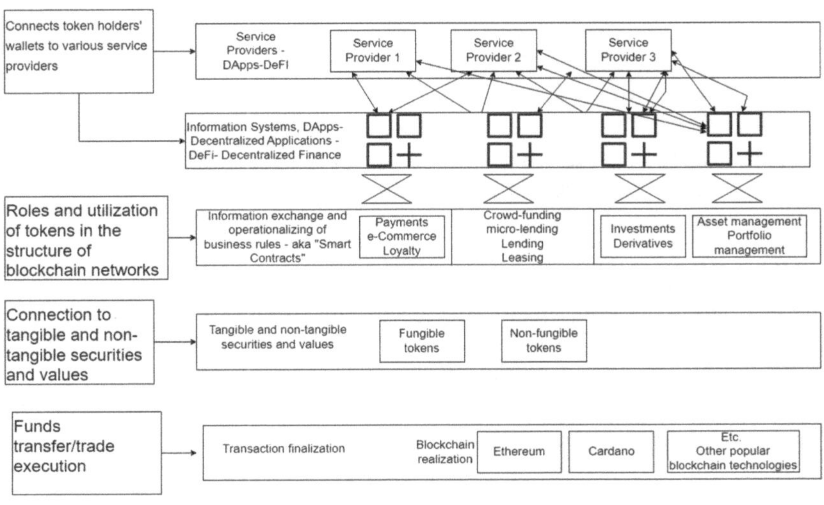

Fig. 1 Enterprise and technology architecture layers—DApps/DEFI

The blockchain functions as the foundation for trustless execution and acts as a settlement and dispute resolution layer.

2. Possession Layer (Tangible and Intangible Securities and Values): This layer includes all assets issued on top of the transaction finalization layer. These include both tangible and intangible securities and values, commonly referred to as tokens. It encompasses all additional digital assets that leverage the underlying blockchain infrastructure.
3. Protocol Standards Layer (Information Exchange & Business Logic Implementation): This layer introduces standardized frameworks tailored for specific use cases, such as decentralized exchanges, lending markets, derivatives, and on-chain asset management. These standards are typically implemented through smart contracts and are accessible to users or applications (e.g., DApps, DeFi platforms). As a result, the protocols built here are highly interoperable.
4. Application Layer (Information Systems, DApps, DeFi Interfaces): This layer enables the creation of user-facing applications that interact with underlying blockchain protocols. These applications, often referred to as Decentralized Applications (DApps) or Decentralized Finance (DeFi) interfaces, typically use a web browser-based front end to abstract complex smart contract interactions, enhancing usability and accessibility for end-users.
5. Service Provider Layer (Aggregators & User-Centric Platforms): An extension of the application layer, this layer consists of service providers that offer platforms connecting multiple protocols and applications. They typically provide comparison tools, ratings, aggregated data, and user-friendly interfaces. These platforms simplify complex tasks by integrating multiple services, enhancing the overall user experience.

The digital FinTech ecosystem consists of robust and modern payment systems, simplified and efficient processes for opening accounts, disbursement of government assistance and subsidies, and access to credit for individuals and small businesses, enabled by credit assessments derived from broad and reliable data sources. It also includes microloans, crowdfunding platforms, cross-border payments, and remittance services (Fig. 2).

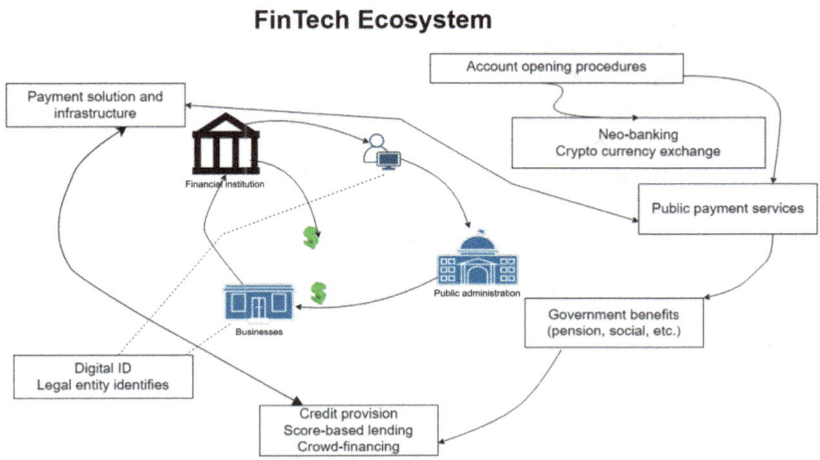

Fig. 2 Components within the FinTech Ecosystem

6 Discussion

The comparative analysis of fintech regulation across the United States and the European Union reveals not only divergent regulatory philosophies but also differing outcomes in market dynamics and innovation. The United States' fragmented regulatory structure, while promoting innovation and competition, often creates operational inefficiencies for fintech firms due to its inconsistent and multi-layered compliance landscape. This decentralized model, as Arner et al. (2016) suggest, tends to prioritize market dynamism but can inadvertently foster regulatory arbitrage and gaps in consumer protection (Arner et al., 2016). Conversely, the EU's harmonized and prescriptive approach—exemplified by PSD2 and GDPR—offers clearer compliance pathways and stronger consumer safeguards. However, this structure may limit flexibility, particularly in rapidly evolving sectors like crypto assets, where regulatory uncertainty and legal fragmentation still pose challenges, as noted by Ferreira and Sandner (2021).

Thematic insights from the reviewed literature highlight that the EU's fintech regulation fosters innovation in structured domains like PayTech and RegTech through mechanisms such as open banking and regulatory sandboxes, PSD2's XS2A rule, in particular, has significantly lowered entry barriers and spurred competition, affirming the EU's commitment to pro-competitive regulation. Moreover, stringent data privacy frameworks have not only enhanced consumer trust but also driven the adoption of RegTech solutions aimed at regulatory compliance. Nevertheless, the EU's high compliance costs and rigid regulatory frameworks may deter new entrants in less mature fintech segments, particularly crypto assets and crowdfunding. Despite these challenges, the EU's regulatory ecosystem has laid a foundation for sustained fintech growth by balancing innovation with risk mitigation—although a more flexible, adaptive approach may be necessary to fully capitalize on emerging technologies and global regulatory convergence.

As the fintech landscape continues to evolve, several emerging trends are shaping the regulatory environment in both the USA and the EU. One notable trend is the increasing emphasis on regulatory sandboxes, which allow fintech companies to test their products in a controlled environment under regulatory supervision. The Financial Conduct Authority (FCA) in the UK has pioneered this approach, and similar initiatives are being explored in the USA and EU (Arner et al., 2015). These sandboxes provide a valuable opportunity for regulators to engage with fintech firms, fostering collaboration and knowledge-sharing. Another trend is the growing focus on sustainability and ethical considerations in fintech regulation. The European Union has been at the forefront of this movement, with initiatives aimed at promoting sustainable finance and responsible lending practices (European Commission, 2020). This focus on sustainability reflects a broader societal shift toward responsible business practices and is likely to influence regulatory frameworks in both regions moving forward.

Both the USA and the EU face significant challenges in regulating the fintech sector. One major challenge is the rapid pace of technological innovation, which often outstrips the ability of regulators to respond effectively. As noted by Arner et al. (2015), the emergence of technologies such as blockchain and artificial intelligence presents unique regulatory dilemmas that require agile and forward-thinking approaches. In the United States, the lack of a cohesive regulatory framework can lead to confusion and uncertainty among fintech companies, hindering their ability to innovate and compete (Magnuson, 2018). In the European Union, while the regulatory framework is more unified, the implementation of regulations can vary significantly across member states. This disparity can create barriers to entry for fintech firms seeking to operate in multiple jurisdictions (Zetzsche et al., 2017). Furthermore, the complexity of complying with regulations such as the GDPR can be particularly burdensome for smaller fintech startups, potentially stifling innovation (European Commission, 2019).

7 Conclusion

The regulatory landscape for fintech in the USA and EU is characterized by distinct approaches, challenges, and emerging trends. While the United States adopts a more fragmented and innovation-driven regulatory framework, the European Union emphasizes consumer protection and harmonization. Both regions face significant challenges in adapting to the rapid pace of technological change, and emerging trends, such as regulatory sandboxes and a focus on sustainability, are likely to shape the future of fintech regulation. As the fintech ecosystem continues to evolve, ongoing dialog between regulators, industry stakeholders, and consumers will be essential to ensure a balanced approach that fosters innovation while safeguarding the interests of all parties involved.

Acknowledgements The paper development was partially supported by project no. TKP2021-NVA-29, which has been implemented with the support provided by the Ministry of Culture and Innovation of Hungary from the National Research, Development and Innovation Fund, financed under the TKP2021-NVA funding scheme.

Competing Interests The authors have no conflicts of interest to declare that are relevant to the content of this chapter.

References

Aldboush, H. H. H., & Ferdous, M. (2023). Building trust in fintech: An analysis of ethical and privacy considerations in the intersection of big data, ai, and customer trust. *International Journal of Financial Studies, 11*(3), 90. https://doi.org/10.3390/ijfs11030090

Arner, D. W., Barberis, J., & Buckley, R. P. (2015). The evolution of FinTech: A new post-crisis paradigm. *Georgetown Journal of International Law, 47*, 1271. https://heinonline.org/HOL/Page?handle=hein.journals/geojintl47&id=1282&div=&collection=

Borgogno, O., & Manganelli, A. (2021). Financial technology and regulation: The competitive impact of open banking. *Market and Competition Law Review*

P, *5*(1). https://doi.org/10.34632/MCLAWREVIEW.2021.10010. https://revistas.ucp.pt/index.php/mclawreview/article/view/10010

Cambounet, B. (2023). Psd3: Modernizing payment and financial services data. Sopra Banking Software. https://www.soprabanking.com/insights/psd3-european-commission-new-proposals/.

Carr, B., Weinstein, C., & Behar, D. (2020). Divergent paths to open banking in UK and US. Law360. https://www.lw.com/insights/2020/11/divergent-paths-to-open-banking

Dorfleitner, G., Hornuf, L., & Kreppmeier, J. (2023). Promise not fulfilled: Fintech, data privacy, and the gdpr. *Electronic Markets*, *33*(1), Article33. https://doi.org/10.1007/s12525-023-00622-x

EIT Digital. (2023). A balancing act between disruption and regulation: Fintech report. Brussels: EIT Digital. https://www.eitdigital.eu/fileadmin/2023/ecosystem/downloads/makers-shapers/EIT-Digital_Fintech-Report.pdf

European Commission. Crypto-assets - European Commission. https://finance.ec.europa.eu/digital-finance/crypto-assets_en

European Parliament "and" of the Council. (2016). Regulation (EU) 2016/679 of the European Parliamentment and of the Council of 27 April 2016 on the protection of natural persons with regard to the processing of personal data and on the free movement of such data, and repealing Directive 95/46/EC (General Data Protection Regulation). *Regulation (Eu)*, *2016*, 679.

European Parliament "and" of the Council. (2018). For a more competitive and innovative European financial sector. https://finance.ec.europa.eu/publications/fintech-action-plan-more-competitive-and-innovative-european-financial-sector_en (Online; Accessed 9. Mar. 2025)

European Securities and Markets Authority. (2024). Markets in crypto-assets regulation (mica). https://www.esma.europa.eu/esmas-activities/digital-finance-and-innovation/markets-crypto-assets-regulation-mica

"European-Parliament" "and" "of the Council": Payment Services Directive (2025). https://finance.ec.europa.eu/regulation-and-supervision/financial-services-legislation/implementing-and-delegated-acts/payment-services-directive_en. (Online; Accessed 9. Mar. 2025)

"European-Parliament" "and" "of the Council": Sustainable finance (2025). https://finance.ec.europa.eu/sustainable-finance_en. (Online; Accessed 9. Mar. 2025)

"European-Parliament" "and" "of the Council" FinTech action plan. (2018). For a more competitive and innovative European financial sector. https://finance.ec.europa.eu/publications/fintech-action-plan-more-competitive-and-innovative-european-financial-sector_en. (Online; Accessed 9. Mar. 2025)

{{"European-Parliament"}{"and"} {"of the Council"}}. (2025). Digital operational re-silence act (DORA). https://www.eiopa.europa.eu/digital-operational-resilience-act-dora_en

Ferrarini, G. (2017). Regulating fintech: Crowdfunding and beyond. *European Economy*, *3*(2), 121–142.

Ferreira, A., & Sandner, P. (2021). Eu search for regulatory answers to crypto assets and their place in the financial markets' infrastructure. *Computer Law & Security Review*, *43*, 105632. https://doi.org/10.1016/j.clsr.2021.105632

Feyen, E., Frost, J., Gambacorta, L., Natarajan, H., & Saal, M. (2021). *Fintech and the Digital Transformation of Financial Services: Implications for Market Structure and Public Policy*. BIS Papers, 117. Bank for International Settlements.

Financial Stability Board (FSB). (2020). The use of supervisory and regulatory technology by authori- ties and regulated institutions: Market developments and financial stability implications. Tech. rep., FSB, Basel. (Report published October 9, 2020).

Goo, J. J., & Heo, J. (2020). The impact of the regulatory sandbox on the fintech industry, with a discussion on the relationship between regulatory sandboxes and open innovation. *Journal of Open Innovation: Technology, Market, and Complexity*, *6*(2), 43. https://doi.org/10.3390/joitmc6020043

Hagerty, B. (2024). Stablecoin draft bill text. https://www.hagerty.senate.gov/wp-content/uploads/2024/10/Stablecoin-Draft-Text.pdf

Hornuf, L., & Schwienbacher, A. (2017). Should securities regulation promote equity crowdfunding? *Small Business Economics*, *49*(3), 579–593.

Hutukka, P. (2024). Fintech law in the European Union, the United States and China: Regulation of financial technology in comparative context. *Maastricht Journal of European and Comparative Law*, *31*(5), 559–594. https://doi.org/10.1177/1023263x241298416

Kapsis, I. (2020). A Truly Future-Oriented Legal Framework for Fintech in the EU. *European Business Law Review*, *31*(Issue 3), 475–514. https://doi.org/10.54648/eulr2020020

KPMG. (2024). Ten key regulatory challenges of 2025. Tech. rep., KPMG Interna- tional. https://kpmg.com/kpmg-us/content/dam/kpmg/pdf/2024/ten-key-regulatory-challenges-of-2025.pdf.Report

Legal Nodes. (2023). Mica regulation explained. https://legalnodes.com/article/mica-regulation-explained

Magnuson, W. (2018). Regulating Fintech. *Vanderbilt Law Review*, *71*, 1167. https://heinonline.org/HOL/Page?handle=hein.journals/vanlr71&id=1211&div=&collection=

McCarthy, J. (2022). The regulation of RegTech and SupTech in finance: Ensuring consistency in principle and in practice. *Journal of Financial Regulation and Compliance*, *31*(2), 186–199. https://doi.org/10.1108/jfrc-01-2022-0004

Nolan, P. (2025). Fintechs against financial fortresses: The battle for data access. Center for European Policy Analysis. https://cepa.org/article/a-fintech-turning-point-how-much-data-should-banks-share/

"Office of the Comptroller of the Currency". (2016). OCC Enforcement Actions. https://www.occ.treas.gov/news-issuances/news-releases/2016/nr-occ-2016-83.html. (Online; Accessed 9. Mar. 2025).

Polasik, M., Huterska, A., Iftikhar, R., & Mikula, Š. (2020). The impact of payment services directive 2 on the paytech sector development in Europe. *Journal of Economic Behavior & Organization*, *178*, 385–401. https://doi.org/10.1016/j.jebo.2020.07.010

Pop, C. (2025). EU vs US: What Are the Differences Between Their Data Pri- vacy Laws? https://www.endpointprotector.com/blog/eu-vs-us-what-are-the-differences-between-their-data-privacy-laws. (Online; Accessed 13. May 2025).

Preziuso, M., Koefer, F., & Ehrenhard, M. (2023). Open banking and inclusive finance in the European union: Perspectives from the dutch stakeholder ecosystem. Tech. Rep. EIF Working Paper 2023/94, European Investment Fund. https://www.eif.org/news_centre/publications/eif_working_paper_2023_94.pdf

Ringe, W. G., & Ruof, C. (2020). Regulating Fintech in the EU: The Case for a Guided Sandbox. *European Journal of Risk Regulation*, *11*(3), 604–629. https://doi.org/10.1017/err.2020.8

Schär, F. (2020). Decentralized Finance: On Blockchain- and Smart Contract-based Financial Markets. https://doi.org/10.2139/ssrn.3571335; https://papers.ssrn.com/abstract=3571335

U.S. Commodity Futures Trading Commission. (2021). Cftc orders tether to pay $41 million over misleading claims. https://www.cftc.gov/PressRoom/PressReleases/8450-21

U.S. Congress. (2023). Clarity for payment stablecoins act of 2023. House Bill 4766. https://www.congress.gov/bill/118th-congress/house-bill/4766

U.S. Securities and Exchange Commission. (2023). Sec investigates paxos over bussed stablecoin. https://www.sec.gov/news

Vezzoso, S. (2018). Fintech, access to data, and the role of competition policy. *SSRN Electronic Journal*. https://doi.org/10.2139/ssrn.3106594

Winch, C.: Are data protection and open banking compatible? (2025). https://www.ukfinance.org.uk/news-and-insight/blogs/are-data-protection-and-open-banking-compatible. [Online; Accessed 13. May 2025].

Zetzsche, D. A., Arner, D. W., Buckley, R. P., & Weber, R. H. (2019). The future of data-driven Finance and RegTech: Lessons from EU Big Bang II. *SSRN Electronic Journal*. Publisher: Elsevier BV. https://doi.org/10.2139/ssrn.3359399

Zetzsche, D. A., Buckley, R. P., Barberis, J. N., & Arner, D. W. (2017). Regulating a revolution: From regulatory sandboxes to smart regulation. *Fordham Journal of Corporate and Financial Law*, *23*, 31. https://heinonline.org/HOL/Page?handle=hein.journals/fjcf23&id=37&div=&collection

PART III

Societal Perspective of Transparency in Fintech

Knowledge and Use of Fintech Products by the Young Generations: A Zero-Inflated Ordinal Data Model

Maria Iannario, Claudia Tarantola, Alessandra Tanda, and Belma Ozturkkal

Traditional models for ordinal dataOrdinal data, such as cumulative models with logitLogit/probit link functions, face limitations in explaining the excess of zero observations Excess of zero observations. This issue arises

M. Iannario (✉)
Department of Political Sciences, University of Naples Federico II, Naples, Italy
e-mail: maria.iannario@unina.it

C. Tarantola
Department of Economics, Management and Quantitative Methods, University of Milan, Milan, Italy
e-mail: claudia.tarantola@unimi.it

A. Tanda
Department of Economics and Management, University of Pavia, Pavia, Italy
e-mail: alessandra.tanda@unipv.it

B. Ozturkkal
Department of International Trade and Finance, Kadir Has University, Istanbul, Türkiye
e-mail: belma.ozturkkal@khas.edu.tr

J. Osterrieder et al. (eds.), *Transparency in FinTech*, Palgrave Studies in Financial Services Technology,
https://doi.org/10.1007/978-3-032-03523-3_7

especially when zeros may indicate two distinct situations: non-participation/absolute non-knowledge and infrequent participation/unconditional knowledge. The phenomenon of excess zeros commonly limits the effectiveness of traditional regression models in contexts where respondents provide graded perceptions on specific items or experiments that identify increasing levels of evaluation. This situation frequently occurs with ordinal scales that include an anchor representing the absence of a symptom, activity, or knowledge, such as "none", "never", or "normal". In such cases, standard methodologies may fall short in accurately modeling the distribution of ordinal outcomes. Extensions of these methodologies can better accommodate the excess of zeros (zero-inflated data) by distinguishing between structured zeros and sampling zeros. These advanced models enable a more precise analysis of ordinal scale data, accounting for instances where some subjects are likely to respond, while others are not.

Our work fits into this scenario, exploring the determinants of non-knowledge, distinguishing between true *non-knowers* and those who might express varying levels of understanding in different circumstances after a brief introduction to the topic. This analysis seeks to understand both the respondents' choice of answers and the intensity of their declared knowledge.

The data consists of 599 Italian respondents, belonging to the categories of Millennials and Generation Z, selected through non-probabilistic convenience sampling via the survey on "Knowledge and Use of Fintech Products," which was conducted as part of the European project CA19130 Fintech and Artificial Intelligence in Finance.

The online self-administered questionnaire asked participants to gauge their knowledge level of several financial tools using a six-point ordinal response scale, ranging from 0 = "no knowledge" to 6 = "expert". Additionally, a four-question test was included to assess their numeracy. Among the items designed to evaluate the knowledge of financial instruments, *Cryptocurrencies* were selected for our analysis. Cryptocurrencies have gained popularity since the 2008 paper by Nakamoto (White et al., 2020), although their everyday use remains limited in terms of currency and they have become relatively more popular as investment assets, especially among educated and young, digitally native investors (Auer & Tercero-Lucas, 2022). Their development has been under scrutiny by policymakers and regulators, and while approaches are diversified across different jurisdictions, there is consensus on the ability of cryptocurrencies to disrupt the financial market and potentially improve financial inclusion, but also on the potential risks related to these instruments (Gomber et al., 2018; Monrat et al., 2019; Zetzsche et al., 2020). To the best of our knowledge, still little is known about cryptocurrency knowledge and use by Millennials and Generation Z.

Preliminary results indicate that a greater knowledge of cryptocurrencies corresponds to a self-assessment of also having greater knowledge of other financial instruments, such as blockchain, and, in general, of Artificial Intelligence instruments. Women, on the other hand, declare less knowledge. Extreme responses, such as selecting "zero knowledge", are more common among individuals with lower educational qualifications and those in the lowest income bracket.

Extensions in a bivariate context, where more than one item among the digital services is under study, as well as analyses on marginal effects and potential indicators for group comparisons.

1 Introduction

This study investigates the knowledge and competence of Italian Millennials and Generation Z regarding financial products, with the aim of identifying potential drivers of their knowledge levels and suggesting policy initiatives to improve financial literacy and reduce household exposure to risks.

The Fintech wave that began after the Great Crisis of 2008 introduced a number of innovations in financial markets, making extensive use of advanced technologies. Among these innovations, investors have become familiar with peer-to-peer platforms, robo-advisors, crowdfunding, instant payments, digital wallets, and cryptocurrencies. Additionally, the use of underlying technologies such as machine learning, artificial intelligence, and blockchain has become more widespread (Locatelli et al., 2021). Despite the rapid development and growing market presence of these innovations, understanding and knowledge of them remain somewhat limited, even among market actors, e.g., investors.

Understanding financial instruments is crucial for investors when evaluating the appropriateness and suitability of various types of investments and assessing the risks associated with specific financial instruments. This applies not only to financial asset investments but also to payment instruments, robo-advisory services, and alternatives to fiat money, such as cryptocurrencies.

Since their introduction in 2008 with the birth of Bitcoin, different cryptocurrencies have been developed with the aim of either replacing or complementing fiat money. Bitcoin, Ethereum, and other cryptocurrencies have experienced varying degrees of success. Although the growth of cryptocurrencies has been impressive considering their young age, their overall use in everyday life remains limited, and their (relatively) greater success has been found as an investment asset (Auer & Tercero-Lucas, 2022). Cryptocurrencies are considered a highly risky investment asset, but they might have the potential to increase financial inclusion. For this reason, the authorities monitor their development closely (Gomber et al., 2018; Monrat et al., 2019; Zetzsche et al., 2020).

Little is known about the diffusion of cryptocurrencies among young people and their understanding and knowledge of cryptocurrencies. Young people, indeed, generally exhibit a lower level of financial literacy than their older peers and might also be subject to behavioral biases (overconfidence, herding behavior, fear of missing out) that can lead them to build risky portfolios without being aware of it (Chhatwani & Parija, 2023; Kaur et al., 2024; Sudzina et al., 2023). This can constitute a serious policy concern regarding the protection of investors and the ability of young people to plan for their future investments, considering the riskiness and expected performance of cryptocurrencies.

Previous studies have investigated the knowledge of cryptocurrencies among young generations, with a focus on specific countries. To the best of our knowledge, no study has specifically examined the Italian population of Millennials and Generation Z. Given the importance of this topic and the relatively limited evidence on cryptocurrency literacy among these groups, we have chosen to focus on this innovative asset in this contribution.

In detail, this study investigates the usage patterns, knowledge levels, and demographic determinants of cryptocurrency engagement using a comprehensive model analysis. The latter aims to elucidate the factors influencing cryptocurrency adoption and the extent of user knowledge across different demographic segments. Understanding cryptocurrency and financial literacy is crucial, as it equips individuals with the skills needed to navigate the complexities of digital finance, make informed investment decisions, and manage risks. Just as financial literacy is essential for understanding traditional assets, it is equally important for effectively engaging with cryptocurrencies.

Young Italians provide an interesting sample for analysis. Recent surveys indicate that financial literacy is generally low among young investors (Barajas et al., 2020; Klapper et al., 2015). The Bank of Italy has also reported that individuals under 35 years old demonstrate lower levels of financial literacy compared to their older peers (Lambroglia et al., 2023). Given that financial literacy and education are critical tools in preventing issues such as over-indebtedness, vulnerability to fraud, behavioral biases (e.g., overconfidence), and excessive risk-taking, it is vital to understand the knowledge and competence of young individuals in managing traditional financial matters.

Moreover, the rise of Fintech has further complicated the financial landscape. While Fintech has contributed to increased financial inclusion and lowered costs through heightened competition, it has also increased certain risks. The digital nature of financial services and products can heighten exposure to risks, especially for unwary investors—this is particularly relevant in the case of cryptocurrencies.

The paper employs data collected via a survey on the knowledge and use of Fintech products. The survey was distributed as part of the European project CA19130 Fin-AI, "Fintech and Artificial Intelligence in Finance," funded by the European Commission. The survey, administered in Italian to improve the response rate, was distributed through student organizations.

The sample consists of 599 responses from Italian university students born between 1980 and 2000 (see Ng et al., 2010 for related work). The sample is almost evenly split between male and female participants, with 55% being women. Preliminary findings indicate that the level of competence and knowledge about this technology and cryptocurrencies is low, with many individuals admitting to being unaware of these innovations.

The results of this research will help define important policy implications and pave the way for future studies. While our findings could, in principle, be extended to other countries, the composition of the sample likely influenced the results. More sophisticated statistical techniques could enhance our analyses, and gathering new responses from different countries would provide a broader understanding of cryptocurrency knowledge among Millennials and Generation Z, the target population explored in this study.

2 Literature Review on Cryptocurrencies and Financial Literacy

Nakamoto's 2008 Bitcoin paper has been cited 34,273 times as of August 2024. Bitcoin gained popularity as a decentralized digital currency, offering an alternative to traditional financial systems. Cryptocurrency, a digital or virtual currency that uses cryptography for security, has garnered significant interest from researchers, investors, and policymakers since the inception of Bitcoin. Surveys are an essential tool for understanding the financial choices individuals make regarding cryptocurrencies like Bitcoin. They provide insights into the motivations and demographic profiles of cryptocurrency users, helping researchers and policymakers grasp the factors driving adoption and usage.

Numerous important studies have focused specifically on surveys conducted in the area of cryptocurrency. These studies offer valuable insights into cryptocurrency usage, knowledge, and, in some cases, focus on younger generations. However, most of them concentrate on single countries, and only a few explicitly investigate the Generation Z population. To the best of our knowledge, none of these studies has examined the Italian context.

Drawing on repeated large-scale surveys of U.S. households from 2018 to 2022, Weber et al. (2023) examines the cryptocurrency investment decisions of households compared to other financial assets. Cryptocurrency investors are generally younger, white, male, and more libertarian compared to those who do not hold crypto. They anticipate significantly higher returns from cryptocurrency and perceive cryptocurrency as safer and a better hedge against inflation than other households do. Stix (2021) uses data from three nationally representative surveys conducted in Austria in 2018 and 2019 to understand more about the purchase and investment of cryptocurrencies and their investors, where cryptocurrency owners are more knowledgeable and risk-tolerant than other investors. Colombo and Yarovaya (2024) conduct an investor survey in Brazil of 573 investors, showing that young, male, risk-tolerant individuals with strong cryptocurrency literacy are more likely to own and invest in cryptocurrencies, highlighting the impact of investor sophistication. Ante et al. (2023) illustrate three distinct groups of Turkish cryptocurrency owners as payment users, crypto investors, and crypto traders, which differ by demographics, income, education, and purchase intentions. The findings suggest that Turkish cryptocurrency owners can inform ongoing regulatory processes and encourage further research on cryptocurrency adoption in emerging markets. Ozturkkal and Ceritoğlu (2024) examine cryptocurrency asset allocation among households using microdata from the 2019 Household Financial Perception and Attitude Survey by the Presidential Finance Office, covering 15,041 individuals across 49 provinces in Türkiye. They explore the risks and demographic factors, such as age, education, household size, and regional NUTS 12 classifications, influencing crypto investments. Using binary regression models, the findings reveal significant demographic differences in risk perception and asset allocation. Notably, vocational school graduates show a higher tendency to invest in cryptocurrencies, while higher education levels are linked to greater diversification in crypto assets. In another study, Ante et al. (2022) investigate a nationally representative survey and 255 cryptocurrency investors. The study indicates that higher net income, greater cryptocurrency knowledge, and stronger ideological motivation for owning cryptocurrency all contribute positively to returns. Gignac et al. (2023), with 372 first-year psychology students, predict intelligence to be negatively related to cryptocurrency investments through a survey analysis.

Akana and Li (2022), studying the Federal Reserve Bank of Philadelphia's 2022 survey, demonstrate that almost a quarter of U.S. households owned cryptocurrency, with ownership more common among younger, Hispanic, or Black individuals with higher incomes and greater use of mobile payment and banking services. Income, education, and other asset ownership are positively related factors for ownership of cryptocurrencies, where motivations for ownership vary. Hackethal et al. (2022), using 10,000 investors' German online banking data, show that cryptocurrency investors are active traders with investment biases and risky portfolios compared to other investors. They are prone to stocks with high media sentiment, have a probability of using technical analysis, and significantly increase their trading activity after their first cryptocurrency purchase. Additionally, they have a tendency to shift their portfolios to riskier securities after purchase. Jalan and Matkovskyy (2023) analyze Nordic countries' investor demographic characteristics to understand digital investment attitudes. They demonstrate variations in youth interest across different regions in crypto assets or NFTs. Both males and females show interest in crypto assets, though males exhibit higher interest. The investment objectives vary, and the investors tend to have low debt levels.

Financial literacy is the ability to understand and effectively use various financial skills, including personal financial management, budgeting, and investing. Lusardi and Mitchell (2022, a) measures of financial literacy are widely regarded as the most accepted and authoritative in the field. Further, Lusardi and Mitchell (2022, b) highlight the different levels of financial literacy between developed and developing countries, emphasizing its importance for successful retirement planning and financial security. They point out demographic disparities, demonstrating that women typically exhibit lower financial literacy compared to men, and younger and older individuals have less financial knowledge than middle-aged men. Additionally, those with more financial education and those actively planning for retirement tend to have higher levels of financial literacy. Similarly, Lusardi and Mitchell (2007) show that Baby Boomers who actively engage in retirement planning and possess higher financial literacy tend to accumulate greater wealth and are better prepared for retirement. Van Rooij et al. (2011) examine over 2000 household portfolio investments in the Netherlands from the De Nederlandsche Bank Survey, emphasizing that financial literacy plays a crucial role in stock market participation, revealing that individuals with higher financial literacy are more likely to invest in stocks, whereas those with lower financial literacy lack understanding of key financial concepts in general, such as risk diversification and the functioning of the stock market. Financial literacy is crucial for cryptocurrency investment because it enables investors to understand the risks, evaluate market dynamics, and make informed decisions in a highly volatile and complex market.

Besides, Balutel et al. (2024) use traditional financial literacy measures on Canadian Bitcoin owners and present that a major part possesses low cryptocurrency knowledge and low financial literacy. Furthermore, there are gender differences in crypto literacy, as female Bitcoin owners have lower Bitcoin knowledge compared to male owners, although no significant gender differences were measured in overall financial literacy among Bitcoin owners.

Moreover, Bonaparte (2022) finds that a household's investment time horizon, alongside other variables like education, stock market participation, and saving attitudes, influences the probability of owning cryptocurrency. With education, being male, and being white, this likelihood increases. Education and stock ownership influence cryptocurrency ownership propensity positively, while financially literate individuals invest less in cryptocurrency. In a similar vein, Zhao and Zhang (2021) investigate financial literacy and cryptocurrency investment, revealing a positive correlation predominantly influenced by investment experience. Additionally,

Fujiki (2020) demonstrates that Japanese cryptocurrency investors are typically young, male, higher-income, and possess specific financial behaviors and literacy levels. He distinguishes Japanese crypto-asset investors as users of noncash payment methods and investors in risky assets.

There are also perspectives that focus on behavior. Luo et al. (2023) investigate five personality traits, collecting data from all investors and investors having crypto investments, to understand the relationship between personality traits and investment choices. The study contributes to understanding the differences in investor personality traits. Nemeczek and Weiss (2023) explore the socioeconomic traits, behavioral preferences, and spending habits of individuals who own cryptocurrencies. Using data from an app for German personal finance management, they conduct a survey to understand the behavioral factors that influence financial decisions. By merging survey data with the customers' security account information, cryptocurrency investors are determined to be often young, male, students or self-employed, and tend to be risk-seeking and impatient, generally avoiding financial advisory services and preferring to make independent decisions due to their self-reported high financial literacy. Additionally, crypto investors tend to spend more on travel, electronics, and food delivery, and less on health. A different perspective is provided by Steinmetz (2023), documenting that recent research has started to examine the links between cryptocurrency use and gambling as a financial speculation tool, recognizing similarities in financial speculation and gambling behaviors. With a study of 3864 Germans identifying differences among sole gamblers, sole cryptocurrency users, and those involved in both, specified as crypto-gamblers, the findings show that dual users are typically young, male, well-educated, and financially stable, with higher knowledge and trust in cryptocurrency compared to others. The study also reveals three user groups based on their level of involvement with cryptocurrency, highlighting potential risks of over-involvement and providing insights for future research and regulation.

Among the most recent papers on the topic, Khan et al. (2023) study financial literacy on fintech matters among Malaysian millennials and find that they have average knowledge of fintech literacy, with more familiarity with peer-to-peer lending. With reference to cryptocurrencies, the authors find that older millennials have lower knowledge than their younger peers.

3 Survey Data and General Overview

The data come from the survey on 'Knowledge and Use of Fintech Products,' administered as part of the European project CA19130 Fintech and Artificial Intelligence in Finance. Data were collected from a sample of respondents, considering variables such as age, gender, education, and income. In this section, we focus only on the variables used in the models, with all variables reported in the appendix.

The sample consists of 599 Italian young people (Millennials and Generation Z), of whom 55% are women and 45% are men. We now provide a brief description of the variables included in our model.

The *gender* variable is coded as 0 for males and 1 for females.

The variable *cryptocurrencies* is derived from responses to a question assessing the level of knowledge regarding the following services/tools, where the tool in question is cryptocurrencies. It is measured using a 6-point scale, where 0 represents "do not know at all" and 5 represents "know perfectly well".

The variable *AI* is calculated from the response to the question as the level of knowledge of the following services/tools, where the tool is *artificial intelligence,* and it is measured at five levels, with "do not know at all" being 0 "know perfectly well" being 5.

Variable *age* indicates the ages of respondents. The average age of the respondents is 23 years, the minimum age is 18, and the maximum age is 42 years.

Education is reported at various increasing levels, ranging from compulsory school to bachelor's, master's, or PhD. More specifically, the variable *education* is categorized as follows: 1 for "compulsory schooling", 2 for "diploma", 3 for "bachelor's degree", 4 for "master's degree", and 5 for "postgraduate degree". We observe that 50.4% of the respondents have an education level higher than a bachelor's degree.

The variable *income* has five levels: Less than 600 euro = 1, Between 600 and 1500 euro = 2, Between 1500 euro and 3000 euro = 3, Between 3000 euro and 5000 euro = 4, Greater than 5000 euro = 5.

The variable *blockchain* is the response to the question, "Have you ever used one of these instruments?". The answers are as follows: "Yes, regularly," corresponding to 1; "Yes, sometimes," corresponding to 2; and "No, never," indicated with 3.

The survey also assessed participants' familiarity, use, and knowledge of other financial instruments such as peer-to-peer lending platforms,

Table 1 Panel A: Tabulation of cryptocurrencies

Cryptocurrencies	*Freq.*	*Percent*	*Cum.*
0	286	47.75	47.75
1	106	17.70	65.44
2	70	11.69	77.13
3	70	11.69	88.81
4	38	6.34	95.16
5	29	4.84	100.00
Total	599	100.0	
Panel B: Tabulation of cryptocurrency use			
1	480	80.13	80.13
2	73	12.19	92.32
3	46	7.68	100.00
Total	599	100.0	
Panel C: Tabulation of cryptocurrencies when gender is male			
0	101	37.41	37.41
1	38	14.07	51.48
2	40	14.81	66.30
3	42	15.56	81.85
4	27	10.00	91.85
5	22	8.15	100.00
Total	270	100.0	
Panel D: Tabulation of *cryptocurrencies* when gender is female			
0	185	56.23	56.23
1	68	20.67	76.90
2	30	9.12	86.02
3	28	8.51	94.53
4	11	3.34	97.87
5	7	2.13	100.00
Total	329	100.0	

crowdfunding, cryptocurrencies, robo-advisors, instant payments, and instant insurance. The survey evaluated the knowledge of the technology (0 = "I don't know/never heard of"; 5 = "I know them perfectly") on machine learning, artificial intelligence, internet of things, biometric recognition, DLT/blockchain, and cloud computing.

Table 1 Panel A provides the zero counts of cryptocurrency responses as 47.75%, with almost half of the sample making the problem of zero counts more evident. Table 1 Panel B reports *cryptocurrency use*. Zero counts for cryptocurrencies are much higher for female respondents than for male respondents (Table 1 Panels C and D).

3.1 Statistical Model

Let Y be a discrete random variable that assumes the ordered values of $0, 1, \ldots, J$ and let r denote a binary variable indicating the split between Regime 0 ($r = 0$, for "zero respondents/non participants")-and Regime 1 ($r = 1$ for "respondents/participants"), which is related to the latent variable $r^* = x'\beta + \in$ where x is a vector of p individual characteristics (covariates) that determine the choice of regimes, β is a p-vector of unknown regression parameters, and $\in$ is a random variable with cumulative distribution function $G_\in(.)$.

Thus, the probability of an individual being in Regime 1 is given by

$$Pr(r = 1|x) = Pr(r^* > 0|x) = G_\in(x'\beta),$$

where we assume $G_\in(.)$ strictly increasing and symmetric around zero.

Standard choices for the distribution function are the *logit* link function, $G(t) = 1/(1 + e^{-t})$, corresponding to the logistic distribution, or the *probit* link function, $G(t) = \Phi(t)$, with Φ the cdf of the standard normal distribution (in our proposal the latter has been selected). Conditional on $r = 1$, respondents levels under Regime 1 are represented by $\tilde{Y}(\tilde{Y} = 0, 1, \ldots, J)$, which is generated by a cumulative link model based upon a second underlying latent variable $\tilde{Y}^*$, where

$$\tilde{Y}^* = z'\gamma + u,$$

with z being a vector of covariates with unknown parameters γ and $u \sim G_u(.)$.

The observed ordinal variable $\tilde{Y}$ takes as values the labels 0 if $\tilde{Y}^* \leq 0$, J if $\tilde{Y}^* \geq \alpha_{J-1}$ otherwise,

$$\tilde{Y} = j \Leftrightarrow \alpha_{j-1} < \tilde{Y}^* \leq \alpha_j \; j = 1, \ldots, J-1$$

where $\alpha_j \, (j = 1, \ldots, J-1)$ are the intercept values to be estimated in addition to the covariate coefficients γ.

Specifically, to observe $Y = 0$ we require either that $r = 0$ (the individual is a non participant) or jointly that $r = 1$ and $\tilde{Y} = 0$ (the individual is a zero respondent/participant).

To observe a positive score, instead, we require jointly that the individual is a participant ($r = 1$) and $\tilde{Y}^* > 0$.

If we assume that the error terms from the first-stage equation and the second-stage cumulative outcome equation, that is, e and u, are not correlated the probability mass function of the Zero Inflated Ordinal model is

$$\Pr(Y \mid z, x) = \begin{cases} \Pr(Y = 0 \mid z, x) = \Pr(r = 0 \mid x) + \Pr(r = 1 \mid x) \\ \quad \Pr(\tilde{Y} = 0 \mid z, r = 1), \\ \Pr(Y = j \mid z, x) = \Pr(r = 1 \mid x) \Pr(\tilde{Y} = j \mid z, r = 1), \\ \quad j = 1, \ldots, J, \end{cases}$$
$$= \begin{cases} \Pr(Y = 0 \mid z, x) = \left[1 - G_\varepsilon(x^\top \beta)\right] + G_\varepsilon(x^\top \beta)\, G_\varepsilon(-z^\top \gamma), \\ \Pr(Y = j \mid z, x) = G_\varepsilon(x^\top \beta)\left\{G_\varepsilon(\alpha_j - z^\top \gamma) - G_\varepsilon(\alpha_{j-1} - z^\top \gamma)\right\}, \\ \quad j = 1, \ldots, J-1, \\ \Pr(Y = J \mid z, x) = G_\varepsilon(x^\top \beta)\, [1 - G_\varepsilon(\alpha_{J-1} - z^\top \gamma)]. \end{cases}$$

In this way, the probability of a zero score has been inflated, as it is a combination of the probability of zero from the cumulative model framework and the probability of non-participation (zero expression) from the split logit/probit model.

Notice that the choice of distribution function $G()$ allows to consider the Zero Inflated Ordinal Probit (ZIOP) as in Harris and Zhao (2007) or Zero Inflated Ordinal Logit (ZIOL) models.

Once the full set of probabilities has been specified and, given a sample of size N from the population, the parameters of the full model can be estimated using maximum likelihood (ML) criteria. The log-likelihood function is

$$\ell(\theta) = \sum_{i=1}^{N} \sum_{j=0}^{J} h_{ij} \; ln \; Pr(Y = j | z_i, x_i, \theta)$$

where θ=(α', β', γ') and the indicator function h_{ij} is 1 if individual i chooses outcome j and zero otherwise.

As described above, the observed realization of the random variable Y can be viewed as the result of two separate latent equations with uncorrelated error terms. However, these correspond to the same individual, so it is likely that the two terms $\in$ and u corresponding to the latent variables may be related. Then the model presents the latter two terms which follow a bivariate normal distribution with correlation coefficient ρ whilst maintaining the identifying assumption of unit variances.

Testing between the models with or without correlation can be based on a simple *t*-test on $\rho = 0$, using the standard errors from the estimated Hessian. Further inferential details concerning also the ***marginal effects*** are in Harris and Zhao (2007) where details on formalization and inferential aspects can be assessed.

4 Empirical Results

In this study, we estimated a zero-inflated ordinal probit model using the function ZIOPROBIT in Stata. The response variable in the model is cryptocurrencies. We considered covariates of the cumulative link component variables: gender, blockchain, and AI, while for the inflation part (excess of zeros), we included income and education. The results are presented in Table 2. It is noticeable that answers related to greater

Table 2 Zero inflated probit model

Cryptocurrencies	*Coefficient*	*Standard error*	z	*p-value*	*(95% Conf. Interval)*	
Gender	−0.28	0.10	−2.67	0.01	−0.49	−0.07
	0.63	0.05	13.59	0.00	0.54	0.73
Blockchain						
AI	0.26	0.04	6.36	0.00	0.18	0.34
Inflate						
Constant	−1.03	0.94	−1.09	0.27	−2.89	0.81
Income	0.30	0.16	1.85	0.06	−0.02	0.62
Education	0.63	0.34	1.79	0.07	−0.06	1.31
α_1	0.64	0.11				
α_2	1.44	0.12				
α_3	2.13	0.14				
α_4	3.14	0.18				
α_5	3.96	0.21				

knowledge of cryptocurrencies correspond to a self-assessment of also having greater knowledge of other financial instruments, such as blockchain and, in general, AI. The sign for the gender variable shows less knowledge expressed by women. Regarding the inflation part, both income and education present a positive effect; this means that people with a higher education or income level do not select zero.

To assess the impact of each explanatory variable on the response variable, we compute what are known as Marginal Effect (ME) measures, as described by Greene (2008), Long and Freese (2014), and Long and Mustillo (2018), and in particular by Agresti and Tarantola (2018) when an ordinal response variable is taken into account. The ME reflects how a change in a particular explanatory variable influences the response variable while keeping all other explanatory variables constant. These measures are straightforward to understand and can be derived from any type of explanatory variable. The ME can be interpreted similarly to regression coefficients in a standard regression model, showing how the probability of being at a specific level changes when transitioning from the level under examination to the reference level.

By setting the values of the other explanatory variables in different ways, we can derive three distinct types of Marginal Effect (ME) measures. The first type, the Average Marginal Effect (AME), involves calculating the ME for a specific explanatory variable for each observation in the sample and then averaging these values. Alternatively, Marginal Effects at Representative Values (MER) can be computed by selecting specific, representative values for the other explanatory variables that are particularly relevant to the issue being studied. Lastly, Marginal Effects at the Mean (MEM) are determined by fixing all remaining explanatory variables at their mean values. For binary variables, the ME corresponds to the discrete change.

Our analysis focuses primarily on the marginal effects for the extreme categories of the ordinal scale concerning cryptocurrencies. This focus is driven by several factors. Often, ordinal response models tend to place special emphasis on the highest and lowest categories, as these often represent the most significant outcomes. For example, in certain fields, these categories may reflect critical states, such as the "best" or "worst" outcomes (e.g., "full recovery" versus "death"). Furthermore, cumulative link models imply monotonic changes in the probabilities of the extreme categories as any explanatory variable increases, while the probabilities for intermediate categories may not exhibit the same pattern of monotonicity.

Among the alternative measures in the following, we consider AME, which can be interpreted as the sample average of the marginal effects.

Table 3 Average marginal effects

	dy/dx	*Std. Err.*	z	*p-value*	*(95% Conf. Interval)*	
Gender (discrete change with baseline value man)						
0	0.07	0.026	2.67	0.008	0.019	0.125
5	−0.01	0.005	−2.68	0.007	−0.027	−0.004
Blockchain						
0	−0.160	0.011	−13.99	0.000	−0.183	−0.138
5	0.036	0.004	9.29	0.000	0.028	0.043
AI						
0	−0.065	0.009	−7.02	0.000	−0.083	−0.047
5	0.014	0.003	5.72	0.000	0.009	0.019
Inflate						
Income						
0	−0.017	0.009	−1.78	0.074	−0.036	0.002
5	0.001	0.001	1.75	0.080	−0.000	0.003
Education						
0	−0.036	0.020	−1.81	0.071	− 0.075	0.003
5	0.002	0.001	1.90	0.057	− 0.000	0.005

Furthermore, AME measures are quite stable when we add an explanatory variable to the model that is uncorrelated with the variable whose effect we are describing; see Mood (2010) for further details. In Table 3, we report the estimated ME, standard errors obtained via the Delta method, and the corresponding 95% confidence intervals.

For the dichotomous variable *gender,* we notice that the probability of selecting value zero for the variable *cryptocurrency* is 7% higher for women than for men.

The remaining variables are all positively associated with the maximum value of the ordinal scale of the response one. For example, an increase of one unit of variable *AI* corresponds to an increase of 1.4% in the probability of selecting category 5 of variable *cryptocurrency.* A similar interpretation holds for the remaining variables.

5 Conclusion

With the rapid diffusion of Fintech innovations, the financial markets have benefited from more efficient instruments and solutions. However, these solutions often come with an additional level of risks or even new types of risks. Investors and financial users might be unaware of these additional risks and complexities introduced by Fintech in many areas of their everyday lives, e.g., payments, savings, and investment decisions. The knowledge and understanding of financial matters is a key objective of policymakers because financially literate households make better decisions and are less likely to be subject to behavioral biases (e.g., Lusardi & Mitchell, 2011b).

Among the various innovations, cryptocurrencies hold particular importance. Indeed, although their diffusion as "currency" has remained relatively limited, they are growing in popularity as investment assets. However, they are considered extremely risky (especially due to their high volatility), and investors might be unaware of their risks. To date, still little is known about the level of knowledge regarding cryptocurrencies, especially among young people who are more likely to engage in crypto investments. The existing literature on cryptocurrency surveys provides valuable insights but also highlights the need for continued research, especially in the face of rapidly evolving technologies and market dynamics.

This study contributes to the growing body of literature on digital finance by highlighting key demographic trends and providing an analytical framework for understanding cryptocurrency adoption. These insights can inform policymakers, educators, and financial institutions aiming to foster informed and inclusive participation in the evolving cryptocurrency market. In particular, focusing on the generational target group investigated in the study, an assessment of the low perception of knowledge among women may imply actions aimed at supporting their understanding of these concepts. The same consideration applies to income and educational qualifications; findings show that those with an elementary education and low income have a higher propensity to report zero knowledge of the cryptocurrency phenomenon. Future surveys should aim for cross-cultural comparisons to build a more robust understanding of the global cryptocurrency landscape. Additionally, future studies should integrate a cross-country dimension of Fintech financial literacy, including cryptocurrencies. A homogeneous, integrated policy effort in this field is desirable to globally improve the level of financial literacy in the Fintech domain, empower households with the tools to make better decisions, contribute to greater investor protection, and, ultimately, strengthen financial stability.

Acknowledgment Maria Iannario gratefully acknowledges the support of the Marie Sklodowska-Curie Actions under the European Union's Horizon Europe research and innovation program for the Industrial Doctoral Network on Digital Finance (acronym: DIGITAL, project no. 101119635) and PRIN 2022 – CUP: E53C24002270006.

Appendix

Appendix A1 Variables employed in the survey

Variable name	*Definition and coding*
Gender	Gender of the respondent, 0 = male, 1 = female
Age	Year of the age of respondent
Family	Members household size 1, 2, 3 or 4 or more than 4
Who you live with	I live alone = 1, I live with a partner = 2, I live with underage children = 3, I live with older children = 4, I live with my parents = 5, other = 6
Level of education	Compulsory schooling = 1, diploma = 2, bachelor's degree = 3, master's degree = 4, postgraduate degree = 5
Subject area in which you study or have studied (if more than one area, indicate the last)	Mathematical and Computer Sciences = 1, Physical sciences = 2, Chemical Sciences = 3, Earth Sciences = 4, Biological Sciences = 5, Medical Sciences = 6, Agricultural and Veterinary Sciences = 7, Civil Engineering and Architecture = 8, Industrial and Information Engineering = 9, Ancient, Philological-Literary and Historical-Artistic Sciences = 10, Historical, Philosophical, Pedagogical and Psychological Sciences = 11, Legal Sciences = 12, Economic and Statistical Sciences = 13, Political and Social Sciences = 14, None/Non-study = 15, Other = 16
Employment status	Homemaker = 1, Unemployed or Unemployable = 2, Self-employed or self-employed = 3, Employee = 4, Retired = 5, Student = 6, Student worker = 7
What sector do you work in	Economics/ Business/ Finance = 1, STEM (Science, Technology, Engineering, Mathematics) = 2, Other (Humanities, health, social sciences, etc.) = 3, None = 4
Income	Less than 600 euro = 1, Between 600 and 1500 euro = 2, Between 1500 euro and

(continued)

Appendix A1 (continued)

Variable name	*Definition and coding*
	3000 euro = 3, Between 3000 euro and 5000 euro = 4, Greater than 5000 euro = 5
How easily do you reach the end of the month	1 is easily 10 hardly
Level of knowledge of the following services/tools:	0 do not know, 5 know perfectly well
crowdfunding	
Cryptocurrencies	
Instant Insurance	
Instant payments	
Roboadvisor	
"peer to peer" ("p2p")	
Cloud computing	
DLT/Blockchain	
Intelligenza artificiale	
Internet of Things	
Machine learning	
Biometric recognition	
Have you ever used one of these instruments	yes regularly = 1, yes sometimes = 2, no, never = 3
crowdfunding	
Cryptocurrencies	
Instant Insurance	
Instant payments	
"peer to peer" ("p2p")	
roboadvisor	
Level of knowledge of the following services/tools:	0 do not know at all, 5 know perfectly well
Benchmark	
Bonds	
Eequity	
Exchange traded fund	
Iannarionvestment fund	
Key investor information document (KIID)	
Mifid	
Stock indexes	
Suitability assessment questionnaire	
ETF (investment fund). what information would you like to have before making decisions? benchmark past performance	0 = not important; 5 = extremely important, I don't know = 6

(continued)

Appendix A1 (continued)

Variable name	*Definition and coding*
Annual fee	
Gull description of included assets	
Information on risk class	
Past performance	
Volatility	
Other fees	
What is your level of knowledge on the following topics? investment and financing opportunities linked to crowdfunding	0 = don't know; 5 = exactly know
Investment and financing opportunities related to the financial sector	
Relationship between monetary policy and interest rates	
Relationship between risk and return for financial investments	
Tisk associated with financial debt instruments	
Imagine that you owe €1,000 on your credit card and that the interest rate applied is 20% (compound annual interest rate). Assuming the interest rate remains unchanged, how many years should pass before the debt doubles?	Two years = 1, three to five years = 2, six to ten years = 3, don't know = 4
What is your level of knowledge of the following financial 'objects'? Financial crisis	0 = don't know; 5 = know perfectly
Sustainable finance	
Quantitive easing	
GDP	
Rating	
Spread	
Inflation rate and purchasing power	
Indicate in which of the following situations you recognise yourself	0 = disagree/not at all; 5 = extremely agree
It is very complicated for me to understand the financial language	
My financial background, and related to its instruments, is not satisfactory	
I am very stressed when I have to make financial decisions	
I have a lot of difficulty in making the right financial decisions on a daily basis	

(continued)

Appendix A1 (continued)

Variable name	*Definition and coding*
I have great difficulty in making long-term financial decisions	
Real estate is the best investment solution	
How good are you at ... ?	0 = not very good; 5 = extremely good
Working with fractions	
Working with percentages	
Calculate a 15% tip	
Understand how much a t-shirt will cost with the 25% discount	
When listening to weather forecasts, do you prefer percentages to be used (e.g. 'there is a 20% chance of rain today') or only words (e.g. 'there is a small chance of rain today')?	1 = I always prefer percentages; 6 = I always prefer words
When people describe to you the possibility of something happening, do you prefer them to use words ("it rarely happens") or numbers ("there is a 1% chance of it happening")?	1 = I always prefer words; 6 = I always prefer numbers
Do you find numerical information useful?	1 = never; 6 = always
Imagine you roll a 5-sided die 50 times. On average, how many times will the die show an odd number? (1, 3 o 5)	5 out of 50 throws = 1, 25 out of 50 throws = 2, 30 out of 50 throws = 3, none of the above = 4
In a small town of 1000 people, 500 people are part of the choir and of these, 100 are men. among the 500 inhabitants who are not members of the choir, 300 are men. what is the probability that a randomly drawn man is a member of the choir? give the probability as a percentage.	10% = 1, 25% = 2, 40% = 3, none of the above = 4
Imagine that you roll a rigged die (6-sided) and that the probability of the die showing a 6 is twice the probability of any other number. on average, making 70 throws, how many times will the die show the number 6?	20 out of 70 throws = 1, 23 out of 70 throws = 2, 35 out of 70 throws = 3, none of the above = 4
In a forest, 20% of mushrooms are red, 50% brown and 30% are white. a red mushroom is poisonous with a 20% probability. A mushroom that is not red is poisonous with a 5% probability. what is the probability that a poisonous mushroom in the forest is red?	4% = 1, 20% = 2, 50% = 3, none of the above = 4

References

Agresti, A. (2010). *Analysis of Ordinal Categorical Data* (2nd ed.). J.Wiley & Sons.

Agresti, A., & Tarantola, C. (2018). Simple ways to interpret effects in modeling ordinal categorical data. *Statistica Neerlandica*, *72*, 210–223.

Akana, T., & Li, G. (2022). Cryptocurrency Ownership: Insights From the CFI COVID-19 Survey of Consumers. Consumer Finance Institute Survey Brief (December).

Ante, L., Fiedler, F., Steinmetz, F., & Fiedler, I. (2023). Profiling Turkish cryptocurrency owners: Payment users, crypto investors and crypto traders. *Journal of Risk and Financial Management*, *16*(4), 239.

Ante, L., Fiedler, I., Meduna, M. V., & Steinmetz, F. (2022). Individual cryptocurrency investors: Evidence from a population survey. *International Journal of Innovation and Technology Management*, *19*(04), 1–24.

Auer, R., & Tercero-Lucas, D. (2022). Distrust or speculation? The socioeconomic drivers of US cryptocurrency investments. *Journal of Financial Stability*, *62*, 101066.

Balutel, D., Felt, M. H., Nicholls, G., & Voia, M. C. (2024). Bitcoin awareness, ownership and use: 2016–20. *Applied Economics*, *56*(1), 33–58.

Barajas, A., Beck, T., Belhaj, M., Naceur, S. B., Cerra, V., & Qureshi, M. S., 2020. Financial inclusion: What have we learned so far? What do we have to learn? *IMF working paper, WP/20/157.*

Bonaparte, Y. (2022). Time horizon and cryptocurrency ownership: Is crypto not speculative? *Journal of International Financial Markets, Institutions and Money*, *79*, 101609.

Chhatwani, M., & Parija, A. K. (2023). Who invests in cryptocurrency? The role of overconfidence among American investors. *Journal of Behavioral and Experimental Economics*, *107*, 102107.

Colombo, J. A., & Yarovaya, L. (2024). Are crypto and non-crypto investors alike? Evidence from a comprehensive survey in Brazil. *Technology in Society*, *76*, 102468. https://doi.org/10.1016/j.techsoc.2024.102468

Downward, P., Lera-López, F., & Rasciute, S. (2011). The Zero-Inflated ordered probit approach to modelling sports participation. *Economic Modelling*, *28*, 2469–2477.

Fujiki, H. (2020). Who adopts crypto assets in Japan? Evidence from the 2019 financial literacy survey. *Journal of the Japanese and International Economies*, *58*, 101107.

Gignac, G. E., Jones, C., Mason, N., Yuen, I., & Zajenkowski, M. (2023). Predicting attitudes toward cryptocurrencies and stocks: The divergent roles of narcissism, intelligence and financial literacy. *Personality and Individual Differences*, *215*, 112382.

Gomber, P., Kauffman, R. J., Parker, C., & Weber, B. W. (2018). On the fintech revolution: Interpreting the forces of innovation, disruption, and transformation in financial services. *Journal of Management Information Systems*, *35*(1), 220–265.

Greene, W. (2008). *Econometric Analysis* (6th ed.). Pearson Prentice Hall.

Hackethal, A., Hanspal, T., Lammer, D. M., & Rink, K. (2022). The characteristics and portfolio behavior of bitcoin investors: Evidence from indirect cryptocurrency investments. *Review of Finance*, *26*(4), 855–898.

Harris, N. M., & Zhao, X. (2007). A zero-inflated ordered probit model, with an application to modelling tobacco consumption. *Journal of Econometrics*, *141*.

Jalan, A., & Matkovskyy, R. (2023, September 21) *Cryptocurrency Adoption in the Nordic Countries: Helicopter View on the Survey*. Available at SSRN: https://ssrn.com/abstract=4738642; https://doi.org/10.2139/ssrn.4738642.

Kaur, M., Jain, J., & Sood, K. (2024). "All are investing in Crypto, I fear of being missed out": Examining the influence of herding, loss aversion, and overconfidence in the cryptocurrency market with the mediating effect of FOMO. *Quality and Quantity*, *58*(3), 2237–2263.

Khan, M. T. I., Liew, T. W., & Lee, X. Y. (2023). Fintech literacy among millennials: The roles of financial literacy and education. *Cogent Social Sciences*, *9*(2), 281046.

Klapper, L., Lusardi, A., & van Oudheusden, P., 2015. Financial Literacy Around the World: Insights from the Standard & Poor's Ratings services global financial literacy survey. https://gflec.org/wp-content/uploads/2015/11/Finlit_paper_16_F2_singles.pdf

Lambroglia, S., Marinucci, M., Stacchini, M., & Vassallo, P. (2023). *Surveys on Financial Literacy and Digital Financial Skills in Italy: Adults*. Statistics of Bank of Italy.

Locatelli, R., Schena, C., & Tanda, A. (2021). A historical perspective on disruptive technologies. In King et al. (Eds.), *Disruptive Technology in Banking and Finance: An International Perspective on FinTech* (pp. 9–45).

Long, J. S., & Freese, J. (2014). *Regresson Models for Categorical Dependent Variables Using Stata*. Stata Press.

Long, J. S., & Mustillo, A. S. (2018). Using predictions and marginal effects to compare groups in regression models for binary outcomes. *Sociological Methods & Research*. doi: https://doi.org/10.1177/0049124118799374

Luo, J., Cao, Q., & Zhang, S. (2023). How do personality traits affect investors' decision on crypto market including cryptocurrencies and NFTs? *Review of Behavioral Finance*.

Lusardi, A., & Mitchell, O. S. (2007). Baby boomer retirement security: The roles of planning, financial literacy, and housing wealth. *Journal of Monetary Economics*, *54* (1), 205–224. Financial Planning Ability, Risk Perception And Household Portfolio Choice 2173. https://doi.org/10.1016/j.jmoneco.2006.12.001

Lusardi, A., & Mitchell, O. S. (2011a). *Financial Literacy and Planning: Implications for Retirement Wellbeing (No. W17078)*. National Bureau of Economic Research.

Lusardi, A., & Mitchell, O. S. (2011b). Financial literacy around the world: An overview. *Journal of Pension Economics and Finance*, *10*(4), 497–508. https://doi.org/10.1017/S1474747211000448

Monrat, A. A., Schelén, O., & Andersson, K. (2019). A survey of blockchain from the perspectives of applications, challenges, and opportunities. *Ieee Access*, *7*, 117134–117151.

Nemeczek, F., & Weiss, D. (2023). Insights on crypto investors from a german personal finance management app. *Journal of Risk and Financial Management*, *16*(4), 248.

Ng, E. S., Schweitzer, L., & Lyons, S. T. (2010). New generation, great expectations: A field study of the millennial generation. *Journal of Business and Psychology*, *25*, 281–292.

Ozturkkal, B., & Ceritoğlu, E. 2024. Household Perspectives on Cryptocurrency: Demographic Determinants and Risk Perceptions. Unpublished Working Paper

Steinmetz, F. (2023). The interrelations of cryptocurrency and gambling: Results from a representative survey. *Computers in Human Behavior*, *138*, 107437.

Stix, H. (2021). Ownership and purchase intention of crypto-assets: Survey results. *Empirica*, *48*(1), 65–99.

Sudzina, F., Dobes, M., & Pavlicek, A. (2023). Towards the psychological profile of cryptocurrency early adopters: Overconfidence and self-control as predictors of cryptocurrency use. *Current Psychology*, *42*(11), 8713–8717.

Van Rooij, M., Lusardi, A., & Alessie, R. (2011). Financial literacy and stock market participation. *Journal of Financial Economics*, *101*(2), 449–472.

Weber, M., Candia, B., Coibion, O., & Gorodnichenko, Y. (2023). *Do You Even Crypto, Bro? Cryptocurrencies in Household Finance (No. W31284)*. National Bureau of Economic Research.

White, R., Marinakis, Y., Islam, N., & Walsh, S. (2020). Is Bitcoin a currency, a technology-based product, or something else? *Technological Forecasting and Social Change*, *151*, 119877.

Zetzsche, D. A., Arner, D. W., & Buckley, R. P. (2020). Decentralized finance. *Journal of Financial Regulation*, *6*(2), 172–203.

Zhao, H., & Zhang, L. (2021). Financial literacy or investment experience: Which is more influential in cryptocurrency investment? *International Journal of Bank Marketing*, *39*(7), 1208–1226. https://doi.org/10.1108/IJBM-11-2020-0552

Regional Fintech Report for Türkiye, Romania, and Bulgaria

Belma Ozturkkal, Ceylan Onay Sahin, Canan Yıldırım, Vasile Alecsandru Strat, Deyan Radev, Georgi Penev, Daniel Traian Pele, Cătălina Chinie, Florin Grosu, Flavius Cosmin Darie, Codruța Mare, Virgil Damian, and Ioana Coita

B. Ozturkkal (✉)
Department of International Trade and Finance, Kadir Has University, Istanbul, Türkiye
e-mail: belma.ozturkkal@khas.edu.tr

C. O. Sahin
School of Business and Law, University of Brighton, Brighton, UK
e-mail: C.OnaySahin@brighton.ac.uk

C. Yıldırım
Rennes School of Business, Rennes, France
e-mail: canan.yildirim@rennes-sb.com

V. A. Strat
Dean of Bucharest Business School, Bucharest University of Economic Studies, Bucharest, Romania
e-mail: vasile.strat@bbs.ase.ro

J. Osterrieder et al. (eds.), *Transparency in FinTech*, Palgrave Studies in Financial Services Technology,
https://doi.org/10.1007/978-3-032-03523-3_8

1 Introduction

The development of financial technologies, particularly in the areas of artificial intelligence, open banking, and blockchain, is increasingly recognized as a crucial driver of economic growth and financial inclusion in emerging economies (see, e.g., Beall, 2018; EBRD, 2022). These technologies have the potential to disrupt traditional financial systems by introducing innovative business models, enhancing financial accessibility, and fostering greater efficiency and transparency. For economies in

D. Radev · G. Penev
Faculty of Economics and Business Administration, Sofia University "St. Kliment Ohridski", Sofia, Bulgaria
e-mail: D.Radev@feb.uni-sofia.bg
e-mail: g.penev@feb.uni-sofia.bg

D. T. Pele
Department of Statistics and Econometrics, Bucharest University of Economic Studies, Bucharest, Romania
e-mail: danpele@ase.ro

C. Chinie · F. Grosu · F. C. Darie
Faculty of Business Administration in Foreign Languages, Bucharest University of Economic Studies, Bucharest, Romania
e-mail: catalina.chinie@fabiz.ase.ro
e-mail: florin.grosu@fabiz.ase.ro
e-mail: flavius.darie@fabiz.ase.ro

C. Mare
Faculty of Economics and Business Administration, and the Center for Interdisciplinary Data Science, Babeș-Bolyai University, Cluj-Napoca, Romania
e-mail: codruta.mare@econ.ubbcluj.ro

V. Damian
Faculty of Finance, Insurance and Stock Exchanges, Bucharest University of Economic Studies, Bucharest, Romania
e-mail: virgil.damian@fin.ase.ro

I. Coita
Faculty of Economics, University of Oradea, Oradea, Romania;
University of Sofia 'St. Kliment Ohridski', Sofia, Bulgaria;
University of Economics in Bratislava, Petržalka, Slovakia
e-mail: coita.iflorina@gmail.com

transition, like those in Southeastern Europe and Türkiye, the adoption and integration of fintech solutions can bridge significant gaps in financial services, particularly for underbanked populations and small and medium-sized enterprises (SMEs). This paper provides a comprehensive analysis of the fintech landscapes in Türkiye, Romania, and Bulgaria, exploring their ecosystems, regulatory environments, and government support structures. By leveraging the findings from recent fintech surveys in these countries and drawing insights from both quantitative and qualitative data, the study aims to offer a comprehensive understanding of the opportunities and challenges these emerging markets face in their journey toward digital financial transformation.

This paper begins with an introduction and a detailed overview of the Fintech Survey design, along with a review of the related literature. It then proceeds to analyze the Fintech markets in Türkiye, Romania, and Bulgaria, covering the Fintech ecosystems, regulatory environments, and government support, followed by conclusions drawn from the market analyses and survey results for each country. The study also provides a summary of the survey findings across all three countries and concludes with overarching insights into the Fintech landscape in this region.

2 Fintech Survey Design and Related Literature

The development of the fintech ecosystems in Türkiye, Romania, and Bulgaria has been the focus of several recent studies, which highlight the rapid growth and unique challenges in these emerging markets. One significant finding is that these ecosystems are still in their early stages but have shown strong potential, driven by a combination of local innovation and the entry of foreign investors. For example, in Romania, the fintech sector has gained momentum due to increasing mobile device usage, internet penetration, and support from large financial institutions. The use of electronic payments has surged, placing Romania among the countries with high growth potential in the region (Bălţoi, 2020). Similarly, in Türkiye, with a young population and widespread adoption of mobile devices, regulations on digital payments enacted in 2013 have accelerated the growth of the sector, and fintech solutions have significantly contributed to the financial inclusion of underbanked populations and SMEs (Bayram et al., 2022). Additionally, Türkiye possesses a unique central location between Europe and the MENA regions, as well as a young and tech-savvy talent pool. Accordingly, the Istanbul Finance

Center project of the government aims to make it a fintech hub for the whole region (Sakarya & Aksu, 2021).

This chapter benefits from the findings of the Fintech ecosystem reports of Bulgaria, Romania, and Türkiye, respectively held in 2023 and 2024, and rests upon the Fintech definition of the Financial Stability Board: "a technologically enabled innovation in financial services that could result in new business models, applications, processes, or products with an associated material effect on financial markets and institutions and the provision of financial services" (Financial Stability Board, 2022). Within this definition, a fintech company may operate under various domains. The World Economic Forum initially defined these domains as payments, deposits and lending, capital raising, investment management, insurance, and market provisioning (World Economic Forum, 2015). Later on, Ankenbrand et al. (2018) developed a more streamlined approach that introduced analytics, distributed ledger technology, and banking infrastructure alongside payments, deposits and lending, and investment management as new domains, which Laidroo et al. (2021) further improved by adding insurtech. However, these reports have examined fintech firms under two main categories, following CCAF, World Bank, and World Economic Forum reports: providers of financial services (digital lending, digital capital raising, digital payments, digital asset exchange, insurtech, and wealthtech) versus providers of technology and support services (cybersecurity and digital identity, credit and data analytics, regtech, and enterprise technology provisioning) (CCAF, World Bank and World Economic Forum, 2020).

The reports integrate information gathered through various methods, including desk research, a survey conducted in spring-summer 2023 for Romania and Bulgaria, and spring 2024 for Türkiye, as well as semi-structured interviews from the same period. The surveys used in these studies combined elements from the 2022 Romanian ecosystem report, the Bulgarian Fintech 2022 report, and the Turkish Fintech 2024 report, adapting a questionnaire previously used by TalTech. The survey primarily focused on the business models of Bulgarian, Romanian, and Turkish FinTech companies, adapting the Business Model Canvas developed by Osterwalder and Pigneur (2010). This model explores nine building blocks of any business: key activities, partnerships, resources, value propositions, customer relationships, channels and segments, cost structure, and revenue streams. The analysis is enriched by following Eickhoff et al. (2017), who revisit the Business Model Canvas from the lens of FinTech businesses and propose a fintech oriented model, where the blocks consist of six components: product/service offering, dominant technology, value propositions, delivery channel, customers, and revenue stream. Additionally, the survey included sections on the use of artificial intelligence (AI) in relation to the EU AI Act and GDPR compliance issues. To complement the quantitative data, qualitative insights were obtained through interviews with representatives from Bulgarian, Romanian, and Turkish FinTech companies, as well as discussions with members of the Bulgarian, Romanian, and Turkish FinTech Associations.

3 Fintech Market Analysis for Türkiye, Romania, and Bulgaria

This section presents an overall view of the fintech ecosystem in respective countries, with a focus on regulatory developments and institutional support available to fintechs. Each country section is followed by its respective survey findings.

3.1 Türkiye

Fintech Ecosystem in Türkiye

Türkiye has substantial potential for the fintech sector, thanks to its young population, interest in technology, and digitalization. Furthermore, the fintech ecosystem is an important area for improving financial inclusion in the country.

Regulations in the fintech field date back to the early 2010s. With the mandatory introduction of new-generation payment devices in 2012, many fintech startups began to emerge in this area. The number of startups grew rapidly after 2015, when the authorities started to issue licenses to e-money and payment institutions (The State of the Turkish Fintech Ecosystem Report, 2023)

In the early 2010s, banks in Türkiye were among the first institutions to support startups and the startup ecosystem by launching incubators and acceleration programs. In recent years, banks have continued to establish numerous venture capital funds to invest in fintech and other sectors.

With the 26 fintechs established in 2023, there are a total of 696 fintechs currently active. When we examine fintech verticals, as of the end of 2023, there are 268 payment technology startups, 108 banking technology startups, and 100 blockchain and cryptocurrency startups in Türkiye. These are followed by corporate finance solutions, insurance technology startups, and financing solutions (The State of the Turkish Fintech Ecosystem Report, 2023).

In 2023, the areas with the most fintech startups were banking technologies, blockchain and cryptocurrency, financing, and payment technologies. Equity-based crowdfunding has also become one of the most preferred areas for entrepreneurs in recent years, with nine platforms receiving establishment permits in 2023 alone (The State of the Turkish Fintech Ecosystem Report, 2023).

Fintech strategies play an important role in fostering the sustainable growth and development of the financial technology sector. It's important to align the different expectations and objectives of the stakeholders within the fintech ecosystem under a common strategy. Today, in preparing the country for the future, it is vital for governments to promote fintech, regulate it in the public interest, and ensure that regulations are aligned with the industry. These considerations are essential in shaping national strategies for financial technologies. Therefore, in Türkiye, the National Fintech Strategy Document (NFSD) has been developed with the aim of addressing the priorities and elevating Türkiye's fintech ecosystem on the global stage (The State of the Turkish Fintech Ecosystem Report, 2023).

Fintech Regulatory Environment and Government Support in Türkiye

While the law on the prevention of money laundering dates back to 1996 in. Türkiye, the Law on Payment and Securities Settlement Systems, Payment Services, and Electronic Money Institutions was enacted in 2013. In 2019, secondary legislation on equity-based crowdfunding was passed and amended in 2021 to include debt-based crowdfunding. In the following years, laws on payment systems and electronic communications were amended to enable open banking services and digital onboarding. As of 2021, legislation to enable QR codes and 24/7 payments was in place, and open banking legislation was aligned with PSD2 to enable Banking as a Service (BaaS). More recently, the CBRT has enacted the "Regulation on the Disuse of Crypto Assets in Payments."

The Central Bank of Türkiye (CBRT) oversees payment and electronic money institutions, while the Banking Regulation and Supervision Agency regulates digital banking, BaaS, and Buy Now Pay Later financing. The Capital Markets Board of Türkiye monitors crowdfunding, equity, and asset management platforms, and insurance is regulated by the Insurance and Private Pension Regulation and Supervision Agency.

Conclusions From the Turkish Fintech Market Analysis

Türkiye's fintech sector has witnessed remarkable growth. Banks in Türkiye were among the early supporters of fintech innovation, launching incubators and acceleration programs to nurture startups and the broader startup ecosystem. This support has continued, with banks establishing numerous venture capital funds in recent years to invest in fintech and other sectors. The Türkiye Fintech Survey, conducted by the authors of this chapter (Sahin, Yıldırım, Ozturkkal), Fintech Association Türkiye, and KPMG, was used during Istanbul Fintech Week (IFW) 2024, which is a global venue for discussion and knowledge exchange in the changing financial services industry to award fintech companies and banks. In its first three editions, IFW hosted more than 10,000 participants from around 30 countries. Nevertheless, the sector faces challenges like limited resource availability, evolving regulatory landscapes, and fierce competition for skilled talent. Despite these obstacles, Türkiye's dynamic entrepreneurial culture, robust IT infrastructure, and rich talent pool provide a favorable environment for fintech growth, though expanding into international markets continues to pose a significant challenge for local companies.

Fintech Survey Results Türkiye

Fintech Report Türkiye, prepared in collaboration with Fintech Association Türkiye and KPMG Türkiye, focuses on the current state and future of the Fintech industry in Türkiye. The report includes enterprise technology provisioning, digital lending, payments, and regtech, as hypothesized by most of the Fintech market. This analysis encompasses the current state, operational activities, technological innovations, and growth potential of the Fintech sector.

The data collected from the survey provides a comprehensive analysis of the current state and future potential of the Turkish fintech sector. The survey results are presented in detail in the Fintech Report Türkiye 2024 and include recommendations to contribute to the sector's development, as well as an evaluation of the regulatory landscape of the country.

Overall, 43 fintechs in Türkiye participated in this survey conducted in Spring 2024. Based on their current phase of development, the participants fall into three categories: Profitable Companies: 53%, Growth Phase Companies: 40%, and Under Construction/Preparations: 7%. These numbers show that there is a competitive and flourishing fintech ecosystem with established players as well as upcoming new players. The majority of surveyed Turkish fintechs prefer to run primary business functions in-house (51%), where Programming and Engineering (23.2%) and Sales (18.1%) represent the top two primary activities Turkish fintechs pursue daily. Marketing and running daily operations share similar time spent (15.5%), while fintechs spend 11.61% of their time on regtech and fraud prevention. Only 15% of fintechs have outsourced programming and engineering, and 13% have outsourced marketing activities. Programming and engineering activities are delegated mainly by fintechs that are in growth stages or under construction, showing the need to incorporate software development skills. On the other hand, marketing activities are primarily delegated by fintechs in growth stages.

The majority of the companies surveyed (74%) are directly involved in providing financial services, while a smaller portion (26%) does not offer financial services directly. Additionally, 55% report supporting the provision of financial services by another company.

Regarding the primary services provided, the most common is digital payments, with 53%, followed by digital lending, with 25% of the companies providing this service. The rest of the services include digital capital raising (9%), digital assets exchange (3%), insurtech (3%), and wealthtech (6%).

Digital platforms are the primary technology fintechs use, with 20% of fintechs indicating them in their top three technology uses. Transaction processing systems account for 15% of technology usage, while AI and decision support systems equally represent the third dominant technology category, with a 12% share each. These findings highlight the importance of interoperability, efficiency, and speed of settlements, accompanied by optimized decision-making in the fintech ecosystem. Marketplaces for exchanging information closely follow with an 11% share, representing the rise of digital trading platforms. Database systems and blockchain technologies each have a 7.6% share, flagging the importance of data management and secure storage.

Surveyed Turkish fintech companies report that their main value propositions are monetary value (17%), customization (14%), convenience (13%), financial risk management (11%), collaboration/coordination (8%), intermediation (7%), unification/consolidation (6%), customer insight, security, and transparency, with 5% each.

Regarding their service type, the majority of companies (53%) are engaged in both B2B and B2C services, highlighting a balanced approach to market engagement. There is also a substantial focus on B2B services, with 42%, while a much smaller portion of companies (5%) cater solely to the B2C market.

63% of the surveyed companies are in the expansion stage of their development. The largest segment of companies (56%) has received first-round investments, while 44% of the companies are yet to receive first-round investments, highlighting potential funding gaps. 54% of surveyed fintechs operate in both domestic and international markets, and 16% report that foreign sales represent up to 20% of their income, while 11% report foreign sales of up to 50%. Western Europe represents the biggest market for surveyed Turkish fintechs (40%), followed by the Middle East (23%), Eastern Europe (19%), and the US (9%). Similarly, Western Europe (63%), the Middle East (61%), and Eastern Europe (53%) are also indicated as the top three regions where surveyed fintechs aim to expand their operations in the next five years. 49% indicate economic uncertainty as the most important threat to their business in the next 12 months.

Most of the surveyed fintechs (33%) have over 100 employees, while small to medium-sized companies represent the second-largest segment (30%), which have between 10 and 49 employees. Medium-sized companies with 50–99 employees make up 16% of the participants. The rest of the participants could be considered micro businesses.

More than three-quarters of respondents indicate that they employ AI in their operations. About 65% state that they have established designated roles for verifying AI-generated results. However, many respondents lack a facility to explain AI-generated outcomes to their customers. These findings suggest that while Turkish fintechs are dynamic and proactive in embracing AI technologies, they need to improve their capabilities in validating and communicating AI-generated outcomes to customers. Additionally, a relatively high number of respondents chose not to answer questions regarding designated roles for checking AI results and facilities for explaining AI outcomes. This could be due to the sensitivity of the issue or a lack of awareness within the industry.

Almost all respondents indicate that they are knowledgeable about the Kişisel Verilerin Korunması Kanunu (KVKK), the local personal data protection law, whose obligations are critically important for the industry. Additionally, over 95% of respondents state that their companies comply with these obligations. This suggests that the industry takes KVKK seriously, recognizing its significant legal consequences and its impact on customer confidence.

More than 70% of respondents indicate awareness of the AI Act, yet only around 40% are taking steps to comply with it. This disparity may be attributed to the lack of specific AI regulations in Türkiye.[1] It is also notable that a significant number of respondents did not answer the questions regarding the AI Act. These findings highlight the potential challenges the AI Act poses for the industry and underscore the need for industry organizations and regulatory bodies to support companies in preparing for compliance.[2]

3.2 Romania

Fintech Ecosystem Romania

The Romanian fintech sector has witnessed substantial growth, significantly narrowing the gap with more established fintech ecosystems in the region. Although still relatively young, the Romanian fintech landscape has matured, driven by new funding rounds, increased collaboration within the ecosystem, and notable exits.

Central to the ecosystem are the fintech companies themselves, represented by RoFintech, which has strengthened its ties with other stakeholders in Romania and established partnerships with fintech associations across the region. RoFintech serves as the primary channel for banks, insurance companies, and large consulting firms to support and collaborate with fintech entities, enhancing the ecosystem's cohesion.

[1] As of June 2024, "On June 25, 2024, a bill for the regulation of AI in Tükiye was presented before parliament. The Bill is currently with the parliamentary committee review in accordance with Turkish legislative process." pls see: https://www.whitecase.com/insight-our-thinking/ai-watch-global-regulatory-tracker-turkey).

[2] See, for example, Truby et al. (2020) on AI regulation in the financial sector.

A pivotal aspect of this growth is the close collaboration between government bodies, the Financial Supervision Authority, the Ministry of Finance, and fintech companies. The National Bank of Romania (NBR), acting as both the central bank and the National Competent Authority (NCA), has played a crucial role in fostering this development, aligning with the broader regulatory framework of PSD2. This collaboration has allowed startups to be actively involved in significant regulatory processes at both national and EU levels, facilitating a more adaptable regulatory environment.

Accelerators and incubators are integral to the Romanian fintech ecosystem. Programs such as Techcelerator, InnovX, Founder Institute, and Commons Accel have been instrumental in the emergence of new fintech companies. Additionally, BCR's announcement of the first fintech corporate venture capital (VC) fund in Romania marks a significant milestone. Expected to become operational in 2024, this fund represents a natural progression from InnovX, BCR's accelerator program, and will provide crucial financial support for further development within the ecosystem.

Educational institutions and research entities are becoming increasingly active in the fintech ecosystem. Major universities in Romania are now offering both long-term and short-term programs dedicated to fintech, addressing the human capital needs of fintech companies. These educational initiatives are essential, given the significant talent competition faced by local fintechs, particularly against global players and banks that are building in-house fintech teams.

Universities are also bridging the gap between regulators and the fintech ecosystem by joining support programs and participating in research projects with both regulators and fintech companies. This collaborative research environment is expected to lead to fintech spinoffs founded by faculty members and executives from existing companies, further enriching the ecosystem.

The existing financial sector in Romania provides a robust market for fintech companies. Banks and insurance companies are actively supporting the ecosystem through commercial partnerships, enhancing the market reach and operational capabilities of fintech firms. However, the development of the ecosystem is sometimes hindered by slow cooperation and coordination among various players. Many believe that only joint efforts involving fintech companies, the government, and universities can overcome these obstacles.

RoFintech is seen as the leader of the Romanian fintech sector, known for its structured and coordinated activities. It acts as the official voice of fintech startups, representing them in dealings with other stakeholders both within Romania and in Brussels. Despite its influential role, RoFintech's activities are limited by its budget, which relies on membership fees. While more companies have joined RoFintech since 2022, significant players are still outside the organization, indicating room for growth and broader participation.

Romania's business environment is conducive to starting and growing fintech companies, thanks to the large financial sector, accessible early-stage capital, and local tech talent. However, expanding into international markets and building global companies remains challenging. Many local fintechs have started taking steps toward international expansion, setting a precedent for others to follow.

A major concern within the ecosystem is the fierce competition for talent. Local fintechs are competing not only with each other but also with global players like Klarna and Stripe, which have recently entered the Romanian market. Banks are also forming in-house fintech teams, further intensifying the competition for skilled professionals. To address this, fintech companies are collaborating with local universities on research projects, although these initiatives are still in the early stages compared to more mature ecosystems in the region.

The Romanian fintech ecosystem is on a promising trajectory, characterized by increased collaboration, support from various stakeholders, and significant investment. The establishment of corporate venture funds, active participation by educational institutions, and efforts toward regulatory cooperation are all positive signs of maturation. Addressing the challenges of talent acquisition and international expansion will be crucial for sustaining this growth. As more success stories emerge, the ecosystem is likely to attract greater investment and talent, further solidifying Romania's position in the regional fintech landscape.

Despite some limitations, the Romanian entrepreneurship culture is robust, characterized by an entrepreneurial mindset, creativity, and openness to innovation and technology. The development of digital infrastructure and the widespread use of English as a business language have fostered the emergence and global growth of fintech companies.

Although state support for startups has increased, fintech-specific support remains limited. The state's main role is to shape the political and legal framework, offering relative freedom for fintech activities. However, inadequate regulation and difficult access to open data pose significant challenges. On a positive note, the National Bank and the Financial Supervision Authority have improved their collaboration with RoFintech, which could help mitigate these regulatory issues.

Romania offers a favorable business environment and culture, strong IT infrastructure, and access to talent and industry-specific knowledge, which are conducive to fintech sector growth. However, obstacles such as limited resources, lack of stakeholder cooperation, insufficient state support, an inadequate legal framework, and potential difficulties in accessing capital could hinder further development.

Fintech Regulatory Environment and Government Support in Romania

The Financial Supervisory Authority (ASF), established in 2013, oversees insurance, private pensions, and capital markets in Romania. Additionally, ASF is responsible for regulating crowdfunding platforms under Law No. 244/2022. ASF is part of the EU Supervisory Digital Finance Academy (EU SDFA), which provides training to enhance financial supervisors' understanding of fintech and promotes a unified approach across Europe.

ASF has launched the FinTech Hub and InsurTech Hub to foster innovation in Romania's financial markets. The InsurTech Hub, involving universities, professional associations, insurance companies, and IT firms, serves as an innovation accelerator. These hubs facilitate collaboration, discussions, and events on the latest regulatory trends.

Separately, the National Bank of Romania (NBR) gained authority over payment service providers with the enactment of Law 209/2019, which aligns with PSD2 (EU Directive 2366/2015). To support fintech innovation, the NBR launched the Romanian FinTech Innovation Hub, a platform for communication between financial service providers and the NBR.

Conclusions From the Romanian Fintech Market Analysis

The Romanian fintech sector has seen rapid growth, closing the gap with more established ecosystems in the region. This progress is driven by increased funding, tighter collaboration among ecosystem players, and the involvement of organizations like RoFintech, which represents the sector and fosters partnerships with banks, insurance companies, and consulting firms. Government and regulatory bodies, including the

National Bank of Romania (NBR) and the Financial Supervisory Authority (ASF), have also enhanced their cooperation with fintech companies, promoting innovation through initiatives like the FinTech Hub and InsurTech Hub. However, challenges such as limited resources, inadequate regulation, and fierce competition for talent persist. Despite these obstacles, Romania's strong entrepreneurial culture, robust IT infrastructure, and access to talent create a favorable environment for fintech growth, though expanding into international markets remains a challenge for local companies.

3.3 Bulgaria

Fintech Ecosystem Bulgaria

The fintech sector in Bulgaria has experienced remarkable growth over the past decade, with a significant concentration in the nation's three largest cities: Sofia, Plovdiv, and Varna. Sofia, the capital city, serves as the nucleus of this burgeoning industry, hosting 131 of the 156 fintech firms operating in the country. The city's competitive advantages are well-documented and widely acknowledged, encompassing a well-educated workforce, the presence of the country's leading technical and economic universities, robust physical and digital infrastructure, and strategic geographical positioning.

The transformation of Bulgaria's financial sector began after the dissolution of the communist regime, shifting from a centrally planned economy to a market-oriented one. Initially driven by public sector initiatives to enhance the efficiency of the Bulgarian National Bank, the impetus for digital finance innovation transitioned toward private consumer needs by the turn of the twenty-first century (Radev and Penev, 2024a). This shift underscored a broader transformation within the country, where market dynamics began to play a central role in shaping the direction of financial innovation.

Despite its origins in the 1990s, the fintech industry in Bulgaria is relatively young but rapidly expanding. According to the BFA Annual Fintech Report 2022, 92% of Bulgarian fintech firms are classified as small and medium-sized enterprises (SMEs), each with an annual turnover of less than €50 million and employing fewer than 250 people (BFA, 2022). The industry's business models are diverse, with digital payments emerging as the most prominent, accounting for 25% of the sector. This is followed by enterprise technology provisioning (18%) and digital asset exchange (15%) (BFA, 2022). Notably, fintech firms specializing in digital payments are the primary contributors to the sector's revenue, generating 54% of the BGN 1.828 billion (~EUR 0.9 billion) total revenue in 2021 (BFA, 2022).

The Bulgarian fintech ecosystem includes both indigenous companies, such as Paynetics, Borica, and Paysera Bulgaria, and foreign direct investments from firms like Paysafe, SumUp, and Nuvei. Despite the smaller size of the credit and data analytics segment, it still plays a crucial role in revenue generation, accounting for 8% of the sector's total revenue (BFA, 2022).

The Bulgarian Fintech Association (BFA), established in 2017, plays a pivotal role in the ecosystem. It employs the Quadruple Helix Model of Innovation to drive the sector's development, which involves collaboration between academia, industry, government, and civil society to foster innovation and development within the sector (BFA, 2022). With 72 member organizations, including fintech companies, two universities, VC funds, and banking institutions, BFA's efforts include publishing annual reports, supporting educational activities, and organizing awareness campaigns and hackathons. The BFA's efforts have been pivotal in creating a conducive environment for fintech innovation, facilitating the exchange of knowledge and best practices among stakeholders, and promoting Bulgaria as a regional leader in fintech development.

Sofia's vibrant startup scene and growing number of VC funds with local expertise are vital to the ecosystem. In 2018, the Bulgarian Stock Exchange (BSE) expanded its funding options for start-ups through the launch of the Bulgarian Enterprise Accelerator Market (BEAM), which has already facilitated the first Initial Public Offering (IPO) of a fintech company (BSE, 2023a). Additionally, the BSE has initiated the BeamUp Lab program, aimed at promoting and encouraging the growth of Bulgarian start-ups (BSE, 2023b). Legal firms specializing in digital finance are also increasing, indicating growing interest from the legal sector.

Education is a cornerstone of the Bulgarian fintech ecosystem, with top universities and specialized training institutions located in Sofia. The best universities and faculties in economics and finance, such as the Faculty of Economics and Business Administration at Sofia University and the University of National and World Economy, provide highly regarded finance and accounting programs (Radev & Penev, 2024b). The Faculty of Law at Sofia University is known for producing legal experts interested in digital finance. The Technical University of Sofia and the Faculty of Mathematics and Informatics at Sofia University produce a significant number of IT engineers annually. Private institutions like SoftUni and Telerik Academy offer software-engineering training and requalification programs.

In 2021, there were 12,900 university and high school students enrolled in STEM programs, potentially contributing to the fintech workforce (BFA, 2022). Bulgarian academia is increasingly incorporating financial innovation into its curricula, with private sector representatives often sharing their experiences through lectures and case studies (Radev & Penev, 2024b). This strong emphasis on education and talent development is crucial for sustaining the growth of the fintech sector in Bulgaria and ensuring a steady supply of skilled professionals to meet the industry's evolving needs.

The fintech industry in Bulgaria is notable for its high level of gender parity, with women constituting 44% of the workforce as of 2023. This is particularly significant, given the traditionally male-dominated nature of the technology and finance sectors. The average age of employees in the Bulgarian fintech industry is 35.4 years, indicating a young and adaptable workforce that is well-suited to the rapidly evolving fintech landscape (BFA, 2022). The presence of a diverse and dynamic workforce is a key asset for the industry, contributing to its ability to innovate and respond to emerging challenges and opportunities.

Bulgaria offers several advantages for fintech, blockchain, and cryptocurrency companies, including modern infrastructure, an experienced workforce, low operating expenses, a favorable tax structure, and a supportive ecosystem. These factors make Bulgaria an attractive destination for startups seeking international growth. The highly skilled workforce and business-friendly climate are likely to drive further development and innovation, attracting more companies and investors to the region. Bulgaria's strategic efforts to foster a conducive environment for fintech growth position it as a leader in these emerging industries, promising continued expansion and success.

Fintech Regulatory Environment and Government Support in Bulgaria

The Bulgarian government and parliament have played a pivotal role in establishing the legal and regulatory foundations necessary for the fintech sector's growth. The financial sector in Bulgaria is highly regulated and segmented, with regulatory oversight divided between the Bulgarian National Bank, which oversees the banking sector, and the Financial Supervision Commission (FSC), which regulates the non-banking sector, including the capital, insurance, and pension markets, as well as investment funds and intermediaries (Radev & Penev, 2024b).

The government's support for the fintech industry is also evident in its efforts to transpose EU directives and regulations into national law. Key examples include the implementation of the EU's Payment Services Directive 2 (PSD 2) and the Anti-Money Laundering (AML) framework, which provide a regulatory framework that aligns with European standards (Radev & Penev, 2024b). Another significant advantage for fintech companies operating in Bulgaria is the country's low-tax environment. Over the past two decades, Bulgaria has maintained a relatively low flat income tax rate of 10%, which offers substantial competitive advantages for fintech companies compared to their Western European counterparts (Radev & Penev, 2024b). This favorable tax regime, combined with competitive salaries that are close to Western European levels, makes Bulgaria an attractive location for fintech firms seeking to optimize their operational costs while retaining access to a highly skilled workforce.

Conclusions the Bulgarian Fintech Market Analysis

The Bulgarian fintech environment has evolved significantly, driven by historical shifts, robust educational institutions, supportive organizational structures, and a favorable regulatory and tax framework. While challenges remain, such as the need for greater coordination among stakeholders and enhanced regulatory clarity, the overall outlook for the Bulgarian fintech sector is positive. The continued development of digital infrastructure, strong government support, and a dynamic startup ecosystem ensure that Bulgaria will remain at the forefront of fintech innovation in the coming years.

Fintech Survey Results for Romania and Bulgaria

A considerable number of fintech companies in Romania and Bulgaria are in the growth phase and not yet profitable (41.3%). Fintech companies in both countries are currently in the construction or preparatory stages (7.9%). This suggests a vibrant startup ecosystem with ongoing entrepreneurial activity. Both countries also have profitable fintech companies (50.8%), indicating successful business models and sustainable operations in the market. The majority of fintech businesses in Bulgaria and Romania (68.3%) are actively engaged in the provision of financial services, indicating a wide range of products and services available in the market. These services include payment solutions (22.0%), lending (14.6%), digital wallets (14.6%), investment/asset management (9.8%), capital raising, including crowdfunding (8.5%), and others. Among the respondents, 49.2% operate both within the home market as well as internationally, 38.1% operate only in the home market, while 12.7% are only internationally present, without operating in the home market. The main external markets where respondents operate are the UK (16.3%) and Romania (11.6%), followed by the USA, Switzerland, Spain, Germany, and Austria, with a percentage of 7% each. Most Romanian and Bulgarian fintech companies want to expand their activities within the EU (19.3%). The main blockers for expanding to foreign markets are the difficulty in establishing networks and contacts abroad, cultural differences, and limited experience in exports.

Fintech companies offering support services mainly focus on RegTech (27.6%), Digital Identity—security, KYC, fraud prevention (17.2%), credit analysis (17.2%), and data analysis (13.8%).

A significant number of fintech companies in both Romania and Bulgaria are actively engaged in marketing (16.2%) and sales efforts (29.7%). Other primary activities that fintech companies in the two countries focus on include running daily business operations and serving existing clients (28.8%), as well as programming and engineering (25.2%).

Most Romanian and Bulgarian fintech companies have not delegated any of their activities to third parties (38.8%). Among the companies that have outsourced part of their activities, the majority have done so for programming and engineering tasks (35.8%), while 20.9% have outsourced their marketing activities.

The surveyed fintech companies use a variety of innovative technologies in their operations, among which are digital platforms on which complementary products/services can be developed (12.7%), database systems (12.3%), machine learning (11.8%), and automated transaction processing systems (10.91%), as well as marketplaces for information exchange (9.6%) and artificial intelligence (9.1%). Less-used technologies include decision support systems (5.9%), robotic process automation (3.6%), blockchain

(2.3%), open banking (1.4%), KYC/sanctions screening (0.5%), embedded finance (0.5%), and eCommerce marketplaces (0.5%).

The main value proposition of the surveyed Romanian and Bulgarian fintech companies is intermediation (22.2%), financial risk management (19.1%), transparency (19.1%), automation (12.7%), customization, improving insight (enhancing the customer's knowledge), and monetary value, with a percentage of 11.1% each.

Fintech companies mentioned economic uncertainty as the main threat to their business (69.8%). Several significant tendencies become apparent when one examines the answers provided by the companies regarding the areas that have the greatest development potential over the next three years. The main development interest is focused on open banking, instant payments, wealth management, RegTech, digital currencies, and personal finance.

The most important funding sources for the next three years are seed capital, venture capital, and equity funding, with the former receiving the highest rating among the listed options.

Examining how fintech companies in Romania and Bulgaria use AI in their operations sheds light on their technology landscapes. Data show that firms vary in their deployment of AI, with some embracing it (55.6%) and others opting out or abstaining from answering.

There is a wide range of familiarity with the AI Act among fintech businesses in Romania and Bulgaria, according to the answers provided in response to the query about their awareness of it.

While most respondents said they were aware of the AI Act (58.7%), others declined to answer (6.4%), implying that they were either unaware of the law in question or unsure about it. This discrepancy in knowledge emphasizes how important it is for the fintech industry to spread knowledge and education on laws like the AI Act.

Companies that operate in these countries must be aware of these restrictions, as they have a significant impact on how artificial intelligence applications are regulated, both morally and legally. Most of the respondents mentioned that they were preparing for the AI Act (52.6%), while others responded negatively or chose not to answer. Companies that have confirmed their preparations take a proactive approach, recognizing the importance of aligning operations with forthcoming laws. Those that have not begun preparations may face difficulties in understanding the requirements or implementing the necessary modifications. Respondents who chose not to respond may still be considering their approach or may be in the early stages of internal deliberations.

4 Summary of the Fintech Surveys for All Countries: Türkiye, Romania, and Bulgaria (TR, RO, BG)

Figure 1 reports the fintech company's compliance with regulations by country. There is a very limited number of companies lacking regulatory compliance. Most companies responded to this question regarding local data regulation or GDPR compliance as "yes."

There are two companies from the Bulgaria and Romania survey that are not based in Romania or Bulgaria. Therefore, we named those companies "other," although they are included in the survey sample. Tables 1 and 2 report AI information for the fintech companies, and the survey findings indicate that most of the companies use AI in their operations, with 63 of the 99 companies surveyed in Table 1. Twenty-four of the companies do not use AI, and 12 did not want to respond to the question.

Table 2 provides information on the AI results check of the 99 fintech companies. The survey findings indicate that 47%, about half, of the companies have a designated person to check the AI results in their company. Thirty-seven percent of the companies do not have a designated person to check the AI results, and 15% did not want to respond to the question.

The companies want to expand to the EU, UK, Far East, Middle East, Western Europe, Canada, individual European countries such as Italy,

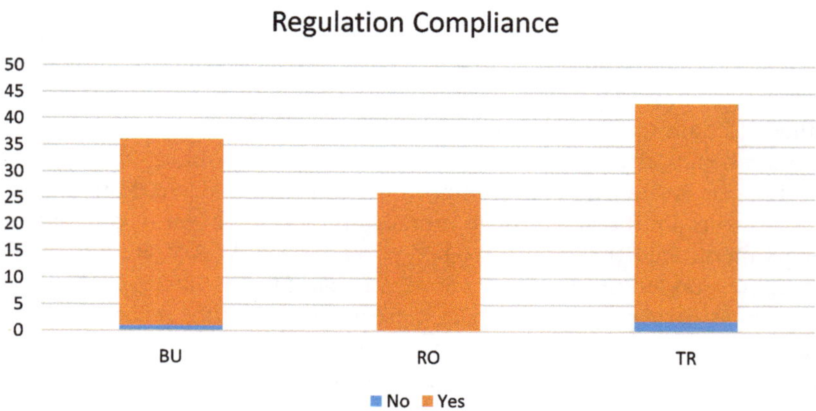

Fig. 1 Is your company compliant with the following regulations (local/GDPR)?

Table 1 AI use: "Do you use AI in your company?"

Country	*Yes*	*No*	*I do not want to respond*	*Total*
TR	33	8	2	43
RO	11	8	3	22
BG	19	8	7	34
Total	63	24	12	99
Total (%)	64	24	12	100

Table 2 AI results check: "Do you have a specific person checking the AI results in your company?"

Country	*Yes*	*No*	*I do not want to respond*	*Total*
TR	28	11	4	43
RO	8	10	4	22
BG	11	16	7	34
Total	47	37	15	99
Total (%)	47	37	15	100

Spain, France, Greece, Germany, Austria, Switzerland, Hungary, Poland, Ukraine, Nordic countries, Benelux, Romania, Türkiye, Africa, Japan, US, Latin America, and regionally.

Table 3 reports that most of the companies expect moderate growth, significant growth, and large growth in the workforce next year. There is a small number of companies expecting no growth, moderate decline, and significant decline in the workforce, as less than 10% of the companies surveyed.

Table 4 shows that most of the companies, 71%, provide financial services, while 29% of the companies do not provide financial services.

Table 5 demonstrates the primary services the companies are involved in by country and in total. Payments, digital payments, and digital lending are important primary services. Some companies perform multiple operations and provide multiple services. There are some companies performing crowd-funding and fundraising activities. Compared to previous fintech services, the companies surveyed focus less on wealthtech, insurance, and brokerage as primary services. Twenty-nine companies did not respond to the question.

Table 3 Workforce: "Expected change in workforce in the next year"

	Large growth	*Moderate decline*	*Moderate growth*	*No growth*	*Significant decline*	*Significant growth*	*Total*
TR			12	1	1	29	43
RO	4	2	15	1			22
BG	6		24	4			34
Total	10	2	51	6	1	29	99
Total (%)	10	2	52	6	1	29	100

Table 4 Financial service: "The company provides a financial service itself"

Country	*No*	*Yes*	*Total*
TR	11	32	43
RO	6	16	22
BG	12	22	34
Total	29	70	99
Total (%)	29	71	100

Table 5 Primary services: "The company is involved in providing the following primary services"

	TR	*RO*	*BG*	*Total*
B2C digital platform/marketplace to facilitate digital transactions		1		1
BI solutions for SMEs		1		1
Capital raising (incl crowdfunding)		2		2
Capital raising (incl crowdfunding), Investment/asset management		1		1
Capital raising (incl crowdfunding), Payments, Investment/asset management, Insurance				0
Crypto currency exchange and wallet services outsourced to a Lithuanian entity			1	1
Digital Assets Exchange	1			1
Digital Capital Raising	3			3
Digital CFO			1	1

(continued)

Table 5 (continued)

	TR	*RO*	*BG*	*Total*
Digital Lending	**8**			**8**
Digital Payments	**17**			**17**
Digital wallet		1		1
fraud and compliance			1	1
Fully digital bank, Payments, Digital wallet, Cards, BaaS, Digital currencies			1	1
Fully digital bank, Payments, Investment/asset management, Digital wallet			2	2
Insurance		1		1
Insurtech	1			1
Investment/asset management			1	1
Lending			3	3
Lending, Capital raising (incl crowdfunding)		1		1
Lending, Capital raising (incl crowdfunding), Investment/asset management			1	1
Lending, Digital wallet		1		1
Lending, Fully digital bank, Payments, Investment/asset management, Digital wallet, The above selected are tailored solutions/services we can develop for our clients		1		1
Lending, Mortgage loans			1	1
Lending, Payments, Digital wallet			1	1
Lending, Payments, Investment/asset management, Trading or brokerage		1		1
Lending, Payments, Trading or brokerage, Digital wallet		1		1
Payments		**3**	**2**	**5**
Payments, Account Information		1		1
Payments, Digital wallet		1	1	2
PFM			1	1
Trading or brokerage			2	2
Trading or brokerage, Digital wallet, eCommerce platform for pre-orders and Fintech solution—micro wallets			1	1
Training		1		1
Wealthtech	2			2
(blank)	11	4	14	29
Total	43	22	34	99
Total (%)	43	22	34	100

Table 6 Business threat: "What is the most important threat to your business in the next 12 months" (only one answer)

	TR	*RO*	*BG*	*Total*	*Total (%)*
Economic uncertainty	21	15	23	59	60
Regulatory uncertainty	11			11	11
Technological competition	6			6	6
Corrupt regulators			1	1	1
Different wars in world		1		1	1
Competition		1	1	2	2
Fast changing regulations			1	1	1
Fast growing competitors			1	1	1
Funding		1		1	1
High inflation rates			2	2	2
Unfair competition	1			1	1
Lack of development funding		1		1	1
Market maturity (under-developed)		1		1	1
Partnerships and new clients			1	1	1
Political uncertainty	4			4	4
Regulatory			1	1	1
Regulatory delays for major obstacles and adoption for innovative financial solutions		1		1	1
Regulatory volatility		1		1	1
To find new investors			1	1	1
War in Ukraine			2	2	2
Total	43	22	34	99	100

Table 6 illustrates that fintech companies see economic uncertainty as a major threat for the next 12 months. Fifty-nine of the 99 companies (60%) reported economic uncertainty as the major threat to their business. Political uncertainty (reported by four Turkish fintech companies) and high inflation rates (reported by two Bulgarian fintech companies) are other factors identified as the most important threats and can be included in this category. Eleven percent of the companies reported regulatory uncertainty as the major threat, and all of these fintech companies are from Türkiye. There are three other responses related to regulatory volatility, delays or obstacles, or corrupt regulators, which were reported by companies from Romania and Bulgaria. Technological competition is the third most important threat to business, and this response was reported exclusively by fintech companies from Türkiye.

5 Conclusion

This study employs two individual Fintech Survey studies by gathering data from Türkiye, Romania, and Bulgaria from 99 fintech companies. Payments, digital payments, and digital lending are important primary services for the companies surveyed. Most of the companies expect moderate growth, significant growth, and large growth in the workforce next year. The insights from the 99 fintech companies surveyed from Türkiye, Romania, and Bulgaria serve as a valuable resource for policymakers, fintech companies, investors, and stakeholders as they navigate the rapidly evolving fintech landscape. By tackling the challenges and capitalizing on the opportunities highlighted, the fintech sector can continue to drive sustainable growth and contribute to a more inclusive and dynamic financial ecosystem. Moving forward, collaboration between public and private sectors will be crucial to fully unlocking the potential of fintech for the benefit of all. This report provides regulators with critical insights into the evolving fintech landscape, helping them to develop informed policies that balance innovation with investor protection and ensure a more stable financial system.

Acknowledgment This work is supported by COST Action 19130 Fintech and Artificial Intelligence in Finance—Towards a transparent financial industry (FinAI) and through the project IDA Institute of Digital Assets, CF166/15.11.2022, contract number 760046/23.05.2024, through the project AI for Energy Finance (AI4EFin), CF162/15.11.2022, contract number 760048/23.05.2024, financed under the Romania's National Recovery and Resilience Plan, Apel nr. PNRR-III-C9-2022-I8, and through the project "A better understanding of socio-economic systems using quantitative methods from Physics" funded by the European Union—NextgenerationEU and the Romanian Government, under National Recovery and Resilience Plan for Romania, contract no 760034/23.05.2023, cod PNRR-C9-I8-CF255/29.11.2022, through the Romanian Ministry of Research, Innovation and Digitalization, within Component 9, Investment I8". This study is also supported by the Bulgarian National Fund's scientific programme "Fundamental Studies 2023", project number KP-06-N75/9 from 07.12.2023, and by the European Union-NextGenerationEU, through the National Recovery and Resilience Plan of the Republic of Bulgaria, project No BG-RRP-2.004-0008. We gratefully acknowledge the support of the Marie Skłodowska-Curie Actions under the European Union's Horizon Europe research and innovation program for the Industrial Doctoral Network on Digital Finance, acronym: DIGITAL, Project No. 101119635". This work was also supported from the National Scientific Program "Petar Beron i NIE" in Bulgaria,

BG-175467353-2023-14-0004 - 2023 and Fellowships for Excellent Researchers R2–R4 RRP, Slovakia, 09I03-03-V04-00502- 2023.

References

Ankenbrand, T., Dietrich, A., & Bieri, D. (2018). *IFZ FinTech Study 2019: An overview of Swiss FinTech*. Institute of Financial Services. Zug IFZ.

Bălţoi, I.-C.-M. (2020). The fintech ecosystem in Romania. *Proceedings of the International Conference on Business Excellence, 14*(1), 273–281. https://doi.org/10.2478/picbe-2020-0026

Bayram, O., Talay, I., & Feridun, M. C. (2022). Fintech promote sustainable finance? Policy lessons from the case of Turkey. *Sustainability, 14*(19), 12414. https://doi.org/10.3390/su141912414

Beall, A. (2018). *To escape Brexit, UK startups are flocking to Eastern Europe*. Published on 19.10.2018. Retrieved August 10, 2024, from https://www.wired.co.uk/article/brexit-uk-fintechs-eastern-europe

BFA. (2022). *Fintech Bulgaria, annual fintech report*. https://fintechbulgaria.org/annual-fintech-report-2022/

BSE. (2023a). *ITF Group: A fintech company with ambition*. https://beam.bse-sofia.bg/en/itf_group.

BSE. (2023b). *This is BeamUpLab, Bulgarian Stock Exchange*. https://beamuplab.space/en/.

CCAF, World Bank and World Economic Forum. (2020). *The global Covid-19 FinTech market rapid assessment report*. University of Cambridge, World Bank Group and the World Economic Forum.

Central Bank of Türkiye. https://www.tcmb.gov.tr/wps/wcm/connect/EN/TCMB%20EN/Main%20Menu/Announcements/Press%20Releases/2021/ANO2021-17

Central Bank of Türkiye website: Official Gazette Number 28690. https://www.tcmb.gov.tr/wps/wcm/connect/e43f22de-0731-4dd7-bb43-5c843e981221/%C3%96deme±Sistemleri±Kanunu.pdf?MOD=AJPERES&CACHEID=ROOTWORKSPACE-e43f22de-0731-4dd7-bb43-5c843e981221-nbMmg7-

EBRD. (2022). *Diagnostic of Estonia, Latvia and Lithuania, European Bank for reconstruction and development*. Retrieved April 6, 2022.

Eickhoff, M., Muntermann, J., & Weinrich, T. (2017). What do FinTechs actually do? A taxonomy of FinTech business models. *ICIS 2017 Proceedings*, 22. http://aisel.aisnet.org/icis2017/EBusiness/Presentations/22

Financial Stability Board. (2022). *FinTech*. https://www.fsb.org/work-of-the-fsb/financial-innovation-and-structural-change/fintech/#:~:text=The%20FSB%20defines%20FinTech%20as,the%20provision%20of%20financial%20services

Fintech Report Türkiye. (2024). *Ceylan Onay Sahin, Canan Yildırım, Belma Ozturkkal* (unpublished manuscript).

FSC. (2023). Fintech innovation hub, financial supervision commission. Retrieved December 29, 2023, from https://www.fsc.bg/?page_id=15962&lang=en

Laidroo, L., Koroleva, E., Kliber, A., Rupeika-Apoga, R., & Grigaliuniene, Z. (2021). Business models of FinTechs—Difference in similarity? *Electronic Commerce Research and Applications, 46*. https://doi.org/10.1016/j.elerap.2021.101034

Official Gazette Türkiye. (1996). *Law no. 4208 on prevention of money laundering date: November 9*. https://ms.hmb.gov.tr/uploads/sites/2/2019/04/LawNo_4208OnPreventionOfMoneyLaundering-Abolished.pdf

Official Gazette Türkiye. (2020). *The regulation on banks' information systems and electronic banking services dated March 15th*. https://www.resmigazete.gov.tr/eskiler/2020/03/20200315-10.htm

Osterwalder, A., & Pigneur, Y. (2010). *Business model generation: A handbook for visionaries, game changers, and challengers*. Wiley.

Presidency of Türkiye sourced Fintech strategy document National Fintech Strategy. *Finance office of the presidency of Türkiye*. Retrieved August 23, 2024. https://www.cbfo.gov.tr/en/national-fintech-strategy-document

Radev, D., & Penev, G. (2024a). Brexit and the Fintech revolution in Europe: Lessons from the Bulgarian Digital Finance Cluster. *Competitiveness Review, ahead-of-print No. ahead-of-print*. https://doi.org/10.1108/CR-07-2022-0108

Radev, D., & Penev, G. (2024b). The digital transformation of financial services: Evolution and competitiveness of Bulgaria's emerging Fintech cluster. In R. Beck, D. Fornahl, C. Ketels, & M. Kiese (Eds.), *Beyond innovation hotspots: Clusters for competitiveness and transformation in real regions*. Edward Elgar Publishing.

Sakarya, Ş., & Aksu, M. (2021). Fintech ecosystem in Turkey: An evaluation in terms of financial markets and financial stability. In S. Bozkuş Kahyaoğlu (Ed.), *The impact of artificial intelligence on governance, economics and finance, Volume I. Accounting, finance, sustainability, governance & fraud: Theory and application*. Springer. https://doi.org/10.1007/978-981-33-6811-8_2

The State of the Turkish Fintech Ecosystem Report. (2023). *Presidency of the Republic of Türkiye Finance Office İstanbul, Türkiye*. https://www.cbfo.gov.tr/sites/default/files/2024-08/the-state-of-fintech-ecosystem-in-turkiye-report.pdf

Strat, V. A., Radev, D., Pele, D. T., Chinie, C., Grosu, F., Darie, F. C., Mare, C., Damian, V., & Coita, I. (2024). *Fintech report Romania & Bulgaria*. Available at SSRN. https://ssrn.com/abstract=4821258

Truby, J., Brown, R., & Dahdal, A. (2020). Banking on AI: Mandating a proactive approach to AI regulation in the financial sector. *Law and Financial Markets Review, 14*(2), 110–120.

World Economic Forum. (2015). *The future of financial services*. https://www3.weforum.org/docs/WEF_The_future__of_financial_services.pdf

World Bank legislation summary page for Türkiye. Retrieved August 23, 2024. https://www.worldbank.org/en/topic/fintech/brief/global-fintech-enabling-regulations-database

A Bibliometric Analysis of Transparency AI in FinTech with Emphasis on Gender Dynamics

Joana Dias, Gonçalo Leitão, Bernardete Ribeiro, and Catarina Silva

Special emphasis is placed on gender dynamics, examining publication and collaboration patterns among researchers of different genders. By synthesizing existing literature, this work aims to offer detailed insights to inform strategic initiatives that address the evolving challenges and opportunities in the expanding field of Fintech AI applications.

J. Dias
Faculty of Economics and INESC Coimbra, University of Coimbra, Coimbra, Portugal
e-mail: joana@fe.uc.pt

G. Leitão · B. Ribeiro · C. Silva (✉)
CISUC/LASI, Department of Informatics Engineering, Faculty of Sciences and Technology, University of Coimbra, Coimbra, Portugal
e-mail: goncalomiguelleitao@gmail.com
e-mail: bribeiro@dei.uc.pt
e-mail: catarina@dei.uc.pt

J. Osterrieder et al. (eds.), *Transparency in FinTech*, Palgrave Studies in Financial Services Technology,
https://doi.org/10.1007/978-3-032-03523-3_9

1 Introduction

The financial technology (Fintech) sector has witnessed exponential growth in recent years, revolutionizing traditional banking and financial services. Fintech encompasses a wide range of innovative technologies and platforms aimed at enhancing financial processes, including payments, lending, investments, and insurance. This digital transformation has reshaped the financial landscape, fostering greater accessibility, efficiency, and convenience for consumers and businesses alike. However, alongside the proliferation of Fintech solutions, concerns have emerged regarding the ethical and societal implications of these technologies, particularly in areas such as data privacy, security, and transparency.

Artificial Intelligence (AI) plays a pivotal role in driving innovation within the Fintech industry, enabling advanced analytics, automation, and personalized services. AI-powered algorithms are increasingly utilized for tasks such as risk assessment, fraud detection, and customer service, offering unparalleled efficiency and accuracy. However, the opacity and complexity inherent in AI algorithms raise significant challenges in ensuring transparency, explainability, and accountability. As AI systems become more sophisticated and pervasive in financial decision-making, the need for transparency and interpretability becomes paramount to foster trust, mitigate risks, and uphold ethical standards. Achieving transparency in AI algorithms is essential not only for regulatory compliance but also for ensuring fairness, accountability, and user trust in Fintech applications.

Gender dynamics in machine learning are, therefore, crucial to prevent algorithms from perpetuating gender ideologies that disadvantage minorities and have hence been often studied Leavy et al. (2018). Nevertheless, an analysis of gender dynamics within the context of research in AI in Fintech is crucial for understanding and addressing potential biases, disparities, and opportunities that may exist in this research field. Despite advancements in gender equality, disparities persist in various domains, including research in technology and finance. It is known that the integration of AI in Fintech has the potential to either exacerbate or mitigate existing gender inequalities, depending on how it is developed, deployed, and regulated. The identification of existing biases and their respective implications in AI-driven Fintech is essential to promote inclusivity, diversity, and fairness.

In this work, we do not analyze the existence of gender bias within AI in Fintech outcomes, but we do analyze what seems to be happening in this research field through a comprehensive examination of gender-related patterns. By elucidating the gender dimensions of AI in Fintech research, we can identify opportunities for empowerment, innovation, and social impact, driving toward a more equitable and inclusive financial ecosystem.

To achieve these goals, this study adopts a bibliometric approach, leveraging quantitative analysis of scholarly literature to explore trends, patterns, and themes in Transparency AI in Fintech research, with a specific emphasis on gender dynamics. Through a systematic examination of publication outputs, authorship patterns, citation networks, and thematic content analysis, we aim to provide nuanced insights into the current state-of-the-art and identify opportunities for further research and innovation in this critical domain.

The rest of the paper is organized as follows. Section 2 presents the bibliometric methodology that was used in this work, detailing the proposed approach, including data sources, pre-processing, and data analysis. Section 5 discusses the results obtained. Finally, Sect. 6 concludes the paper with the conclusions and future lines of research.

2 Bibliometric Study

Bibliometric analysis is a tool that allows us to retrieve information from the vast amount of publication data that is available, specifically considering the authors and keywords of the existing publications. It can contribute to the understanding of a particular subject area, uncovering the main topics that are being researched, as well as pinpointing paths for future work that have not yet been explored. This analysis can detect leading research topics and identify topic clusters, offering crucial insights into the progression of the literature and highlighting both well-established and emerging areas within a field.

Although a bibliometric analysis does not have to follow a strict protocol and workflow as systematic reviews do, there are some good practices that should be followed. The workflow applied in this work is inspired by the PRISMA protocol, as depicted in Fig. 1.

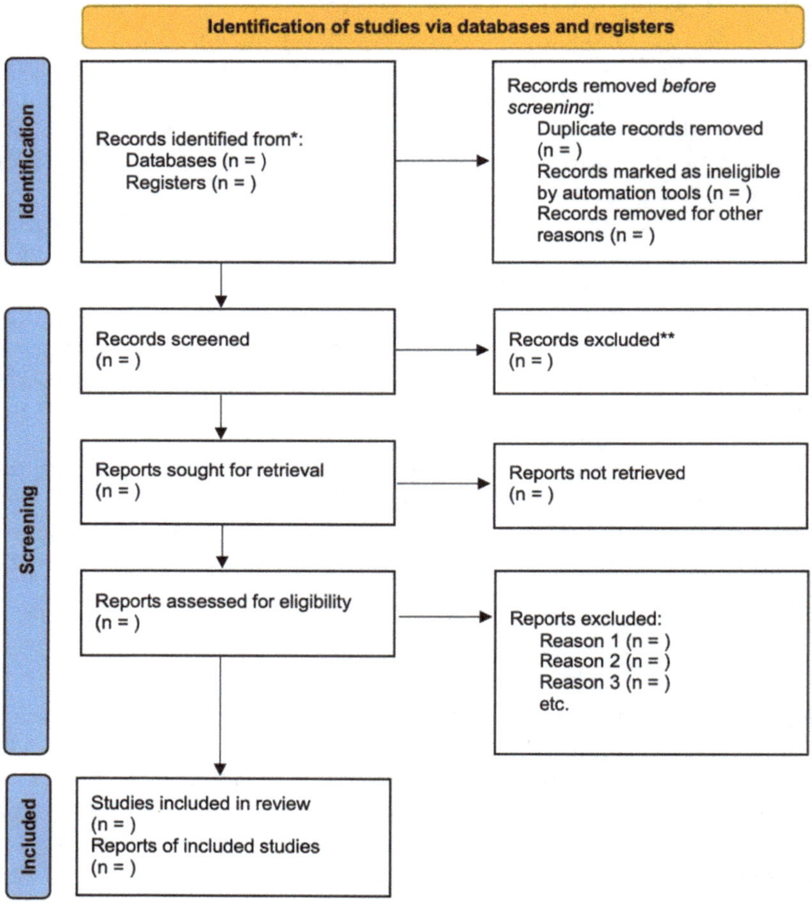

Fig. 1 Preferred reporting items for systematic reviews and meta-analyses (PRISMA) statement protocol Page et al. (2021)

2.1 *Data Source and Selection*

The bibliometric analysis conducted was based on data retrieved from the Scopus database on the 26th of November, 2023. A query was defined, and only the publications that complied with all the conditions established were further analyzed. The query used was as follows:

```
(
  TITLE-ABS-KEY(financ* OR fintech)
  AND TITLE-ABS-KEY((artificial AND intel*) OR (machine AND
   learn*)
    OR (AI) OR (ML))
  AND TITLE-ABS-KEY(ethics OR privacy OR explainability OR trans-
   parency OR trust OR responsible)
)
  AND PUBYEAR > 2016
  AND PUBYEAR < 2024
  AND (
    LIMIT-TO (DOCTYPE, "ar")
    OR LIMIT-TO (DOCTYPE, "cp")
)
```

This query defines that works published as journal articles or conference proceedings between 2016 and 2024 are being considered (notice that although the query was performed in 2023, there were already several works published with a date of 2024). These works must contain words that may be related to the topic of AI applied to finance, also considering ethical or explainability concerns. These words can appear in the title, abstract, or keywords. With this query, a total of 1284 publications were retrieved.

The abstracts of each and every publication retrieved were read by four different persons, who independently voted on whether that work should or should not be included in this analysis. The works to be included were those that were selected by at least 3 out of 4 possible votes. After this screening process, a total of 396 works were considered for further analysis.

The list of the total 1284 works and the 396 selected works, including Scopus links, can be accessed at https://bit.ly/papersGenderStudy, as including them in the bibliography of this paper is not feasible.

2.2 *Data Analysis*

After having selected the final set of publications, these data can be analyzed. There are different software tools available for performing this analysis and visual representation of the data. In this work, VOSviewer[1] was chosen Eck and Waltman (2010). This is a software tool that enables the creation, visualization, and exploration of bibliometric networks and has gained significant popularity for analyzing and reviewing academic research, being extensively used in recent years in different scientific areas. The use of VOSviewer was complemented by the use of Gephi[2], for better visualization and cluster identification, as well as for the calculation of some network measures.

2.3 *Results*

Two main analyses were first conducted based on the co-occurrence of keywords and considering the authors' connection network.

I. Keyword Co-occurrence

Figure 2 presents the keyword co-occurrence network. This is a visual representation of how often pairs of keywords appear together in a set of academic publications. The co-keyword analysis provides valuable insights by identifying the most popular, trending, and dominant research paths in the field. In this analysis, the content of publications is examined, assuming that frequently co-occurring keywords share a thematic relationship. This helps visualize the interconnections among different research topics and identify relationships and patterns within a research field by highlighting frequently co-occurring terms. To delve deeply into the analysis of this network, it is possible to identify and independently visualize the clusters that are revealed (see Fig. 3).

Cluster 1: Ethical and Transparent AI/ML in Fintech Decision-Making

This cluster considers works that are focused on AI/ML applications in financial institutions, where there is an increasingly critical need for transparency and ethical practices. Decisions made by these models, particularly in risk assessment and credit scoring, must be transparent and justifiable. This is crucial for maintaining the trust of stakeholders and complying with regulatory standards. The emphasis on decision-making within this cluster highlights the transformative impact of machine learning on

[1] https://www.vosviewer.com.

[2] https://gephi.org.

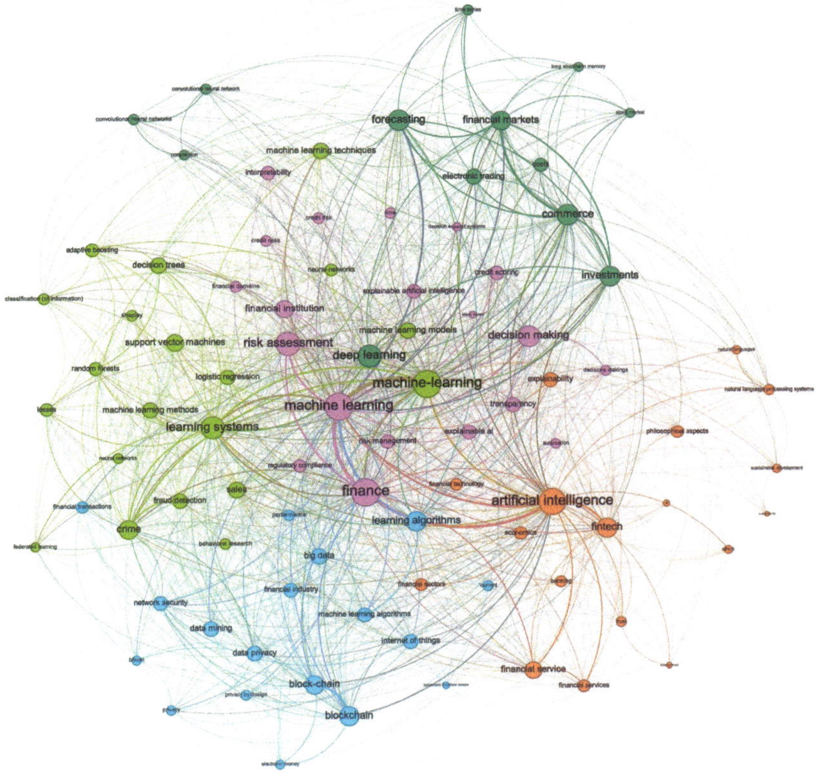

Fig. 2 Keyword co-occurrence network

traditional financial practices. It also points to the ethical implications of automated decision systems, where biases and inaccuracies can have significant repercussions. Therefore, ensuring that machine learning models are interpretable is essential for ethical decision-making, fostering fairness, and preventing discrimination.

Cluster 2: Advanced AI/ML Methods for Fintech Security and Compliance
This cluster seems to be the most technical one, as it showcases a myriad of different AI/ML methods that are being used in this field. These methods are employed to enhance various applications within the financial sector,

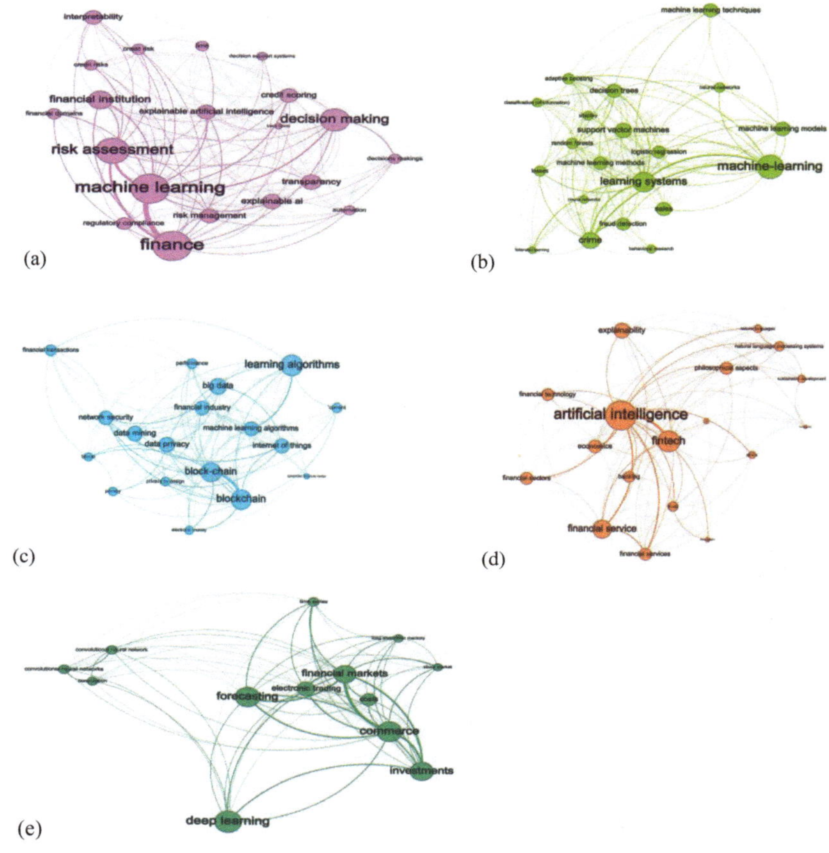

Fig. 3 Clusters representation. **a** Cluster 1: Ethical and transparent AI/ML in Fintech decision making. **b** Cluster 2: Advanced AI/ML methods for Fintech security and compliance. **c** Cluster 3: Innovations in secure and transparent digital Fintech. **d** Cluster 4: Interdisciplinary perspectives on ethical AI in Fintech. **e** Cluster 5: Advanced AI for Fintech forecasting and optimization

particularly highlighting their role in improving crime and fraud detection, indicating a broader interest in utilizing these technologies to safeguard financial systems, ensure ethical practices, and maintain trust and compliance. It is also interesting to note the different levels of explainability that may be associated with these various models and methods, and the improved outcomes that may be achieved from their complementary and ensemble use, particularly regarding the compromise between accuracy and interpretability.

Cluster 3: Innovations in Secure and Transparent Digital Fintech
This cluster is defined by keywords such as blockchain, data privacy, network security, financial transactions, big data, and electronic money. It focuses on the intersection of technology and finance, particularly considering digital currencies and secure financial transactions. This cluster suggests research aimed at exploring the use of decentralized ledger technology for secure and transparent financial transactions, addressing concerns and advancements in protecting personal and financial data in digital transactions. There has been research dedicated to developing methods and protocols to safeguard financial networks from cyber threats and attacks that must be efficient and able to guarantee reliability in digital financial transactions but, at the same time, also need to guarantee transparency. Overall, this cluster is composed of research fields that seek to innovate and secure digital financial systems while addressing concerns related to privacy, security, and the efficient management of financial transactions.

Cluster 4: Interdisciplinary Perspectives on Ethical AI in Fintech
This cluster features keywords such as artificial intelligence, philosophical aspects, natural language processing, explainability, financial services, and economics. This cluster considers works that present an interdisciplinary focus on the integration of AI in the financial sector, examining the ethical and philosophical implications of using AI in finance, discussing the morality of AI decisions, the impact of AI on employment in the financial sector, and the broader societal implications of AI-driven financial systems.

The interaction of these developments with human decision-makers is a crucial aspect of this cluster, considering, among other things, the use of natural language processing systems. Ensuring that AI systems are explainable and transparent helps build trust and allows humans to understand and validate AI-driven decisions. Addressing ethical and philosophical questions helps align AI developments with societal values, ensuring that technological advancements benefit humanity while mitigating potential negative consequences. This comprehensive approach underscores the importance of considering both technological and human factors in the evolution of AI in financial services.

Cluster 5: Advanced AI for Fintech Forecasting and Optimization
Overall, this cluster considers the use of AI, particularly deep learning and neural networks, in forecasting and optimizing financial activities, namely time series. It reflects ongoing efforts to apply different advanced technologies to improve investment strategies, specifically through better market analysis. The main focus is the application of advanced AI and machine learning techniques to predict and optimize financial and commercial activities. These technologies are capable of analyzing complex and vast datasets, enabling more accurate predictions of market trends, stock prices, and investment opportunities. By processing historical time series data, neural networks can identify patterns and make informed forecasts about future market movements, aiding investors in making strategic decisions. These advancements aim to increase efficiency, reduce risks, and maximize returns in financial markets.

II. Evaluation metrics
To enrich the outcomes of the co-keyword analysis, we evaluated several network metrics that provide a more nuanced understanding of the importance of research components beyond what is captured by publications or citations alone. The metrics analyzed using Gephi were as follows:

- **Average degree**: The degree of a node represents the number of direct connections it has with other nodes in the network. In our analysis, the average degree is 40.045. This indicates that, on average, each keyword is connected to approximately 40 other keywords, suggesting a strong level of interconnection among topics.
- **Average weighted degree**: The weighted degree takes into account not only the number of connections but also the strength or frequency of these connections. The average weighted degree of our network is 103.528, revealing that some nodes have significantly more robust connections than others. This metric highlights the varying importance of relationships between keywords based on their co-occurrence in the documents.
- **Eigenvector centrality**: Eigenvector centrality measures the influence of a node based on its connections and those of its neighbors. A higher eigenvector centrality score indicates greater importance

within the network, as the node is linked to other highly connected nodes. In our network, most keywords have eigenvector centrality scores close to 1, signifying that they each play a significant role in transmitting information to other prominent keywords.

III. Authors' Collaboration

This analysis was also complemented by examining the authors' collaboration network. This is a network that maps out and analyzes the collaborative relationships between researchers (Fig. 4). Each node represents an individual author, while each edge between nodes signifies a co-authorship relationship, indicating that the connected authors have worked together on one or more publications. The nodes are labeled with the names or identifiers of the authors, and the edges represent their collaborative relationships. Analyzing authors' collaboration networks can serve multiple purposes. It helps in identifying key researchers who are central to the field, understanding collaboration patterns, and evaluating the impact of research based on collaborative connections. Additionally, these networks facilitate networking and collaboration by providing insights into potential partners and research groups. The average degree of the network is under 2 (1.807), with a weighted degree of 2.434.

IV. Gender Dynamics

In the analysis of the authors' network, gender analysis was also conducted. For each publication, the gender of the first author was identified. To streamline this process, ChatGPT[3] was employed to automatically categorize the gender of each first author as Female, Male, or Undetermined. In cases where ChatGPT was unable to determine the gender—accounting for only 15% of instances—a manual search was performed to accurately identify it. Ultimately, 69% of the first authors were identified as men, while 31% were identified as women.

Figure 5 presents the two co-keyword networks generated, considering the works with a first author who is either a woman or a man, respectively.

The most prominent keywords, such as "machine learning" and "finance," are central to both networks. These keywords are connected with many other topics, indicating their critical importance in Fintech

[3] https://chatgpt.com/.

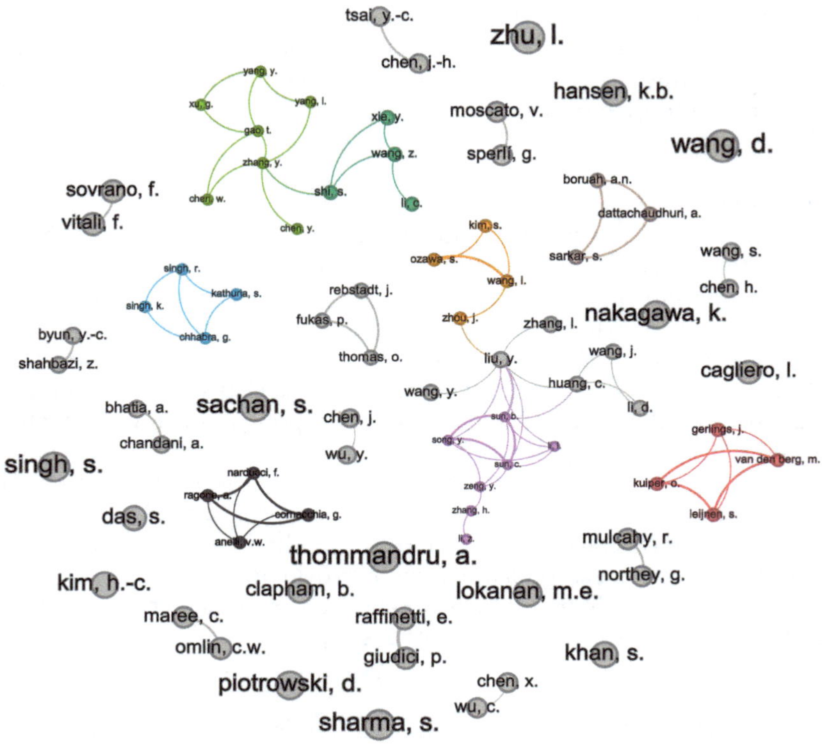

Fig. 4 Authors collaboration network

research. The male-authored network presents a central cluster of highly interconnected keywords with a clear emphasis on machine learning and finance, indicating strong integration of these themes in their research. The female-authored network shows less dense and more spread-out clustering. The network is more fragmented, with fewer interconnections, implying a more diverse set of research topics. There is a special interest in decision-making aspects within Fintech.

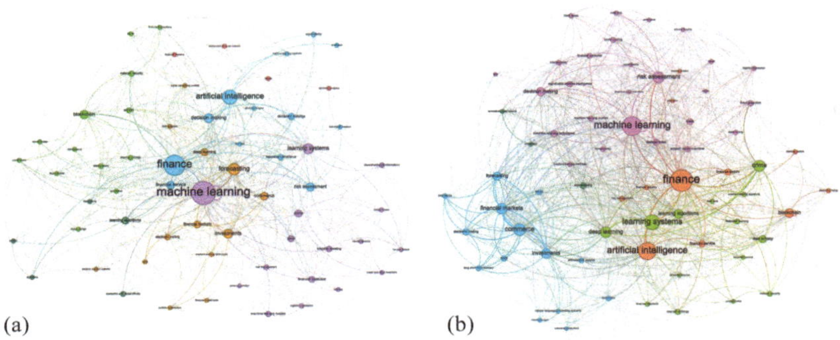

Fig. 5 Keyword co-occurrence with gender dynamics. **a** First author is a woman. **b** First author is a man

3 Discussion of Results

Regarding the co-occurrence of keywords and the clusters identified, there seem to be some gaps in the existing literature that could represent interesting future research opportunities. It appears there is a lack of comprehensive standards and guidelines for ethical AI use in finance. Individual efforts have been put into place, but specific guidelines do not seem to exist. It is also of paramount importance to understand the implications of initiatives like the EU AI Act in Fintech. The EU AI Act represents a significant step toward establishing comprehensive guidelines for the ethical and transparent use of AI in general, and in Fintech in particular. By addressing key research gaps and promoting standardization, transparency, and ethical considerations, the Act provides a robust framework for future developments in the field. Another interesting gap seems to be research that explicitly considers the legal implications of AI in Fintech. The legal implications related to transparency, equity, and fairness in Fintech are expected to become increasingly significant as the industry continues to grow and innovate. Fintech companies must be required to provide clear and accessible information about their services, data usage, and decision-making processes. How this transparency can be defined by law, and how law can contribute to equity and fairness, should also be central concerns for research in this area, requiring interdisciplinary research teams.

It also seems that there is an insufficient research effort on the long-term societal impacts of AI-driven financial decisions. This may be caused by the fact that it is a rather new research topic. It would be important to study the impact of AI in Fintech on individual lives, as well as on employment and societal structures.

There appears to be a significant gap in integrating blockchain technology with traditional financial systems, particularly in terms of harmonizing these decentralized solutions with established financial infrastructure. Additionally, the potential for combining AI with classical portfolio optimization methods, such as those derived from the seminal work of Markowitz, has not been sufficiently explored. This integration could offer new insights and enhancements to investment strategies and represent a step toward greater transparency.

Analyzing the authors' network reveals a clear need for greater collaboration and integration among researchers. Although there are several active research groups in this field, the current level of integration and cooperation is relatively low, as evidenced by the existing publications. This suggests that, while researchers are engaged individually or in small teams, there is substantial room for improvement in collaborative efforts and joint initiatives to advance the field more effectively. Overall, while there is active and interconnected research in Fintech with contributions from both genders, there is a noticeable gender imbalance. Male authors dominate and are more central in key research areas, suggesting an opportunity to increase diversity and promote more female participation and leadership in Fintech research. This could lead to a more balanced and inclusive research community, fostering diverse perspectives and innovations in the field.

4 Conclusions and Future Work

This bibliometric analysis reveals that the field of AI in Fintech is still developing and lacks maturity. While many researchers are engaged in important work, including research on transparency and ethics, the research community remains fragmented. There is also a noticeable absence of integration between AI and established methodologies that have long been used in the financial sector. Combining AI with these traditional approaches could enhance model transparency and decision interpretability, which is crucial given the significant impact AI in finance has on our daily lives. There is also a clear gender imbalance in terms of female versus male researchers working on these matters. It would be interesting to investigate whether this imbalance has any impact on research outcomes.

Acknowledgements The author acknowledges the support and research collaboration of the COST Action 19130—Fintech and Artificial Intelligence in Finance. This work is partially financed through national funds by FCT—Fundação para a Ciência e a Tecnologia, I.P., in the framework of the Project UIDB/00326/2025 and UIDP/00326/2025, and by FCT—Fundação para a Ciência e a Tecnologia, I.P., in the framework of the Project UIDB/00326/2025, UIDP/00326/2025, UIDB/00308/2020.

References

Eck, N. J. V., & Waltman, L. (2010). Software survey: Vosviewer, a computer program for bibliometric mapping. *Scientometrics*, *84*(2), 523–538.

Leavy, S.: Gender bias in artificial intelligence: The need for diversity and gender theory in machine learning. In *2018 IEEE/ACM 1st International workshop on gender equality in software engineering (GE)* (pp. 14–16).

Page, M. J., McKenzie, J. E., Bossuyt, P. M., Boutron, I., Hoffmann, T. C., Mulrow, C. D., Shamseer, L., Tetzlaff, J. M., Akl, E. A., Brennan, S. E., Chou, R., Glanville, J., Grimshaw, J. M., Hr´objartsson, A., Lalu, M. M., Li, T., Loder, E. W., Mayo-Wilson, E., McDonald, S., & Moher, D. (2021). The prisma 2020 statement: An updated guideline for reporting systematic reviews. *BMJ (Clinical Research Ed.)*, *372*(71). https://doi.org/10.1136/bmj.n71

PART IV

The Role of Transparency in Promoting Financial Inclusion

Transparency and Financial Inclusion in Central Eastern European Countries: A Path to Economic Empowerment

Albulena Shala, Rezarta Perri, Maria Iannario, and Claudia Tarantola

Compared to Western and Northern Europe, South Eastern European Countries (SEECs) exhibit lower levels of banking penetration, digital payment adoption, and access to financial services, making them a particularly relevant case study for analyzing financial inclusion dynamics. Moreover, these countries display heterogeneous financial

A. Shala (✉)
Faculty of Economics, Univeristy of Pristina, Prishtinë, Kosovo
e-mail: albulena.shala@uni-pr.edu

R. Perri
Economic Faculty, Unveristy of Tirana, Tirana, Albania
e-mail: rezartaperri@feut.edu.al

M. Iannario
University of Naples Federico II, Naples, Italy
e-mail: maria.iannario@unina.it

C. Tarantola
Università degli Studi di Milano, Milan, Italy
e-mail: claudia.tarantola@unimi.it

J. Osterrieder et al. (eds.), *Transparency in FinTech*, Palgrave Studies in Financial Services Technology,
https://doi.org/10.1007/978-3-032-03523-3_10

infrastructures, with some nations (e.g., Bulgaria, Croatia) showing strong progress, while others (e.g., Serbia, Montenegro) still facing barriers to financial accessibility.

Examining CEECs allows us to capture the diverse trajectories of financial inclusion and the effectiveness of different policy measures. CEECs are also experiencing a shift from traditional banking to digital finance. This makes them a useful place to study factors such as the number of ATMs and points of sale, how people save money, and the transition from traditional banking to digital finance, and how these elements affect new financial systems. Understanding these trends can provide valuable insights into strategies for promoting financial inclusion in other developing and transitioning economies.

1 Introduction

Financial inclusion promotes economic growth, financial development, and inclusivity. It improves access to financial services for the poor, which can help reduce poverty and income inequality. Recently, there have been numerous policy initiatives aimed at promoting financial inclusion. For instance, the World Bank has made the Global Financial Inclusion (Global Findex) a comprehensive database available to evaluate and track the progress of financial inclusion across member nations. Additionally, the Alliance for Financial Inclusion was established in 2008 as a network of policymakers dedicated to improving financial inclusion strategies in developing and emerging market economies. Research by Allen et al. (2014) and Demirgüç-Kunt et al. (2008) indicates that having a bank account increases savings, empowers women, boosts household consumption, and fosters productive investments.

Financial inclusion (FI) has gained prominence in recent years as a crucial component of global sustainable development. Access to financial services impacts economic opportunities, particularly for the poor, because it enables them to save, invest, and take advantage of credit (Subbarao, 2009). The majority of individuals now have access to formal financial services, which has improved the economy and the financial system's overall efficiency. However, as the majority of developing nations lack access to financial services, these advantages are only available to industrialized countries.

Access to finance, according to proponents of financial inclusion, must be improved to achieve inclusive growth and development (World Bank, 2014).

However, there is growing disapproval of the idea that financial inclusion is merely a new label for microfinance, whose efficacy in reducing poverty is increasingly being questioned (Mader, 2018). The narrative that emphasizes individual access to financial services and entrepreneurship as a means of escaping poverty is challenged by opponents of financial inclusion (Bateman & Chang, 2012). They also dispute the generalization that there is a direct link between financial inclusion and reduced poverty and inequality (Mader, 2018).

The literature widely agrees on the necessity of approaching FI as a multidimensional concept; however, there is less consensus regarding its primary dimensions. While there is broad agreement in the literature that composite indices offer a comprehensive approach to measuring FI, there is no agreement on the most effective way to do so. FI is widely seen as a crucial factor in determining a nation's economic development. As a result, it is now the focus of economic policymaking on a global scale, and because of this, more academics and decision-makers are becoming interested in it.

This chapter makes significant contributions to the literature. The purpose of this chapter is to evaluate the financial inclusion and transparency of Central and Southern European countries (CEECs). However, since many of the indicators presented in the literature to measure financial inclusion are not found in the main databases, we are limited to using a small number of indicators.

2 Literature Review

A growing body of research demonstrates how inclusive financial markets lower rates of poverty and inequality by enabling people to control their spending, obtain bank loans, and purchase insurance (Mader, 2018). Additionally, financial inclusion fosters the growth of both new and existing innovative businesses, generating jobs that boost national savings (Ajide, 2020). Finally, financial inclusion improves the economic empowerment of youth, women, and other previously excluded groups, as well as their active engagement in the financial system (Hendriks, 2019).

The research on financial inclusion can be broadly divided into two groups. Using field studies, the first strand examines the effects and determinants of financial inclusion on individuals and households. For instance, Brune et al. (2011) demonstrate how improved financial access through commitment savings accounts in rural areas of Malawi benefits poor households. These households could keep their savings for agricultural inputs, creating access to funds for lean times, and, as a result, their well-being was improved. According to Allen et al. (2014), commercial banks can increase access to finance for people in Kenya by targeting underprivileged households. The second strand is more concerned with global patterns and the effects of financial inclusion across countries. Honohan (2008) discovered that country-specific structural factors are important for financial access. Macroeconomic-level studies use country-level panel data comparisons to show the general relationship between financial inclusion, economic growth, and employment. Financial inclusion, according to Sarma (2008), is the process of ensuring that all participants in an economy can access and easily use formal financial institutions. Financial inclusion ensures that people, households, and businesses in a community have sufficient access to formal financial services and products such as transactions, credit cards, payments, savings, and insurance, and that these are provided sustainably. Singh and Singh Kondan (2011) define financial inclusion. Joshi (2014) mention that there is no universally accepted definition of financial inclusion; it is the process of ensuring that people have simple access to and use financial services from formal financial institutions in a timely, adequate, and low-cost manner, particularly for the financially disadvantaged group. According to the World Bank (2014), financial inclusion (FI) refers to people and businesses having access to reasonably priced financial goods and services that satisfy their requirements and are implemented in a way that is ethical and long-lasting.

In academic literature, the concepts of "financial inclusion" and "financial exclusion" are frequently discussed. Financial exclusion, as defined by Wilson (2012) and Buckland (2012), is characterized as a lack of access to financial services. Exclusion is influenced by factors like location, the cost of services, and the degree of knowledge one has about the advantages of financial services. Financial exclusion is the result of people or groups in a community having limited access to formal financial services for a variety of potentially discriminatory reasons (Sinclair, 2001). Beck and De La Torre (2006) highlight that an underdeveloped financial system can impose high costs on individuals seeking financial services, posing challenges to economic growth and the financial inclusion of certain societal groups.

Conversely, an inclusive financial system aims to maximize access and usage while minimizing involuntary exclusions (Cámara & Tuesta, 2014).

The distinction between voluntary and involuntary financial exclusion must also be made. Voluntary exclusion, according to the World Bank (2014), is a situation in which a section of the population or a company chooses not to use financial services, either because they don't need them or due to cultural or religious reasons. In contrast, involuntary exclusion results from low income, a high-risk profile brought on by prejudice, and flaws and faults in the financial system. Since it may be addressed with suitable economic programs and policies to enhance income and repair market failures and defects, this involuntary factor, which is seen as a barrier to financial inclusion, requires policy and research activities.

Developing nations are formulating strategies to enhance literacy, reduce gender discrimination, and create suitable employment opportunities. Financial inclusion would positively affect this aspect. For instance, Atkinson and Messy (2013) argue that fiscal strategy methods and policies can help to lessen discrimination in the world of finance. This necessitates modifications to the financial level of the policy framework. Anti-discrimination laws have the potential to benefit disadvantaged populations and advance economic growth.

Grohmann et al. (2018) and Wang and Guan (2017) both conducted studies that found formal financial services were more inclusive in families led by men. They identified that men were more likely to have access to or use formal financial services, whereas women, particularly in certain cultural and socioeconomic contexts, faced barriers such as gender discrimination, limited access to financial education, and lower levels of financial literacy.

This finding ties into broader discussions about gender inequality in financial inclusion and the need for targeted policies and programs to address these disparities. For example, promoting financial literacy and reducing structural barriers for women can help improve financial inclusion and empower women in various economic contexts.

In a separate study, Sarma (2012) used data from the Global Financial Inclusion (Global Findex) database of the World Bank to show the positive and significant correlation between development and financial inclusion. Sarma (2012) studied socioeconomic variables like income, literacy, and urbanization to demonstrate that the growth of the financial and banking sectors is closely tied to financial inclusion. The study revealed a close association between the Human Development Index and the financial inclusion index. As demonstrated by Demirgüç-Kunt and Klapper (2013), income and education are two essential factors for gaining access to financial services. This is further supported by the proposal of Kairiza et al. (2017), which asserts a significant correlation between financial inclusion and factors including literacy, population, and income.

According to Bruhn and Love (2014), the usage of formal financial services by the poor can also be referred to as financial inclusion. Financial inclusion refers to expanding the number of (usually poor) people who have access to formal financial services, primarily through holding formal bank accounts, which helps to reduce poverty and promote economic growth. An inclusive financial system is desirable and will provide opportunities for all people, particularly the poor, to access and move funds, grow capital, and reduce risk. Improving financial inclusion helps reduce poverty and promote economic growth by empowering individuals who were previously excluded from the formal financial system. With access to financial services, people can invest in education, build savings, and start businesses. These opportunities allow them to improve their economic well-being, create wealth, and contribute to broader societal growth. Financial inclusion also fosters entrepreneurship, which drives innovation and job creation, creating a positive feedback loop for economic development.

For households in poverty, financial inclusion has various advantages. Financial inclusion benefits the banking industry by lowering the risk of procyclicality. For example, if financial inclusion were to significantly increase the number of small savers, banks' deposit bases would grow and remain stable, reducing their reliance on "non-core" financing, which is more volatile during crises (Khan, 2011). It enables people with modest incomes to save for the future, which promotes financial stability and encourages a high level of use of bank deposits, which helps secure a more solid deposit base for banks during difficult times (Han & Melecky, 2013).

Additionally, expanding financial inclusion offers low-income households opportunities to save, invest, and access credit (Ellis et al., 2010). Moreover, since low-income populations are relatively resistant to economic cycles, incorporating them into the financial sector enhances the stability of deposit and loan bases. Higher levels of financial inclusion encourage greater participation of various economic sectors in the formal financial system. As the formal sector's share increases, the effectiveness of using interest rates as a primary tool for macroeconomic stability is strengthened, benefiting economic growth (Cecchetti & Kharroubi, 2012).

According to Dev (2006), when self-help organizations and microfinance institutions join inclusion programs, financial inclusion can be seen as both a commercial opportunity and a social obligation because these two actors are crucial to improving financial inclusion. Using information gathered from bank regulators, Beck et al. (2007) were among the first to assess the inclusiveness of financial systems. The number of bank branches and ATMs per person and per square kilometer, the number of deposit and loan accounts per person, and the average size of deposits and loans relative to Gross Domestic Product (GDP) per capita are key indicators used to assess access to and usage of banking services. These metrics were developed to provide a comprehensive view of financial inclusion across 99 countries, offering valuable insights into the availability, accessibility, and utilization of banking services globally. As a result, the authors created new indicators of bank access, such as dimensions of access and usage of financial services for three types of services, including deposits, loans, and payments.

Measures of financial inclusion can vary from study to study, depending on the specific context, objectives, and methodologies employed. This variability highlights the importance of creating a shared body of literature and standardized indicators that enable cross-country and cross-study comparisons. A common framework would ensure consistency, improve the comparability of findings, and facilitate the development of policies that are more targeted and effective in promoting financial inclusion. Establishing such a shared understanding is crucial for advancing research and informing policymakers aiming to address financial disparities and promote sustainable economic development. For instance, Honohan (2008) developed a financial access indicator that measures only one aspect of financial inclusion—the proportion of the adult population in each economy who has access to formal financial intermediaries. For economies where financial access statistics are available, this composite financial access index was created using household survey data. Additionally, Sarma (2008), followed by Sarma and Pais (2011), created an indicator of financial inclusion. Financial inclusion is described as "a process that ensures the accessibility, availability, and utilization of the formal financial system for all members of an economy" (Sarma, 2008, p. 5; Sarma & Pais, 2011, p. 13). Their normalized index converts data on the availability, use, and accessibility of banking services into a single number between 0 and 1, with 0 denoting total financial exclusion and 1 denoting total inclusion. Amidžic et al. (2014) developed a financial inclusion indicator that was a composite of variables from various dimensions, including outreach (geographic and demographic penetration), usage (deposits and lending), and quality (disclosure requirement, dispute resolution, and cost of usage). Each measure is first normalized, statistically identified for each dimension, and then aggregated using statistical weights, with the aggregated value being calculated after a weighted geometric mean.

Also, it has been widely accepted to use mobile phone penetration as a stand-in for mobile banking when measuring financial inclusion (Chauvet & Jacolin, 2017). In light of this, mobile money accounts have developed into a crucial tool for carrying out financial transactions for many households in developing nations (Mehrotra & Nathanael, 2016). In earlier studies, the financial inclusion index was solely produced by considering financial services associated with banking. However, other financial services, such as insurance, pensions, and offerings from microfinance, financial institutions, and fintech, have also received recent attention in the financial inclusion space.

The concept is more broadly defined in more recent definitions, which take into account the use, cost, and quality of financial services in addition to access to formal financial institutions (see Allen et al., 2016, Demirgüç-Kunt et al., 2017). The "access" dimension in these multifaceted definitions of financial inclusion refers to the availability or potential use of financial services, whereas the "use" dimension refers to the actual usage of such services (Beck et al., 2007). Typically, the "cost" component of financial inclusion is defined as including both financial and non-financial costs associated with using and accessing financial services, such as bank fees or proximity (Arora, 2010). Finally, the "quality" component evaluates how well consumers are informed and protected, as well as whether financial services are meeting their demands (Mialou et al., 2017). For some, increasing access to a variety of financial services, such as insurance, pensions, and securities markets, constitutes financial inclusion (World Bank, 2014). However, because financial inclusion (FI) is a multidimensional concept, it cannot be effectively measured by simple measures like bank account ratios or the number of ATMs (Cámara & Tuesta, 2014). The most commonly utilized indicators are the number of bank branches, ATMs, bank credit, and bank deposits. However, after the global financial crisis of 2007, world leaders and politicians rethought their approach and realized that continued FI development is crucial. Consequently, as policymakers' awareness of the significance of FI has grown, so too has their attention turned to FI measurement. Researchers occasionally develop different measures.

The International Monetary Fund and the World Bank, in particular, have been in charge of data collection operations on a global scale. The World Bank's Financial Inclusion dataset (Global Findex), which provides individual-level data on the use of financial services in 148 countries; the International Monetary Fund's Financial Access Survey, which provides aggregate data on the supply of and access to financial services for 189 countries; and the World Bank's Enterprise Survey, which provides firm-level data, are three of the most significant international data sources on financial inclusion.

3 Methodology

As the objective of this study is to analyze transparency and financial inclusion with a focus on the CEEC, we adopt a methodological approach focusing on documentation review and secondary resource analysis. We use comparative data analysis across CEE countries over a number of years, with a particular emphasis on indicators pertaining to banking systems, financial inclusion, and financial infrastructure. Among the important data points included in this analysis are:

1. ATM Density (ATMs per 100,000 adults): This measures the dispersion and availability of automated teller machines (ATMs), which is a sign of how easily accessible banking services are.
2. Branch Density: This metric, which counts the number of physical bank branches per 100,000 adults, provides information about the structure of traditional banking and how it has evolved in response to trends in digital banking.
3. Usage of Debit Cards (per 1000 adults): This indicates the use of debit cards as a payment mechanism, which may signify a transition from cash-based to electronic payment systems.
4. POS Terminal Density (per 100,000 adults): This measure indicates how many point-of-sale (POS) terminals are available, serving as a sign of how widely card payment systems are utilized in the retail and service sectors.
5. Savings at Financial Institutions (percentage of population aged 15 and over): This statistic shows the proportion of adults who save at

official financial institutions, which is a sign of financial inclusion and the growth of financial systems.

6. Transparency Index: The T-Index, which represents the accessibility of public data in every country, reflects computer-mediated transparency. By displaying the information that governments have agreed to share (de jure) and the amount they actually share (de facto), it accomplishes this. The above data points have been accessed via open-source databases published mainly by the World Bank.

4 Results

The following tables present data sourced from the World Bank open-source datasets. According to the data in Table 1, the number of ATMs per 100,000 adults varies by area, with the Baltic States showing a decline and Southeastern European countries often having larger numbers. While the decrease in some countries might be caused by the growing use of digital and mobile banking options, the rise in others most likely reflects the development of banking infrastructure and a move toward broader financial inclusion. The availability of ATMs tends to increase across southern and southeastern Europe (such as Croatia, Montenegro, North Macedonia, Bosnia, and Serbia), which may reflect these countries' expanding economies and financial inclusion.

Compared to its regional competitors, Croatia has one of the highest rates of ATMs per 100,000 adults. A robust ATM network is indicated by the comparatively high numbers of ATMs in Bulgaria and Romania, which exceed 90 per 100,000 adult population. With comparatively low rates, Serbia and Albania are at the lower end of the spectrum, which may indicate a greater reliance on non-ATM channels or less access to banking infrastructure.

The countries with the largest declines in branch counts are those with the highest adoption rates of digital banking: Estonia, Lithuania, and Bulgaria. In contrast, countries like Montenegro and North Macedonia exhibit more gradual or stable changes, which may indicate either a delayed adoption of digital banking or a preference for maintaining traditional banking services (Table 2).

Despite a decline from 59.82 branches per 100,000 individuals in 2011 to 50.87 branches in 2017, Bulgaria still has one of the highest numbers of

Table 1 ATMs per 100,000 adults

Country/ Years	*2012*	*2013*	*2014*	*2015*	*2016*	*2017*	*2018*	*2019*	*2020*	*2021*	*2022*
Albania	35.68	35.31	34.55	34.98	33.81	31.47	31.71	30.64	29.99	31.42	…
Bulgaria	92.8	93.43	92.98	92.42	95.7	95.13	94.67	93.4	94.33	91.36	…
Bosnia and H.	41.56	44.61	46.84	49.9	50.12	51.1	53.89	55.84	58.24	58.02	…
Czechia	45.71	49.06	49.6	50.87	52.65	55.65	55.64	57.1	57.98	57.17	…
Estonia	83.59	79.56	76.7	72.61	70.01	67.99	67.77	67.92	65.68	64.6	…
Croatia	113	114.12	117.08	123.4	127.81	140.38	140.01	147.31	156.8	141.54	…
Hungary	56.49	57.13	57.84	57.25	59.43	60.94	60.93	60.56	60.94	59.96	…
Lithuania	51.83	49.88	51.19	49.01	48.27	46.75	46.69	46.93	38.5	37.84	30
Latvia	72.94	68.53	62.9	63.04	61.29	61.88	61.96	61.34	58.25	57.42	57.87
North Macedonia	49.65	54.05	55.6	60.67	59.99	59.41	59.63	60	59.96	57.13	56.69
Montenegro	69.6	71.56	70.94	76.09	77.85	80.83	80.98	87.05	81.12	81.7	77.06
Poland	56.27	58.35	63.46	68.49	…	…	71.87	70.92	70.51	67.94	66.82
Romania	64.96	63.84	65.07	68.57	66.69	66.69	66.83	64.71	64.39	62.79	…
Serbia	46.6	44.89	44.36	45.75	50.66	45.77	30.68	31.55	31.7	31.65	31.21
Slovak Republic	54.7	56.22	58.93	59.52	60.11	60.69	71.87	70.92	70.51	67.94	66.82
Slovenia	101.56	100.74	96.05	95.4	95.28	93.66	35.74	34.31	33.53	30.78	31.03
Kosovo	35.68	36.26	36.45	39.97	38.33	36.01	36.01	35.32	33.86	34.95	…

Source World Bank

Table 2 Branches per 100,000 adults

Country	*2012*	*2013*	*2014*	*2015*	*2016*	*2017*	*2018*	*2019*	*2020*	*2021*
Albania	24.02	23.41	21.94	21.85	21.51	20.56	19.536	18.706	18.607	...
Bulgaria	61.15	60.58	60.21	60.14	48.39	50.87	52.80	57.89	60.25	...
Bosnia and H.	31.75	32.45	33.31	30.42	28.94	28.32	30.53	30.01	29.92	29.85
Czechia	23.84	24.3	24.22	23.69	22.36	21.29	21.26	20.57	18.30	...
Estonia	16.02	13.95	12.39	11.15	10.43	10.09	9.68	8.93	7.92	...
Croatia	35.62	34.65	33.91	33.6	32.83	32.5	30.05	28.36	27.09	26.84
Hungary	16.08	15.41	15.5	15.13	14.71	14.64	14.20	23.42	23.36	...
Lithuania	19.27	18.08	16.24	14.55	13.45	13.62	11.45	10.08	10.46	11.18
Latvia	24.64	21.6	20.4	18.05	17.1	16.45	14.70	9.74	7.05	6.64
North Macedonia	24.65	24.76	24.87	24.69	25	25.64	24.23	24.19	23.23	22.42
Montenegro	40.56	42.42	41.89	42.97	44.24	43.56	43.62	40.85	38.10	25.75
Poland	33.97	32.98	32.96	31.14	31.02	29.29	29.73	28.95	25.76	23.21
Romania	33.16	31.61	30.72	28.68	27.98	26.63	25.58	23.66	22.56	...
Serbia	38.07	33.91	30.6	29.77	29.72	28.23	17.94	17.38	16.61	15.45
Slovak Republic	26.63	26.9	27.99	28.27	28.26	26.91	25.60	24.81	23.32	...
Slovenia	38.49	34.45	31.85	31.19	30.64	29.47	10.68	10.57	9.54	8.79
Kosovo	22.9	21.79	20.28	20.35	19.97	16.74	16.16	15.47	15.13	...

Source World Bank

branches. This may reflect a more extensive or traditional banking system. As one of the most advanced countries in terms of digital banking services, Estonia has one of the lowest numbers of bank branches, with just 10.09 branches per 100,000 individuals in 2017.

According to Table 3, debit cards are becoming more and more popular in the majority of the nations on the list, with substantial rises in Albania, Kosovo, and Estonia. Debit card usage is still strong in countries like Latvia and Bulgaria, despite small reductions, suggesting that these nations have already attained rather high penetration levels. In the meantime, nations like Lithuania, Romania, and Montenegro show robust growth, indicating that banking services and the use of electronic payments will continue to spread throughout these areas.

In terms of debit card adoption, Estonia and Slovenia lead the way, with Estonia's strong growth reflecting its high level of digital payments. Debit card usage has significantly increased in Albania and Kosovo, likely indicating the growing financial systems in both countries and a rising use of electronic payment methods. Although Bulgaria continues to dominate the region in terms of total card adoption, the decline in debit card usage may be attributed to market saturation or other economic factors. While

Table 3 Debit cards per 1000 adults

Country	*2011*	*2012*	*2013*	*2014*	*2015*
Albania	304.00	312.06	318.33	335.82	349.91
Bulgaria	1100.83	1152.39	1105.39	1010.15	984.84
Czechia	888.89	921.73	978.91	1049.64	1060.65
Estonia	1253.5	1281.26	1298.56	1330.22	1359.67
Croatia	1951.88	1844.52	1728.18	1785.86	1809.32
Hungary	902.84	906.29	898.36	886.68	896.25
Lithuania	1346.44	1266.47	1209.52	1146.79	1231.08
Latvia	1041.85	1076.02	1076.51	1047.16	1021.62
Montenegro	605.41	610.95	688.99	702.41	766.10
Poland	767.68	821.35	872.83	919.41	901.26
Romania	658.80	675.27	705.93	721.12	738.95
Serbia	878.90	815.81	862.05	872.33	904.80
Slovak Republic	988.47	867.79	905.98	947.98	985.09
Slovenia	1421.57	1438.6	1435.98	1355.05	1361.16
Kosovo	425.16	461.36	491.15	516.96	645.76

Source World Bank

Poland and Latvia have experienced slight declines, they still maintain high levels of card adoption, which remain above the global average.

According to the data in Table 4, the region's POS terminal use is generally on the rise, which is indicative of better financial infrastructure and a growing reliance on electronic payments. While nations like Bulgaria, Czechia, and Lithuania exhibit significant growth in POS usage, Estonia and Croatia lead in the availability of POS terminals. Despite still having a lower number of POS terminals, nations like Kosovo and Albania are making progress. Both technological developments and a regional shift toward cashless payment methods are probably responsible for this surge.

In terms of POS terminals per 100,000 adults, Estonia and Croatia are unquestionably in the lead, reflecting their robust digital economies and widespread use of electronic payment systems. Estonia, in particular, stands out as one of the most developed countries in this area, with Croatia following closely behind. High rates of POS terminal adoption are also seen in Bulgaria and the Czech Republic, signaling both increased customer demand for electronic transactions and advancements in card payment infrastructure. While Albania and Kosovo still lag behind more developed nations in terms of POS penetration, both show strong growth.

Table 4 POS terminals per 100,000 adults

Country	*2011*	*2012*	*2013*	*2014*	*2015*
Albania	224.55	230.07	243.45	278.64	283.26
Bulgaria	1012.2	1090.64	1127.84	1224.86	1494.18
Czechia	1141.7	1132.53	1067.54	1128.79	1595.24
Estonia	2649	2430.61	2471.42	2601.45	2871.58
Croatia	2763.99	2502.83	2552.54	2759.55	2889.29
Hungary	995.78	1009.83	10,739.49	1243.28	1326.59
Lithuania	1476.08	1270.01	1369.97	1562.78	1872.46
Latvia	1398.88	1413.38	1509.14	1678.2	1845.31
Montenegro	2020.02	2143.35	2202.54	2526.34	2245.92
Poland	825.22	895.76	1008.8	1230.74	1433.14
Romania	735.97	746.48	758.88	775.59	778.74
Serbia	967.44	1048.35	1004.65	1080.97	1106.56
Slovak Republic	869	879.85	912.47	993.7	1171.31
Slovenia	1940.87	2194.96	2019.98	1866.56	2161.37
Kosovo	584.25	661.05	690.68	712.74	748.09

Source World Bank

Their rising numbers suggest a positive trend in card payment adoption and financial inclusion. Meanwhile, Romania and Serbia exhibit slower but steady progress, highlighting a growing preference for electronic payments and a moderate improvement in POS terminal availability.

The Table 5 highlights distinct geographical variations in formal savings behavior and financial inclusion. Strong growth and high levels of savings at financial institutions indicate well-developed banking systems and robust financial infrastructure in Central and Eastern European countries such as the Czech Republic, Estonia, and the Slovak Republic. The most notable improvement is observed in Bulgaria, suggesting that efforts to expand access to financial services have been effective. While nations like Kosovo, Serbia, and Montenegro currently lag behind in savings rates, they show promise for future growth as their financial institutions continue to advance.

The data across all tables indicates a trend of increasing financial inclusion, particularly in Central and Eastern Europe. Countries with well-established banking systems, such as the Czech Republic, Estonia, and the Slovak Republic, have experienced rapid growth in digital payments,

Table 5 Saved at a financial institution (% age 15+)

Country/Years	*2011*	*2014*	*2017*	*2021*
Albania	8.56	7.48	8.66	9.66
Bulgaria	4.8	14.34	27.8	23.12
Bosnia and Herzegovina	6.08	8.82	9.79	18.66
Czechia	35.48	37.57	45.31	59.77
Estonia	28.87	31.64	46.93	61.78
Croatia	12.23	27.28	35.79	25.23
Hungary	17.25	19.3	23.65	31.9
Lithuania	20.49	28.26	33.95	46.88
Latvia	13.32	25.31	27.51	42.87
North Macedonia	7.78	13.74	17.27	14.84
Montenegro	3.36	5.29	10.1	…
Poland	17.99	20.81	32.56	36.43
Romania	8.69	13.27	13.58	18.69
Serbia	3.17	8.72	11.98	18.93
Slovak Republic	36.84	43.96	49.87	58.93
Slovenia	28.85	32.51	31.22	39.85
Kosovo	4.95	7.21	8.7	10.33

Source World Bank

ATM accessibility, and savings deposits. Meanwhile, Croatia and Bulgaria have made significant progress in encouraging saving and improving financial service accessibility. However, Kosovo, Serbia, and Montenegro still face challenges and have relatively lower levels of financial inclusion.

To see how the Transparency Index is progressing and to compare it with the indicators above, Table 6 displays Transparency Index (T-Index) scores for a number of countries in the years 2021, 2023, and 2024 for the following categories: total score (TIN_TSC), de facto score (DF_TSC), and de jure score (DJ_TSC). The De Facto Index rates 14 crucial websites for data accessibility and coverage, while the De Jure Index examines legal transparency (a nation's transparency legislation).

These indices highlight differences in both the practical access to information and the legal frameworks that support it, offering insightful information about each nation's digital landscape and governance. Researchers and policymakers can pinpoint areas for development and promote a more open and accessible digital environment by examining these scores.

In most countries, de facto scores (DF_TSC) are higher than de jure scores (DJ_TSC), indicating that many have systems or practices in place that go beyond the provisions of laws or constitutions. For example, Bulgaria received a de jure score of 6 in 2024 but a de facto score of 11. Many countries appear to have higher de jure scores in 2023 than in 2021, which may be due to more laws or constitutional amendments being made to conform to de facto practices. With consistently high scores over all years, particularly for the de jure and de facto components, Estonia stands out as having a strong legal and governance framework. Over the course of the three years, Romania's scores have remained relatively constant at 17. While nations with lower scores (such as Serbia and North Macedonia) may still be working to improve or may be having difficulties bringing their governance into line with their legal frameworks, those with higher total scores (such as Estonia, Romania, and Slovakia) probably have both de facto and de jure strong legal frameworks.

5 Conclusions

Bulgaria and the Czech Republic consistently show high numbers of ATMs per 100,000 adults, reflecting a well-developed ATM infrastructure. The data clearly demonstrate a trend toward increasing ATM access, with Estonia and Croatia also showing strong availability and consistent development over time. Although countries like Montenegro, North

Table 6 Transparency index among countries

Country	*DF_TSC*	*DJ_TSC*	*TIN_TSC_2021*	*DF_TSC*	*DJ_TSC*	*TIN_TSC_2023*	*DF_TSC*	*DJ_TSC*	*TIN_TSC_2024*
Albania	8.5	4	12.5	8.5	6	14.5	9.5	6	15.5
Bosnia & H.	10.5	4	14.5	9	4	13	9.5	5	14.5
Bulgaria	10.5	5	15.5	11	6	17	11	6	17
Croatia	12	5	17	13	6	19	12	6	18
Estonia	**12.5**	**5**	**17.5**	**13**	**6**	**19**	**13**	**6**	**19**
Greece	7.5	5	12.5	7.5	6	13.5	10.5	6	16.5
Hungary	8.5	4	12.5	8	5	13	8.5	5	13.5
Kosovo	...	...	...	11.5	4	15.5	12.5	4	15.5
Czech R.	9	5	15	9.5	6	15.5	9.5	6	15.5
Latvia	12	5	17	11.5	6	17.5	11.5	6	17.5
Lithuania	11.5	5	16.5	12.5	6	18.5	12.5	6	18.5
Montenegro	10.5	5	15.5	11	6	17	11.5	6	17.5
N Macedonia	8.5	3	11.5	10	5	15	10.5	5	15.5
Poland	10.5	4	14.5	9	5	14	9	5	14
Romania	12	5	17	12	6	18	12	6	18
Serbia	11	3	14	10.5	4	14.5	10.5	5	15.5
Slovak R.	**12.5**	**5**	**17.5**	**13**	**6**	**19**	**13**	**6**	**19**
Slovenia	11	4	15	12.5	5	17.5	12	5	17

Note

DF_TSC	T-Index de facto score (0–14)
DJ_TSC	T-Index de jure score (0–5) for 2021 and (0–6) for 2023
TIN_TSC	T-Index total score (de facto + de jure—0-19) for 2021 and (0–20) for 2023
TIN_FL	T-Index de jure fulfillment out of 20 components (Note: 19 components for 2021)
2024	The scores for T-Index 2024 are composed of 14 de-facto components and 6 de-jure components

Source **https://corruptionrisk.org/transparency/**

Macedonia, and Serbia still trail behind more developed nations, their modest gains reflect a growing banking infrastructure. In nations such as Bosnia and Herzegovina and Albania, ATM density has grown more slowly, yet these countries continue striving for improved accessibility.

The data also indicates a decline in the number of bank branches in several nations, which signals the shift toward online banking. Slovenia and Estonia show notable drops in branch numbers, likely due to their widespread use of digital banking. In contrast, North Macedonia and Montenegro have seen steady or gradual increases in branch density, suggesting that traditional banking services remain valued. Bulgaria continues to have a high number of branches, possibly reflecting a more traditional or expansive banking system.

Estonia, Croatia, and the Czech Republic lead in POS terminal density, thanks to their robust digital economies and widespread electronic payment systems. POS usage is also high and growing in the Slovak Republic and Bulgaria, suggesting rising consumer demand for card-based transactions. While Albania and Kosovo show slow POS adoption, both are growing rapidly, pointing to a gradual shift toward electronic payments. Serbia and Romania exhibit stable progress, indicating continuous advancements in the infrastructure supporting card payments.

In terms of savings, countries like the Slovak Republic, Estonia, and Czechia show high and increasing savings rates, a sign of strong financial inclusion and sophisticated financial institutions. Bulgaria stands out with a remarkable increase in savings, from 4.8% in 2011 to 27.8% in 2017, reflecting successful efforts to expand access to savings accounts. Lithuania, Poland, and Croatia show moderate growth, indicating advancements in both financial services and saving habits. However, Kosovo, Serbia, and Montenegro continue to face challenges in achieving higher levels of financial inclusion. From the data, Estonia and Slovakia have the highest total scores in 2024 (19 points), which suggests they are among the "best" in this context, especially in terms of the T-Index.

In conclusion, financial inclusion plays a critical role in reducing poverty and fostering economic growth by providing individuals with the tools to invest in education, save, and pursue entrepreneurial ventures. However, the varying measures of financial inclusion across studies highlight the need for a shared and standardized framework to enhance comparability and guide policy development. A common set of indicators will not only strengthen the body of research but also ensure that efforts to promote financial inclusion are targeted and effective. Ultimately, this collective approach can drive more inclusive and sustainable economic development globally.

References

Ajide, F. M. (2020). Financial inclusion in Africa, does it promote entrepreneurship? *Journal of Financial Economic Policy, 12*(4), 687–706.

Allen, F., Carletti, E., Cull, R., Qian, J. Q., Senbet, L., & Valenzuela, P. (2014). The African financial development and financial inclusion gaps. *Journal of African Economies, 23*(5), 614–642.

Allen, F., Demirguc-Kunt, A., Klapper, L., & Peria, M. S. M. (2016). The foundations of financial inclusion: Understanding ownership and use of formal accounts. *Journal of Financial Intermediation, 27*, 1–30. https://doi.org/10.1016/j.jfi.2015.12.003

Amidžic, G., Massara, M. A., & Mialou, A. (2014). *Assessing countries' financial inclusion standing-A new composite index.* International Monetary Fund.

Arora, R. U. (2010). Measuring financial access. *Griffith Business School Discussion Papers Economics, 1*(7), 1–21.

Atkinson, A., & Messy, F. A. (2013). Promoting financial inclusion through financial education: OECD/INFE evidence, policies and practice.

Bateman, M., & Chang, H. J. (2012). Microfinance and the illusion of development: From hubris to nemesis in thirty years. *World Economic Review, 1.*

Beck, T., & De la Torre, A. (2006). *The basic analytics of access to financial services* (*4026*). World Bank Publications.

Beck, T., Demirguc-Kunt, A., & Peria, M. S. M. (2007). Reaching out: Access to and use of banking services across countries. *Journal of Financial Economics, 85*(1), 234–266.

Bruhn, M., & Love, I. (2014). The real impact of improved access to finance: Evidence from Mexico. *The Journal of Finance, 69*(3), 1347–1376.

Brune, L., Giné, X., Goldberg, J., & Yang, D. (2011). Commitments to save: A field experiment in rural Malawi. World Bank Policy Research Working Paper, (5748).

Buckland, J. (2012). *Hard choices: Financial exclusion, fringe banks, and poverty in Urban Canada.* University of Toronto Press.

Cámara, N., & Tuesta, D. (2014). *Measuring financial inclusion: A muldimensional index.* BBVA Research Paper, (14/26).

Cecchetti, S. G., & Kharroubi, E. (2012). *Reassessing the impact of finance on growth.*

Chauvet, L., & Jacolin, L. (2017). Financial inclusion, bank concentration, and firm performance. *World Development, 97*, 1–13.

Demirgüç-Kunt, A., Honohan, P., & Beck, T. (2008). *Finance for all? Policies and pitfalls in expanding access.* World Bank.

Demirgüç-Kunt, A., & Klapper, L. (2013). Measuring financial inclusion, explaining variation in the use of financial services across and within countries. *Brookings Papers on Economic Activity, 2013*(1), 279–340.

Demirgüç-Kunt, A., Klapper, L., & Singer, D. (2017). Financial inclusion and inclusive growth: A review of recent empirical evidence. World Bank Policy Research Working Paper, No. 8040, Washington, DC.

Dev, S. M. (2006). Financial inclusion: Issues and challenges. *Economic and Political Weekly*, 4310–4313.

Ellis, K., Lemma, A., & Rudd, J. (2010). Financial inclusion, household investment and growth in Kenya and Tanzania. *Project Briefing*, *43*, septiembre.

Grohmann, A., Klühs, T., & Menkhoff, L. (2018). Does financial literacy improve financial inclusion? Cross country evidence. *World Development*, *111*, 84–96.

Han, R., & Melecky, M. (2013). *Financial inclusion for financial stability: Access to bank deposits and the growth of deposits in the global financial crisis.* World Bank policy research working paper, (6577).

Hendriks, S. (2019). The role of financial inclusion in driving women's economic empowerment. *Development in Practice*, *29*(8), 1029–1038.

Honohan, P. (2008). Cross-country variation in household access to financial services. *Journal of Banking and Finance*, *32*(11), 2493–2500.

Joshi, V. K. (2014). Financial inclusion: Urban-poor in India. *SCMS Journal of Indian Management*, *11*(4), 29.

Kairiza, T., Kiprono, P., & Magadzire, V. (2017). Gender differences in financial inclusion amongst entrepreneurs in Zimbabwe. *Small Business Economics*, *48*(1), 259–272.

Khan, H. R. (2011). *Financial inclusion and financial stability: Are they two sides of the same coin.* Address by shri HR Khan, deputy governor of the reserve bank of india, at Bancon, 1–12.

Mader, P. (2018). Contesting financial inclusion. *Development and Change*, *49*(2), 461–483.

Mehrotra, A., & Nadhanael, G. V. (2016). Financial inclusion and monetary policy in emerging Asia. In *Financial inclusion in Asia* (93–127). Palgrave Macmillan.

Mialou, A., Amidzic, G., & Massara, A. (2017). Assessing countries' financial inclusion standing—A new composite index. *Journal of Banking and Financial Economics*, *2*(8), 105–126.

Sarma, M. (2008). *Index of financial inclusion.* Working Paper, No. 215, Indian Council for Research on International Economic Relations, New Delhi.

Sarma, M. (2012). *Index of Financial Inclusion–A measure of financial sector inclusiveness.* Centre for International Trade and Development, School of International Studies Working Paper Jawaharlal Nehru University. Delhi, India.

Sarma, M., & Pais, J. (2011). Financial inclusion and development. *Journal of International Development*, *33*(2), 279–285.

Sinclair, S. P. (2001). *Financial exclusion: An introductory survey*. CRSIS, Edinburgh College of Art/Heriot Watt University.

Singh, K., & Singh Kondan, A. (2011). 9 Financial Inclusion, Development And Its Determinants: An Empirical Evidence of Indian States. *Asian Economic Review*, *53*(1), 115.

Subbarao, D. (2009). *Financial inclusion: Challenges and opportunities*. Reserve Bank of India's Bankers Club, Kolkata, December, 9.

Wang, X., & Guan, J. (2017). Financial inclusion: Measurement, spatial effects and influencing factors. *Applied Economics*, *49*(18), 1751–1762.

Wilson, T. A. (2012). Supporting social enterprises to support vulnerable consumers: The example of community development finance institutions and financial exclusion. *Journal of Consumer Policy*, *35*(2), 197–213.

World Bank. (2014). *Global financial development report 2014: Financial inclusion*. Washington, DC. © World Bank. https://openknowledge.worldbank.org/handle/10986/16238. License: CC BY 3.0 IGO.

Transparency and Financial Governance: Possible Ways to Enhance Corporate Transparency

Stefania Mierlita, Adriana Tiron-Tudor, and Liana Stanca

1 Introduction

Governance of an organization encompasses the principles, procedures, mechanisms, and practices by which organizations are controlled and operated through their structure of management and stakeholders (Srivastava, 2023). The interests of stakeholders need to be balanced in developing and implementing effective governance activities (Nicolò et al., 2024). On the other hand, the reputation and profitability of a firm can be destroyed by inadequate corporate governance (Douglas et al., 2018). Among the core principles of corporate governance are transparency, accountability, equity, and risk management (Tiron-Tudor & Deliu, 2024).

Thus, companies should publicly and transparently express the responsibilities and duties of both the management and the board in order to increase stakeholder reliability. To validate and protect the integrity of

S. Mierlita · A. Tiron-Tudor (✉) · L. Stanca
Faculty of Economics and Business Administration, Babes-Bolyai University, Cluj-Napoca, Romania
e-mail: stefania.mierlita@econ.ubbcluj.ro
e-mail: adriana.tiron@econ.ubbcluj.ro
e-mail: liana.stanca@econ.ubbcluj.ro

J. Osterrieder et al. (eds.), *Transparency in FinTech*, Palgrave Studies in Financial Services Technology,
https://doi.org/10.1007/978-3-032-03523-3_11

financial reporting and the firm's operations, they also need to have internal processes and policies in place. Balanced and timely disclosure of significant issues pertaining to the company is necessary to guarantee that investors have access to accurate and transparent information. From a governance perspective, the case of financial sector organizations represents an extremely relevant topic, at least due to the following two arguments.

First, the emergence of new digital technologies has ushered in the digital finance era, bringing new opportunities and risks. Several academics are optimistic regarding the effect of digitalization, revealing that automating and optimizing internal company procedures may lead to higher profitability and productivity, while simultaneously boosting production, reducing expenses, and minimizing errors (Ebrahim et al., 2021; Musina, 2020; Parida et al., 2019; Rodin et al., 2019). However, AI-driven algorithms have the capacity to adversely impact individuals' rights and dignity, thereby raising ethical issues that require resolution (Tiron-Tudor et al., 2024). By training software engineers and technical teams to understand the moral implications of related algorithms and the value of ethics, such ethical dilemmas can be prevented. These algorithms have the potential to be more impartial and less biased compared to human judgment, which is nonetheless prone to prejudice. There are several strategies to avoid such biases. Data preprocessing can eliminate bias in the data before it is used to build a model, fairness metrics can help set better goals for models, and regular auditing, monitoring, and stakeholder engagement can provide even more confidence.

Second, organizations from the financial sector, including retail or investment banks, insurance providers, exchange and clearing houses, and others, given the nature of their services, significantly impact society and thus are socially responsible. The general expectation is that they will positively impact society (Nicolò et al., 2024).

In a more connected financial system, risks can rapidly diffuse throughout multiple financial institution areas, worsening throughout the system and affecting the real economy (Srivastava, 2023). Also, the significant impact of financial organizations' governance failures suggests room for improvement in internal control systems, audit techniques, oversight processes, and regulatory frameworks. Therefore, institutions in the financial sector require reliable systems, strong governance norms, and robust controls. The presence of vulnerabilities in the governance structure of such institutions may lead to operational risks, which can then escalate into credit, reputation, liquidity, market risks, or a combination of them. This situation adds a further burden on monitoring techniques, as frequent issues with control, supervision, and audit mean that a single failure is capable of erasing all past accomplishments in the public's judgment (Douglas et al., 2018).

In this frame, transparency can contribute to robust governance of financial sector organizations in several ways, including improving risk assessment, reducing systemic risks, increasing commitment to regulatory compliance, enhancing regulatory oversight, enhancing policy effectiveness, and promoting financial stability. Each of these elements is discussed below.

2 Improving Risk Assessment

Transparency improves risk assessment and contributes to better financial governance (Yoro, 2024). From a managerial perspective, transparent practices are crucial for effective risk assessment and management (Chang-Mo & Donghyun, 2022). Within the company, transparent practices enable organizations to improve risk assessment, evaluate threats, and prioritize the ones to address. Moreover, they encourage collaboration among different departments, breaking down silos that often hinder effective risk management. Thus, it is crucial to build trust, cultivate an integrity-based culture within firms (Efunniyi et al., 2024) and engage employees in risk management efforts.

Identifying potential risks that might affect the financial stability of a business or the financial sector is a crucial aspect of effective risk assessment, covering market, credit, and operational risks, as well as other factors. To improve risk assessment, a thorough process for identifying and lowering possible risks is necessary (Efunniyi et al., 2024). Second, internal controls and early warning systems can help identify signs of new risks so that steps can be taken to reduce them before they worsen (Efunniyi et al., 2024).

With advanced data processing technologies and blockchain, transparency ensures data integrity and security (Ebrahim et al., 2021). Additionally, sharing data can significantly improve how organizations handle and reduce risks (Wang, 2024). AI development and machine learning open up new ways to find problems, improve risk management, and strengthen oversight systems (Kiron et al., 2018). However, at the same time, many companies have become aware of digital and AI risks and their digital responsibility.

As a result, they have started to assess the risks, update their procedures, and become transparent in how they use AI technologies, following ethical guidelines and aligning their AI practices with broader regulatory expectations (Tóth & Blut, 2024).

3 Reducing Systemic Risks

Systemic risk is an important issue in financial governance. It refers to the links between the financial system's riskiness and specific financial organizations' riskiness (Iqbal & Vähämaa, 2019). Iqbal et al. (2015) also describe it as the impact of a financial sector institution on the financial system's risk. Making financial networks more open can significantly reduce systemic risk. One way to do this is to make the liability of each bank visible to other banks and to make it illegal for banks to borrow from systemically risky nodes (Thurner & Poledna, 2013).

Central banks significantly reduce systemic risks in the financial sector (Andrieş et al., 2020). Below, we emphasize the purpose of central bank transparency in avoiding systemic risks. Over the past 20 years, central banks have increased their level of transparency, which has led to concerns about how this impacts systemic risk (Andrieş et al., 2020; Zhang et al., 2023). Market participants can benefit from this transparency, as it provides more information, enhancing their decisions (Demertzis & Hughes Hallett, 2007; Van der Cruijsen & Demertzis, 2007). Conversely, confusion and misunderstanding can result from having too much information, which is why an ideal degree of transparency is necessary (Van der Cruijsen et al., 2010). Providing excessive information can overload market participants, leading to uncertainty and potential increases in systemic risk. As central bank transparency impacts systemic risk, Zhang et al. (2023) suggest that enhancing independence can mitigate this impact, making it a crucial factor in financial governance. Transparency is frequently researched alongside central bank independence, as the latter creates conditions for the former to be effective (Dudchenko, 2020). Transparent and independent central banks can reduce systemic risks by fostering financial stability and trust (Andrieş et al., 2020; Dudchenko, 2020).

Transparency in central banking can have both beneficial and adverse effects on financial institutions. It enhances information transmission, helping investors make informed decisions (Van der Cruijsen & Demertzis, 2007). Nevertheless, it can also encourage risky behaviors among financial sector organizations, which could increase systemic risk through a collective approach (Andrieş et al., 2020). This dual effect highlights the complexity of transparency's role in financial governance. Research shows that central bank transparency influences systemic risk in both developed and developing nations through a nonlinear effect. In particular, it has an upside-down U-shaped impact in developing countries (Zhang et al., 2023) and a positive nonlinear effect in developed countries (Van der Cruijsen et al., 2010). This indicates that, in developed countries, increased transparency initially reduces systemic risk; however, it may elevate it beyond a certain point. In contrast, in the context of developing countries, it initially raises systemic risk before reducing it as public trust grows.

Developed markets are generally more transparent than developing ones, influencing how transparency affects systemic risk (Dincer & Eichengreen, 2010). In developed countries, transparency can raise the volatility of exchange rates, whereas it does not affect emerging ones (Weber, 2019). Greater transparency can improve financial stability in developing countries by reducing information asymmetry in the credit market (Tibertoa et al., 2020). However, excessive transparency can lead to information overload, creating uncertainty and potentially increasing systemic risk (Dudchenko, 2020). Beyond a threshold, more information becomes counterproductive, emphasizing the importance of a balanced strategy for transparency (Van der Cruijsen et al., 2010).

4 Transparency Enhances Policy Effectiveness and Promotes Financial Stability

A significant advantage of transparency is that it mitigates information asymmetry among stakeholders. This improved information flow helps prevent misuse and supports informed decision-making (Ali et al., 2022). It builds investor confidence, encourages rational investment decisions (Yoro, 2024), enhances corporate governance, and reduces risks (Bui & Krajcsák, 2023).

Transparency involves stakeholders in decision-making (Manes-Rossi et al., 2019), enhancing the effectiveness of financial policies and corporate governance. It also provides stakeholders with thorough information, which is crucial for mitigating uncertainty and promoting well-informed decision-making. Moreover, good auditing ensures accurate financial statements, boosting investor confidence and improving policy frameworks (Darmawan, 2023). Clear policy communication enhances understanding and compliance. Clear and timely disclosures of financial data and information about company activities allow market players to respond quickly to developments and reduce uncertainty. Yoro (2024) shows that greater openness is linked to increased trading and reduced stock price volatility, supporting the idea that more openness helps maintain market stability.

Transparency provides essential information that aids in the assessment of management performance and the company's overall health, thereby reducing the likelihood of poor management and the risk of fraud (Wang, 2024). Applying international reporting standards, such as IFRS (International Financial Reporting Standards), also significantly enhances stakeholder trust through transparent regulatory reporting (Efunniyi et al., 2024). Moreover, transparency enhances management and board decision-making by delivering accurate data for resource allocation, risk management, and long-term planning, as well as encouraging ethical behavior and responsibility while discouraging misconduct and abuse of power (Wang, 2024). Furthermore, by motivating people to disclose unethical behavior, a good whistleblower policy increases transparency and strengthens adherence to regulations (Srivastava, 2023).

Transparency in financial governance extends its benefits beyond policy effectiveness, contributing to financial stability. To maintain the financial industry's stability, a strong corporate governance framework that prioritizes transparent disclosure—fostering trust and reducing uncertainty by enabling the public and stakeholders to understand and evaluate the company—is necessary (Ştefănescu, 2014). Trust is critical for investors and creditors, who rely on accurate and timely financial data to assess an entity's financial condition (Fung, 2014). Governance transparency at the country level also positively enhances the accuracy of analyst forecasts (Bhat et al., 2006), supporting financial stability by reducing market uncertainty. Open and honest corporate governance contributes to financial stability, ensuring that companies act in ways that benefit all stakeholders (Augustine, 2012). Regular earnings reports and meetings, which keep investors informed and engaged while fostering market stability, further strengthen this alignment (Efunniyi et al., 2024). Moreover, using information and communication technologies to disseminate financial statements has enhanced transparency, reduced information asymmetry, and supported effective policy implementation (Bertot et al., 2010).

5 Transparency: Increasing Commitment to Regulatory Compliance

Transparency is crucial in increasing commitment to regulatory compliance in the financial sector. Transparency can strengthen a firm's commitment to regulatory frameworks, responsible conduct, and effective risk management by encouraging adherence to regulatory requirements, open communication, and prompt disclosures. Different approaches exist in this sense. Financial institutions that are transparent about their operations and financial health are held accountable for their actions. This enhanced accountability encourages adherence to regulatory requirements and ethical practices (Fülöp, 2012).

Transparency improves market efficiency by conveying management's dedication to maximizing shareholder value and using responsible risk management techniques, as well as by offering accurate and trustworthy information (Darmawan, 2023). Organizations' clear procedures ensure they maintain strong internal systems for managing risks and running the business (Kashyap & Iveroth, 2021).

Complying with regulations is essential to ensuring organizations provide stakeholders with reliable information for informed decision-making (Efunniyi et al., 2024; Rahmah & Iskandar, 2021). However, despite fostering trust and credibility, organizations face challenges in maintaining compliance due to the complexity of differing global regulatory frameworks (Efunniyi et al., 2024).

Rigid regulations driven by financial scandals have forced management to place a higher priority on compliance and ethical behavior. Strict reporting procedures and adherence to key regulatory frameworks, such as GDPR (the General Data Protection Regulation) and SOX (the Sarbanes-Oxley Act), are essential for enhancing transparency in corporate governance (Efunniyi et al., 2024). These regulations protect stakeholders by ensuring accurate financial reporting, preventing fraud, and restoring market trust through stricter disclosures, increased accountability, and improved audit standards (Wang, 2024). Following financial scandals, SOX, the European Union's Market Abuse Regulation, and the Dodd-Frank Act introduced specific rules that are difficult to circumvent. They also imposed stricter penalties for non-compliance, which further emphasized the importance of adhering to these regulations (Efunniyi et al., 2024; Muslim, 2024).

Blockchain, AI, and big data analytics are new technologies that help businesses comply with regulations. They do this by making transactions more honest and transparent, reducing fraud and manipulation, which is important for building stakeholder trust (Ebrahim et al., 2023; Muslim, 2024). However, maintaining regulatory compliance requires transparency in how AI models make financial judgments (Tiron-Tudor et al., 2024).

Despite the benefits, achieving adequate transparency remains challenging. Enforcing regulations is essential to guaranteeing adherence to governance and accounting standards (Hermalin & Weisbach, 2003). However, significant challenges arise from varying regulations and rules, as well as the difficulty of ensuring uniform compliance procedures across borders (Efunniyi et al., 2024). Additionally, while transparency is crucial, its implementation could have unclear effects on regulatory and organizational goals (Kashyap & Iveroth, 2021).

6 Transparency: Enhancing Regulatory Oversight

The foundation of contemporary economies is the financial services sector. It is distinguished by a complex environment in which consumer protection, risk, and innovation must all exist in a delicate relationship. Thus, the international financial crisis and the aftermath of financial scandals have highlighted the critical role of transparency in financial governance. Companies are under increasing pressure to demonstrate their ability to combat financial fraud effectively through transparent practices and technological advancements (Currie et al., 2018). Researchers have identified the lack of transparency as a significant weakness, which limits investors' ability to assess risks accurately (Barth & Landsman, 2010). Moreover, stock exchanges and regulators worldwide have acknowledged the value of transparency, leading to the development of several regulations designed to guarantee the transparency of companies' accurate and timely financial disclosures (Bhat et al., 2006; Fung, 2014).

Regulations enforced at both national and worldwide levels play a crucial role in preserving this balance. These frameworks safeguard consumers, improve market stability, and address new issues as they develop. Robust regulatory oversight disincentivizes inappropriate behavior and reassures stakeholders of a company's commitment to transparency (Sari, 2023). Regulatory oversight also enhances transparency by ensuring the regulations are appropriately applied, lowering systemic risks, and protecting financial markets (Costello et al., 2019).

Regulatory frameworks that promote transparency help detect and mitigate financial fraud, supporting the financial markets' general integrity and stability (Wang, 2024). For example, the Sarbanes-Oxley Act (SOX) emphasizes the significance of transparency in financial reporting through stringent disclosure requirements that enhance regulatory oversight and improve the quality and reliability of financial disclosures (Bhat et al., 2006; Darmawan, 2023). SOX has underscored the importance of transparency in improving market integrity and discouraging fraudulent strategies (Li, 2010). By imposing fines for non-compliance, these regulations highlight the significance of transparent financial reporting, which is critical for mitigating financial risks and fostering investor confidence (Darmawan, 2023). Additionally, the Committee of Sponsoring Organizations demonstrates the importance of strong internal control procedures in ensuring openness and honesty (Sari, 2023). These procedures should include risk assessment and monitoring systems. Such practices are crucial for fostering integrity, particularly in an evolving regulatory environment. Technology, such as real-time reporting dashboards and board portals, has been integrated into governance practices to enhance transparency and improve regulatory oversight (Musina, 2019; Sari, 2023).

The main international standard-setting body for prudent bank supervision is the Basel Committee on Banking Supervision (BCBS). It offers a venue for frequent collaboration on banking oversight issues, bringing together 45 members, including central banks and bank supervisory bodies from 28 jurisdictions. The BCBS issued a globally accepted set of regulations to improve bank supervision, treatment, and regulation, recognized as Basel III. These measures represent the basic norms that are applicable to banks operating internationally.

Predatory lending, unfair credit evaluations, and deceptive financial products are less likely to occur due to the EU Markets in Financial Instruments Directive II (MiFID II), in force since 2018 (European Union, 2014), which sought to improve investor protection and enhance investment product transparency. Financial organizations' treatment of consumer data is impacted by the EU General Data Protection Regulation (GDPR) (2018), which has emerged as the international norm for data privacy. Hence, regulations in Europe are designed to safeguard sensitive consumer data and guarantee that institutions in the financial sector have strong systems against cyber threats. In this context, concerns over operational resilience, which depend more and more on digital infrastructure and crucial third-party service providers, are rising as a result of accelerated digitalization in the financial sector. Clear guidelines for the security of financial organizations' information systems and networks, including banks, investment businesses, and insurance providers, are established under the EU Digital Operational Resilience Act (DORA) (European Union, 2022). According to DORA, institutions in the financial sector must improve their cybersecurity safeguards, keep an eye on operational risks throughout their digital environment, as well as implement new third-party risk management guidelines.

In 2010, the European System of Financial Supervision (ESFS) was implemented to track systemic risks. Thus, a distinct supervisory architecture was established, consisting of a board, namely the European Systemic Risk Board (ESRB), and three European supervisory authorities (ESAs): the European Banking Authority (EBA), the European Securities and Markets Authority (ESMA), and the European Insurance and Occupational Pensions Authority (EIOPA). First, the ESRB oversees the EU's financial system, and prevents and mitigates systemic risk. Using "soft powers", the ESRB issues suggestions or precautions to mitigate major systemic risks threatening the EU's financial stability. The ESRB's activity is complemented by the activities of the three European supervisory authorities (ESAs).

EBA's role is ensuring the stability and efficacy of the financial system in Europe. Its primary responsibilities include creating uniform regulations for banks in the European Union, guaranteeing fair competition, and protecting financial services customers. Next, ESMA serves multiple roles within the financial regulatory framework. As a regulator, it formulates regulatory guidance for both supervisors and entities under its jurisdiction, while also drafting mandatory technical regulations. By establishing shared supervisory priorities, conducting peer evaluations, promoting collaborative supervisory activities, and planning training sessions, it fosters supervisory consistency throughout the EU. Furthermore, many service providers and financial infrastructures are directly supervised by ESMA. It acts as a central repository for regulatory data, guaranteeing data quality while supplying market participants and supervisors with infrastructure. ESMA functions as a market observer, conducting stress tests and releasing research reports on risks that impact financial stability. On the international stage, it represents the EU's collective interests, engaging with non-EU regulators to foster cooperation and international standards. Additionally, ESMA advises the European Commission, Council, and Parliament on securities and market supervision. Lastly, EIOPA is the heart of the EU's insurance and occupational pensions supervision. It aims to foster financial stability and confidence in these markets.

7 Conclusion

A good corporate governance may improve the performance at the company level and also at the sector level, especially if we refer to the financial sector, where institutions are interconnected. The lessons learned from the financial institutions' governance failures of 2007–2008 were that even banks operating in some of the most developed governance environments in the world, such as the United States (US) and the United Kingdom (UK), face risks related to weak governance. Transparency plays a crucial role in avoiding weak governance and the risks related to failure. Thus, in this chapter, we propose some possible ways to enhance corporate transparency with a specific focus on improving risk assessment, reducing systemic risks, and enhancing regulatory oversight.

References

Ali, S., Zhongxin, W., Ali, Z., Usman, M., & Zhuoping, Y. (2022). Does financial transparency substitute corporate governance to improve stock liquidity? The emerging market of Pakistan provides evidence in this regard. *Frontiers in Psychology*, *13*, 1003081. https://doi.org/10.3389/fpsyg.2022.1003081

Andrieş, A. M., Nistor, S., & Sprincean, N. (2020). The impact of central bank transparency on systemic risk: Evidence from Central and Eastern Europe. *Research in International Business and Finance*, *51*, 100921. https://doi.org/10.1016/j.ribaf.2018.06.002

Augustine, D. (2012). Good practice in corporate governance: Transparency, trust, and performance in the microfinance industry. *Business and Society*, *51*(4), 659–676. https://doi.org/10.1177/0007650312448623

Barth, M. E., & Landsman, W. R. (2010). How did financial reporting contribute to the financial crisis? *European Accounting Review*, *19*(3), 399–423. https://doi.org/10.1080/09638180.2010.498619

Bertot, J. C., Jaeger, P. T., & Grimes, J. M. (2010). Using ICTs to create a culture of transparency: E-government and social media as openness and anti-corruption tools for societies. *Government Information Quarterly*, *27*(3), 264–271. https://doi.org/10.1016/j.giq.2010.03.001

Bhat, G., Hope, O. K., & Kang, T. (2006). Does corporate governance transparency affect the accuracy of analyst forecasts?. *Accounting & Finance*, *46*(5), 715–732. https://doi.org/10.1111/j.1467-629X.2006.00191.x

Bui, H., & Krajcsák, Z. (2023). The impacts of corporate governance on firms' performance: From theories and approaches to empirical findings. *Journal of Financial Regulation and Compliance*, *32*(1), 18–46. https://doi.org/10.1108/JFRC-01-2023-0012

Chang-Mo, K., & Donghyun, K. (2022). Risk management transparency and compensation. *Journal of Corporate Finance*, *75*, 102245.

Costello, A. M., Granja, J., & Weber, J. (2019). Do strict regulators increase banks' transparency? *Journal of Accounting Research*, *57*(3), 603–637. https://doi.org/10.1111/1475-679X.12255

Currie, W. L., Gozman, D. P., & Seddon, J. J. (2018). Dialectic tensions in the financial markets: A longitudinal study of pre-and post-crisis regulatory technology. *Journal of Information Technology*, *33*(4), 304–325. https://doi.org/10.1057/s41265-017-0047-5

Darmawan, A. (2023). Audit quality and its impact on financial reporting transparency. *Golden Ratio of Auditing Research*, *3*(1), 32–45. https://doi.org/10.52970/grar.v3i1.375

Demertzis, M., & Hughes Hallett, A. (2007). Central bank transparency in theory and practice. *Journal of Macroeconomics*, *29*(4), 760–789. https://doi.org/10.1016/j.jmacro.2005.06.002

Dincer, N., & Eichengreen, B. (2010). Central bank transparency: Causes, consequences, and updates. *Theoretical Inquiries in Law*, *11*(1), 75–123. https://doi.org/10.2202/1565-3404.1237

Douglas, C., Johan, S., & Peter, R. (2018). Developments in financial institutions, governance, agency costs, and misconduct. *Journal of International Financial Markets, Institutions and Money*, *54*, 1–14. https://doi.org/10.1016/j.intfin.2017.06.004

Dudchenko, V. Y. (2020). Interaction of Central bank independence and transparency: Bibliometric Analysis. *Business Ethics and Leadership*, *4*(2), 109–115. https://doi.org/10.21272/bel.4(2).109-115.2020

Ebrahim, R., Kumaraswamy, S., & Abdulla, Y. (2021). FinTech in Banks: Opportunities and Challenges. In Y. Albastaki, A. Razzaque, & A. Sarea (Eds.), *Innovative Strategies for Implementing FinTech in Banking* (p. 100–109). IGI Global Scientific Publishing. https://doi.org/10.4018/978-1-7998-3257-7.ch006

Efunniyi, C. P., Abhulimen, A. O., Obiki-Osafiele, A. N., Osundare, O. S., Agu, E. E., & Adeniran, I. A. (2024). Strengthening corporate governance and financial compliance: Enhancing accountability and transparency. *Finance and Accounting Research Journal*, *6*(8), 1597–1616. https://doi.org/10.51594/farj.v6i8.1509

European Union. (2014). Directive 2014/65/EU of the European Parliament and of the Council of 15 May 2014 on markets in financial instruments and amending Directive 2002/92/EC and Directive 2011/61/EU (MiFID II). *Official Journal of the European Union, L 173*, 349–496. available at: https://eur-lex.europa.eu/eli/dir/2014/65/oj/eng

European Union. (2022). Regulation (EU) 2022/2554 of the European Parliament and of the Council of 14 December 2022 on digital operational resilience for the financial sector and amending Regulations (EC) No 1060/2009, (EU) No 648/2012, (EU) No 600/2014, (EU) No 909/2014 and (EU) 2016/1011. *Official Journal of the European Union, L 333*, 1–79. available at: https://eur-lex.europa.eu/eli/reg/2022/2554/oj/eng

Fülöp, M. T. (2012). *Audit in Corporate Governance*. Cluj-Napoca, Romania: Alma Mater Publishing House.

Fung, B. (2014). The demand and need for transparency and disclosure in corporate governance. *Universal Journal of Management*, *2*(2), 72–80. https://doi.org/10.13189/ujm.2014.020203

Hermalin, B. E., & Weisbach, M. S. (2003). Boards of directors as an endogenously determined institution: A survey of the economic literature. *Economic Policy Review*, *9*(1), 7–26. https://doi.org/10.2139/ssrn.380180

Iqbal, J., Strobl, S., & Vähämaa, S. (2015). Corporate governance and the systemic risk of financial institutions. *Journal of Economics and Business*, *82*, 42–61. https://doi.org/10.1016/j.jeconbus.2015.06.001

Iqbal, J., & Vähämaa, S. (2019). Managerial risk-taking incentives and the systemic risk of financial institutions. *Review of Quantitative Finance and Accounting*, *53*(4), 1229–1258. https://doi.org/10.1007/s11156-018-0780-z

Kashyap, S., & Iveroth, E. (2021). Transparency and accountability influences of regulation on risk control: The case of a Swedish bank. *Journal of Management and Governance*, *25*(2), 475–508. https://doi.org/10.1007/s10997-020-09550-w

Kiron, D., Prentice, P. K., Ferguson, R. B., & Kruschwitz, N. (2018). Reshaping business with artificial intelligence. *MIT Sloan Management Review*, *59*(1), 1–16. https://doi.org/10.1162/itgg_a_00084

Li, C. (2010). The impact of SOX section 404 on the association between audit fees and audit reporting lags. *Auditing: A Journal of Practice and Theory*, *29*(2), 195–210. https://doi.org/10.2308/aud.2010.29.2.195

Manes-Rossi, F., Aversano, N., & Tartaglia Polcini, P. (2019). Popular reporting: Learning from the US experience. *Journal of Public Budgeting, Accounting and Financial Management*, *32*(1), 92–113. https://doi.org/10.1108/JPBAFM-01-2019-0013

Musina, A. A. (2020). Digitalization of Banking – The Way to Create a «Bank of the Future.». *Intelligence. Innovations. Investment*, *6*, https://doi.org/10.25198/2077-7175-2019-6-10

Muslim, M. (2024). Managerial Finance Tactics in the Era of Enhanced Regulation Following Financial Scandals. *Advances in Management & Financial Reporting*, *2*(1), 1–10. https://doi.org/10.60079/amfr.v2i1.202

Nicolò, G., Zanellato, G., Esposito, B., & Tiron-Tudor, A. (2024). Cultural dimensions and sustainability disclosure in the banking sector: Insights from a qualitative comparative analysis approach. *Business Strategy and the Environment*, *33*(8), 8086–8101. https://doi.org/10.1002/bse.3911

Parida, V., Sjödin, D., & Reim, W. (2019). Reviewing literature on digitalization, business model innovation, and sustainable industry: Past achievements and future promises. *Sustainability*, *11*(2). https://doi.org/10.3390/su11020391

Rahmah, E. D. D., & Iskandar, Y. (2021). The effect of profitability and financial risk on earning management of mobile telecommunication operators registered in indonesia stock exchange period 2015–2018. *Nusantara Science and Technology Proceedings*, *4*(4), 362–368. https://doi.org/10.11594/nstp.2021.1041

Rodin, B. K., Ganiev, R. G., & Orazov, S. T. (2019). «Fintech» in digitalization of banking services. In *International Scientific and Practical Conference on Digital Economy (ISCDE 2019)* (830–833). Atlantis Press. https://doi.org/10.2991/iscde-19.2019.31

Sari, R. (2023). Enhancing corporate governance through effective oversight and accountability. *Advances: Jurnal Ekonomi and Bisnis*, *1*(6), 344–356. https://doi.org/10.60079/ajeb.v1i6.291

Srivastava, A. (2023). Governance in financial institutions: Key elements and preventing the failures. *Asian Journal of Economics and Banking*, *7*(3), 424–434. https://doi.org/10.1108/AJEB-05-2022-0049

Ştefănescu, C. A. (2014). Transparency and disclosure requirements–An analysis of corporate governance codes. *Atlantic Economic Journal*, *42*(1), 113–114. https://doi.org/10.1007/s11293-013-9386-y

Thurner, S., & Poledna, S. (2013). DebtRank-transparency: Controlling systemic risk in financial networks. *Scientific Reports*, *3*(1888). https://doi.org/10.1038/srep01888

Tibertoa, B. P., de Moraesb, C. O., & Corrêac, P. P. (2020). Does transparency of central banks' communication affect the credit market? Empirical evidence for advanced and emerging markets. *North American Journal of Economics and Finance*, *53*, 101207. https://doi.org/10.1016/j.najef.2020.101207

Tiron-Tudor, A., & Deliu, D. (2024). The Sustainability Performance of SMEs in Industry 5.0: A Proposal for a Synergetic Digital Sustainable Development Maturity Model (SDSDMM). *Eastern European Economics*, 1–45. https://doi.org/10.1080/00128775.2024.2442306

Tiron-Tudor, A., Rodgers, W., & Deliu, D. (2024). The accounting profession in the Twilight Zone: Navigating digitalization's sided challenges through ethical pathways for decision-making. *Accounting, Auditing & Accountability Journal, Ahead-of-print*. doi: https://doi.org/10.1108/AAAJ-12-2022-6173

Tóth, Z., & Blut, M. (2024). Ethical compass: The need for Corporate Digital Responsibility in using Artificial Intelligence in financial services. *Organizational Dynamics, 53*(2), 101041. https://doi.org/10.1016/j.orgdyn.2024.101041

Van der Cruijsen, C., & Demertzis, M. (2007). The impact of central bank transparency on inflation expectations. *European Journal of Political Economy, 23*(1), 51–66. https://doi.org/10.1016/j.ejpoleco.2006.09.009

Van der Cruijsen, C. A., Eijffinger, S. C., & Hoogduin, L. H. (2010). Optimal Central bank transparency. *Journal of International Money and Finance, 29*(8), 1482–1507. https://doi.org/10.1016/j.jimonfin.2010.06.003

Wang, J. (2024). The impact of financial information transparency on corporate governance effectiveness. *Transactions on Economics, Business and Management Research, 10*, 298–302. https://doi.org/10.62051/5kh49x75

Weber, C. S. (2019). The effect of central bank transparency on exchange rate volatility. *Journal of International Money and Finance, 95*, 165–181. https://doi.org/10.1016/j.jimonfin.2019.04.002

Yoro, M. (2024). Impact of financial reporting transparency on investor decision-making. *American Journal of Accounting, 6*(1), 25–36. https://doi.org/10.47672/ajacc.1785

Zhang, X., Liang, Q., & Lee, C. C. (2023). How does central bank transparency affect systemic risk? Evidence from developed and developing countries. *The Quarterly Review of Economics and Finance, 88*, 101–115. https://doi.org/10.1016/j.qref.2022.12.005

PART V

The Future on Fintech Organizations and their Transparency

Fintech 5.0: From Shadows to Clarity—The Future of Transparency in Financial Organizations

Delia Deliu and Andreea Moldovan

1 Introduction

Over the past two decades, financial technology (Fintech) has transformed the way individuals, businesses, and institutions interact with financial services (Goldstein et al., 2019; Puschmann, 2017; Schueffel, 2016). What began with digital banking and mobile payments has expanded into automation-driven financial platforms and data-intensive solutions that continually push the boundaries of innovation (Putra et al., 2024; Giglio, 2022).

Yet with growing sophistication has come greater opacity. Algorithmic lending, proprietary trading systems, and AI-driven financial decision-making have created processes that are often difficult for consumers (and even regulators) to interpret (Setiawan & Maulisa, 2020; Zetzsche et al., 2017). Many of these technologies function within *obscured frameworks*, where financial outcomes emerge from hidden processes with little transparency regarding how decisions are made, how risks are assessed, or how

D. Deliu (✉) · A. Moldovan
Faculty of Economics and Business Administration, West University of Timişoara, Timişoara, Romania
e-mail: delia.deliu@e-uvt.ro
e-mail: andreea.moldovan@e-uvt.ro

J. Osterrieder et al. (eds.), *Transparency in FinTech*, Palgrave Studies in Financial Services Technology,
https://doi.org/10.1007/978-3-032-03523-3_12

biases are mitigated (Chou, 2019; Soundararajan & Shenbagaraman, 2024). This lack of clarity has fueled growing concerns among regulators, policymakers, and consumers, raising fundamental questions about accountability, fairness, and trust in Fintech (Aldboush & Ferdous, 2023; Müller & Kerényi, 2019). Thus, as Fintech continues to evolve, driven by rapid technological advancements, it is not only reshaping financial services but also redefining expectations of transparency, trust, and regulatory compliance (Leong & Sung, 2018; Zetzsche et al., 2017).

The emergence of *Fintech 5.0* has amplified these issues, as the sector's reach now extends beyond transactional innovation into areas that affect market integrity and global financial stability (Arner et al., 2015; Chakraborti et al., 2025). Organizations are increasingly deploying Artificial Intelligence (AI), Machine Learning (ML), Blockchain Technology (BT), Decentralized Finance (DeFi), and tokenized assets to promote efficiency, drive accessibility, expand financial inclusion, and transform traditional service models (Arner et al., 2016; Farcane & Deliu, 2020; Philippon, 2016; Tohang et al., 2021). But as these technologies scale, *transparency* has become a central concern, one that will ultimately determine the credibility and sustainability of the sector (Addy et al., 2024; Bhat et al., 2024).

Transparency in this context extends beyond ethics or regulatory compliance; it represents a bedrock for trust and long-term stability within financial markets. Unlike traditional banks that have historically relied on insured deposits and deeply embedded trust mechanisms to withstand financial crises (Deliu, 2020; Thakor & Merton, 2024), many Fintech organizations operate without such buffers. Their dependence on investor confidence leaves them far more exposed when transparency breaks down, creating vulnerabilities that can quickly escalate into systemic risks.

Although Fintech platforms excel in harnessing Big Data (BD) to evaluate creditworthiness with remarkable precision (Buchak et al., 2018), they cannot replicate the institutional trust embedded in traditional banks. The absence of deposit guarantees or long-standing oversight makes them more exposed to reputational risks when transparency is lacking. This means that when Fintech lenders fail to meet transparency expectations, they face significant reputational risks, which can erode investor confidence and lead to financial instability. The collapses of cryptocurrency exchanges like FTX and Mt. Gox serve as cautionary tales of how a lack of financial transparency can result in catastrophic losses for investors (Aspris et al., 2021; Foley et al., 2019).

At the same time, Fintech companies operate in rapidly evolving technological and regulatory landscapes (Anagnostopoulos, 2018), often across jurisdictions with uneven legal standards (Chen & Bellavitis, 2020). While automation, algorithmic decision-making, and decentralized networks offer efficiency (Saini, 2023), they also introduce new complexities concerning data privacy, financial risk disclosure, and corporate accountability (Arner et al., 2022; Dorfleitner et al., 2023; Goldstein et al., 2019; Putra et al., 2024). In this context, the emergence of Fintech 5.0, expected to integrate hyper-personalization, sustainability, and ethical finance, presents a unique opportunity to build transparency-first financial ecosystems that balance innovation with regulatory responsibility (He et al., 2023).

The evolution of Fintech, from its earliest stages to the anticipated emergence of Fintech 5.0, highlights the growing importance of transparency in financial ecosystems. Fintech 1.0 (1866–1967) marked the birth of globalized finance, with early telecommunication networks and international banking systems laying the groundwork for modern financial services (Arner et al., 2015). Afterward, the advent of Fintech 2.0 (1967–2008) saw the rise of digital banking and electronic payments, improving efficiency but also introducing challenges related to financial fraud and regulatory oversight (Frame & White, 2014; Trautman, 2015). The 2008 financial crisis exposed significant gaps in regulatory frameworks (Deliu, 2020; Farcane et al., 2011), leading to the emergence of Fintech 3.0 (2008–2020), a period characterized by startups, BT, and AI-driven financial services disrupting traditional banking (Farcane & Deliu, 2020; Philippon, 2016).

Today, in the Fintech 4.0 (2020–present) era, financial interactions are increasingly powered by DeFi, Central Bank Digital Currencies (CBDCs), and AI-driven investment platforms (Riantama et al., 2020; Schär, 2021). However, as these technologies become more sophisticated and create numerous opportunities, risks related to algorithmic accountability, risk transparency, and consumer protection have emerged.

Fintech 4.0 has brought many advancements, but it has also amplified concerns about regulatory oversight, data security, and fairness in financial decision-making (Addy et al., 2024). These concerns will define the shift to Fintech 5.0, the next frontier in financial technology, where hyper-personalization, ethical finance, and regulatory harmonization will redefine transparency in the financial industry (He et al., 2023). In this phase, transparency is expected to become the foundation of financial trust (Boot et al., 2021), balancing innovation with regulatory responsibility.

Fintech organizations are not monolithic; they encompass a wide range of financial service providers with distinct business models, operational structures, and transparency challenges (Gomber et al., 2017; Varga, 2017). Neobanks and Challenger Banks, for example, operate exclusively through digital platforms, relying on open banking frameworks and API integrations to deliver seamless services. These institutions improve financial accessibility, but also challenges related to data privacy and cybersecurity (Arner et al., 2022; Dorfleitner et al., 2023; Vives, 2019). DeFi platforms, built on BT and Smart Contracts, promise transparent and auditable transactions by eliminating intermediaries (Farcane & Deliu, 2020). Yet their lack of standardized governance exposes users to high risks and potential financial instability (Auer & Claessens, 2018). Regulatory Technology (RegTech) firms have also become central players in the Fintech ecosystem, offering automated compliance tools, AI-based fraud detection, and advanced risk assessment systems (Anagnostopoulos, 2018; Kumar et al., 2025; Putra et al., 2024). Although these solutions improve transparency, they also rain concerns about the interpretability of ML models and the ethical consequences of algorithmic decision-making (Brummer & Yadav, 2018). Cryptocurrency exchanges and digital asset platforms face even greater challenges. The collapses of FTX and Mt. Gox revealed major gaps in Proof-of-Reserves (PoR) mechanisms, financial solvency practices, and investor protection (Aspris et al., 2021; Foley et al., 2019).

These examples illustrate how weaknesses in transparency can lead to severe market failures and erode trust in the broader Fintech ecosystem. Thus, despite their variety, all Fintech organizations share a common challenge: balancing operational efficiency with transparency and regulatory compliance (Boot et al., 2021). Those that fail to meet transparency expectations risk consumer distrust, regulatory scrutiny, and reputational damage, ultimately jeopardizing their long-term sustainability (Addy et al., 2024; Bhat et al., 2024).

As Fintech 5.0 emerges, organizations must move out of the shadows of opacity and step into the light of transparency, embracing openness and trust as foundational principles. Fintech transparency operates across two core dimensions: internal (governance, risk management, and compliance) and external (stakeholder disclosures), ensuring ethical management, trust, and regulatory oversight (Böhme et al., 2015; He et al., 2023). In an era of increasingly digitized and AI-driven financial systems, transparency will be critical not only for regulatory compliance but also for shaping consumer trust, investment confidence, and overall financial stability. Navigating these complexities effectively is essential for fostering ethical innovation and mitigating systemic risks in the industry.

This chapter therefore investigates the future of Fintech organizations and their transparency policies by addressing the following three questions:

- RQ1. How do different types of fintech organizations approach transparency in Fintech 5.0?
- RQ2. What are the challenges of balancing internal and external transparency?
- RQ3. How can regulatory frameworks evolve to promote responsible fintech transparency?

By exploring these questions, the chapter provides a strategic roadmap for understanding the transparency dilemmas in Fintech 5.0 and offers recommendations for building sustainable and accountable financial ecosystems.

2 The Future Landscape of Fintech Organizations

2.1 *The Evolution of Fintech: From Fintech 1.0 To Fintech 5.0*

The evolution of Fintech can be traced through several distinct phases, each shaped by technological breakthroughs, regulatory shifts, and evolving consumer behaviors (Fig. 1). Over time, Fintech has transitioned from the early digitization of banking systems to the development of AI-driven, DeFi ecosystems, fundamentally reshaping transparency policies, regulatory oversight, and trust in financial services (Arner et al., 2015; Setiawan & Maulisa, 2020; Varga, 2017).

Fintech 1.0 marked the initial digitization of financial services, when traditional banks began adopting basic digital solutions to improve operational efficiency and accessibility. Fintech 2.0 emerged in the wake of the 2008 financial crisis, introducing mobile banking, Peer-to-Peer (P2P) lending, and early BT trials, disrupting traditional financial institutions and forcing regulatory frameworks to adapt (Farcane & Deliu, 2020; Setiawan & Maulisa, 2020). Fintech 3.0 saw the widespread adoption of AI, open banking, and DeFi, fostering automation, financial inclusion,

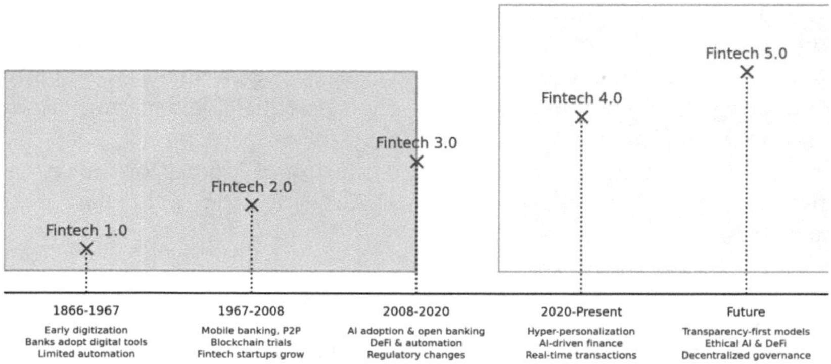

Fig. 1 Desirable evolution of Fintech transparency: from shadows to clarity

and data-driven decision-making (Addy et al., 2024). The current phase, Fintech 4.0, is characterized by hyper-personalization, advanced ML, and real-time financial services, enabling digital platforms to tailor financial products to individual users with unprecedented precision (Riantama et al., 2020).

Looking ahead, the trajectory of Fintech 5.0 is expected to be marked not only by technological breakthroughs but also by a growing emphasis on transparency and accountability. Ethical governance and consumer trust will need to stand alongside innovation as defining elements of financial evolution (Cabarkapa et al., 2024; Kumar et al., 2025), shaping both the legitimacy and the long-term resilience of future Fintech systems.

The transition from manual banking systems and centralized control in Fintech 1.0 to the AI-powered, decentralized ecosystems envisioned in Fintech 5.0 highlights a growing focus on governance, compliance, and transparency as defining pillars of financial innovation (Boot et al., 2021; Chakraborti et al., 2025). As we enter this new phase, financial organizations will focus on hyper-personalized, ethical, and regulatory-compliant solutions (Setiawan & Maulisa, 2020), integrating principles such as the explainability of AI (XAI), decentralized governance, and tokenized financial transparency (He et al., 2023).

As technology moved from underground (transatlantic cables) to above-ground (mobile networks, BT, AI), financial systems also transitioned from opacity to transparency, fostering trust. The 2008 financial crisis exposed banking's black-box nature, shifting consumer mindsets from passivity to financial empowerment (Deliu, 2020; Farcane & Deliu, 2020). This drove Fintech toward customer-centric models, aligning with Maslow's hierarchy of needs, where, once financial security is achieved, individuals seek self-directed decision-making (Boot et al., 2021). Now, in Fintech 5.0, rapid decision-making poses new challenges. Psychological heuristics, particularly trust, help consumers navigate information overload (Müller & Kerényi, 2019). Trust has shifted from authoritarian (banks, regulators) to community-based (BT, algorithms) models (Müller & Kerényi, 2019). Beyond technology, three drivers shape this transition: growing consumer demand for transparency, regulatory mandates, and the need for enhanced identity protection (Dorfleitner et al., 2023).

In this framework, Fintech 5.0 must balance transparency, security, and compliance, determining whether *firms will embrace trust-first models (clear pathways) or remain opaque (shadowed systems), risking consumer and regulatory backlash.*

Fintech 1.0 (1866–1967): The Foundation of Financial Globalization
The origins of Fintech 1.0 can be traced back to the late nineteenth century, when advances in communication and computation began reshaping financial services (Jalal et al., 2023). The invention of the telegraph and the deployment of transatlantic cables in the 1860s enabled near-instantaneous international financial transactions, allowing financial markets to operate across borders more efficiently (Moore, 2000). These innovations laid the groundwork for globalized finance, facilitating trade and investment beyond local markets.

During this period, financial systems were highly centralized, with banks, stock exchanges, and insurance companies serving as the primary institutions controlling financial transactions (Leong & Sung, 2018). These entities operated under emerging legal and regulatory frameworks, which varied significantly across jurisdictions. Transparency in finance was largely an internal concern, as there were no standardized disclosure requirements for consumers or regulators. Early financial regulations were primarily focused on preventing fraud, managing systemic risks, and ensuring institutional stability rather than on promoting openness or consumer rights (Frame & White, 2014).

By the early twentieth century, financial institutions increasingly relied on mechanized systems for bookkeeping and transactions, with the introduction of early computing machines such as the punched-card systems developed by IBM in the 1920s. These systems improved financial record-keeping, enhancing efficiency and reducing human error. However, access to financial data remained exclusive to institutions, reinforcing the opaque nature of financial decision-making during this time.

The mid-twentieth century saw groundbreaking advancements in payment systems, which would later form the foundation for modern digital transactions. The introduction of charge cards (precursors to modern credit cards) began with Diners Club in 1950, followed by the launch of Visa in 1958 and Mastercard in 1966. These innovations marked the first steps toward a cashless economy, reducing reliance on physical currency and manual processing, and introducing new layers of financial security and convenience (Mishkin, 2007).

Although Fintech 1.0 lacked the transparency frameworks seen in later stages, it established the infrastructure for global financial integration. The expansion of electronic financial systems, alongside growing regulatory oversight, laid the groundwork for the future evolution of digital banking, financial transparency, and consumer protections in the decades to come.

Fintech 2.0 (1967–2008): The Rise of Digital Banking and Electronic Finance

The second phase of Fintech, spanning 1967–2008, was defined by the digitalization of financial services, significantly improving efficiency, accessibility, and transaction speed. This period saw the emergence of electronic payment systems, ATMs, and digital banking, transforming how individuals and businesses managed their finances (Legowo et al., 2021; Trautman, 2015).

The introduction of computers and mainframe technology in the 1970s enabled financial institutions to automate transactions, leading to Electronic Funds Transfers (EFTs) and credit card networks, reducing reliance on cash and manual bookkeeping (Arner et al., 2015). The launch of the first ATM by Barclays in 1967 marked a shift toward self-service banking, allowing access to funds beyond traditional banking hours (Bátiz-Lazo & Wardley, 2007). By the 1980s, digital technology accelerated High-Frequency Trading (HFT), algorithmic risk management, and cross-border financial transactions. However, the growing reliance on computerized systems also created systemic risks. This became evident during Black Monday in 1987, which was the largest single-day stock market crash at the time. The event highlighted the dangers of automated trading and prompted regulators to introduce circuit breakers as a safeguard against extreme volatility (Bookstaber, 2007).

As financial markets globalized, major regulatory reforms facilitated financial liberalization and integration. The Single European Act (1986) removed capital movement restrictions within the European Economic Community, fostering cross-border financial activity (Commission of the European Communities (CEC), 1986). The UK's Big Bang (1986) deregulated the London Stock Exchange, increasing competition and financial innovation (Mullineux, 2012). This trend continued with the Maastricht Treaty (1992), which laid the foundation for the euro and deepened financial integration within the EU (Arner et al., 2016; Giglio, 2022). These regulatory changes transformed investment banking, enabling the growth of derivatives, mortgage-backed securities, and structured financial products. The combination of technological advancements, increased competition, and evolving regulations set the stage for modern Fintech innovation and globalization.

By the late 1990s and early 2000s, internet-based banking gained traction, with traditional banks adopting online banking platforms that allowed consumers to manage finances remotely. Secure encryption technologies bolstered confidence in digital transactions, accelerating the expansion of online financial services. Simultaneously, early fintech disruptors emerged, offering alternative financial solutions. Online payment systems like PayPal (1998) and Skrill (2001) facilitated seamless digital transactions, reducing reliance on traditional bank transfers (Alcalá Consuegra & Zabaraín García, 2012; Trautman, 2015). P2P lending platforms such as Prosper (2005) and Zopa (2005) revolutionized lending by enabling direct financial interactions, bypassing banks (Milne & Parboteeah, 2016). Robo-advisors, pioneered by Betterment (2008) and Wealthfront (2008), democratized investment management through algorithm-driven portfolio optimization (Alois, 2015; Philippon, 2016; Phoon & Koh, 2018). These innovations empowered consumers with greater financial autonomy, reducing dependence on traditional banking structures and paving the way for more decentralized financial services.

Although Fintech 2.0 improved both efficiency and accessibility, it also brought new challenges in transparency, cybersecurity, and regulatory oversight. The growing complexity of digital transactions made financial activities harder to monitor, whereas the rapid expansion of unregulated Fintech firms created vulnerabilities in areas such as financial stability, fraud detection, and anti-money laundering (AML) controls (Achim et al., 2023). The 2008 global financial crisis exposed major regulatory weaknesses, particularly in derivatives trading, mortgage-backed securities, and shadow banking (Boot et al., 2021). In response, policymakers introduced sweeping financial reforms to strengthen oversight and restore trust. The Dodd-Frank Act (2010) imposed stricter banking regulations, enhanced derivatives market oversight, and improved consumer protections ("Restoring American Financial Stability Act of 2010"). Internationally, the Basel III Framework (2010) reinforced banking resilience by increasing capital reserve requirements and improving risk management practices (Cecchetti & Schoenholtz, 2017; Goodhart, 2011; Toniolo, 2005). These reforms aimed to restore financial stability and transparency in the rapidly evolving digital economy.

Fintech 2.0 marked the transition from manual, paper-based banking to fully digital financial ecosystems. Innovations such as ATMs, electronic payments, online banking, and Fintech startups laid the foundation for a consumer-driven financial industry (Trautman, 2015). However, increasing complexity, regulatory gaps, and cybersecurity threats underscored the need for stronger financial oversight. The 2008 crisis served as a catalyst for regulatory change, paving the way for Fintech 3.0, where technologies like BT, AI, and DeFi would further revolutionize the financial sector.

Fintech 3.0 (2008–2020): The Emergence of Platform-based Finance and Fintech Startups

The 2008 global financial crisis exposed critical weaknesses in traditional banking, including risk management failures, regulatory gaps, and declining consumer trust. In response, Fintech 3.0 emerged, characterized by the rise of platform-based financial services, DeFi, and Fintech startups (Tohang et al., 2021). Consumers, disillusioned with traditional banks, turned to technology-driven alternatives that offered greater efficiency, transparency, and accessibility.

During this phase, financial services shifted away from institutional control, embracing cloud computing, AI, and mobile technology to deliver digital-first, user-centric financial solutions. This disrupted traditional banking, empowering startups and tech firms to redefine payments, lending, insurance, and investments.

The financial instability following 2008 created an opportunity for Fintech startups to challenge traditional banking dominance. With consumers frustrated by high fees and inefficiencies, digital-first platforms gained traction by offering faster, cheaper, and more transparent financial services.

One major success was Stripe (2010), which revolutionized online payments by providing a developer-friendly API that simplified payment processing for businesses. Similarly, InsurTech startups like Lemonade (2015) and Metromile (2011) leveraged AI and automation to streamline underwriting, personalize insurance policies, and reduce operational costs, making insurance more accessible and cost-effective (Kumar et al., 2025). Fintech innovation extended beyond payments, redefining borrowing, investing, and financial management through AI-driven automation, personalized financial tools, and real-time analytics (Tohang et al., 2021). These transformations marked a shift toward consumer-empowered finance, reducing reliance on traditional intermediaries.

The proliferation of smartphones fueled mobile payment adoption, changing consumer spending habits. Companies like Apple Pay (2014), Samsung Pay (2015), and Google Wallet (2011, later Google Pay in 2018) introduced secure, contactless payment solutions, allowing instant transactions with biometric authentication and tokenization for fraud prevention. The growing acceptance of digital wallets accelerated the transition to a cashless economy, promoting financial inclusion in both developed and emerging markets.

Crowdfunding platforms have transformed capital-raising mechanisms, enabling startups and individuals to secure funding without traditional financial intermediaries. Platforms like Kickstarter (2009) and Indiegogo (2008) have allowed entrepreneurs to attract investors directly, decentralizing access to capital. P2P lending models have further disrupted venture capital and private equity, fostering financial inclusion and automated investment processes.

The emergence of Bitcoin (2009) and Ethereum (2015) introduced BT and DeFi, shifting financial transactions away from centralized intermediaries. BT enabled transparent, secure, and autonomous financial interactions, reducing fraud risks and ensuring publicly verifiable transactions (Farcane & Deliu, 2020). Ethereum's smart contracts further expanded BT applications, enabling automated lending, insurance claims, and digital asset transfers. DeFi platforms allowed users to borrow, lend, and trade assets without banks, promoting financial self-sovereignty (Schär, 2021). However, despite enhancing transparency, BT and cryptocurrencies raised regulatory and security concerns, including fraud, market manipulation, and compliance with AML regulations. The absence of central oversight led to increased calls for regulatory frameworks to balance innovation with consumer protection.

The rapid expansion of Fintech prompted regulatory changes to enhance competition and financial transparency. One of the most significant policy changes during this period was the Revised Payment Services Directive (PSD2) by the European Union in 2018. This required banks to securely share customer financial data with third-party Fintech firms via open banking APIs. Additionally, it increased competition and innovation by allowing Fintech companies to build alternative financial solutions. Ultimately, it strengthened consumer data protections, ensuring that users had greater control over their financial information (Saini, 2023; Vives, 2019). Open banking regulation marked a shift from closed banking ecosystems to a more transparent, consumer-driven financial infrastructure. It paved the way for Fintech firms to provide tailored banking, lending, and investment services, further disrupting traditional financial models.

Despite its many benefits, the rapid expansion of digital financial services also introduced significant challenges. One major concern was AI-driven decision-making and algorithmic bias, as many Fintech firms increasingly relied on ML models for credit scoring, lending approvals, and risk assessments. The opacity of these AI models raised concerns about unexplained rejections, potential biases, and fairness in financial decision-making (Brummer & Yadav, 2018). Consumers and regulators questioned how these algorithms assessed creditworthiness and determined financial risk, emphasizing the need for explainable AI (XAI) and greater transparency in automated financial processes. Another critical challenge was cybersecurity and data privacy risks (Dorfleitner et al., 2023). As Fintech platforms became more reliant on digital transactions, they also became more vulnerable to cyberattacks, data breaches, and identity theft. Regulators struggled to enforce uniform security standards, leading to inconsistencies in consumer protection measures and creating potential gaps in digital financial security. Ensuring robust encryption, secure authentication protocols, and compliance with global data protection regulations became essential for maintaining trust in Fintech services. Additionally, the rise of DeFi enhanced transaction transparency, but it also complicated regulatory oversight. The lack of a central governing authority in DeFi systems raised concerns about fraud, money laundering, and market instability, as decentralized platforms often operated outside traditional financial regulations. Policymakers faced mounting pressure to develop frameworks that could balance financial innovation with risk mitigation without stifling technological progress.

Thus, the Fintech 3.0 era revolutionized finance through platform-based models, digital wallets, crowdfunding, and BT-powered financial ecosystems (Tohang et al., 2021). It fostered competition, accessibility, and decentralization but also exposed critical gaps in AI ethics, cybersecurity, and DeFi regulation. As Fintech 4.0 emerged, the focus shifted toward hyper-personalization, real-time analytics, and heightened regulatory scrutiny, setting the stage for the next phase in Fintech evolution.

Fintech 4.0 (2020–present): AI, BT, and DEFI

Fintech 4.0 marks the deep integration of AI, BT, DeFi, and digital identity verification into mainstream financial systems. This period is characterized by automated financial decision-making, digital-only banking, and decentralized P2P financial ecosystems (Riantama et al., 2020).

The COVID-19 pandemic accelerated the mass adoption of digital financial services, with social distancing and remote work driving reliance on mobile payments, digital banking, and AI-driven financial tools (Nicoletti, 2017, 2021, 2025). Fintech firms responded with more personalized, data-driven solutions, challenging traditional banking models with seamless, digital-first experiences.

On the one hand, Fintech 4.0 has enhanced efficiency, security, and transparency. On the other hand, it has introduced new challenges related to algorithmic bias, cybersecurity, regulatory oversight, and consumer protection. As innovation advances, governments and financial regulators face increasing pressure to develop frameworks that balance technological progress with financial stability.

AI has fundamentally transformed finance, driving credit assessments, fraud detection, personalized banking, and automated investment management (Gomber et al., 2017). AI-powered chatbots and virtual assistants now handle customer inquiries, dispute resolutions, and financial advice, reducing costs and improving the customer experience. A major shift in AI-driven lending is the use of alternative data sources (e.g., mobile usage, e-commerce behavior, social media) to assess creditworthiness in real-time.

Although these developments have widened financial access, they have also sparked concerns about algorithmic bias and the lack of transparency in decision-making. Regulators now demand explainability in AI credit assessments, ensuring fair, transparent lending. AI-driven HFT platforms analyze massive datasets to predict market movements and execute trades in milliseconds, giving institutions a competitive edge. However, these automated trading systems have also increased market volatility, prompting debates about their long-term impact on financial stability. In response to these concerns, regulators are emphasizing AI governance frameworks, particularly XAI methodologies that allow both consumers and regulators to understand AI-driven financial decisions.

The rise of Neobanks (Challenger Banks) has been one of the most disruptive trends of Fintech 4.0. These fully digital financial institutions operate without physical branches, offering low fees, real-time analytics, and AI-driven financial planning. Major Neobanks such as Monzo and Revolut (UK) provide commission-free international transactions, budgeting tools, and real-time spending insights. Similarly, N26 (Germany) integrates AI-driven financial planning and automated savings. Digital identity verification, powered by companies like Onfido and Jumio, enhances fraud prevention and account security through facial recognition and biometric authentication. Neobanks emphasize financial transparency, offering clear fee structures and open banking frameworks that allow users to securely link multiple accounts through APIs. However, AML compliance, data security, and consumer protection remain major regulatory challenges. Moving forward, transparency policies in neobanking will focus on robust data privacy protocols, real-time financial health reporting, and consumer trust (Dorfleitner et al., 2023). As open banking evolves, Neobanks are expected to reshape digital finance, balancing security, transparency, and regulatory accountability.

BT has become a foundation for financial trust, offering secure, decentralized, and tamper-proof transactions. By enabling publicly verifiable financial records, BT reduces fraud risks and increases accountability. Governments are also exploring CBDCs as a BT-based alternative to cash, promising faster transactions and financial inclusion. However, concerns about privacy, government surveillance, and regulatory control remain central to CBDC debates (Carrière-Swallow & Haksar, 2021).

DeFi is among the most transformative fintech innovations, enabling borrowing, lending, and trading through BT-based P2P financial networks. Unlike traditional banking, DeFi platforms operate without intermediaries, using smart contracts to automate transactions and facilitate real-time audits. By eliminating third parties, DeFi enhances efficiency and transparency, allowing users full control over financial assets. However, despite its benefits, DeFi introduces significant risks. Flash loan attacks, where hackers exploit vulnerabilities in smart contracts, have resulted in multi-million-dollar losses due to unsecured lending mechanisms. Additionally, liquidity crises pose a serious challenge, as DeFi platforms lack lender-of-last-resort protections, making them highly susceptible to market crashes and extreme volatility. Another major concern is the lack of consumer protection, as DeFi operates largely outside traditional regulatory frameworks, leaving users vulnerable to fraud, hacking, and asset instability (Auer & Claessens, 2018). Financial regulators, including the Financial Action Task Force (FATF) and the European Securities and Markets Authority (ESMA), are pushing for AML compliance and real-time transaction monitoring (Chang et al., 2020). Governance transparency and security measures will be essential in ensuring DeFi's long-term stability and legitimacy (Jalal et al., 2023).

Embedded finance is reshaping consumer transactions by embedding financial services within non-financial platforms. An example is the rapid rise of Buy Now, Pay Later (BNPL), which enables consumers to divide purchases into interest-free installments. Leading providers (e.g., Klarna, Afterpay, Affirm), dominate Western markets, while companies like Axio are expanding rapidly in emerging markets. Amazon's $150 M acquisition of Axio illustrates the convergence of retail, payments, and consumer credit, signaling a broader shift toward integrated financial ecosystems. Although BNPL provides financial flexibility and accessibility, it also raises concerns regarding hidden fees, mounting consumer debt, and regulatory challenges. In response, regulators have introduced stricter transparency and responsible lending requirements, mandating clear disclosure of repayment terms, stronger risk assessment practices, and enhanced consumer protections.

Fintech 4.0 has transformed financial services by making them smarter, faster, and more efficient. However, as AI, BT, and DeFi continue to evolve, the industry faces significant challenges, including cybersecurity risks, algorithmic biases, and regulatory uncertainty. Looking ahead, Fintech 5.0 is expected to prioritize several areas of development. One of the main focuses will be on ethical AI and bias mitigation, ensuring that financial decision-making processes are fair, transparent, and free from discriminatory biases. Additionally, the integration of sustainable finance principles, particularly Environmental, Social, and Governance (ESG) criteria, will shape the next generation of fintech solutions, promoting financial practices that align with global sustainability goals. Furthermore, regulatory harmonization will become increasingly important, as governments and financial authorities work toward establishing global fintech standards that enhance consumer protection, financial stability, and cross-border compliance.

To adapt to these rapid changes, financial institutions can adopt three strategies for integrating digital transformation: stepwise (gradual tech adoption), big bang approach (rapid large-scale innovation), or emergent approach (continuous real-time adaptation) (Nicoletti, 2021, 2025). By embedding automation, AI, and real-time analytics, financial firms can offer seamless, data-driven financial services tailored to individual needs. As Fintech innovation accelerates, transparency, security, and regulatory alignment will be critical to shaping the future of Fintech 5.0.

Fintech 5.0 (Future): Hyper-Personalized, Sustainable, and Ethical Finance
The next phase of Fintech, Fintech 5.0, is expected to represent a shift from purely profit-driven innovations to a model that integrates hyper-personalization, sustainability, and ethical financial practices (Saini, 2023). Unlike previous Fintech revolutions, which emphasized efficiency, automation, and decentralization, this phase will prioritize financial transparency, inclusivity, and responsibility, ensuring that financial institutions operate with a greater sense of accountability toward consumers, regulators, and society at large (He et al., 2023; Nicoletti, 2021).

Incorporating ESG principles, Fintech 5.0 will need to align financial models with sustainability goals. Financial institutions will be expected to improve transparency in governance, lending practices, and investment decisions to ensure fairer access to credit, ethical investment frameworks, and stronger consumer protections (Boot et al., 2021). Furthermore, with the continued development of Quantum Computing (QC), tokenized assets, decentralized identity verification, and AI-powered compliance monitoring, the future of Fintech will involve greater automation and more sophisticated transparency measures.

At its core, Fintech 5.0 seeks to integrate trust, security, and financial inclusion into financial ecosystems worldwide. The widespread adoption of AI-driven platforms, cognitive computing, BDA, and robotic process automation (RPA) will enable banks and financial service providers to develop new business models, streamline operations, and improve decision-making processes (Addy et al., 2024; Nicoletti, 2021, 2025).

- *Hyper-Personalization in Financial Services and AI-Driven Finance*

Fintech is undergoing a profound transformation, driven by advancements in AI, BT, QC, and regulatory innovations. These developments are not only streamlining financial operations but also introducing new business models that prioritize efficiency, security, and inclusivity. A defining feature of Fintech 5.0 is the emergence of hyper-personalized financial services, where banking and investment products are tailored to individual user preferences, behaviors, and risk profiles (Chakraborti et al., 2025).

Financial institutions will increasingly leverage real-time data analytics, AI-powered cognitive solutions, and predictive modeling to offer services that dynamically adapt to consumer spending habits, savings goals, and investment strategies. AI-driven solutions will enhance customer engagement by analyzing vast datasets to provide automated portfolio management, predictive loan approvals, and targeted financial recommendations. ML models will play a central role in assessing users' financial behavior, determining the most suitable credit options, savings plans, and investment opportunities for each individual.

In addition to offering tailored financial solutions, AI-powered chatbots and virtual assistants are expected to grow increasingly sophisticated, helping users make more informed financial decisions while limiting the need for direct human involvement. Such advancements not only streamline operations but also enable institutions to lower costs and simultaneously enhance customer satisfaction.

However, with increased personalization comes growing concerns over data privacy, AI ethics, and algorithmic bias (Dorfleitner et al., 2023). Regulators will need to ensure that AI-driven financial decisions remain transparent, explainable, and free from biases that could disadvantage certain demographic groups. The demand for XAI will grow, requiring financial institutions to demonstrate how ML algorithms assess risk, approve loans, or set credit limits.

AI and ML are already transforming financial services by enabling predictive analytics, fraud detection, and automated decision-making. AI-powered robo-advisors provide personalized investment strategies, while ML-driven risk assessment models improve credit scoring accuracy, enhancing both customer experiences and operational efficiency (Bartram et al., 2020). By reducing costs for financial institutions, AI is helping create a smarter, more inclusive, and highly automated financial landscape.

- *Quantum Finance and Cryptographic Transparency*

The emergence of QC is set to revolutionize financial modeling, risk assessment, and portfolio optimization, as it enables complex calculations to be processed exponentially faster than traditional computing systems. Quantum algorithms will enhance derivatives pricing, market simulations, and HFT, offering unprecedented precision in financial forecasting and investment strategies.

However, the rise of quantum technology also presents a significant threat to traditional cryptographic security. Current encryption methods that safeguard financial transactions, identity verification, and BT networks could become vulnerable to quantum decryption. This challenge necessitates the development of quantum-resistant encryption methods, ensuring that digital assets and financial transactions remain secure in the quantum era. Financial institutions will need to invest in post-quantum cryptographic frameworks to future-proof security and maintain consumer trust in a rapidly evolving digital finance landscape.

- *RegTech-Powered Compliance and Financial Transparency*

RegTech is playing a crucial role in automating compliance processes, helping financial institutions navigate the increasingly complex regulatory landscape (Anagnostopoulos, 2018). AI-driven monitoring, real-time transaction auditing, and BT-based identity verification are allowing firms to adhere to global financial regulations more efficiently while reducing compliance costs and mitigating fraud-related risks.

As regulatory scrutiny increases, RegTech firms and compliance-focused Fintechs are expected to lead efforts in enhancing financial transparency (Anagnostopoulos, 2018). These organizations will leverage AI and ML models to improve risk assessment, fraud detection, and regulatory reporting. The integration of BT-based compliance mechanisms will further strengthen financial oversight, ensuring that transaction histories remain immutable and verifiable in real time.

Future transparency policies in RegTech-powered compliance will likely include real-time compliance monitoring, automated audits, and open financial reporting to ensure full adherence to regulatory frameworks (Monroy & Corredor, 2019). As financial authorities continue tightening regulations, FinTech firms must embrace regulatory alignment to build trust, reduce financial crime risks, and create a more accountable financial ecosystem.

- *Sustainability, ESG-Driven Finance and Ethical FinTech*

As the financial industry evolves, sustainability and ESG compliance are set to become core pillars of Fintech 5.0. The emphasis will shift toward ethical finance, ensuring that corporate decision-making and investment strategies align with social responsibility, environmental impact, and governance transparency (Addy et al., 2024). Financial institutions will be expected to integrate ESG principles into their operations, fostering a more responsible and sustainable financial ecosystem (Rerung et al., 2024).

A very important aspect of sustainable Fintech will be the promotion of green finance initiatives, directing capital toward renewable energy projects, carbon-neutral investments, and climate-conscious financial products. Impact investing will also play a significant role, encouraging capital allocation toward businesses that prioritize fair labor practices, diversity and inclusion policies, and ethical supply chain management. To reinforce corporate accountability, BT-based financial reporting will enable real-time verification of ESG compliance, allowing regulators, investors, and consumers to track environmental and social impact transparently (Tiron-Tudor & Deliu, 2024).

The integration of Fintech solutions into sustainability-driven finance is already reshaping markets. Green finance initiatives, impact investing, and carbon credit trading platforms are leveraging BT and AI, and digital payment solutions to promote ethical and environmentally responsible financial practices. Additionally, digital inclusion efforts are expanding access to financial services for underserved populations, ensuring that financial progress remains equitable and accessible.

Governments and financial regulators are moving toward stricter ESG reporting standards, requiring financial institutions to disclose environmental and social impact metrics (Rerung et al., 2024). The integration of real-time ESG analytics will enable investors to assess the ethical footprint of their financial decisions, helping to shift global capital flows toward more sustainable economic activities. In this new era of Fintech 5.0, transparency, sustainability, and ethical governance will become essential components of a future-proof financial system (Addy et al., 2024; Bhat et al., 2024).

- *DeFi, Smart Contracts, and the Future of Financial Inclusion*

As Fintech 5.0 continues to evolve, DeFi is expected to expand its role in delivering financial services without intermediaries. By eliminating the need for traditional banks and brokers, DeFi will offer direct, borderless financial solutions, particularly benefiting underbanked and emerging markets. This shift will enhance financial accessibility, empowering individuals who previously lacked access to formal banking services.

DeFi platforms leverage BT to facilitate P2P lending, yield farming, and decentralized exchanges (DEXs) (Aspris et al., 2021). By integrating smart contracts (i.e., self-executing agreements stored on BT networks), DeFi enhances financial transparency, reduces counterparty risk, and automates transactions without relying on centralized authorities. These innovations increase efficiency and security, making financial services more inclusive and resilient.

However, despite its transformative potential, DeFi faces significant regulatory and security challenges. The absence of clear oversight raises concerns about market manipulation, financial fraud, and smart contract vulnerabilities. Since DeFi operates outside traditional financial regulations, consumers are often left unprotected against hacking, exploitative lending practices, and liquidity risks.

As DeFi expands, regulators are expected to intensify demands for accountability and stronger governance transparency. Financial authorities across the globe will work toward frameworks that can curb risks without undermining the advantages of decentralization. Responsible governance will therefore become a central priority, striking a balance between financial innovation and consumer protection, while helping to prevent systemic risks and encourage the growth of a more transparent and inclusive financial ecosystem.

- *Embedded Finance and the Future of Ethical Fintech*

Another dominant feature of Fintech 5.0 will be the further expansion of embedded finance, where financial services become an invisible yet integral part of everyday transactions. E-commerce platforms, social media applications, and digital marketplaces will integrate seamless financial services, allowing users to access credit, savings, and investment tools within their existing digital ecosystems.

Amazon's recent acquisition of Axio, an Indian Buy Now, Pay Later (BNPL) startup, for over $150 million highlights how embedded finance is transforming the industry. This move signals that BNPL services, digital lending, and seamless payment solutions will continue to grow, particularly in emerging economies.

However, as embedded finance becomes more prevalent, financial regulators will need to establish safeguards to ensure that these services are offered ethically and responsibly, preventing predatory lending and hidden financial risks.

Consequently, Fintech 5.0 represents a fundamental shift in the financial sector, where technological innovation is balanced with ethics, transparency, and sustainability (Chakraborti et al., 2025). Unlike earlier Fintech revolutions that focused solely on automation and profitability, this phase emphasizes trust, responsible AI usage, and regulatory compliance.

By integrating hyper-personalized AI-driven finance, ESG compliance, DeFi, and embedded financial services, Fintech 5.0 aims to build a financial ecosystem that is more inclusive, secure, and ethically responsible. As the industry moves forward, the success of Fintech 5.0 will be defined not just by technological advancements but also by its ability to create a transparent and socially responsible financial world (Table 1).

Consequently, Fintech 5.0 will be defined by hyper-personalization, quantum-driven security enhancements, and AI-powered compliance frameworks, ensuring that financial systems remain transparent, secure, and ethically responsible in the digital age.

3 The Future of Transparency in Fintech 5.0

As Fintech enters its next evolutionary phase, commonly referred to as Fintech 5.0, transparency is poised to become one of the most critical factors shaping the industry's future (Allen et al., 2021; Menat, 2016). While earlier phases of Fintech were driven primarily by efficiency, automation, and speed, the emerging paradigm emphasizes openness, explainability, and accountability. This shift marks the transition from opaque, proprietary decision-making models to transparent, auditable, and ethically sound financial systems, requiring organizations to prioritize accountability and openness.

Traditionally, many Fintech organizations operated with secrecy, leveraging exclusive access to financial data and proprietary algorithms as competitive advantages. However, as regulatory scrutiny intensifies and consumer expectations evolve, financial firms face mounting pressure to adopt transparent business models. In this new era, transparency goes

Table 1 The evolution of Fintech: from Fintech 1.0 to Fintech 5.0

Pillar	*Fintech 1.0 (1866–1967)*	*Fintech 2.0 (1967–2008)*	*Fintech 3.0 (2008–2020)*	*Fintech 4.0 (2020–present)*	*Fintech 5.0 (future)*
Core characteristics	Early digitization of finance, introduction of telegraph, transatlantic cables, and early computing systems. Financial institutions relied on centralized models with minimal transparency	The rise of digital banking, electronic payments, ATMs, and credit cards. Introduction of EFT systems. The 1987 market crash highlighted risks associated with financial technology	The emergence of platform-based finance, mobile wallets, crowdfunding, and P2P lending. Expansion of BT, cryptocurrencies, and DeFi	Integration of AI, BT, and DeFi in mainstream financial services. Proliferation of digital-only Neobanks, automated trading, biometric identity verification, and RegTech compliance monitoring	Hyper-personalized financial services, ESG-driven finance, XAI, and sustainable financial models. Implementation of decentralized identity systems, tokenized financial reporting, and real-time AI-driven compliance monitoring
Main technologies	Telegraph networks, transatlantic cables, early mechanical computing, paper-based financial transactions	ATMs, credit cards, EFT, computerized banking systems, internet banking, early mobile banking	BT, mobile wallets, AI-driven automation, robo-advisors, cryptocurrency platforms, open banking APIs, cloud computing	AI-powered financial decision-making, biometric authentication, DeFi, RegTech solutions for compliance monitoring, digital	QC, tokenized assets, XAI, decentralized identity verification, real-time compliance monitoring, ESG-

(continued)

Table 1 (continued)

Pillar	*Fintech 1.0 (1866–1967)*	*Fintech 2.0 (1967–2008)*	*Fintech 3.0 (2008–2020)*	*Fintech 4.0 (2020–present)*	*Fintech 5.0 (future)*
				identity verification, CBDCs	driven finance models
Major innovations	Globalized financial communications, first iterations of risk management, structured financial products	Introduction of online banking, credit scoring models, risk management tools, HFT, and early automation	Emergence of Fintech startups disrupting traditional banking, rise of mobile payments, crowdfunding, P2P lending, and robo-advisors	Development of AI-driven investment management, biometric verification, DeFi platforms, and real-time regulatory compliance technologies	Expected adoption of ethical AI, quantum-secured transactions, AI-driven sustainable finance, and enhanced consumer data control
Regulatory changes	Minimal regulation, primarily focused on preventing fraud and ensuring financial stability. The emergence of formal banking regulations to standardize financial operations	Financial liberalization through the Big Bang (1986) in the UK, the Maastricht Treaty (1992) enabling EU financial integration, and the Basel II framework improving international banking regulations	Introduction of the Revised Payment Services Directive (PSD2) in 2018, enforcing open banking. Initial cryptocurrency regulations introduced as Bitcoin and Ethereum gained adoption. Post-2008 crisis regulatory reforms	Stronger AML/KYC compliance measures, introduction of CBDC discussions, real-time AI-driven fraud monitoring, and RegTech solutions for automated regulatory compliance	Mandatory ESG disclosures for financial institutions, AI ethics and explainability standards, DeFi governance frameworks, full transparency in BT-based financial reporting

(continued)

Table 1 (continued)

Pillar	*Fintech 1.0 (1866–1967)*	*Fintech 2.0 (1967–2008)*	*Fintech 3.0 (2008–2020)*	*Fintech 4.0 (2020–present)*	*Fintech 5.0 (future)*
			like Dodd-Frank Act (2010) focused on risk mitigation and financial transparency		
Challenges and risks	Lack of transparency, reliance on manual processes, risk of financial fraud due to weak regulatory frameworks	Systemic financial risks, security vulnerabilities in early electronic systems, need for more robust international regulatory frameworks	Cybersecurity threats, regulatory uncertainty surrounding BT and cryptocurrency, privacy concerns with AI-driven financial services	Ethical concerns about AI decision-making, privacy risks with biometric verification, lack of regulation in DeFi markets, and compliance challenges	Ensuring ethical AI use, balancing personalization with privacy, enforcing sustainability mandates, and addressing regulatory complexities in tokenized financial models
Impact on consumers	Limited financial accessibility, manual banking processes, reliance on cash transactions	Increased access to digital banking, greater financial inclusion, improved transactional efficiency	More consumer control over financial choices, wider access to alternative lending and investment options, rise of self-service banking	Frictionless banking experiences through Neobanks, greater use of AI-powered financial planning tools, improved transaction security	Fully customized financial services, decentralized identity ownership, real-time financial transparency, and AI-assisted wealth management

(continued)

Table 1 (continued)

Pillar	*Fintech 1.0 (1866–1967)*	*Fintech 2.0 (1967–2008)*	*Fintech 3.0 (2008–2020)*	*Fintech 4.0 (2020–present)*	*Fintech 5.0 (future)*
Transparency focus	Limited transparency, with most financial operations conducted internally within banks. Customers had little visibility into institutional financial practices	Regulatory oversight increased, but consumer financial data remained under institutional control. Financial disclosures improved, but transparency remained a secondary concern	BT introduced public ledger transparency, increasing openness in financial transactions but raising concerns over regulatory oversight in decentralized systems	AI-driven compliance monitoring provided real-time risk assessment, BT improved transactional transparency, and digital banks offered greater visibility into account management and fees	A fully transparent financial ecosystem, with BT-based financial reporting, decentralized identity verification, and AI-powered real-time compliance ensuring regulatory adherence and accountability

beyond regulatory necessity and increasingly serves as a defining factor of competitiveness. Financial technology must not only be intelligent and efficient but also comprehensible, fair, and auditable.

The need for transparency in fintech extends beyond regulatory compliance; it is an essential component of a resilient and sustainable financial ecosystem (Bouafia et al., 2024). Opaque financial decision-making can lead to algorithmic biases, discriminatory lending practices, and regulatory non-compliance, potentially excluding marginalized communities and reinforcing economic disparities. For example, AI-driven credit scoring models have been found to inadvertently perpetuate racial and socioeconomic biases, resulting in unfair lending practices (Abbas, 2024).

Moreover, the fragmented nature of global financial regulations introduces challenges for Fintech firms operating across multiple jurisdictions. With rapidly evolving policies on AI, financial disclosures, and data protection, firms must continuously adapt to shifting regulatory landscapes or risk legal and reputational consequences (Pantielieieva et al., 2020). Consumers, too, are increasingly aware of financial opacity, and a lack of transparency can erode trust, hinder Fintech adoption (Jünger & Mietzner, 2020), and amplify regulatory scrutiny.

History has repeatedly demonstrated the dangers of financial opacity. The 2008 global financial crisis was exacerbated by complex and opaque financial instruments, which even industry professionals struggled to fully understand. More recently, the collapse of high-profile crypto exchanges like FTX and Mt. Gox has underscored the risks associated with opaque financial structures and non-transparent governance (Aspris et al., 2021; Foley et al., 2019). Without proactive transparency measures, fintech risks replicating past failures, especially as algorithmic trading, DeFi, and AI-driven lending models become more widespread.

In the modern financial landscape, trust has become one of the most valuable yet fragile assets a financial institution can possess. Unlike trust in social media platforms, where users entrust their data, trusting a bank involves direct financial risk, making trust harder to gain and easier to lose (Thakor & Merton, 2024). The digitization of financial services has empowered consumers, allowing them to switch banks, withdraw funds, or terminate financial relationships almost instantly. This newfound autonomy has weakened traditional loyalty structures, forcing Fintech firms to actively cultivate and maintain consumer trust through transparent, ethical practices.

In this era of Industry 6.0 and information democratization, transparency is more than just a business practice, respectively a core strategic imperative shaping consumer perceptions, investment decisions, and regulatory policies (Leong & Sung, 2018). For Fintech companies, where security, reliability, and automation underpin every transaction, transparency is essential for safeguarding reputation, maintaining compliance, and fostering long-term sustainability. A single instance of misconduct, mismanagement, or fraud can cause irreparable reputational damage, particularly in today's volatile and hyper-connected financial environment.

A recent study (Thakor & Merton, 2024) suggests that trust in financial innovations operates as a binary phenomenon: it is either fully present or entirely absent. This implies that when investor confidence erodes, the response, instead of being a gradual reassessment, is an abrupt withdrawal from the technology or platform (Shkolnyk & Zakharkina, 2022). As long as trust remains intact, occasional disruptions may exert minimal impact on Fintech adoption (Vives, 2019). However, a single major trust failure could trigger a widespread loss of confidence, leading to market instability and regulatory interventions.

Transparency in Fintech is multi-dimensional, encompassing both internal and external elements. Understanding these two dimensions is essential for evaluating how Fintech organizations balance regulatory compliance, consumer trust, and operational integrity. Internal transparency refers to governance structures, decision-making processes, and regulatory compliance measures within a financial institution. Firms that embrace internal transparency foster ethical financial management, fraud prevention, and accountable leadership (Böhme et al., 2015; Gomber et al., 2017). External transparency, on the other hand, pertains to public disclosures of financial, operational, and governance-related information. This includes how companies communicate with consumers, regulators, and investors, ensuring that financial systems remain fair, competitive, and ethically aligned (He et al., 2023).

The central challenge for Fintech firms is determining how much transparency is sufficient while balancing proprietary data protection, security concerns, and regulatory expectations (Goldstein et al., 2019). For example, traditional banks are subject to capital adequacy disclosures and strict financial reporting frameworks, whereas many crypto-based Fintech firms operate with opaque balance sheets, leading to unexpected collapses and investor losses (Foley et al., 2019). Similarly, AI-driven financial services present unique transparency challenges since many credit-scoring algorithms and investment models operate as "black-box" systems with little explainability. The growing demand for XAI is a response to these concerns, as regulators push for greater clarity in automated decision-making processes (Brummer & Yadav, 2018; Campbell-Verduyn, 2018).

3.1 *Internal Transparency: Governance and Accountability*

Internal transparency in Fintech refers to how financial organizations manage and disclose information within their structures, covering governance policies, decision-making processes, compliance mechanisms, and operational reporting (Addy et al., 2024). Companies that prioritize internal transparency benefit from greater accountability, improved regulatory adherence, and enhanced internal risk management (Pantielieieva et al., 2020). In an industry where automation, AI, and data analytics play increasingly prominent roles, maintaining clear internal governance structures is crucial for ensuring ethical financial practices and trustworthiness.

The integration of AI in financial decision-making presents new challenges for transparency and accountability (Petrovska et al., 2020). As AI systems assume greater responsibility in loan approvals, credit scoring, algorithmic trading, and fraud detection, concerns regarding bias, liability, and unintended consequences demand rigorous oversight and ethical safeguards (Fletcher & Le, 2021; Giglio, 2022; Turksen et al., 2024). The lack of explainability in AI-driven models, often referred to as black-box algorithms, has prompted increasing regulatory scrutiny. Stakeholders now demand greater clarity on how financial decisions are made, particularly when they impact consumers' creditworthiness, investments, or access to financial services (Percy et al., 2021). Accountability is widely recognized as the cornerstone of AI governance, ensuring transparency and trust in financial innovation (Bartram et al., 2020; Giglio, 2022; Novelli et al., 2024; Varga, 2017).

Internal transparency is both a regulatory requirement and a core component of trust-building in Fintech. Fintech originally emerged as a solution to restore confidence in financial systems following the 2008 global financial crisis, offering greater accessibility, efficiency, and consumer empowerment (Goldstein et al., 2019; Jalal et al., 2023; Tohang et al., 2021). However, as the industry has expanded, so too have concerns surrounding the ethical implications of AI, BDA, and algorithmic financial management (Petrovska et al., 2020). Consumers expect not just seamless access to financial services but also transparency in how these services operate (Shkolnyk & Zakharkina, 2022).

As Fintech organizations increasingly incorporate AI-driven decision-making, concerns related to ethics, privacy, and consumer well-being have intensified. Algorithmic bias, lack of human oversight in AI-led financial decisions, and opaque ML models have created growing regulatory and ethical challenges (Rizinski et al., 2022; Hermansyah et al., 2023; Bouafia et al., 2024). Moreover, the impact of Fintech on consumer psychology has also emerged as a critical issue. The rise of techno-stressors, such as information overload, misinformation, and AI-induced decision-making anxiety, complicates the user experience (Deliu, 2024; Deliu & Olariu, 2024). Customers often feel overwhelmed by complex financial products that lack clear explanations, contributing to distrust in Fintech platforms (Alcalá Consuegra & Zabaraín García, 2012). Transparency can mitigate these concerns, improving consumer confidence, financial literacy, and long-term customer loyalty.

At the same time, Fintech firms must balance internal transparency with the imperative for innovation and growth. The record-breaking $34 billion in venture capital funding for Fintech startups (The Economist, 2021) underscores the industry's rapid expansion. However, customer loyalty is now more critical than market relevance, as consumers increasingly prioritize institutions that align with their ethical values and uphold strong governance standards. By integrating transparency, ethical AI practices, and consumer-focused business models, Fintech firms can differentiate themselves in an increasingly competitive landscape.

As Industry 6.0 redefines the intersection of finance and technology, internal transparency will play a crucial role in leadership, governance, and long-term sustainability. Established frameworks, such as the Upper Echelons Theory (Hambrick & Mason, 1984) emphasize the role of top executives in shaping organizational accountability. Fintech firms that embed robust governance mechanisms, ethical decision-making practices, and internal audit structures will be better positioned to navigate regulatory challenges and retain consumer trust.

Fintech firms that prioritize internal transparency establish well-defined governance frameworks, outlining clear roles and responsibilities for board members, executives, compliance officers, and stakeholders (Tiron-Tudor & Deliu, 2024). Transparent corporate structures ensure that decision-making processes remain accountable and subject to internal scrutiny. Organizations that conduct regular internal audits, maintain independent oversight bodies, and foster open communication within the company benefit from stronger regulatory compliance and ethical leadership (Böhme et al., 2015; Campbell-Verduyn, 2018).

Internally transparent Fintech firms ensure that compliance procedures are well-documented, accessible, and frequently updated to align with global regulatory changes. Automated compliance monitoring tools, AI-driven risk assessments, and RegTech solutions help organizations maintain real-time oversight of financial operations (Anagnostopoulos, 2018). Compliance transparency also minimizes the risk of regulatory penalties and fosters a culture of ethical decision-making (Allen et al., 2021).

Financial transparency within Fintech firms requires real-time documentation of financial activities, internal risk assessments, and operational performance reports (Rerung et al., 2024). Organizations that provide employees with access to relevant internal data foster a culture of ethical accountability and informed decision-making. Transparent internal reporting systems also enhance collaboration between departments, ensuring that risk management strategies are proactively adjusted in response to evolving financial trends.

By ensuring internal transparency across governance, compliance, and financial reporting, fintech organizations can strengthen their regulatory standing, enhance risk management strategies, and establish long-term trust with both regulators and consumers.

3.2 *External Transparency: Public Trust and Regulatory Compliance*

External transparency refers to how openly Fintech firms communicate with customers, investors, regulators, and the broader public. This includes financial disclosures, open-source data practices, customer privacy policies, and regulatory reporting. High levels of external transparency foster consumer trust, reduce fraudulent activities, and ensure adherence to global financial standards (Rabbani et al., 2020).

As regulatory scrutiny increases and consumer expectations shift toward ethical financial practices, Fintech firms must navigate the delicate balance between transparency and data privacy (Aldboush & Ferdous, 2023; Dorfleitner et al., 2023). While regulators demand greater accountability, real-time compliance monitoring (Rerung et al., 2024), and open financial disclosures, consumers expect secure, private, and personalized financial services (Zetzsche et al., 2017). Striking this balance is one of the greatest challenges facing Fintech organizations today (Monroy & Corredor, 2019).

In a world of intensified financial surveillance, external transparency plays a pivotal role in maintaining public trust (Chou, 2019; Rabbani et al., 2020). Fintech firms must ensure clear communication about data collection, storage, and usage to address both regulatory requirements and consumer concerns regarding privacy and security (Dorfleitner et al., 2023). Financial surveillance involves monitoring transactions, analyzing financial behaviors, and sharing data with regulatory authorities to prevent fraud, money laundering, and financial crimes (Zetzsche et al., 2017). While these measures enhance financial security, they also raise concerns about data privacy, surveillance capitalism, and consumer autonomy (Dorfleitner et al., 2023). Consumers expect Fintech firms to: (i) ensure data privacy by adopting secure storage and processing mechanisms; (ii) demonstrate integrity through ethical AI-driven financial decision-making; and (iii) foster security by preventing fraud, protecting sensitive information, and limiting unnecessary data exposure. For Fintech firms, compliance with financial surveillance mandates requires implementing robust Know Your Customer (KYC) protocols (Botha, 2024), AML systems (Daugaard et al., 2024), and continuous transaction monitoring (Turksen et al., 2024). These practices involve collecting vast amounts of consumer data, which, if not managed transparently, can lead to public distrust and regulatory backlash.

Additionally, the Fintech industry operates in a rapidly evolving regulatory landscape, shaped by heightened financial surveillance and growing consumer awareness. As governments and regulatory bodies impose stricter compliance measures to prevent financial crimes, safeguard consumer rights, and ensure data integrity, Fintech firms must maintain a delicate balance between transparency and trust (Dorfleitner et al., 2023).

Fintech is described as a technology-enabled disruptor of financial services that facilitates innovation while simultaneously increasing financial complexity. Today, Fintech companies must acknowledge frameworks such as the General Data Protection Regulation (GDPR) and the California Consumer Privacy Act (CCPA), which mandate data protection and consumer transparency (Dorfleitner et al., 2023). In the same vein, the European Union AI Act requires XAI and ethical compliance in financial services, while the Open Banking Standards encourage data-sharing frameworks that enhance transparency and competition. Adhering to these regulations requires advanced planning, real-time reporting, and technology-driven compliance solutions. As such, Fintech firms must integrate automated compliance monitoring, ensuring continuous alignment with legal mandates without compromising consumer privacy.

However, the tension between transparency and privacy is a defining challenge in modern Fintech governance. Transparency, a key factor in consumer trust and regulatory compliance, requires clear disclosures on financial data collection, processing, and usage. However, excessive transparency risks exposing sensitive consumer information, potentially compromising data security and user privacy.

Research highlights the importance of striking a balance, where Fintech firms adopt anonymization techniques to protect user identities while enabling financial audits (Dorfleitner et al., 2023). Additionally, they can create data minimization strategies to collect only essential financial information (Carrière-Swallow & Haksar, 2021), as well as secure data-sharing protocols that restrict access to authorized parties only (Bouafia et al., 2024).

Consumer expectations further complicate the transparency-privacy dynamic. Users demand ethical data handling and robust privacy protections, expecting Fintech companies to: (i) offer control over personal data, including opt-in/opt-out mechanisms; (ii) provide clear, accessible privacy policies explaining data usage; and (iii) demonstrate the benefits of transparency, such as fraud prevention and enhanced security.

Fintech firms must embed privacy-first frameworks into their transparency policies, ensuring consumer rights, regulatory compliance, and trust-building remain top priorities.

Thus, Fintech firms can enhance consumer trust by providing clear and comprehensible financial product disclosures, transparent transaction fees, and robust data privacy policies (Dorfleitner et al., 2023). The implementation of open APIs and real-time transaction monitoring further strengthens transparency by allowing consumers to track and manage their financial interactions with greater clarity.

Structured public reporting mechanisms, including audited financial statements, regulatory filings, and corporate sustainability reports, play a crucial role in building investor and stakeholder confidence (Addy et al., 2024; D. Arner et al., 2022; Bhat et al., 2024; Tiron-Tudor & Deliu, 2024). The integration of BT-based financial disclosures provides an immutable and verifiable record of financial transactions, ensuring greater transparency and accountability in external reporting.

Fintech firms that prioritize external transparency actively engage with regulators and compliance authorities, ensuring full adherence to financial laws and industry standards. Participation in regulatory sandboxes, public hearings, and cross-border compliance initiatives demonstrates a commitment to ethical financial practices and transparent operations (Zetzsche et al., 2017).

4 The Four Transparency Models for Fintech 5.0

As financial technology advances toward Fintech 5.0, transparency emerges as a pivotal factor in determining the sustainability, trustworthiness, and regulatory compliance of Fintech organizations. Four distinct models illustrate how the presence (or absence) of internal and external transparency may shape the future of financial services. Each model outlines its core characteristics, governance structures, regulatory implications, AI oversight, financial disclosure practices, and its impact on consumer trust and financial stability (Fig. 2).

At one extreme, the Full Transparency Model represents the best-case future, where Fintech firms fully embrace transparency, ensuring trust,

Fig. 2 The four transparency models in Fintech 5.0

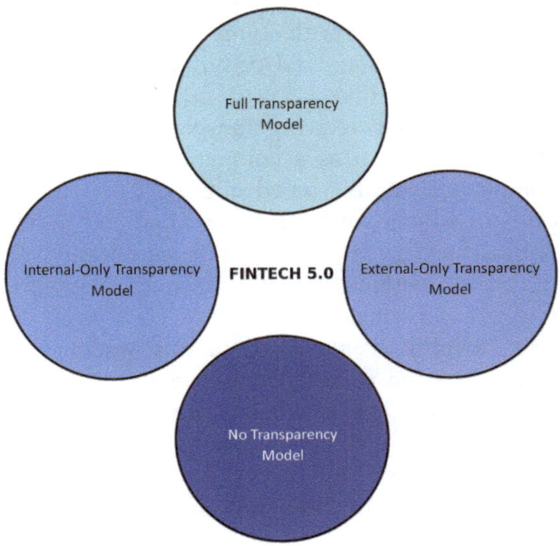

fairness, and responsible AI-driven decision-making. At the other extreme, the No Transparency Model illustrates the worst-case outcome, where unchecked AI, opaque financial models, and financial secrecy lead to systemic risks, fraud, and consumer distrust.

Between these extremes, the External-Only Transparency Model describes a world where regulation enforces transparency, but Fintech organizations remain reluctant to change, leading to a surface-level commitment to transparency without meaningful internal governance reforms. The Internal-Only Transparency Model represents a model where Fintech firms operate with strong internal controls and self-regulation but limit external disclosures, creating trust asymmetries between companies, regulators, and consumers.

Each possibility is synthesized in Table 2, outlining the organizations' governance structures, financial transparency policies, and their impact on market stability, compliance, and ethical AI adoption (Table 2).

4.1 Full Transparency Model

The Full Transparency Model envisions a future where Fintech organizations maximize both internal and external transparency, transforming financial services into an open, trust-driven ecosystem. Unlike traditional financial institutions that rely on opaque decision-making, Fintech firms in this model operate with complete visibility, ensuring that risk assessments, capital reserves, and AI-driven decisions are accessible for public and regulatory scrutiny.

Rather than perceiving transparency as a regulatory burden, firms in this model leverage it as a competitive advantage. Through XAI, real-time compliance, and BT-based auditing, Fintech companies establish an environment where consumers, investors, and regulators have equal access to critical financial data. This shift significantly reduces fraud, misinformation, and unethical financial practices, making the Fintech industry more resilient and consumer-centric.

A defining characteristic of this model is the full auditability of AI-driven decision-making frameworks. Lending, credit scoring, fraud detection, and trading algorithms are no longer black-box systems but are instead fully explainable and subject to oversight. Consumers and regulators can access detailed breakdowns of financial decisions, strengthening accountability and eliminating algorithmic bias.

Table 2 Transparency models in Fintech 5.0: overview and core characteristics

Pillar	*1. Full transparency model*	*2. External-only transparency model*	*3. Internal-only transparency model*	*4. No transparency model*
Overview	The ideal future for Fintech, where both internal and external transparency are maximized. Organizations embrace radical openness, ensuring full disclosure of governance, risk management, financial data, and AI decision-making. Trust, fairness, and accountability are integral to the Fintech ecosystem	Fintech firms comply with strict external transparency regulations but maintain opaque internal governance and decision-making. Transparency is regulator-enforced, not voluntary, requiring firms to disclose financial data, operational risks, and AI decision-making only as legally mandated.	Fintech firms maintain strong internal transparency and accountability while restricting external disclosures. Proprietary financial technologies, AI models, and risk frameworks remain hidden, leading to trust asymmetries between firms, regulators, and consumers	The worst-case scenario, where Fintech firms operate with minimal internal and external transparency. AI-driven financial services, algorithmic trading, and digital assets lack oversight, resulting in systemic risks, financial instability, and consumer distrust
Core characteristics	Fintech organizations embrace complete internal and external transparency, ensuring consumer trust, regulatory compliance, and ethical AI integration. Every decision, risk assessment, and financial transaction remains fully visible to all stakeholders	Fintech organizations do not voluntarily adopt transparency but comply with regulatory mandates that enforce disclosure. While external transparency improves, internal governance and AI decision-making remain proprietary and opaque	Fintech firms ensure ethical governance and compliance but restrict external transparency, providing minimal disclosures to regulators, investors, and customers. Operating under self-regulation, they conceal proprietary risk models, AI decisions, and operational data	Fintech firms operate in secrecy, with minimal transparency and AI-driven systems replacing human oversight. Profit outweighs ethics, creating financial instability, systemic risks, and potential fraud, while regulators and consumers remain in the dark

(continued)

Table 2 (continued)

Pillar	*1. Full transparency model*	*2. External-only transparency model*	*3. Internal-only transparency model*	*4. No transparency model*
Key features	✔ XAI as the norm ✔ BT-based PoR and transactions ✔ Real-time regulatory oversight and open banking ✔ Public governance of Fintech firms	✔ Mandatory AI ethics and explainability standards ✔ Regulated PoR and public financial disclosures ✔ Open banking standards, but no full transparency ✔ High compliance costs and regulatory arbitrage	✔ Internal compliance and ethical AI governance ✔ Opaque external financial reporting ✔ Selective data-sharing with regulators ✔ Corporate-led innovation and secretive AI models	✔ No XAI or auditing standards ✔ Opaque corporate structures and hidden financial risks ✔ Dark AI and algorithmic decision-making ✔ Minimal public financial disclosures
Characteristics of Fintech firms	✔ XAI ✔ Decentralized governance ✔ Real-time regulatory Compliance ✔ Tokenized financial reporting ✔ Privacy-protected open banking	✔ Regulatory pressure ✔ Surface-level transparency ✔ Fragmented open banking adoption ✔ Algorithmic oversight gaps	✔ Internal AI ethics and risk management ✔ Opaque external disclosures ✔ Selective compliance ✔ Corporate-led innovation	✔ Non-explainable AI (NXAI) ✔ Opaque corporate structures ✔ No public auditing standards ✔ High risk of financial crashes

(continued)

Table 2 (continued)

Pillar	*1. Full transparency model*	*2. External-only transparency model*	*3. Internal-only transparency model*	*4. No transparency model*
Example of future technologies	• AI-generated real-time compliance dashboards for consumers and regulators • BT PoR auditing for all financial institutions •Open APIs with consumer-controlled financial data sharing	• Government-regulated Fintech sandboxes for AI transparency testing • CBDCs with real-time compliance tracking • Machine-readable regulatory reporting standards for Fintech firms	• Privately managed AI-based lending models, with minimal public oversight • Internal-only XAI frameworks for proprietary risk assessment • Selective data-sharing agreements with regulators but not with the public	• AI-driven black-box hedge funds, operating without public disclosure • Algorithmic financial services with undisclosed bias in lending and credit decisions • Unregulated DEXs leading to financial instability
Implications	⊕ Trust-driven competitive advantage ⊕ Lower fraud and market stability ⊕ RegTech & compliance automation growth	⊕ Regulated financial stability ⊖ Compliance costs ⊖ Opaque AI risks	⊕ Efficient internal decision-making ⊖ Consumer distrust risks ⊖ Market imbalances	⊖ Regulatory chaos ⊖ Mass consumer distrust ⊖ Crypto and DeFi failures

BT ensures real-time financial transparency. PoR-systems provide immutable records of liquidity, risk exposure, and capital reserves, preventing financial mismanagement. Unlike traditional institutions that release delayed and selective reports, fintech firms in this model offer continuous, real-time audits, reinforcing corporate integrity and investor confidence.

Regulatory compliance is embedded directly into fintech operations through AI-driven RegTech solutions (Anagnostopoulos, 2018). Governments and regulators are moving away from periodic audits to real-time AI-powered monitoring, detecting violations before they escalate. This proactive compliance approach strengthens financial stability, reduces inefficiencies, and creates a more resilient financial ecosystem.

Governance structures also shift toward decentralization and participatory decision-making. Many firms adopt Decentralized Autonomous Organizations (DAOs), where stakeholders, consumers, and regulatory bodies vote on financial and operational matters. This governance model enhances corporate accountability and public trust, reducing the influence of centralized executive authority.

Consumer empowerment is another important aspect of this model. Unlike traditional banks that monetize financial data without consent, fintech firms implementing open banking frameworks ensure that users retain full ownership of their financial information. Consumers can authorize or deny access to third parties, eliminating unauthorized data sharing while promoting a fair and transparent financial ecosystem.

The adoption of this transparency-first model would reshape Fintech, fostering trust-based financial services and attracting long-term consumer loyalty. The risks of fraud, financial mismanagement, and market manipulation would be significantly reduced due to real-time BT-auditing and AI-powered compliance. Additionally, systemic financial crises could be mitigated by preventing firms from concealing liabilities, risks, or operational weaknesses.

However, this model also presents challenges. Full transparency may compromise proprietary financial strategies, as firms are required to disclose their financial models, investment strategies, and risk assessment frameworks. To balance openness with competitive security, selective disclosure agreements and permissioned BT networks may be necessary. Another challenge lies in the costs of maintaining continuous transparency. Implementing real-time compliance systems, BT-based audits, and decentralized governance demands significant investment in infrastructure and data management.

Despite these challenges, the Full Transparency Model provides a sustainable blueprint for ethical, accountable, and stable financial systems. By embracing open governance, XAI, and BT-based disclosures, Fintech firms can redefine financial services as transparent, inclusive, and consumer-centric. As Fintech advances toward Fintech 5.0, transparency-first business models will set the industry standard for responsible AI, regulatory alignment, and long-term financial sustainability.

4.2 *External-only Transparency Model*

The External-Only Transparency Model envisions a future where Fintech organizations comply with strict external regulatory mandates but do not voluntarily embrace transparency. Unlike the Full Transparency Model, where firms proactively disclose financial and operational data, organizations in this model reluctantly comply with legally enforced transparency requirements. Financial disclosure, AI decision-making audits, and risk assessment reporting are driven by government intervention rather than ethical commitment. While external transparency improves due to regulatory oversight, internal transparency remains opaque. Fintech firms reveal only the minimum legally required information, keeping proprietary AI models, risk frameworks, and governance structures confidential. This results in a superficial level of transparency, where financial institutions appear compliant but operate without fully disclosing their internal decision-making processes.

In this model, regulators play a dominant role in shaping Fintech operations by imposing mandatory audits, AI explainability requirements, and financial disclosure laws. Fintech firms often view these regulations as an operational burden, leading to a compliance-driven approach that prioritizes legal adherence over voluntary openness. While external transparency enhances market stability, it also increases regulatory expenses, slows innovation, and encourages firms to find legal loopholes.

Fintech firms operating under this model exist in a highly regulated financial ecosystem, where compliance is externally enforced rather than internally adopted. Governments mandate PoR-disclosures, requiring companies to report balance sheets, risk exposure, and debt structures. However, these disclosures are often limited to regulatory agencies, restricting public access to key financial information.

AI transparency remains partial and highly regulated. Fintech firms must comply with "Explainability Laws", auditing AI-driven financial decisions that impact credit scoring, lending, and investment recommendations. However, although regulators may be able to evaluate the fairness of AI systems and the safeguards against bias, consumers themselves have limited visibility into these processes, which restricts their ability to question or contest algorithmic decisions. Open banking adoption is also mandated by law, granting customers access to their financial data and allowing third-party service providers to integrate with financial platforms. Despite this, Fintech firms retain control over internal data models, restricting external oversight into trading algorithms, credit decision-making frameworks, and investment risk models.

The enforcement of strict regulatory transparency laws enhances financial system integrity by reducing fraud, preventing market instability, and mitigating financial mismanagement. However, these laws come at a high cost. Fintech firms face significant compliance expenses, as they must invest in automated reporting solutions, continuous auditing, and AI validation systems to meet evolving regulations. The financial and operational burdens of compliance slow innovation and increase overhead costs. As regulatory frameworks tighten, some Fintech firms engage in regulatory arbitrage, relocating their headquarters to jurisdictions with weaker transparency laws to avoid excessive oversight. This weakens global financial oversight, creating an uneven playing field where some regions enforce strict disclosure laws, while others offer secrecy havens for financial institutions seeking fewer restrictions.

Government-mandated transparency strengthens accountability and ensures regulatory compliance, but it does little to foster a culture of voluntary openness. Most Fintech firms disclose information only to the extent required by law. In the same time, though, they keep proprietary AI models, risk strategies, and governance structures hidden from view. Although consumers gain some benefits through regulated access to financial data, they still lack meaningful visibility into how algorithms shape credit scoring, lending, and investment decisions. Regulatory oversight contributes to greater financial stability, yet many firms continue to shield their internal processes, prioritizing competitive advantage over genuine ethical transparency.

As the Fintech industry navigates the complexities of compliance-driven transparency, organizations prioritize legal adherence over ethical financial governance. This model offers a stable but restrictive approach to transparency, where external oversight dictates financial visibility, but internal decision-making remains concealed.

4.3 Internal-only Transparency Model

The Internal-Only Transparency Model envisions a future where fintech firms prioritize internal governance, compliance, and risk management, ensuring robust ethical and regulatory standards. However, these organizations limit external transparency, keeping proprietary financial technologies, AI models, and risk frameworks hidden from public scrutiny. Unlike models that embrace radical openness or operate under strict regulatory mandates, this approach relies on corporate self-regulation, where firms enforce internal accountability mechanisms by restricting financial disclosures beyond what is legally required.

In this model, Fintech firms maintain strong internal oversight, implementing rigorous compliance programs, AI fairness audits, and risk assessments. AI-driven financial tools, such as credit scoring algorithms, lending platforms, and investment recommendation systems, undergo thorough internal monitoring to ensure fairness and accountability. However, these reports remain confidential, leaving consumers with limited insight into how financial decisions are made. Although strong internal governance can reinforce operational integrity, external stakeholders are often left with little more than limited disclosures and regulatory assurances when evaluating the financial stability of Fintech firms.

Unlike externally regulated transparency models, Fintech firms in this framework retain control over financial reporting, choosing not to disclose risk models, financial reserves, or investment strategies to the broader public. Companies only release the minimum legally required financial data, helping them protect proprietary algorithms and maintain a competitive edge. However, this selective disclosure approach raises concerns about financial stability, market integrity, and consumer trust, as investors and customers lack full visibility into how financial products operate. Although these firms limit public financial transparency, they actively engage with regulators, providing selective financial data and risk metrics as part of compliance requirements. Regulators receive high-level risk reports but lack full oversight of AI-driven financial decision-making, making it difficult to monitor market-wide risks. Unlike models where regulatory agencies enforce strict transparency laws, this approach relies on self-regulation, leading to strong internal governance but weaker external enforcement.

Financial reporting under this model remains opaque, with firms disclosing only essential financial data to meet regulatory requirements. Proofs of Reserves (PoRs), liquidity metrics, and risk assessments are shared with government agencies but are not accessible to investors, consumers, or competitors. This dynamic results in a controlled model of transparency in which regulators, rather than the public, hold exclusive access to information about Fintech firms' risk exposure, AI-driven decision-making, and overall financial stability. Proprietary algorithms are guarded as trade secrets, allowing firms to advance financial technologies without external scrutiny. Although these AI-powered products fuel innovation in lending, trading, and investment, the mechanisms behind their decisions remain largely opaque to consumers. This secrecy protects corporate intellectual property but also creates trust asymmetries, as customers cannot fully evaluate how their financial data is processed or how creditworthiness and risk assessments are determined.

The Internal-Only Transparency Model presents significant challenges, particularly in maintaining consumer trust. Without public PoRs, AI explainability, or detailed risk disclosures, skepticism toward Fintech services increases. Consumers struggle to understand financial decisions, limiting adoption and weakening investor confidence. The lack of comprehensive financial disclosures also introduces systemic risks. Since AI-driven trading, lending, and credit scoring platforms operate privately, regulators may struggle to detect financial instability before crises emerge. Hidden risk exposure, opaque debt structures, and proprietary investment models create vulnerabilities that could trigger financial shocks in the event of market downturns or algorithmic failures.

Fintech firms benefit from corporate autonomy, proprietary AI innovation, and lighter regulatory burdens, but these advantages cpme at the cost of eroding public confidence when financial transparency is restricted. Consumers gain access to financial products and services, but without full visibility into AI decision-making frameworks, investment strategies, or financial risk models, concerns about fairness, financial ethics, and algorithmic biases persist.

As the Fintech industry evolves, organizations operating under this model must navigate the tension between innovation and trust. If firms fail to provide sufficient external transparency, they may face increasing regulatory pressure and consumer backlash. Nevertheless, if they expand public disclosures while maintaining internal governance integrity, they could achieve a balance between corporate self-regulation and public accountability. The Internal-Only Transparency Model represents a financial landscape where firms operate with strong internal governance but limited public oversight. This approach supports AI-driven innovation and competitive market positioning. However, it simultaneously creates a fragile trust dynamic between Fintech firms, regulators, and consumers. Moving forward, organizations will need to reassess their approach to transparency, ensuring that consumer trust, financial stability, and regulatory alignment remain intact in the Fintech 5.0 era.

4.4 No Transparency Model

The No Transparency Model represents the worst-case future for Fintech, where both internal and external transparency are absent. In this environment, Fintech organizations operate without oversight, allowing AI-driven financial systems, algorithmic trading platforms, and DeFi services to function in secrecy. Unlike models that emphasize internal self-regulation or external compliance mandates, this model envisions an unregulated, unchecked Fintech ecosystem.

Financial firms in this model prioritize profit maximization over ethical considerations, leading to widespread consumer exploitation, financial discrimination, and increased systemic risk. AI-powered financial decision-making becomes a black-box system, leaving consumers, regulators, and investors without insight into how financial determinations are made. Hidden biases in credit scoring, lending, and investment decisions go unchecked, disproportionately impacting marginalized communities. The lack of transparency fosters financial instability, as undetected risk exposure, opaque investment strategies, and fraudulent activities escalate, often culminating in major market crashes.

Fintech firms in this model deliberately conceal financial data, risk models, and AI-driven decision-making frameworks from both regulators and the public. Unlike the Internal-Only Transparency Model, where strong internal governance provides at least some oversight, firms operating under No Transparency lack any meaningful accountability, exposing them to market volatility, fraud, and unchecked AI biases. With algorithmic financial systems replacing human oversight, Fintech firms depend entirely on AI-powered investment platforms, automated lending decisions, and opaque digital assets. These non-explainable, unaudited AI systems introduce hidden biases, undisclosed risks, and unpredictable financial outcomes, making markets extremely unstable. Corporate governance structures remain opaque, enabling firms to engage in high-risk financial activities without public scrutiny. Without PoRs or real-time financial disclosures, Ponzi schemes, asset manipulation, and speculative trading become widespread, increasing the likelihood of market failures and financial collapses.

A defining feature of this model is the absence of effective regulatory oversight. Governments struggle to keep pace with rapid Fintech innovations, allowing firms to exploit loopholes in financial laws and evade compliance obligations. Unlike models where regulatory agencies enforce transparency laws, this model envisions a system in which financial mismanagement remains undetected until major crises unfold. Without compliance mandates, Fintech firms engage in unchecked algorithmic trading, opaque financial lending, and speculative asset creation, exposing markets to severe instability. Dark AI models (i.e., AI-driven decision-making frameworks that operate without transparency or accountability) replace traditional banking mechanisms, eliminating financial governance structures. Since regulators lack access to financial health reports, AI risk models, and corporate balance sheets, they fail to detect financial mismanagement, hidden liabilities, or emerging crises until it is too late. As a result, governments are forced to intervene only after financial collapses occur, further eroding consumer trust and deepening market uncertainty.

The consequences of this model are severe, leading to widespread financial instability, unchecked AI discrimination, and the erosion of consumer trust in Fintech organizations. The absence of transparency enables fraudulent schemes, unverified financial practices, and speculative market behavior, increasing the likelihood of systemic financial crises. Fintech firms conceal risk models and financial reserves, preventing regulators from accurately assessing financial stability. Unlike models where internal governance offers some level of risk mitigation, firms operating under No Transparency allow hidden risks to escalate into full-scale financial disasters. Consumers face widespread financial discrimination, as AI-driven credit scoring, lending, and investment algorithms operate with hidden biases and non-explainable decision-making. Unlike models where AI systems are auditable and interpretable, Fintech firms in this model deliberately avoid AI transparency, making it impossible for consumers to challenge unfair financial decisions. Additionally, cryptocurrency exchanges, digital asset platforms, and DeFi services collapse due to hidden financial risks and mismanagement, resulting in massive investor losses and market failures. Without PoR-mechanisms, digital financial institutions lack solvency verification, leading to liquidity crises and the breakdown of consumer confidence.

The No Transparency Model represents the most dangerous path for Fintech, where unregulated AI-driven decision-making replaces ethical governance, consumer rights, and financial security. The lack of regulatory oversight allows financial institutions to operate without accountability, resulting in frequent market crashes, fraudulent investment schemes, and speculative trading failures.

To avoid this worst-case future, Fintech organizations and regulatory agencies must prioritize transparency-first financial models, improve AI governance structures, and enforce real-time financial disclosure laws. Without such interventions, the Fintech industry risks widespread financial failures, public distrust, and severe government-imposed restrictions in response to inevitable crises.

Consequently, the four models presented illustrate different potential futures for Fintech organizations regarding transparency. This comparative analysis explores the main differences, strengths, weaknesses, and implications of each model, offering a structured assessment of how Fintech firms may evolve in Fintech 5.0 (Table 3).

The four models represent a spectrum of transparency, ranging from the Full Transparency Model, which embodies complete openness and accountability, to the No Transparency Model, where fintech operates without oversight, fostering secrecy and financial instability. The External-Only Transparency Model ensures compliance through regulatory enforcement, while the Internal-Only Transparency Model prioritizes corporate self-regulation, restricting public access to critical financial data.

Governance structures across these models vary significantly. Decentralized, trust-driven governance defines Full Transparency, where financial decisions are made collaboratively through DAOs, and AI models are fully explainable and bias-free. By contrast, No Transparency lacks any meaningful governance, allowing firms to operate unchecked, with non-transparent AI models and hidden financial risks. In between, External-Only Transparency enforces disclosure laws but retains corporate resistance to openness, while Internal-Only Transparency prioritizes internal ethics and AI fairness but restricts public access to financial disclosures.

AI-driven financial services play a central role in shaping Fintech's future. Transparency in credit scoring, investment strategies, and fraud detection will

Table 3 Transparency models in Fintech 5.0: governance, AI decision-making, and market stability outcomes

Pillar	*1. Full transparency model*	*2. External-only transparency model*	*3. Internal-only transparency model*	*4. No transparency model*
Internal transparency	Y—full internal audits, open governance, XAI	N	Y—strong internal ethics and AI auditing, self-regulation	N
External transparency	Y—public financial reporting, consumer data control, decentralized oversight	Y—government-mandated disclosures, regulated PoRs	N	N
Governance and corporate structure	Decentralized governance (DAOs), public participation, open-source AI audits	Government-enforced compliance, reactive transparency laws	Corporate-led AI ethics and risk management, selective disclosures	No structured governance, hidden decision-making models
AI transparency and algorithmic decision-making	XAI, full public oversight, bias-free decision-making	Regulated AI transparency, limited consumer access to AI explainability	Internally monitored AI, but external algorithmic secrecy	NXAI, black-box decision-making, discriminatory risk assessments
Financial risk, consumer trust, and market stability	Low financial risk, high consumer trust, fraud-resistant financial models	Medium risk, government-enforced stability, compliance-driven trust	Medium-high risk, consumer skepticism, hidden investment strategies	Extreme risk, financial fraud, speculative market volatility

determine whether Fintech enhances fairness and trust or perpetuates discrimination and risk concealment. In Full Transparency, AI is fully auditable and accountable, ensuring fair and ethical financial decisions. External-Only Transparency enforces AI explainability for regulators but not consumers, while Internal-Only Transparency ensures bias-free AI within firms but lacks public disclosure. The No Transparency Model, however, leads to unchecked algorithmic biases, discriminatory lending, and financial manipulation.

Transparency also impacts market stability, financial risk exposure, and consumer confidence. Full transparency fosters trust, financial security, and proactive risk mitigation, preventing crises caused by hidden liabilities and Ponzi schemes. External-only transparency strengthens compliance but suffers from regulatory loopholes, while internal-only transparency creates investor skepticism due to restricted financial visibility. The no-transparency model leads to systemic financial instability, as unverified lending models, concealed risks, and fraudulent digital platforms collapse, triggering market crises and consumer distrust.

Ultimately, the future of Fintech transparency will depend on whether firms embrace openness or prioritize secrecy. The Full Transparency Model offers the most sustainable and stable path, ensuring trust, regulatory alignment, and financial resilience in the Fintech 5.0 era. By adopting transparency-first business models, Fintech organizations can foster ethical financial services, build consumer confidence, and drive long-term industry innovation.

5 Future Transparency Strategies in FinTech 5.0

The four models outlined in this study present diverging paths for the future of Fintech, underscoring the crucial role of transparency in shaping financial organizations, regulatory frameworks, and consumer trust (Table 4). The Full Transparency Model fosters openness, trust, and accountability, ensuring XAI-driven financial services. The External-Only Transparency Model enforces compliance through regulations but maintains internal opacity, potentially stifling innovation and creating inefficiencies. The Internal-Only Transparency Model prioritizes strong internal governance and self-regulation while restricting external disclosures, which may weaken consumer confidence and trigger regulatory scrutiny. Finally, the No Transparency Model poses the greatest risk, where unchecked AI, concealed financial systems, and hidden risks increase the likelihood of fraud, financial crises, and market instability.

Table 4 Transparency models in Fintech 5.0: characteristics, strategic implications, and hypothetical future applications

Pillar	*1. Full transparency model*	*2. External-only transparency model*	*3. Internal-only transparency model*	*4. No transparency model*
Context	*The ideal future: Fintech organizations built on radical transparency*	*Transparency enforced by regulation, not voluntary commitment*	*Fintech firms ensure strong internal accountability but maintain external secrecy*	*The worst-case scenario: unregulated, non-transparent Fintech ecosystem*
Real-world inspiration	Open banking, DeFi, and BT-based auditing ⊕ Ethereum (DeFi and Open-Source Smart Contracts) ⊕ Monzo and Starling Bank (Neobanks) ⊕ OpenAI's XAI ⊕ El Salvador's Bitcoin Adoption	Banks under strict regulations but still operating with opaque internal governance ⊕ EU's PSD2 and Open Banking Regulations ⊕ U.S. Dodd-Frank Act (Post-2008 Regulation) ⊕ China's AI Regulations (2023)	Traditional financial institutions, hedge funds, and corporate-led AI Fintech solutions ⊕JP Morgan's AI-Powered Trading (Hedged Transparency) ⊕ Wealthfront and Betterment (Robo-Advisors) ⊕ Stripe (Fintech Payment Processor) ⊕ Credit Scoring Firms (FICO, Experian)	Collapsed crypto exchanges, unregulated AI trading firms, and secretive hedge funds ⊖ FTX and Mt. Gox (collapsed crypto exchanges) ⊖ Algorithmic trading flash crashes ⊖ AI-Generated credit scoring discrimination (Unregulated AI lending) ⊖ Dark pool trading and market manipulation
Examples of Fintech firms	⊕ Monzo and Starling Bank (Neobanks) ⊕ Ethereum and Public DeFi Platforms ⊕OpenAI for Finance ⊕ DAOs for Lending	⊕ PayPal and Apple Pay (Digital Payment Firms) ⊕ Revolut (Challenger Bank) ⊕ Binance and Coinbase (Crypto Exchanges) ⊕ AI Credit Scoring Systems (FICO, Experian, etc.)	⊕ JP Morgan AI Trading (AI-Powered Hedge Funds) ⊕ Wealthfront and Betterment (Robo-Advisors) ⊕ Stripe (Fintech Payment Processor)	⊖ Shadow banking and HFT firms ⊖ Unregulated DeFi platforms ⊖ Chinese AI loan scams

(continued)

Table 4 (continued)

Pillar	*1. Full transparency model*	*2. External-only transparency model*	*3. Internal-only transparency model*	*4. No transparency model*
			⊕ AI-Driven Loan Platforms (Upstart, LendingClub)	
Industry implications and future outlook	⊕ Higher consumer trust ⊕ Greater market stability and fraud reduction ⊕ Higher compliance costs and open-source challenges	⊕ Financial stability increases ⊖ High operational costs and compliance risks ⊖ Consumer distrust in proprietary AI models	⊕ Strong internal ethics and governance ⊖ Consumer distrust in AI and Fintech services ⊖ Regulators struggle to oversee Fintech growth	⊖ Consumer distrust and financial scandals ⊖ Regulatory chaos and delayed oversight ⊖ AI-powered financial discrimination
Hypothetical future example	**"TrustBank AI"**—A fully transparent Neobank, where all financial decisions, AI models, and risk assessments are open-source, auditable, and explainable in real-time. Customers can audit AI-driven decisions, verify PoRs instantly, and participate in governance via BT-based voting, ensuring a trust-driven financial ecosystem	**"RegBank 2028"**—A Fintech bank that complies with strict government reporting standards but discloses only the minimum required data. AI-driven lending models remain opaque, offering little transparency into financial decision-making for customers	**"FinTrust AI"**—A financial institution that personalizes loans, investments, and insurance using AI but keeps its decision-making processes undisclosed, citing trade secrets. Regulators have limited oversight, while customers trust the brand yet remain skeptical about potential biases in financial decisions	**"DarkBank AI"**—A Fintech lender offering instant AI-driven loans without disclosing the credit evaluation process. Customers receive no explanation for rejections, while unchecked biases lead to financial discrimination. Regulators struggle to intervene, lacking the tools to audit its opaque AI decision-making systems

5.1 The Future of Transparency in Fintech

As the Fintech industry advances toward Fintech 5.0, transparency policies will shape its trajectory, determining whether financial organizations prioritize trust and consumer protection or operate in secrecy, leading to instability (Lokesh, 2024; Nicoletti, 2025). A central question is whether firms will voluntarily embrace transparency or if regulators will need to impose stricter disclosure mandates to ensure accountability (Zetzsche et al., 2017; Dorfleitner et al., 2023).

Transparency extends beyond compliance, forming the basis of consumer trust, financial stability, and the prevention of crises (Petrovska et al., 2020). Firms that embrace full transparency create an open financial ecosystem, leveraging real-time auditing, XAI models, open governance, and BT-based PoRs (Shkolnyk & Zakharkina, 2022). By contrast, firms that operate in secrecy and opacity expose consumers and investors to hidden risks, liquidity crises, and financial losses, as seen in past financial failures like FTX and Mt. Gox.

Models that adopt partial transparency introduce unique challenges. On the one hand, externally regulated models enforce financial disclosure but do not mandate openness in AI models, risk frameworks, or lending practices, leading to superficial compliance rather than meaningful transparency (Müller & Kerényi, 2019). On the other hand, internally governed models strengthen corporate oversight but limit public financial disclosures, creating consumer skepticism and potential regulatory intervention (Rizinski et al., 2022). Thus, the future of Fintech transparency will depend on how firms balance innovation, regulation, and consumer protection. Those that fail to adopt proactive transparency measures may face stricter regulations and consumer backlash, making voluntary transparency policies crucial for financial security and market confidence.

Traces of all four transparency models can already be observed in today's Fintech sector. Radical transparency is evident in Ethereum's DeFi ecosystem and in Neobanks such as Monzo and Starling, which rely on open-source smart contracts, public transaction histories, and verifiable records. Regulatory-driven approaches appear in frameworks like the EU's PSD2 and the U.S. Dodd-Frank Act. These rules require financial disclosures but stop short of demanding openness about how algorithms shape credit, lending, or investment decisions. Many companies therefore disclose only what is legally required, leaving much of their internal activity obscured. Some firms, including JP Morgan, Wealthfront, and Stripe, place emphasis on ethical standards and internal oversight of algorithms but restrict public access to financial reporting. This approach strengthens governance internally, yet it provides limited insight to consumers and investors, which weakens trust. Finally, opaque models persist in areas such as dark-pool trading, high-frequency algorithmic trading, and the collapse of unregulated platforms like FTX. These examples show how hidden risks and unaccountable systems can destabilize markets and invite regulatory intervention.

The level of transparency Fintech firms adopt will have far-reaching implications for regulatory frameworks, consumer trust, and industry competition. Firms that view transparency as a strategic advantage will be better positioned to navigate evolving regulations, attract loyal customers, and ensure financial stability. With increasing regulatory oversight of AI-driven financial services, digital lending platforms, and DeFi ecosystems, Fintech firms must prepare for real-time AI audits, BT-based PoRs, and standardized financial reporting mandates. Companies that embrace transparency will gain a competitive edge. In contrast, those that resist it will face regulatory scrutiny and consumer distrust. Consumer confidence in AI-driven financial services will also be a determining factor in Fintech 5.0 adoption (Chakraborti et al., 2025). Without XAI models, fair lending practices, and open governance, consumers may reject algorithmic financial decision-making in favor of traditional banking models with clearer oversight. Governments will need to develop new legal frameworks to oversee AI-powered financial services, preventing algorithmic bias, financial discrimination, and high-risk lending practices. Collaboration between regulators and industry leaders will be essential to balancing innovation with compliance, ensuring that Fintech remains both competitive and trustworthy.

Fintech transparency in the future represents more than a regulatory obligation; it will become a fundamental necessity for the industry itself (Rerung et al., 2024). Firms that adopt radical transparency will enhance consumer trust, regulatory alignment, and financial stability (Nicoletti, 2025). In contrast, those that embrace secrecy and opacity risk losing consumer confidence, facing regulatory crackdowns, and experiencing financial crises due to unchecked risks (Zetzsche et al., 2017). To build a sustainable and ethical Fintech 5.0 ecosystem, Fintech firms must prioritize real-time financial transparency, XAI governance, and BT-based auditing mechanisms. Failure to do so could result in a future dominated by government intervention, financial collapses, and market instability.

Ultimately, the future of Fintech 5.0 will be defined by how financial organizations choose to embrace or resist transparency (Petrovska et al., 2020; Shkolnyk & Zakharkina, 2022). Policymakers, financial regulators, and Fintech firms must work together to prevent the industry from drifting toward opacity by encouraging transparency-first financial models that balance technological innovation, regulatory compliance, and consumer protection (Rerung et al., 2024).

5.2 *Transparency Strategies and Policies in FinTech 5.0*

As financial services become more automated and data-driven, transparency policies will be crucial in ensuring financial integrity, preventing fraud, and fostering consumer trust. Fintech 5.0 is set to introduce advanced regulatory mechanisms and technological solutions that will reshape how financial institutions operate under public and regulatory scrutiny.

AI-Driven Compliance and Real-Time Auditing. One of the defining innovations of Fintech 5.0 will be the use of AI-powered compliance and monitoring tools. These systems will allow financial institutions to identify suspicious transactions in real time and ensure alignment with AML rules and fraud prevention standards (Putra et al., 2024). At the same time, BT play a growing role in financial reporting. By recording transactions on immutable ledgers, BT will provide regulators with direct access to verifiable financial statements and balance sheets (Zetzsche et al., 2017). By storing all transactions on immutable ledgers, Fintech firms will enhance financial oversight and reduce the risk strengthening oversight and reducing opportunities for manipulation or accounting fraud (Buchak et al., 2018). In parallel, advances in identity verification will further reinforce transparency and security. Decentralized biometric systems, integrating fingerprint scanning, facial recognition, and BT-based identity solutions, are expected to become mainstream. These tools will make identity fraud far more difficult while also preserving consumer privacy and trust in digital financial ecosystems (Aldboush & Ferdous, 2023).

Strengthening Internal and External Transparency Frameworks. To prevent financial fraud, systemic risks, and AI-driven discrimination, Fintech organizations must adopt robust internal and external transparency policies. First, these should include mandatory internal AI explainability audits to ensure financial algorithms are fair, unbiased, and accountable. Second, they should encompass real-time financial disclosures, reducing the risk of hidden financial liabilities and market manipulation. Ultimately, they should involve decentralized governance models that allow consumer participation in financial decision-making.

Governments must implement global transparency standards to prevent Fintech firms from relocating to regulatory havens with weak financial disclosure laws. A Basel-like transparency framework for Fintech could ensure accountability in financial risk exposure, AI decision-making processes, and corporate governance (Bartram et al., 2020). To enhance AI accountability, XAI standards should be enforced, requiring Fintech firms to open-source their risk models, credit scoring algorithms, and lending decision-making frameworks. This would reduce algorithmic bias, increase consumer trust, and prevent hidden financial risks. Additionally, BT-based PoR mandates should become an industry standard, requiring Fintech firms to publicly verify financial reserves in real time (Farcane & Deliu, 2020), reducing the risk of financial speculation and fraudulent accounting practices (Fletcher & Le, 2021).

Regulating AI-Driven Financial Decision-Making. As AI-driven financial models become increasingly dominant, stringent regulatory measures will be essential to prevent bias, discrimination, and financial manipulation (Soundararajan & Shenbagaraman, 2024; Zetzsche et al., 2017). First, policymakers must introduce mandatory AI ethics audits, requiring Fintech firms to document how AI is used in credit scoring, lending, trading, and fraud detection (Farcane & Deliu, 2020). Second, they should institute real-time AI transparency reporting, ensuring that regulators and consumers understand how financial decisions are made. Ultimately, they must establish consumer rights to challenge AI-based financial decisions, allowing individuals to request explanations and appeal unfair AI-driven financial outcomes (Zetzsche et al., 2017). To oversee these regulations, a centralized AI transparency authority should be established to monitor AI-driven financial systems, prevent algorithmic bias, and mitigate market manipulation risks.

Consumer-Centric Financial Transparency Policies. A consumer-first approach to transparency will be necessary to build long-term trust in Fintech services. Fintech firms should adopt open banking frameworks, empowering consumers to access and control their financial data without restrictions (Farcane & Deliu, 2020). Consequently, they will easily understand how financial products work, including AI-driven decisions (Chou, 2019). Additionally, they will receive clear and standardized financial disclosures, preventing hidden fees, unfair lending practices, and deceptive transactions. Additionally, smart contract-based financial agreements should be legally standardized, enabling real-time, immutable, and transparent financial contracts on BT networks. This would allow consumers to verify loan terms, investment risks, and financial obligations independently, reducing reliance on intermediaries. Consumer education initiatives should also be prioritized, ensuring that individuals understand AI-driven financial services, potential risks, and the impact of automated decision-making on their financial well-being.

Financial Market Oversight and Crisis Prevention Measures. To prevent financial instability and mitigate systemic risks, Fintech organizations must adopt standardized financial risk disclosures that allow regulators and consumers to assess market vulnerabilities before they escalate (Auer & Claessens, 2018; Schär, 2021). Regulators should implement continuous financial stability monitoring systems, enabling real-time tracking of: (i) Fintech liquidity risks and debt exposure; (ii) AI-driven market manipulation and high-risk financial activities; and (iii) hidden financial liabilities in digital lending and speculative investments (Cecchetti & Schoenholtz, 2017; Fletcher & Le, 2021). To reduce risks associated with opaque lending models and high-frequency AI trading, policymakers should enforce mandatory liquidity stress tests for Fintech firms, ensuring they maintain adequate reserves to withstand financial downturns. Additionally, a global Fintech Risk Monitoring Authority (FRMA) should be established to monitor cross-border financial risks, ensuring that unverified speculative investments do not trigger large-scale financial crises.

Regulatory Sandboxes and Global Coordination on Fintech Transparency. To promote responsible Fintech innovation, regulators should create regulatory sandboxes, allowing firms to test transparency-driven financial models in real-world environments before full-scale implementation (Zetzsche et al., 2017). These sandboxes will help ensure that new Fintech solutions comply with global transparency mandates, AI ethics guidelines, and consumer protection laws. A Global Fintech Transparency Council (GFTC) should also be established to coordinate international regulatory efforts, preventing Fintech firms from relocating to jurisdictions with weak financial oversight. Governments should work toward cross-border regulatory alignment, ensuring that Fintech organizations adhere to universal financial transparency standards regardless of location.

Hence, the future of Fintech 5.0 will be shaped by how firms integrate transparency-first strategies into their operations. By adopting AI-driven compliance monitoring, BT-based financial reporting, open banking frameworks, and global transparency regulations, Fintech organizations can enhance consumer trust, prevent financial crises, and maintain regulatory alignment (Zetzsche et al., 2017). Firms that proactively embrace transparency will gain a competitive advantage, attracting consumers who prioritize ethical financial services and accountability. In contrast, those that resist transparency will face stricter regulatory scrutiny, financial instability, and potential market exclusion. As Fintech continues to evolve, balancing innovation with transparency will be key to ensuring a stable, consumer-trust-driven financial ecosystem. The adoption of robust transparency policies, AI governance frameworks, and global financial oversight mechanisms will determine whether Fintech 5.0 succeeds as an open, accountable, and secure financial landscape.

Henceforth, the future of Fintech 5.0 hinges on how financial organizations, regulators, and policymakers prioritize and implement transparency-first policies. The Full Transparency Model provides the strongest foundation for Fintech firms seeking to build trust, ensure ethical AI governance, and maintain financial stability. In contrast, firms that resist transparency risk falling into the No Transparency Model, where unchecked AI, hidden financial risks, and regulatory non-compliance lead to market collapses, increased government intervention, and consumer distrust. To ensure a stable and innovative financial ecosystem, Fintech firms must adopt proactive transparency policies, open governance structures, and XAI decision-making frameworks.

Henceforth, the time to act is now. Organizations that do not embrace transparency risk stricter regulation, financial instability, and a decline in consumer confidence in an increasingly oversight-driven financial landscape. By committing to transparency-first strategies, Fintech firms can strengthen long-term trust, encourage ethical innovation, and build a more resilient and consumer-centric industry.

6 Conclusion

The evolution of Fintech 5.0 presents both opportunities and challenges, with transparency emerging as a critical determinant of trust, stability, and regulatory alignment. The four transparency models explored in this study illustrate divergent paths, ranging from fully open financial ecosystems to opaque, high-risk Fintech environments.

The Full Transparency Model represents the ideal future, where fintech firms leverage openness as a competitive advantage, fostering trust, ethical AI deployment, and financial stability. Conversely, the No Transparency Model highlights the risks of unchecked AI, hidden financial liabilities, and regulatory non-compliance, which lead to market collapses and consumer distrust. Between these extremes, partial transparency models reflect varying levels of regulatory oversight and internal governance, each presenting distinct advantages and challenges for the industry.

With the rise of Fintech 5.0, transparency is expected to evolve into a core market necessity rather than remaining solely a matter of regulation. Consumers increasingly demand clarity in AI-driven financial decisions, risk assessments, and transaction processes, making transparency-driven Fintech firms more attractive to investors and customers. Those that adopt transparency-first business models will gain a sustainable market edge. In contrast, those that resist disclosure will face heightened regulatory scrutiny and declining consumer confidence.

Major innovations such as BT-based PoRs, XAI, and DeFi governance will shape trust-driven Fintech ecosystems. By prioritizing open data-sharing, ethical AI standards, and real-time financial disclosures, Fintech firms can position themselves as leaders in the financial revolution. In contrast, those that cling to opacity risk regulatory penalties, consumer skepticism, and financial instability.

Regulatory bodies will play a crucial role in enforcing transparency by establishing global financial disclosure standards, AI ethics guidelines, and real-time auditing mandates. Governments must develop proactive oversight mechanisms, including continuous AI audits, BT-based financial reporting, and consumer protection policies, to ensure Fintech firms remain accountable. A Global Fintech Transparency Authority should be created to prevent regulatory arbitrage, ensuring that firms cannot escape transparency requirements by relocating to jurisdictions with weaker financial oversight.

What was once regarded as a regulatory or corporate obligation in Fintech is now a standard demanded by consumers. As financial literacy improves, consumers are increasingly aware of opaque AI decision-making, hidden fees, and unethical financial practices. This shift forces Fintech firms to prioritize ethical governance, clear communication, and open financial disclosures. If Fintech organizations fail to meet transparency expectations, consumers may shift back to traditional banking models or migrate to transparency-focused Fintech alternatives, pushing non-compliant firms out of the market.

The lessons learned from past financial crises, including the 2008 banking collapse and the downfall of opaque cryptocurrency exchanges like FTX, underscore the dangers of financial secrecy and unregulated risk exposure. To prevent future crises, fintech firms must embrace transparency, implement ethical AI frameworks, and integrate decentralized financial governance models.

Fintech 5.0 stands at a defining moment. Firms can either embrace transparency, leading to a new era of trust-driven financial services, or resist openness, risking market instability and regulatory intervention. The decision Fintech organizations make today will shape the future of global financial stability and consumer confidence. The question remains: *Will Fintech firms choose to build clear pathways of open, transparent, and trust-driven financial models, or remain trapped in shadowy systems of secrecy and opacity?*

References

Achim, M. V., Pisoni, G., Mare, C., Moloney, M., Korba, S., Molnár, B., Bedowska-Sojka, B., & Coita, I. F. (2023). FinTech, regulation, and cybercrime: Opportunities arising from new technologies. Available at SSRN 4620106.

Addy, W. A., Ofodile, O. C., Adeoye, O. B., Oyewole, A. T., Okoye, C. C., Odeyemi, O., & Ololade, Y. J. (2024). Data-driven sustainability: How Fintech innovations are supporting green finance. *Engineering Science & Technology Journal*, *5*(3), 760–773.

Alcalá Consuegra, R. A., & Zabaraín García, M. A. (2012). *A study of electronic payments in B2C eCommerce*. Working paper.

Aldboush, H. H., & Ferdous, M. (2023). Building trust in Fintech: An analysis of ethical and privacy considerations in the intersection of big data, AI, and customer trust. *International Journal of Financial Studies*, *11*(3), 90.

Allen, F., Gu, X., & Jagtiani, J. (2021). A survey of Fintech research and policy discussion. *Review of Corporate Finance*, *1*, 259–339.

Alois, J. D. (2015). *China release draft peer to peer lending rules. Asks for comments*. Crowdfund Insider.

Anagnostopoulos, I. (2018). Fintech and regtech: Impact on regulators and banks. *Journal of Economics and Business*, *100*, 7–25.

Arner, D. W., Barberis, J., & Buckley, R. P. (2015). The evolution of Fintech: A new post-crisis paradigm? *Georgetown Journal of International Law, 47*(1271), 1–45.

Arner, D. W., Barberis, J., & Buckley, R. P. (2016). 150 years of Fintech: An evolutionary analysis. *Jassa, 3*, 22–29.

Arner, D., Buckley, R., Charamba, K., Sergeev, A., & Zetzsche, D. (2022). Governing FinTech 4.0: BigTech, platform finance, and sustainable development. *Fordham Journal of Corporate and Financial Law, 27*(1), 1–71.

Aspris, A., Foley, S., Svec, J., & Wang, L. (2021). Decentralized exchanges: The "wild west" of cryptocurrency trading. *International Review of Financial Analysis, 77*, 101845.

Auer, R., & Claessens, S. (2018). Regulating cryptocurrencies: Assessing market reactions. *BIS Quarterly Review, 9*, 51–65.

Bartram, S. M., Branke, J., & Motahari, M. (2020). *Artificial intelligence in asset management*. CFA Institute Research Foundation.

Bátiz-Lazo, B., Wardley, P. (2007). Banking on change: Information systems and technologies in UK high street banking 1919–1969. *Financial History Review, 14*(2), 177–205.

Bhat, M. A., Khan, S. T., Alkhwaldi, A. F., & Abdulmuhsin, A. A. (2024). Investigating the critical drivers of Fintech adoption to promote business sustainability of SMEs. *Global Knowledge, Memory and Communication.*

Böhme, R., Christin, N., Edelman, B., & Moore, T. (2015). Bitcoin: Economics, technology, and governance. *Journal of Economic Perspectives, 29*(2), 213–238.

Bouafia, K., Molnár, B., & Majid, G. (2024, February). Blockchain technologies for transparency in FinTech. In *International congress on information and communication technology* (pp. 575–585). *Springer Nature Singapore.*

Botha, L. L. (2024). *An investigation on how blockchain technology can transform the know-your-customer (kyc) process* [Master's thesis, Universidade NOVA de Lisboa (Portugal)].

Bookstaber, R. (2007). *A demon of our own design* (pp. 7–32). John Wiley & Sons.

Boot, A. W., Hoffmann, P., Laeven, L., & Ratnovski, L. (2021). Fintech: What's old, what's new? *Journal of Financial Stability, 53*, 100836.

Brummer, C., & Yadav, Y. (2018). Fintech and the innovation trilemma. *Georgetown Law Journal, 107*, 235.

Buchak, G., Matvos, G., Piskorski, T., & Seru, A. (2018). Fintech, regulatory arbitrage, and the rise of shadow banks. *Journal of Financial Economics, 130*(3), 453–483.

Campbell-Verduyn, M. (2018). Bitcoin, crypto-coins, and global anti-money laundering governance. *Crime, Law and Social Change, 69*, 283–305.

Carrière-Swallow, Y., & Haksar, V. (2021). Let's build a better data economy. *Finance & Development, 58*(1), 10–13.

Cecchetti, S. G., & Schoenholtz, K. L. (2017). *Money, banking, and financial markets*. McGraw-Hill.

Chang, V., Baudier, P., Zhang, H., Xu, Q., Zhang, J., & Arami, M. (2020). How Blockchain can impact financial services–The overview, challenges and recommendations from expert interviewees. *Technological Forecasting and Social Change, 158*, 120166.

Chakraborti, J., Aggarwal, S., & Kumar, P. (2025) *FinTech 5.0: The Journey from Cryptocurrency to Neo Banking*.

Chen, Y., & Bellavitis, C. (2020). Blockchain disruption and decentralized finance: The rise of decentralized business models. *Journal of Business Venturing Insights, 13*, e00151.

Chou, A. (2019). What's in the black box: Balancing financial inclusion and privacy in digital consumer lending. *Duke Law Journal, 69*, 1183.

Commission of the European Communities (CEC). (1986). *Single European Act* (Vol. 2). Office for Official Publications of the European Communities.

Daugaard, T. V., Jensen, J. B., Kauffman, R. J., & Kim, K. (2024). Blockchain solutions with consensus algorithms and immediate finality: Toward Panopticon-style monitoring to enhance anti-money laundering. *Electronic Commerce Research and Applications, 65*, 101386.

Deliu, D. (2020). The Impact of a Socio-Economic Crisis on Corporate Governance Effectiveness and Sustainable Development. Acumen: The Current New Coronavirus (COVID-19) Pandemic. *Proceedings of the 35th International Business Information Management Association (IBIMA)*, 1–2.

Deliu, D. (2024). Professional judgment and skepticism amidst the interaction of artificial intelligence and human intelligence. *Audit Financiar, 22*(176), 724–741.

Deliu, D., & Olariu, A. (2024). The role of artificial intelligence and big data analytics in shaping the future of professions in Industry 6.0: Perspectives from an emerging market. *Electronics, 13*(24), 4983.

Dorfleitner, G., Hornuf, L., & Kreppmeier, J. (2023). Promise not fulfilled: FinTech, data privacy, and the GDPR. *Electronic Markets, 33*(1), 33.

Farcane, N., & Deliu, D. (2020). Stakes and challenges regarding the financial auditor's activity in the blockchain era. *Audit Financiar, 18*(157), 154–181.

Farcane, N., Deliu, D., & Gheorghian, M. (2011). Auditing fair values in a sensitive socio-economical context. *Annales Universitatis Apulensis: Series Oeconomica, 13*(2), 364.

Fletcher, G. G. S., & Le, M. M. (2021). The future of AI accountability in the financial markets. *Vanderbilt Journal of Entertainment and Technology Law, 24*, 289.

Foley, S., Karlsen, J. R., & Putniņš, T. J. (2019). Sex, drugs, and bitcoin: How much illegal activity is financed through cryptocurrencies? *The Review of Financial Studies, 32*(5), 1798–1853.

Frame, W. S., & White, L. J. (2014). *Technological change, financial innovation, and diffusion in banking* (pp. 1–5). SSRN.

Giglio, F. (2022). Fintech: A literature review. *International Business Research, 15*(1), 80–85.

Goldstein, I., Jiang, W., & Karolyi, G. A. (2019). To FinTech and beyond. *The Review of Financial Studies, 32*(5), 1647–1661.

Gomber, P., Koch, J., & Siering, M. (2017). Digital finance and Fintech: Current research and future research directions. *Journal of Business Economics, 87*(5), 537–580.

Goodhart, C. (2011). *The Basel Committee on banking supervision: A history of the early years 1974–1997.* Cambridge University Press.

He, M., Song, G., & Chen, Q. (2023). Fintech adoption, internal control quality and bank risk taking: Evidence from Chinese listed banks. *Finance Research Letters, 57,* 104235.

Jalal, A., Al Mubarak, M., & Durani, F. (2023). Financial technology (Fintech). In *Artificial intelligence and transforming digital marketing* (pp. 525–536). Springer Nature Switzerland.

Jünger, M., & Mietzner, M. (2020). Banking goes digital: The adoption of FinTech services by German households. *Finance Research Letters, 34,* 101260.

Kumar, N., Addula, S. R., Seranmadevi, R., & Tyagi, A. K. (2025). Advanced banking solutions for industry 5.0: From industry's perspective. In *Creating AI synergy through business technology transformation* (pp. 1–24). IGI Global.

Leong, K., & Sung, A. (2018). FinTech (financial technology): What is it and how to use technologies to create business value in Fintech way? *International Journal of Innovation, Management and Technology, 9*(2), 74–78.

Legowo, M. B., Subanidja, S., & Sorongan, F. A. (2021). Fintech and bank: Past, present, and future. *Jurnal Teknik Komputer AMIK BSI, 7*(1), 94–99.

Lokesh, Y. R. (2024, March 5). Unveiling the relevance of Fintech 5.0 in today's dynamic financial landscape. *RIMS.* https://rimsbangalore.in/unveiling-the-relevance-of-Fintech-5-0-in-todays-dynamic-financial-landscape/

Menat, R. (2016). Why we're so excited about FinTech. In *The Fintech book: The financial technology handbook for investors, entrepreneurs and visionaries* (pp. 10–12).

Milne, A., & Parboteeah, P. (2016). *The business models and economics of peer-to-peer lending.*

Mishkin, F. S. (2007). *Monetary policy strategy.* MIT Press.

Moore, C. (2000). *Understanding the industrial revolution* (p. 36). Psychology Press.

Monroy, D. A., & Corredor, J. (2019). Regulando Fintech 2.0 y Fintech 3.0: Administración de riesgos y regulación prudencial (Regulating Fintech 2.0 and Fintech 3.0: Risk Management and Prudential Regulation). *Colección Enrique Low Murtra: Derecho Económico, 13.*

Mullineux, A. (2012). *UK banking after deregulation (RLE: Banking & Finance).*

Müller, J., & Kerényi, Á. (2019). The need for trust and ethics in the digital age–Sunshine and shadows in the FinTech world. *Financial and Economic Review, 18*(4), 5–34.

Nicoletti, B. (2017). *The future of FinTech. Integrating finance and technology in financial services.* Palgrave Macmillan Cham.

Nicoletti, B. (2021). *Banking 5.0: How Fintech will change traditional banks in the 'new normal' post pandemic.* Springer Nature.

Nicoletti, B. (2025). *How Fintech will change traditional banks in the "new normal" post pandemic.* Palgrave Studies in Financial Services Technology. Palgrave Macmillan.

Novelli, C., Taddeo, M., & Floridi, L. (2024). Accountability in artificial intelligence: What it is and how it works. *AI and Society, 39*(4), 1971–1882.

Pantielieieva, N., Khutorna, M., Lytvynenko, O., & Potapenko, L. (2020). FinTech, RegTech and traditional financial intermediation: Trends and threats for financial stability. In *Data-Centric Business and Applications: Evolvements in Business Information Processing and Management (Volume 3)* (pp. 1–21). Springer International Publishing.

Percy, C., Dragicevic, S., Sarkar, S., & d'Avila Garcez, A. (2021). Accountability in AI: From principles to industry-specific accreditation. *AI Communications, 34* (3), 181–196.

Petrovska, B., Atanasova-Pacemska, T., Corizzo, R., Mignone, P., Lameski, P., & Zdravevski, E. (2020). Fintech and artificial intelligence in finance-towards a transparent financial industry"(FinAI) CA19130. *Applied Sciences.*

Philippon, T. (2016). *The Fintech opportunity (no. W22476).* National Bureau of Economic Research.

Phoon, K. F., & Koh, C. C. F. (2018). Robo-advisors and wealth management. *Journal of Alternative Investments, 20*(3), 79.

Puschmann, T. (2017). Fintech. *Business and Information Systems Engineering, 59*, 69–76.

Putra, J. M., Mahadewi, E. P., Fahlevi, R., Sanantagraha, A. I., & Sopyan, A. (2024). Fintech transformation: An analysis of era 5.0 technology in digital finance applications. *Seascapeid Journal of Economics, Management, and Business, 1*(2), 23–40.

Rabbani, M. R., Khan, S., & Thalassinos, E. I. (2020). FinTech, blockchain and Islamic finance: An extensive literature review.

Rerung, A., Paranita, E. S., Rina Asmara Agung, A. Y., Budiandru, B., & Tandililing, E. M. (2024). The influence of Fintech innovations, ESG reporting, and blockchain technology on financial transparency and accountability. *The Journal of Academic Science, 1*(2), 111–117.

Riantama, I., Suardhika, I. N., & Yuesti, A. (2020). Financial technology application success in the 4.0 Era. *International Journal of Psychosocial Rehabilitation, 24*(9), 2948–2962.

Rizinski, M., Peshov, H., Mishev, K., Chitkushev, L. T., Vodenska, I., & Trajanov, D. (2022). Ethically responsible machine learning in Fintech. *IEEE Access, 10*, 97531–97554.

(2010). Restoring American Financial Stability Act of 2010". s.3217. Available at: http://frwebgate.access.gpo.gov/cgi-bin/getdoc.cgi?dbname=111_cong_bills&docid=f:s3217as.txt.pdf

Saini, A. K. (2023). The Fintech revolution and future of banking and financial institutions: A quantitative investigation. *PsychologyandEducation, 55*(1), 428–436. https://doi.org/10.48047/pne.2018.55.1.53

Schär, F. (2021). Decentralized finance: On blockchain- and smart contract-based financial markets. *Federal Reserve Bank of St. Louis Review, 103*(2), 153–174.

Schueffel, P. (2016). Taming the beast: A scientific definition of Fintech. *Journal of Innovation Management, 4*(4), 32–54.

Setiawan, K., & Maulisa, N. (2020, March). The evolution of Fintech: A regulatory approach perspective. In *3rd International conference on law and governance (ICLAVE 2019)* (pp. 218–225). Atlantis Press.

Shkolnyk, I. O., & Zakharkina, L. S. (2022). Fintech innovations and transparency of finance: World practices and Ukrainian realities.

Soundararajan, R., & Shenbagaraman, V. M. (2024). Enhancing financial decision-making through explainable AI and Blockchain integration: Improving transparency and trust in predictive models. *Educational Administration: Theory and Practice, 30*(4), 9341–9351.

Subburayan, B., Sankarkumar, A. V., Singh, R., & Mushi, H. M. (2024). Transforming of the financial landscape from 4.0 to 5.0: Exploring the integration of blockchain, and artificial intelligence. *Applications of BlockChain Technology and Artificial Intelligence*, 137–161.

Thakor, R. D., & Merton, R. C. (2024). Trust in lending. *The Review of Economics and Statistics*, 1–45.

The Economist. (2021, July 15). Investment in Fintech booms as upstarts go mainstream. Available at https://www.economist.com/finance-and-economics/2021/07/15/investment-in-Fintech-booms-as-upstarts-go-mainstream. Accessed on January 17, 2025.

Tiron-Tudor, A., & Deliu, D. (2024). The sustainability performance of SMEs in industry 5.0: A proposal for a Synergetic Digital Sustainable Development Maturity Model (SDSDMM). *Eastern European Economics*, 1–45.

Tohang, V., Lo, E., & Anggraeni, A. (2021, January). Financial technology 3.0 adoption in financial and non-financial institutions from modified UTAUT perspective. In *Conference on international issues in business and economics research (CIIBER 2019)* (pp. 1–6). Atlantis Press.

Toniolo, G. (2005). *Central bank cooperation at the bank for international settlements 1930-1973*. Cambridge University Press.

Trautman, L. J. (2015). E-Commerce, cyber, and electronic payment system risks: Lessons from PayPal. *UC Davis Business Law Journal*, *16*, 261.

Turksen, U., Benson, V., & Adamyk, B. (2024). Legal implications of automated suspicious transaction monitoring: Enhancing integrity of AI. *Journal of Banking Regulation*, 1–19.

Varga, D. (2017). Fintech, the new era of financial services. *Vezetéstudomány-Budapest Management Review*, *48*(11), 22–32.

Vives, X. (2019). Digital disruption in banking. *Annual Review of Financial Economics*, *11*(1), 243–272.

Zetzsche, D. A., Buckley, R. P., Barberis, J. N., & Arner, D. W. (2017). Regulating a revolution: From regulatory sandboxes to smart regulation. *Fordham Journal of Corporate & Financial Law*, *23*(11), 1–61.

Conclusion

Advanced breakthrough of technology through AI and ML solutions is swiftly changing Fintech landscape and increasing Transparency of Fintech Markets delivering never seen before potential for improvement of all market deficiencies. Changes of Fintech market every single part in short period of time it is challenging to research topics within the field. While technological advances are difficult to follow they raise in the same time undoubted regulatory challenges and impact societal issues such as balanced development and gender. Due to it we have narrowed our research in the field of three market segments: Integrating Health System Performance and Economic Stability, Wealth and Asset Management and Accounting in the first part of the book. In the second part we are offering research on the Regulatory challenges and Taxation again narrowing our research to areas such as Insurance Fintechs and Crowdfunding platforms. In the third part our research starts from societal perspective focusing on benefits and challenges from the book's main topic on developing countries as well as its impact on Gender Dynamics.

As never seen before increase of AI and ML technologies use in the field of Fintech are offering new standards in the field of transparency and recent increase of the AI driven technology has set new frontiers in the Fintech.

In the first paper of the first part of book we are focusing on Integrating Health System Performance and Economic Stability: A Geospatial and

J. Osterrieder et al. (eds.), *Transparency in FinTech*, Palgrave Studies in Financial Services Technology, ,
https://doi.org/10.1007/978-3-032-03523-3

AI-Driven Approach to TF. The study examines the relationship between health system performance and economic performance in the EU countries, with an impact on financial transparency. The analysis focuses on how recessions affect the medical and economic sectors, highlighting the link between improved medical services and economic stability. It uses geospatial analysis through spatial econometrics and artificial intelligence (AI) to correlate economic and medical data, revealing the effects of major economic events on medical providers from 2007 to 2019, including the 2008 crisis. The study highlights the crucial role of financial transparency in supporting efficient health systems and a resilient economy. Limitations of the study include the heterogeneity of the health and economic systems of the analyzed EU countries, the relatively short observation period, the complexity of the relationships studied, the possible omissions of relevant factors, the variability of data quality, and the trade-off between interpretability and accuracy in AI/econometric modeling, which may affect the generalizability of the conclusions.

The second paper named „Conceptual Framework for Assessing the Use of Artificial Intelligence in Wealth & Asset Management" provides a conceptual framework, including factors to assess the readiness of AI in wealth and asset management companies. It aims to provide guidance for wealth & asset management companies regarding the use of artificial intelligence (AI) and key considerations when assessing usability. Furthermore, it should sensitize data-related issues and foster an understanding of implementation frameworks considering AI systems. Attractive first-adopter trial implementations with low or even no costs, personal connections to an application provider or even the own expertise to develop or set up such an AI application could be reasons to deviate from a best practice approach. Thus, the ideas discussed in this paper and its proposed framework provide various controversies, opening the gates for further research and analysis regarding the appropriateness of AI applications.

The third paper „Empowering Triple-Entry Accounting with Machine Learning: and Blockchaing Unveiling Transparency Through Advanced Analytics" researches the utilization of Machine learning as promising avenue to augment the transparency advantages of triple-entry accounting. By leveraging ML algorithms, anomalies within distributed ledger data can be swiftly identified, flagging potential instances of fraud or errors. Looking ahead, this work underscores the contributions of applying ML to enhance TE accounting systems, yet unresolved challenges persist. Maturing techniques are necessary to address issues surrounding data privacy, regulatory oversight, and decentralized governance. Further engagement with standards bodies and policymakers is crucial. Additionally, targeted use cases and datasets are needed to explore applications in diverse sectors such as supply chain, insurance, and financial markets. Future research should delve into scalable, privacy-aware ML architectures optimized for distributed financial graphs to deepen understanding at a technical level.

In the second part of the book we are providing regulatory perspective of the developments in the field.

In the first paper "Playing by the rules: advances to prudential regulation and supervision of UK insurance startups and insurtech is focused on advances to legal and regulatory challenges in the digital insurance era" is focused on the UK insurance industry, with developments of the regulatory environment and prudential supervision. It presents a critical analysis of existing supervisory practices from the Prudential Regulation Authority (PRA) for the UK re-insurance sector, inclusive of the Lloyd's of London. The aim of this analysis performed is to comment on gaps identified from the latest PRA's approach to insurance supervision and the New Insurer Start-Up Unit Guide, towards the effective supervision of insurance startups and insurtech.

In the second paper "**Taxation** of Crowdfunding Platforms", Taxation of platforms is seen as a protection mechanism to prevent fraudulent activities, as it will ensure transparency and control of the activities of these platforms within the scope of fulfilling documentation and registration obligations. Within the scope of the study, crowdfunding platforms, the functioning and types of these platforms will be explained, and the taxation of equity based platforms according to Turkish Law will be discussed. Paper concludes that Taxation of equity based crowdfunding platforms requires the correct determination of the legal status of the platforms. Crowdfunding platforms themselves are liable for corporate tax, value added tax and other taxes relevant to "offline" businesses.

First paper of the third part "Knowledge and use of Fintech Products by the young generations: a Zero inflated ordinal data model" explores the determinants of non-knowledge, distinguishing between true *non-knowers* and those who might express varying levels of understanding in different circumstances after a brief introduction to the topic- Knowledge and Use of Fintech Products. This analysis seeks to understand both the respondents' choice of answers and the intensity of their declared knowledge.

With the rapid diffusion of Fintech innovations, the financial markets have benefited from more efficient instruments and solutions. However, these solutions often come with additional level of risks or, even, new types of risks. Investors and financial users might be unaware of this additional risk and complexities introduced with Fintech in many areas of their everyday lives, e.g. payments, savings and investments decisions. A homogeneous integrated policy effort in this field is desirable to improve globally the level of financial literacy in the Fintech domain, empower households with the tools to make better decisions and contribute to a greater investor protection and, finally, a stronger financial stability.

Second paper of the third part is Regional Fintech Report for Türkiye, Romania and Bulgaria a developing countries. Paper examines the landscape of fintechs across three countries, focusing on the fintech solutions among businesses and is created from two individual fintech survey studies of (1) Türkiye and (2) Romania and Bulgaria. By gathering data from Türkiye, Romania and Bulgaria, the survey aims to uncover patterns, trends, and regional differences in fintech engagement. There is an investigation of the prevalence of digital payment systems, the adoption of blockchain technology, the influence of regulatory frameworks. This study employs two individual Fintech Survey studies by gathering data from Türkiye, Romania and Bulgaria from 99 fintech companies. The insights from the 99 fintech companies surveyed from Türkiye, Romania and Bulgaria serve as a valuable resource for policymakers, fintech companies, investors and stakeholders as they navigate the rapidly evolving fintech landscape. By tackling the challenges and capitalizing on the opportunities highlighted, the fintech sector can continue to drive sustainable growth and contribute to a more inclusive and dynamic financial ecosystem.

The third paper "A Bibliometric Analysis of Transparency AI in Fintech with Emphasis on Gender Dynamics", conducts a comprehensive bibliometric analysis to chart the current landscape of transparency in AI research within the Fintech domain, identifying key research trends and potential areas for further investigation. Special emphasis is placed on gender dynamics, examining publication and collaboration patterns among researchers of different genders. By synthesizing existing literature, this work aims to offer detailed insights to inform strategic initiatives that address the evolving challenges and opportunities in the expanding field of Fintech AI applications. This bibliometric analysis reveals that the field of AI in

Fintech is still developing and lacks maturity. While many researchers are engaged in important work, including research on transparency and ethics, the research community remains fragmented. There is also a noticeable absence of integration between AI and established methodologies that have long been used in the financial sector.

Combining AI with these traditional approaches could enhance model transparency and decision interpretability, which is crucial given the significant impact AI in finance has on our daily lives. There is also a clear gender imbalance in terms of female versus male researchers working on these matters.

Index

J. Osterrieder et al. (eds.), *Transparency in FinTech*, Palgrave Studies in Financial Services Technology, ,
https://doi.org/10.1007/978-3-032-03523-3

Kolibri 360 GmbH
Ferdinand-Jühlke-Straße 7
99095 Erfurt, Deutschland
produktsicherheit@kolibri360.de